ATTENTION DEFICIT HYPERACTIVITY DISORDER AS A LEARNED BEHAVIORAL PATTERN

A Less Medicinal More Self-Reliant/ Collaborative Intervention

---

Craig Wiener

University Press of America,® Inc.
Lanham · Boulder · New York · Toronto · Plymouth, UK

Copyright © 2007 by
University Press of America,® Inc.
4501 Forbes Boulevard
Suite 200
Lanham, Maryland 20706
UPA Acquisitions Department (301) 459-3366

Estover Road
Plymouth PL6 7PY
United Kingdom

Library of Congress Control Number: 2007926461
ISBN-13: 978-0-7618-3809-8 (paperback : alk. paper)
ISBN-10: 0-7618-3809-0 (paperback : alk. paper)

∞™The paper used in this publication meets the minimum
requirements of American National Standard for Information
Sciences—Permanence of Paper for Printed Library Materials,
ANSI Z39.48—1984

To my sons
Casey and Scott

Table of Contents

Preface

Attention Deficit Hyperactivity Disorder as a Learned Behavioral Pattern: A Less Medicinal More Self-reliant/Collaborative Intervention proposes an alternative way to reduce the incidence of ADHD actions and reactions. ADHD patterning is examined in a conceptual framework with a long tradition in the psychology field: the learning paradigm. While most ADHD therapies are based on medicinal and stringent management, this intervention instead promotes autonomy and collaboration.

In that we are telling increasing numbers of children (and adults) that they have a genetically caused functional delay, it is essential that we evaluate the bases of those claims, and carefully study the consequences of the treatments we select to implement. Substantial resources have been allocated to support traditional interventions, but our recommended approach can potentially yield long-term improvements if we are willing to explore alternatives rather than settle for the status quo.

A collaborative/self-reliant pattern of interaction has been promoted in the workplace and with non-diagnosed children; however, to date, this approach has not yet been advised for ADHD diagnosed individuals. The general assertion is that "out of control" children require greater control as well as chemical readjustment in order to rectify their so-called biological delay. A psychological account is seldom given much credence, especially in the wake of acceptance of biological determinism. Professionals instead orient to "inform" about the biological causes of ADHD and the subsequent necessity to medicate individuals in order to coerce behavior. This trend continues but there seems to be growing concern that we are too quickly endorsing medicinal therapies and patterns of interaction that mimic institutional care; such interventions rarely produce significant long-term improvements for any population.

This current work examines ADHD behavior from the perspective of a Clinical Psychologist. It is a long overdue reformulation of the diagnostic category as it occurs in the world of diagnosed children, adults, and families. Because we have observed that diagnosed individuals can indeed function acceptably when they do what they "want to do," more questions are being raised about the validity of the diagnostic category and traditional explanations for the problematic behaviors. As an alternative we adopt a conceptual framework that emphasizes what the individual learns as she or he encounters various contexts, situations, and circumstances. We do not discount biology, but neither do we endorse the construct of neurological inhibitory delay to account for ADHD patterning. Moreover, we expect that the side effects and shortcomings observed as a result of traditional treatments will be ameliorated through the implementation of our recommended procedures, importantly, if they are applied before age twelve.

This book owes special thanks to Susan Davis for her scholarly copyediting and outstanding effort in helping to prepare this manuscript. It was a pleasure working with her on this as well as my first book *Attention Deficit Hyperactivity Disorder as a Learned Behavioral Pattern: A Return to Psychology.*

Craig Wiener Ed.D.
Worcester, MA
January, 2007

Chapter 1

A Basis for Self-reliant/
Collaborative Interacting

It is now commonly asserted that ADHD is an inherited neurobiological delay of one's ability to inhibit responses, and that any reasonable intervention must be designed to contend with that problem. This current work not only offers a different conceptualization of ADHD, but it also identifies alternative ways to diminish the frequency rates of the behaviors. Rather than account for ADHD behaviors in terms of delayed neurology, the current paradigm understands those behaviors as *conditioned*. While it is an empirical question as to whether this alternative intervention will outperform the commonly practiced interventions according to specified criteria for some diagnosed persons and therapists, it is nonetheless important to consider the time frame of the measurements, the side effects, and the response generalization before passing judgment.

When understanding ADHD patterns as learned, a history of reinforcement coordinates with ADHD patterns as it does with what we recognize as normative behaviors. Non-diagnostic actions are not necessarily more neurologically complex (e.g., touching to alert vs. touching to irritate); but rather they are simply more appropriate, less troublesome, disruptive, or annoying. However, because diagnosed persons do not participate sufficiently, modulate the pace of their actions acceptably, or respect social boundaries, it is presumed that they must possess a neurological delay that causes those deficiencies.

Rather than assert biological causality, the view presented here is that some people (who may also be burdened by other problems) learn to respond with diagnostic patterns too frequently when encountering various kinds of adversity.

While people generally learn to respond to adversity through persistence, adaptation, accommodation, and hard work, we acknowledge that some people (for myriad reasons) learn the opposite. In many instances these individuals evade, encroach, act too quickly or slowly, and/or cease involvement altogether.

While most children learn to behave responsibly over time, and integrate behavior with others in acceptable ways, some children learn to shirk obligations, and behave in a demanding, less accommodating fashion compared to other children in their age group. A more contributing and considerate response pattern is not being shaped. A significant number of these individuals will eventually qualify for an ADHD diagnosis, especially when ADHD responding repeats in school.

For those who do develop diagnostic patterns, we observe that the behaviors occur most severely when individuals lose discretionary authority, feel insecure, receive a negative evaluation, or experience discomfort and rejection; in these cases individuals are conditioned to struggle less. They remain intolerant of inconvenience or disappointment, and are generally less accommodating to others when having to conform to these situations and circumstances. The main aim of this current intervention is to alter these patterns of behavior.

Many health practitioners, parents and caregivers can, for example, interpret ADHD responding as an effective way for diagnosed individuals to divert attention away from conflict, or conversely, as a way to monopolize. The responses could also be conditioned to repeat if they result in reducing restrictions or as a means of rapid escape from interrogation. Some responses may be conditioned so that others must maintain responsibility and function as the child's agent. Each of the aforementioned eventualities may be increasing the frequency rates and/or staying power of ADHD responses over time.

Assigning causation to genetics or biology ignores the correspondence of the behaviors with context, and any shift in frequency rates of the behaviors contingent on the sequence of events occurring after they are expressed. For example, individuals may be conditioned to not read or follow instructions under certain conditions, because by so doing, failure to understand can be avoided, and self-directedness can be maintained. Such events could potentially increase the frequency of the non-accommodating responses under equivalent conditions.

Individuals can also learn to enact behaviors either quickly or slowly, show high activity levels, touch numerous objects within a short period of time, and be conditioned to be risk takers (they run when advised to walk). ADHD behaviors can be reinforced if they reduce the probability of missing out or being held back. Such behaviors can also possibly sequence with an increase in notoriety from onlookers.

The characterization of ADHD outlined here diverges from what is apparently unreliable diagnostic labeling and poorly explained symptom inconsistencies, towards a better understanding of the specifics of context, situation, and circumstance associated with ADHD frequency rates. The approach abandons the formulation that neurological delay is "driving" or circumscribing the person to enact disruptive, feral, uncouth, inappropriate, distracted, inconsiderate, un-motivated, careless behaviors. Variations in symptom expression are no longer seen to be resultant from environmental exacerbations or compensations that influence the posited ever-present bodily deficiency. Diagnosed persons are presumed to be repeating behaviors that have been reinforced and continue to be reinforced with enough frequency to resist their extinction. The reinforcement history does not make the set of behaviors impervious to change, as the careful alteration of reinforcement contingencies is still a viable way to facilitate and condition non-diagnostic patterns.

ADHD is not understood as a permanent obstacle; we presume that diag-nosed children can learn new responses for particular problems and already of-ten demonstrate necessary competencies in situations (e.g., persistence, willing-ness to practice, attentiveness). It is thus advisable that facilitators alter whatever impedes the repetition of the impressive responses. For example, a diagnosed child may be less disorganized when identifying ways to obtain the best price when buying an object with his own money, and/or when remembering to tell a parent to wash clothing for an upcoming school dance, but may not function as competently when spending his parent's money or when preparing for a stipu-lated excursion.

Instead of being less able to perform what is known, ADHD could be un-derstood as a disorder of non-reinforcement to comply or accommodate enough to expectations or commonly held values. Behavioral change can be addressed proactively by altering situational parameters to closely match conditions that cue acceptable responses, and by helping diagnosed persons characterize situa-tions differently so that they are more apt to respond non-diagnostically.

Rather than for us to presume that a child is neurologically delayed when showing ADHD disorganization, we can recall when we had a difficult time remembering where we put our belongings when we have not initially estab-lished routines such as putting keys and scissors in the same place after using them. Diagnosed persons may not be a special case, and they may not be so neu-rologically limited as to be unable to learn simplistic routines that prevent them from receiving an ADHD label.

One might ask if it is their neurology that prevents them from doing more consistent, reliable, acceptable routine behavior, or is it that they have not yet been conditioned to do a very simplistic sequence of behaviors that could easily be enacted automatically without prior mental rehearsal. In our view, children will put toys back in their bins without the necessity of doing an inhibitory re-sponse and any antecedent executive functioning after that *habit* has been estab-lished.

Even if it is the case that many diagnosed children present more complica-tions for training and socialization compared to a random sampling (due to co-occurring functional difficulties), their failure to do very simple routines may be a problem of conditioning, rather than a consequence of a lesser functioning inhibitory system. Intervention might only entail that parents shape diagnosed children to do daily routines more autonomously so that the child learns the necessary sequence of actions with less supervision or parental entanglement.

The various medicinal and interventionist compensations advocated by traditionalists could become less necessary when diagnosed persons participate within a learning approach. Because diagnostic behaviors are less often observed during behavioral acts associated with satisfactory outcomes, ours is an effort to recreate those conditions as much as possible. While traditionalists continue to address a neurological delay, our intervention orients to attend to the gap between what others require and that which the diagnosed person initiates and enjoys.

Attempts are made to obtain their willingness to participate from the outset so that obstacles or negativity associated with what others initiate can be eliminated or reduced, and the probability of conscientious behavior and follow through can be enhanced. We anticipate that when hardship associated with activity *required by others* is diminished, increased non-diagnostic responding will ensue: that assigned and non-assigned conditions will begin to converge. It is probable that diagnosed persons will show competencies in both kinds of conditions when fewer problems exist that are associated with the directives, limits, and expectations of others.

In our view, the traditional interventions now employed to change diagnostic functioning are undermining individuals' self-reliance in the long run. For example, the provision of external representation and directive assistance certainly makes task requirements easier, but it does little to help the diagnosed person learn to solve increasingly complex problems autonomously. Acceptable responding may be elicited, but the end result could be that diagnosed persons have fewer opportunities to function independently without the need for constant assistance.

Without being aware, diagnosed individuals may be being trained towards even greater reliance on the efforts of others (and medication) to help them behave satisfactorily. Traditionalists claim that diagnosed persons need medication and compensation to stop the upsurge of disinhibited responses, but we do not yet know whether that dependency is endemic to the condition, or whether traditional treatment interventions advance a perpetual reliance on it.

As a way to avoid the deeper dependency mentioned above, we attempt here to increase non-diagnostic responding by shaping self-efficacy, the degree to which an individual feels confident and capable of performing a certain behavior in a specific situational context (Bandura, 1977). Skill development might help reduce pessimism and discouragement that can occur when diagnosed individuals must meet the expectations of others. For example, it has been found that people who show positive self-efficacy also have a higher probability of developing effective task strategies (Latham, Winters, and Locke, 1994; Wood and Bandura, 1989). Locke and Latham (2002) note:

The concept of self-efficacy is important in goal-setting theory in several ways. When goals are self-set, people with high self-efficacy set higher goals than do people with lower self-efficacy. They also are more committed to assigned goals, find and use better task strategies to attain goals, and respond more positively to negative feedback than do people with low self-efficacy (p. 706).

Locke and Latham's report suggests that many of the delays associated with diagnosis can be ameliorated by shaping "self-efficacy," and introducing self-set goals. Locke and Latham add that "goal commitment can also be enhanced by leaders communicating an inspiring vision and behaving supportively" (p. 707).

There are numerous studies showing that allowing participation in goal setting often results in people setting higher goals and improved performance when achieving those goals (e.g., Latham and Yukl, 1976, Latham, Mitchell and Dossett, 1978). Similarly, Schein (1969) has formulated a way to increase collaboration in work settings by focusing on the "process" of decision making with the aim that comfortable and harmonious interaction patterns will translate into company success. Even biological determinists Hallowell and Ratey (1995) recommend that intervention incorporate collaborative methods used in business in order to help families learn negotiating techniques. They say that a book written as part of the Harvard Negotiation Project entitled *Getting to Yes: Negotiating Agreement without Giving In*, by Fisher, Ury, and Patton (1991) is a very useful resource for families who are learning to negotiate effectively. If these interventions work successfully in business settings to increase satisfaction, participation, and achievement, they can be replicated in family and school settings (as much as possible) with diagnosed persons as early as possible. The presumption of disability will undoubtedly discourage some people from collaborative/self-reliant intervention.

We anticipate that diagnosed persons will start to imitate the positive behaviors being role modeled during collaborative exchanges: thus they will effectively learn to accommodate the perspectives of others because they regularly practice negotiation and compromise during social interacting. A parental question to the child might be, "I wonder why that person behaved in that way?" then proceed to discuss reasons with the child. Such an exercise can lead towards greater tolerance and empathy for others.

Given the large body of empirical work showing that children (in general) often learn through imitation (Bandura, Ross, and Ross, 1961; Bandura, 1965), we might increase the probability of learning the behaviors recommended by encouraging parents to enact self-reliant/collaborative patterns as often as possible. Even if diagnosed persons are delayed in ability to imitate, role modeling is still a useful method. If loved ones share, demonstrate reliability, exhibit calm when encountering adversity, and show consideration for multiple perspectives rather than self-centered rigidity, diagnosed persons are likely to behave similarly. But the family cannot be the only participants in the learning intervention method.

If teachers do not collect and grade homework, for example, they are not shaping diagnosed children to reliably complete their work. If others do not follow through with what they say, children are also likely to copy those behaviors and behave with less time awareness. One goal is to increase dependability, perspective taking, and the enactment of routines, so it is incumbent upon loved ones to do those behaviors and role model the same interacting within the marital relationship (which children are often keen to copy).

Over time diagnosed persons may recognize that we all have less discretionary input in certain situations and more in others. Such a realization can also help diagnosed persons adapt to the world as it is, since we cannot change everything we desire to change. For that reason alone it is important to emphasize perspective taking during socialization, because it can reduce a "me only" orientation and help the child cope better when accommodation is necessary.

When it does become imperative to unilaterally impose limits, facilitators are advised to do so in a relatively benign fashion and emphasize that the creation of limits is a means of protection, not an attempt to control or belittle the diagnosed person. The best manner in which to enact unilateral solutions is a firm but kind one, and ideally not during angry exchanges; therefore an act of protection will not be confused with mistreatment, vindictiveness, punishment, dislike, or denial. In this approach diagnosed children are conditioned to behave in acceptable ways without the expectation that, to do so, they must also endure suffering or admonishment.

The traditional view advocates reinstatement of parental control and inducing compliance, but we assert that their model does not address the problems with sharing and coordinating differences of opinion which are so prevalent in the diagnosed population. Therefore, instead of pressuring diagnosed persons to comply with commands, directives, and instructions, this alternative intervention focuses on deriving win/win solutions whenever possible. Rather than restore parental control as advised by Robin (2006), success is defined by the frequency of mutually-acceptable self-reliant behaviors, and by the frequency with which behaviors consistent with "social interest" are autonomously enacted. The aim is for diagnosed persons to fully integrate and initiate acceptable actions, rather than copy the behaviors in response to the demands or coercions of others.

Presiding individuals will not be gratified instantaneously or consistently when utilizing non-domineering tactics, but they may notice that weaker individuals accommodate more with less coercion over time. Over the longer term, there may also be recognizable benefits to conciliation and compromise and long-term outcomes may be impressive. For example, instead of insisting that the child stop fidgeting and listen, the parent will convey that the child's point of view is valued and that his participation makes it possible to incorporate his ideas into family decisions. Over a number of trials he will learn to participate with less harping.

Similarly, when the child offers a suggestion it is important to remain supportive, even if some aspects of the idea are unworkable. Such an approach encourages the child to contribute rather than detach over time. The effects may not be immediately evident, but the long-term outcomes will be rewarding.

If we employ a self-reliant/collaborative approach we can potentially help diagnosed persons learn, for example, to complete science fair projects in the same way as they complete other non-assigned projects. They will be encouraged to duplicate their persistence when they convince parents to conform to their initiatives. They might be persuaded to repeat the attentive listening that occurs, as when a parent says something they are "not supposed to hear," as well as retain other useful information in the same way as they recall the latest gossip pertaining to their hobbies.

We observe that many diagnosed children can enact many non-assigned activities without contingency management or interventions designed to offset their disability, and it would seem that their behavior in these circumstances would not qualify them for an ADHD diagnosis. Many diagnosed persons do different non-assigned activities over extended periods of time and show uninterrupted attention, fewer errors of omission and commission, and an ability to work out solutions to complex problems.

Moreover, under conditions of increased discretionary input and less scrutiny by others, despite whether punishments or rewards are added, whether stimulants are used to increase methodical responding, or whether the designated final contingency is immediate or in the distant future, the individual's response pattern can be characterized as aroused, systematic, participatory, and eager. Task completion typically occurs regularly, and the diagnosed person functions with a schedule either alone or under little external supervision.

Traditionalists claim, however, that activities diagnosed individuals initiate and enjoy provide immediate feedback, and thus do not require the executive functioning necessary to complete school-related tasks. The invoking of this argument permits them to retain the disability model. But we argue that ADHD behaviors have not been reinforced when conditions are less disapproving and associated with success and discretionary authority. For example, video game playing allows maneuvering; the respondent can derive his or her own course of action; performance is rarely evaluated by others; and the operator may stop or go in relation to his or her own initiative. Such conditions stand in contrast with those requiring conformity to the expectations of others (especially in school), which may not correlate with comfort and success.

When playing video games a player not only can obtain a simulated motoric adventure, but can also press a button to restart the game at any time after making mistakes. The game has parameters, but individuals need not deal with the whims, preferences, disapproval, and demands of others who may interfere with their discretionary authority or threaten their competence. Dominance can be achieved much like what happens when hunting prey. Although many diagnosed persons will still externalize blame when problems occur during self-instructed activity (e.g., blame the machine), the video game operator retains discretionary influence (i.e., the machine does not talk back) compared to assigned activities.

Rather than infer that ADHD responding occurs in direct relation to the amount of inhibition and executive functioning required for success, history of reinforcement can be invoked to account for the occurrence of problematic behaviors. In this view symptoms are predicted to show less frequently during creative play, compared to situations when others impose constraints and instructions which increase the probability of failing to meet standards, and risk undermining the child's social importance and discretionary authority.

There is the additional claim that ADHD behaviors will usually be frequent when conditions are negative, insecure, irrelevant, restrictive, judgmental, difficult to understand, and/or when resentment is harbored. Not surprisingly, as traditionalists have reported, school is a context that highly correlates with ADHD behavior for the majority of diagnosed children, but during free play it is much more difficult to distinguish between diagnosed children and controls.

However, it is not that free play compensates for ADHD, but rather that ADHD is not reinforced when one does free play. Consistent with that assertion, Murphy et al. (2001) did not find that diagnosed adults had problems with ideational creativity, and Barkley, Edwards, et al. (2001) did not find that diagnosed adolescents had problems with ideational fluency in their laboratory studies to encourage creative responding. Problematic responding in those conditions was absent.

This is not to say that excessive exposure to freedom and indulgence is a desirable way to socialize children. Too much exposure to conditions of boundless freedom may also correlate with reduced arousal and participation when sedate prescriptive tasks and activities are presented. The individual might respond as if something is missing, and/or that he or she is being denied.

Neural biological development may differ as well when individuals are regularly exposed to excessive stimulation. For example, Amen (2001, 29) asserts, "We are being programmed to need more stimulation in order to pay attention." He notes that after video game playing there is an increase in the release of dopamine; this means that there will be less "available later on to do schoolwork, homework, chores, and so on."

Given Amen's concerns, we can direct diagnosed children towards various social and solitary activities and not rely heavily on television to distract the child. Spending inordinate time on solitary activity such as video game playing (especially the simplistic fast-paced games), or television watching may deprive the child of opportunities to develop friendships and negotiating skills. Watching too much television may rob the child of chances to integrate social perspectives, enact and comprehend language exchange, adapt to extenuating circumstances, and contend with the emotionality, inconsistency, evaluation, and disharmony that occurs during social interaction. We are not saying that television watching will cause ADHD, as Christakis et al. (2004) propose; frequent television watching does not help a child develop initiative as well as socially coordinated patterns of behavior.

Despite the lack of a causal relationship between watching television and ADHD (Barkley, 2006d), it is nevertheless helpful for parents to encourage their diagnosed children towards a variety of suitable and intriguing activities to help them build skills towards meeting a wide array of environmental demands. Having televisions in bedrooms is not recommended, for example, when encouraging the child to engage in varied activities; parents can find positive ways to prevent younger children's exposure to programs not designed for them.

It may even be necessary to change how the entire family uses the television so that all family members learn alternative activities instead of watching relatively inane programming that generally hinders a child's biological and behavioral development (Parker-Pope, 2004). Along these lines, Brody (2004) reports that parents can reduce their diagnosed children's inattentive behavior in noteworthy ways by merely changing television viewing patterns. When making these changes, parents can emphasize that more time is available to interact together, and family members can now fulfill obligations as well as pursue hobbies.

Although when altering the frequency of television watching, parents might also show flexibility, as it is helpful that the child find the new patterning agreeable rather than coercive. For instance, if the child deems it important to watch a particular show, the parent must decide whether it would do more harm than good to deny the request. The expectation is that, by encouraging and role modeling new routines over the long term, it will be possible to reduce the amount and type of programming being watched, even if the amount of time watching television varies day to day.

The reinforcement of ADHD patterns

We observe that many different reinforcement histories may influence the occurrence of ADHD responding. Intervention is thus a matter of identifying the sequences of contexts and situations that increase diagnostic as well as non-diagnostic behaviors. In this treatment approach diagnosed persons learn new ways to respond to the adversity that had previously cued the undesired diagnostic pattern. Since very different behavioral responses can be shaped in relation to the same starting point, it is not surprising that ADHD behaviors become frequent regardless of whether or not one has a particular molecular biology, type of parent, or family environment. Many diagnosed persons have learned that failure and disapproval will occur when doing what others require; these individuals may not be reinforced to please others, in that they have continuously experienced impatience and disapproval. ADHD responding will thus provide a quick escape from the hardship associated with compliance. If that pattern is evident, one can ask the diagnosed child "What are you saying no to?" or "What did I say that you didn't like?" whenever lack of accommodation occurs.

Even opposite forms of social patterning such as irresponsible and overly responsible parenting can potentially increase the frequency of these behaviors. For example, lackadaisical parents can inadvertently condition the child to do ADHD responding when the behaviors frequently result in some degree of parental involvement. Their reduced involvement could also lower the probability that the child will learn acceptable socialization and increase the probability of shaping overly intrusive behaviors as well. Consistent with this view, Barkley (2006c) notes that parents of children described as hyperactive and injury-prone play with their children less often and are likely to allow their children to leave the house unattended. In contrast, inordinately protective and worried parents can also condition diagnostic responding more often. In these conditions of socialization the child will characterize the parent as obstructive, annoying, and judgmental rather than helpful. ADHD responding may become the child's way to counteract incessant parental direction and orchestration.

However, ADHD responding can increase and be reinforced more often when the child suffers from significant diminishment of parental involvement, especially after having previously been indulged, when for example, parent meets a new partner, a baby is born, parent works longer hours, or is preoccupied with other concerns. Given the wide range of possibilities for diagnostic responses to be reinforced, it is difficult to identify a circumscribed set of parenting behaviors that correlate with the behavioral set. It is nevertheless recommended that we treat ADHD behaviors as different and reinforced rather than delayed. The increase in frequency of particular ADHD behaviors in particular conditions is taken to mean that the behaviors have been shaped to recur.

A lack of coordination with socially acceptable future events does not determine that a person is functionally delayed. Behaviors such as excessive studying and reading, or a health food diet regime can also relate to problematic biological and psychosocial consequences in the long and the short term. Given that we usually do not invoke a disability model or regard these excessive behaviors as a failure to properly think through troublesome outcomes, we must ask on which grounds are the behaviors we call ADHD any different.

One might also ask if kings and queens or CEOs are "driven" by their neurology or are insufficiently doing mental antecedents when they demand a quick response from their servants. Or are they are conditioned to do these behaviors, in that their servants follow their instructions promptly when they are ordered? We are perplexed as to why neurological delay has to be invoked when individuals respond with ADHD patterns. Even if others do not like the behaviors being emitted, they can nevertheless be understood as reinforced within the circumstances in which they appear.

The current model derives history of reinforcement for each individual as a way to account for behaviors that traditionalists label as inability to self motivate, and/or perform what one already knows. The analysis of past events rather than neurology becomes the method to account for non-responsiveness to instructions, fidgeting in one's seat when confined, touching numerous forbidden objects, seeking other rambunctious children, indulgence that leads to long-term problems, missed appointments, and/or poor effort on assigned tasks.

It is in this sense that some individuals (most often having developmental delays and other atypical circumstances that disrupt age-consistent social patterning) may be reinforced to respond to failure, terse directives, rejection, constraint, criticism, and subordination by acting in ways that are rapid, sluggish, provocative/intrusive, or non-participatory. However, these reactions do not mean that there is a neurological limiting condition that causes the responses, or that there is a reliable correspondence between the degree of psychosocial impairment and the extent of neurological delay.

People can be reinforced to persist less, impose more, squirm, respond hastily, take risks, overreact, not react, and complain, instead of doing acceptable responses (including particular mental actions that could help them solve cumbersome time consuming requirements). While problems mastering particular content, negative temperament, pre- and post-natal brain injuries, particular genes, motor and language problems, asthma, adoption, and depressed and/or single mothers might increase the probability of learning to do ADHD behavior, the increased occurrence of those responses in particular situations may be understood as a function of what transpires when those behaviors are emitted.

In some histories of reinforcement, ADHD behaviors become probable when responding to discontentment, loss of social influence, duress, oppression, unease, avarice, segregation, rebuff, refusal, or curtailment. However, those behaviors are predicted to occur less often when diagnosed persons are under the influence of stimulant medication (which would also be true for the general population), when environmental changes facilitate success, when it is problematic or threatening to not respond in a conciliatory or conscientious fashion, and when events are consistent with the diagnosed person's point of view and preferences.

ADHD behaviors may occur with or without oppositional behaviors, but it is often the case that oppositional behaviors are conditioned when individuals *initially* do ADHD at a young age, approximately between ages three and five. Diagnostic behaviors can increase the probability of angry outbursts, as many people cannot easily remain consistent, calm and non-erratic when ADHD patterning is evident. However, we observe that the behaviors subsumed by Oppositional Defiant Disorder (ODD) are hostile, sullen, or pugnacious responses to dissatisfaction, and are generally typical for older children. The angry behaviors and brooding responses are learned more often when there has been a history of quarreling, inconsistent training, and/or difficult personalities, and are usually learned later in childhood after individuals have developed enough interpersonal authority and physical presence to combat others forcefully.

Although even without the animosity associated with oppositional/defiant patterning, it can be asserted that ADHD behavior is more related to problems with conformity than traditionalists would have us believe. Diagnosed persons are usually unwilling to follow the directives of others; they frequently will not complete assignments, and on many occasions will overstep boundaries. Their agenda apparently takes precedence.

As the child ages, this relatively non-integrated social patterning often continues; motoric intrusiveness will usually diminish, and more sedentary non-participatory behaviors will occur. Generally, we observe that older diagnosed persons become less accessible, although their contributions and accommodations to others remain as deficient as when they were younger. Problems related to the completion of work can carry on into adulthood; when these diagnosed adults are inconvenienced, adjustment to the expectations of others is often minimal—as when they were hyperactive. We observe that the quality and quantity of effort expended when faced with imposed requirements is significantly less compared to responses when doing self-initiated and enjoyable activities.

However, we are not proclaiming that people *want* to do ADHD, or that they have been taught by others to do the behaviors; but rather, interactions and sequences of events have over time shaped and reinforced the responses. Many of us will, for example, find it difficult to manage an infant that has a negative temperament, and many of us will participate less if our failure rates are high. Thus, the probability that non-normative patterning such as ADHD will be reinforced under negative or arduous circumstances is high. Parents raising diagnosed children may not be atypical; instead, circumstances of socialization are allowing for ADHD behaviors to be learned.

As noted, ADHD behaviors are reinforced irrespective of the particular parenting style identified as modal. For example, a child can meet diagnostic criteria and be paired with a responsible, organized, accommodating, and involved parent who is very concerned that the child meet the expectations of others, and is also sensitive to what others deem appropriate and permissible. This parent frequently relieves and shields the child, feels remorse and/or guilt when the child is displeased, and solves problems for him in order to avoid difficulties. When concerned about functional or emotional difficulties, this pattern will intensify.

However, in this case ADHD behaviors are being inadvertently and constantly reinforced. When we examine this interactional pattern in detail, even though bitterness is not extreme, and although the parent frequently complains, overprotects, penalizes, and feels frustrated and exhausted, few would argue that that parent is doing something egregious, unacceptable, or even atypical. As noted by Nigg and Hinshaw (1998) only children showing oppositional and conduct-disordered behaviors typically have parents with personality traits that differ remarkably from controls.

Yet despite the absence of vitriol or inconsistency in the relationship, the parent may nevertheless function as the child's keeper and director. If the parent does most of the orchestrating and accommodating as dramas and hyperbole occur from one situation to the next, the child will not learn to struggle or persist in the face of adversity, or learn to wait patiently when she is not the focal point of mother's concern. The child will not necessarily be learning age-consistent patterns of responsibility and autonomy, or learning to deal calmly, attentively, and effectively with daily displeasures and events. Thus diagnostic behaviors might continue to be reinforced unbeknownst to those who care most.

It would therefore be prudent to first consider history of reinforcement as a logical account for ADHD, and gather a detailed analysis of interactional patterns. For instance, given the patterns in the above scenario, we would not be surprised if that child were to have greater difficulty functioning in groups at school where accommodation is less frequent compared to home life. Teachers usually have less time and inclination to react to every child's discomfort, success, and disappointment similarly to what took place in the household during the child's early life. The child may also feel insecure in a crowded classroom situation and respond as if something is absent or lost, thus amplifying the diagnostic patterning.

In another scenario, ADHD patterning can be reinforced when diagnosed child and parent show similar behaviors. When these conditions are present, the parent's behavior is imitated by the child, and both are reinforced when behaving the same way within the household. Due to the mirroring of behavioral patterns, it is also likely that competition (and conflict) will occur.

Consistent with this interpretation is the finding of increased incidence of oppositional behaviors when both parent and child show ADHD behavioral patterns. Barkley and Edwards (1998) note a 40-50% chance that at least one parent of a defiant child with ADHD will also be diagnosed as ADHD. Fifteen to 20% of these parents will be the mother and 25-30% will be the father. The presumption is that outcomes are always consequences of genetics unfolding (Barkley, 2006a), however, it is important to point out that the influence of a diagnosed parent's anxiety, depression, substance abuse, or marital and employment problems on diagnosed children has not been fully explored.

We might then ask why this area of concern has not had greater attention. The traditionalist belief system is built entirely on the assumption that environment has no seminal influence. Given the lack of empirical work examining parent/child interactions over time, it seems essential to fill this information gap, and to adequately investigate contingencies that reinforce ADHD behavior in each diagnosed person across settings, with different people, and content. We can, for example, explore behavioral patterns that occur when children react to corrective, belittling, tattletale siblings, or catering and interfering grandparents who are at odds with the child's parents.

As with actions in general, there are advantages and disadvantages when enacting ADHD patterns. The fact that others often disapprove does not confirm that the behaviors represent delayed functioning. Hyperactive behaviors may disrupt and tire others, but they also provoke notoriety and excitement. Impulsive responding increases risk and errors, but those actions also diminish the probability of shortfall or denial. Inattentiveness can result in low achievement, but those behaviors also protect the actor. Therefore, it seems that each ADHD symptom can be understood as conditioned despite the pros and cons of the responses.

By identifying the ways in which diagnostic responding is being reinforced, families will be in a better position to diminish the frequency rates of those behaviors. Loved ones can reflect on how they respond to ADHD patterns and try to understand how their treatment is maintaining the child's reactions. For example, they can be less reactionary and disapproving and redirect the child towards socially acceptable behavior in situations. Parents can also set firmer limits on the extent to which they will accommodate during diagnostic responding, and thus require the child to meet them halfway. Parents can role model the behaviors they want their child to imitate; being angry and negative does not help accomplish those goals.

For those adults who take the view that authoritarianism works best, restraint is highly recommended in which commands are seldom given. Observant, firm, reliable, and consistent parental behavior can yield positive interactions over time, and increase the successes achievable when the child participates. The addition of extra contingencies to induce compliance may not be necessary and indeed, the strategy may even be counterproductive.

While many children taking stimulant medications might describe their mood as "feeling funny," and adults often report mood elevation and "euphoria" when taking these medications (DuPaul, Barkley, and Connor, 1998, 516), the current approach attempts instead to induce similar positive and excited responses to socio-cultural requirements *without* the need for diagnosed people to ingest drugs, or be enticed by extra rewards. By changing how diagnosed persons respond to assigned activity and responsibility, we anticipate that productivity, persistence, and arousal will occur even without chemical stimulants, assistance, bribes, or punishment.

However, traditional inquiry has unfortunately *not* made it a priority to study the ways in which ADHD behaviors might be reinforced for those who qualify for the diagnosis. For example, even though a traditional assessment might ask parents what they do when problem behaviors occur, or what the child might do in response to the parent's behavior, such inquiries relate to the extent to which parents obtain compliance from the child (e.g., Barkley and Edwards, 1998).

Given that shortcoming, rather than invariably presume that troublesome parent/child interactions are caused by ADHD delay, researchers could inquire further into reports that mothers of diagnosed children are less responsive to their child's questions, are excessively directive in their style, are strict and negative (DuPaul et al., 2001), and assess the ways in which those patterns influence ADHD responding. Investigators could also note whether ADHD frequency rates increase when discipline is too lax, over reactive and coercive, (Gerdes, Hoza, and Pelham, 2003), and when it is more "tit for tat" (Fletcher et al., 1996), since those patterns also occur frequently within the ADHD population. However, the possible ways in which those more frequent interactions might reinforce ADHD in different contexts and situations has not been a focus of traditional investigation.

Traditionalists are adamant that no one has yet identified social parameters or parenting behaviors that adequately account for the development of ADHD patterning. They refer to data showing genetics and biology as reasonable ways to explain the etiology of the diagnostic pattern. Observed atypical interactions between parents and diagnosed children are understood as a consequence of the difficult neurological patterns exhibited by the child: It is claimed that parents are being adversely stressed, but that parents do not in any way participate in the fostering of those behaviors. Parents are instead responsible for preventing secondary problems by containing the ADHD through increased contingency management, compensations, and ensuring that the diagnosed child takes medication.

A biopsychosocial understanding

We assert here that ADHD patterning is conditioned through a series of events and interactions over time. Biology is only one component of the *biopsychosocial* system that can limit, modify, and influence possibilities. Rather than biology being foremost in affecting behavior, we presume that parameters from different domains influence each other, and that events occurring over time integrate within the biopsychosocial individual. Rather than discount biology when explicating ADHD behavior, we simply remove it from its causal antecedent status.

This alternative reformulation is offered to address the apparent inconsistencies, limitations and contradictions within the accepted traditional paradigm. Because no one has yet identified a discrete impairment or parameter from any domain of study that coincides with the behavioral DSM-IV-TR (The American Psychiatric Association, 2000) criteria in clinically useful ways (Barkley, 2000), it seems more tenable that a confluence of parameters from psychology, biology, and anthropology affect whether particular persons will exhibit ADHD behavior patterns.

Firstly, it is baffling as to why neurological parameters are perceived as the critical determinants of the occurrence of an ADHD response, since all that is required to diminish symptoms is to place diagnosed persons in situations less associated with negativity, uselessness, adversity, failure, and irrelevance. If an activity is analogous to interests and hobbies, we anticipate (as do traditionalists) that performance will be acceptable. One may therefore reasonably intervene simply by facilitating the repetition of the non-diagnostic responding that occurs when the diagnosed person is comfortable and interested.

In this contextual formulation, what is called "goodness of fit" between child and social matrix can account for significant differences in events over time for any biopsychosocial system. We acknowledge that this will be less effective with regard to profoundly mentally deficient individuals whose possibilities for learning are significantly restricted; but this may be a greater concern for the ADHD population where noteworthy variations occur through dissimilarities in conditioning. Unexpected changes may occur as new patterns of reinforcement are introduced over extended time frames. At present some diagnosed children show atypical early behavioral patterning, while others do not show any problematic functioning until much later in childhood. Some non-diagnosed persons show problematic early patterning that correlates with the ADHD diagnosis, yet never qualify for the behavioral criteria at any point in their lives.

Generally, there is significant heterogeneity in behavioral patterns, co-occurring problems, biological patterns, prognoses, responses to intervention, and possibilities for learning within the ADHD diagnostic group. The shaping that occurs is, in our view, not predestined or genetically mapped out; any number of behavioral patterns can be fostered in relation to how loved ones respond.

Our approach is fairly consistent with models used to treat couples, families, and groups, as the interventions used are likely to address behavior as contextual, situational, and circumstantial. The focus is on *interactions between participants* rather than identifying one individual as the cause of a problem within the group. We expect that very different developmental outcomes will occur as a function of the availability of helpful social resources, similar to the findings reported by Werner (1993) in her longitudinal study of individuals facing initial social and functional difficulty.

ADHD becomes a descriptive label for a behavioral pattern that includes a higher than usual rate of provoking, intruding, hastening, delaying, and avoiding. Each of those behaviors is understood as reinforced by an historical pattern. Intervention is aimed at systematically altering the sequences of situations and circumstances (i.e., changing history) in order to impact the frequency rates of those behaviors. Diagnosed persons are claimed to vacillate between the extremes of non-participation and invasiveness, but both of these non-normative extremes present difficulties.

When doing hyperactive/impulsive behaviors, the individual is disruptive to others and at personal risk. Rather than conform to limits and propriety, the individual behaves impudently, narcissistically, and jeopardizes others. Conversely, inattentive behaviors present an opposite social problem; the behaviors create difficulty for others in that greater participation is required but not forthcoming. The individual will avoid, not respond, or disengage from others.

Traditionalists claim, however, that these two atypical responses correspond to an identical neural biological inability to control the self, but this alternative perspective sees these behavioral extremes as particular reinforced responses that occur in various situations and circumstances. They are characterized as infringing or repellent, and occur at particular times given the subject's past history of conditioning.

The symptoms impulsivity, hyperactivity, and inattentiveness are given psychosocial meaning; they are not understood as signs of a delayed neurological system. For example, rather than say he was "driven to distraction," one can say that he has been conditioned to not participate in those circumstances. Instead of saying he was impulsive and could not stop himself, one could assert that he has been reinforced to respond hastily and would have functioned acceptably had he been reinforced to enact some other behavior in his repertoire (including pausing to contemplate alternatives).

A learning paradigm makes it possible to understand the repetition of ADHD behaviors in a very different way as compared to invoking the claim that the behaviors are merely instances of disinhibited neurology. A careful analysis of psychosocial history helps us to very reliably account for the emission of one or another diagnostic response.

Interestingly, Bargh and Chartrand (1999) note that this is apparently the case for what they call "mental processes" as well. These authors state:

> The necessary and sufficient ingredients for automation are frequency and consistency of use of the same set of component mental processes under the same circumstances, regardless of whether the frequency and consistency occur because of a desire to attain a skill, or whether they occur just because we have tended in the past to make the same choices or to do the same thing or to react emotionally or evaluatively in the same way each time. These processes also become automated, but because we did not start out intending to make them that way, we are not aware that they have been and so, when the process operates automatically in that situation, we aren't aware of it (p. 469).

In Bargh and Chartrand's scenario, when we repeat observable or mental actions in response to certain conditions, those behaviors are understood as being automatically cued by situation. Reactions occur without our awareness of which parameters are reinforcing particular mental actions or any other behavioral acts that we do. This is what we refer to as a "force of habit."

So when it is said that diagnosed persons lack awareness or that they cannot stop themselves, those assessments do not support the traditional construction that diagnosed persons are neurologically less able. The reports mean that observers of those behaviors have not yet identified the contingencies that reinforce the responses. However, like other frequently repeated learned behaviors, those responses may be emitted in a seemingly automatic fashion without any immediate understanding of what accounts for their occurrence.

ADHD reacting can be so habitual and pervasive that persons doing those behaviors will also report an inability to change. Diagnosed persons will indicate that they cannot sit still, or that they think about all kinds of different content when others speak or when they try to concentrate. Yet despite those self-reports of helplessness and lack of self-control, the self-appraisals and the frequency and severity of the patterning tell us nothing about the etiology of the reactions. All of the seemingly "driven" patterns of response can nevertheless still be reinforced.

Individuals may be conditioned to be distractible and fidgety in highly repetitious and extreme ways similar to individuals who are shaped to sustain concentration in exceptional ways and show a calm demeanor (e.g., yoga). They might learn to monopolize social interaction, expend minimal effort doing what others instruct, become insecure when excluded or no longer the center of attention, and rely excessively on others to complete work, and *yet* still report that change seems impossible.

Persons doing diagnostic behaviors might report having no knowledge whatsoever of the conditions under which the behaviors occur, nor understand the event sequences that seem to increase the frequency rates of particular behaviors. They may vehemently want to change and report a powerlessness to do so. However, within this conceptual framework their reports of being "driven to distraction" are not imbued with more credibility than other appraisals. The fact that ADHD behaviors are difficult to stop does not mean that they are not also conditioned. When diagnosed persons report that they would like nothing more than to be able to concentrate and complete certain activities, or that they are incapable of resisting distraction, those reactions are also characterized as conditioned. Many of us make these assessments when we have learned particular actions early in development, and when we recognize that it is difficult to change problematic responses. However, other than noting that the behaviors are enacted effortlessly and habitually, it is unclear what is being discriminated when these kinds of reports are made.

Therefore, instead of understanding ADHD responses as less controlled, those reactions are characterized as reinforced. The behaviors may increase the probability of different outcomes such as protecting against disappointment, maintaining discretionary authority, and reducing the probability of denial. While persons doing those behaviors might be functioning in a socially unacceptable fashion, they may still be reinforced to respond in those ways, and they might not be getting exposure to conditioning that would increase more acceptable responding. In the traditional vernacular, they control differently and unacceptably, but it is arguable whether they have an additional delay called ADHD that causes them to behave unacceptably.

The impulsive or poorly regulated diagnosed child appears to be showing less ability to integrate the future into decision making, but our view is that ADHD behaviors are related to the individual's reinforcement history. This view is well illustrated when a diagnosed child informs his parent that he cannot wash the dishes because he has homework to complete, or when he convinces his parents to buy a particular toy for its educational value. When these behaviors occur, we could argue that the diagnosed child is controlling the future extremely competently. It might be asked if his priorities have suddenly changed, or if events that are more likely in relation to those actions are reinforcing the mature responses.

ADHD behaviors are complex to unravel as they may get reinforced when others smirk, show concern, become irritated, upset, and/or compensate and relent after the child acts in a careless, forgetful, risky, intrusive, or indifferent manner. Diagnostic responding might increase if the child does not respond to instructions, as those non-responses can prod others to repeat and solicit further engagement. Reinforced sequencing is also evident when diagnosed children fail to transition with others, and as parents try harder to help them keep pace within the group.

Diagnostic responding might get reinforced (rather than extinguished) when significant others beg, plead, cajole, lecture, pressure, disapprove, and/or become powerlessness and frustrated with the behaviors. It seems that all of those social responses may increase the child's social significance, reluctance, and authority, as well as increase reconciliation when everyone calms down. Sometimes failure to participate and attend may protect the child from being criticized by family members, although the net result is that the child rarely joins in when the family congregates. As noted previously, it is events that follow ADHD responding that either increase or decrease the probability of insecure, under-accommodating, less conciliatory behaviors.

As Skinner (1953, 71) notes "The assertion that early experiences determine the personality of the mature organism assumes that the effect of operant reinforcement is long-lasting." Our alternative approach adopts Skinner's view and examines early patterns of conditioning before discounting the significance that learning might have had on the frequency and severity of observable ADHD behaviors.

Benefits of self-reliant/collaborative interacting

We argue here that by engaging the diagnosed person in a collaborative intervention, an increase in acceptable responding without the need to continuously monitor or pressure the individual will develop. That is, behaviors initially learned with less pressuring and directive cueing will repeat in situations where there is less pressuring and orchestrating, because those behaviors have never been aspects of the conditioning from the outset.

This training problem is evident when a child informs a parent about an acceptable achievement, and the parent states "I'm proud of you, and now you have permission to play outside again." While this parental response might increase the likelihood that the child will continue to show conforming behaviors as long as parent maintains control over the child's actions, if the parent stops doing the behaviors in response to positive attainments, or if the child learns to counter the parent's unilateral decision making, there is an increased probability that the child will function less acceptably. Until the child also learns to achieve in conditions that have nothing to do with parental responses (including their environmental manipulations), appreciated behavior is less likely when parental attachment is reduced.

One could say that traditional intervention conditions a child to respond to parental action to a greater rather than lesser extent, and the child's conditioning is utterly reliant on the parental contribution. The learning alternative intervention proposed here attempts to avoid these problems. Instead, there is increased focus on the child's reaction to achievements when this information is exchanged. For example, a parent will ask the child about his or her response to having successfully completed a task. The child's reaction to what was achieved, and problems the child identifies are the focus of the exchange rather than the parent's appraisal of the child's performance.

If the child avoids (e.g., the child responds by saying "I don't know" or "I don't care"), the parent can discuss this reaction non-critically and try to resolve problems that relate to the responses. For example, the parent might ask "Is it that you don't know or are you holding back from saying what you want?" We expect during the initial stages of treatment that past conditioning will markedly impede positive interaction. The child will likely have learned to anticipate an escalating argument, heightened criticism or blame, or disapproval when parents (and other adults) initiate an interaction pertaining to expected achievements.

However, we are confident that by integrating the child's perspective into the interaction, there will be the increased probability that the exchange will reinforce the child to continue to talk with the parent. The child can also learn how to initiate similar verbal exchanges about future social expectations. Over time, the child will begin to show fewer avoidance behaviors and follow through with behavioral plans derived from less reliance on parental cues, directions, punishments or rewards. Since the child's perspective is incorporated into the social exchange, we predict that the identified behaviors will remain consistent with what the child initiates and enjoys. Like other forms of self-instruct behavior, those actions will show improved reliability, increased self-reliance, consistency of effort, and organization through time.

Since ADHD behaviors can be very taxing for others, and coercion is difficult for the weaker individual, both diagnosed person and loved ones can be reinforced by a social pattern where participants develop their own resources and give support to each other's distress. In contrast to infancy when others must accommodate fully and remain constantly involved in order to promote the baby's survival, the requirement starts to shift, whereby children gradually become less demanding and avoidant and more involved. If it is the case that ADHD behaviors become increasingly intolerable as the child grows older, the earlier that problematic behaviors are extinguished, the better.

Diagnosed persons will learn to do socially acceptable acts primarily when taking an amphetamine and when others impose extra rewards, punishments, coercions, and compensations within the traditional intervention scheme. However, little is being done to condition diagnosed persons to enact those same behaviors in situations where the manager is less involved, or when medication is not enhancing performance; both manager and medication are necessary to keep spurring the behavioral acts.

The child primarily learns to function in a highly contrived environment heightened by medication and management that are both unlikely to persist as the child ages, or if problems arise with the pharmacological treatments. While traditional methods are the quickest ways to induce change, they have not proved to be the best long-term (fewest side effects) way to induce change that will repeat across conditions. Learning and traditional approaches each attempt to increase participation, help one to develop routines, instigate effective problem solving strategies and organization of behavior over time, but the learning approach places less emphasis on medicating or reliance on others to instigate and direct.

Rather than stimulate participation and acceptable methodical responding with amphetamines, additional rewards, and other compensations as a way to make societal requirements seem plausible, achievable, and exciting, the current model accomplishes those ends by maintaining the diagnosed person's discretionary input by increasing instances of reciprocal exchange, and by shaping independent accomplishments. We expect that these changes will promote better arousal and persistence to parallel what happens when diagnosed persons do activities that they initiate and enjoy.

When behaviors are induced by others we understand that they have been conditioned to occur in the presence of those who direct the action (i.e., as long as the parent beats the drum, the child rows the boat). But when the monitoring system is removed, the frequency rates of the behaviors may often diminish. For example, if a diagnosed child is told that he will be punished for touching a particular object, the system works as long as someone is available to monitor compliance. But compliance is less guaranteed when no one is in the room, because not touching is conditioned in relation to the coercion and the probability of punishment being given by someone who facilitates those outcomes.

Since a very different sequencing of events is probable in relation to touching a forbidden object without the monitor, very different behaviors may be enacted when no one is around. Given this unknown, we think it worthwhile to develop an intervention to shape typical responding using less directive supervision. We also advise that we avoid adding token systems to induce new behaviors, in that these solutions often result in side effects such as significant drop off in compliance when they are discontinued. Much like what happens when a child is forced to eat a certain food and then does not eat the food when older, behaviors might not repeat frequently in non-coercive conditions if they are coercively reinforced.

Therefore, instead of helping diagnosed individuals better follow rules, this alternative intervention helps them better contribute to *making* rules, and to better *cooperate* with the rules. Parents are encouraged to facilitate agreeable social arrangements whenever possible, and are also discouraged from using harsh and patronizing approaches. The expectation is that positive interaction will affect the frequency with which diagnosed children coordinate acceptably with parents and other authority figures. In other words, diminish such responses as finishing quickly, antagonistic behavior, and disengagement when social importance is diminished, or when children are otherwise uncomfortable with how they are treated.

The current approach attempts to train new patterning with less point of performance directing and contingency management. Even if traditional interventions were progressively thinned as the child matures (Barkley, 2006f), diagnosed persons might still be influenced by the contingencies managed by the parent that are being given in less quantity or further apart. They might remain preoccupied with the bribes and punishments that the parent imposes, and very little would be accomplished regarding the conditioning of behaviors unrelated to specific parental actions.

The alternative goal is to condition diagnosed persons to initiate socially acceptable behaviors and achievements without unilateral coercions imposed by others. While the dogmatic approaches obtain the assent of others, follow-through will be less frequent as a result when pressuring conditions are removed. Dogmatism could also train participants to struggle for discretionary authority rather than to cooperate, since the *modus operandi* is to shift the other person towards adopting one's own views rather than towards compromise.

However, many people seem to fear that significantly worse outcomes will occur if traditional intervention is *not* employed. Instead of designing interventions geared towards strengthening weaker characteristics and teaching individuals new skills, most will proceed as if medication, coercion, and extra contingencies are essential for normalcy. They will assert that all other interventions will simply be a disservice to the inherently delayed diagnosed person.

It is generally recognized that adults who seek treatment must necessarily learn some self-management, but it is also claimed that meeting diagnostic criteria means that one must always maintain external support (including use of medication). Adherents assert that the best anyone can do is ingest medication for a lifetime, create a support system so that less thinking is required to meet expectations, and increase the frequency of the rewards and punishments.

Those advocating compensatory treatments also point out that many younger diagnosed children have problems with fine motor skills needed for personal care and craftsmanship tasks or have difficulty communicating. Diagnosed children are typically viewed as less able to be responsible, and this often results in others' skepticism that they will follow through adequately without monitoring (Barkley and Edwards, 1998). However, maintaining the dependence of diagnosed children on the discretionary authority of others is not likely to help them behave satisfactorily without supervision. This may be one of the reasons why traditional methods have not produced impressive long-term results, especially when treatments stop.

The common belief that diagnosed persons are less able to be responsible and to anticipate distant future consequences implies that if they make agreements with others, their neurological limitation will undermine their ability to follow through. Traditionalists assert that diagnosed persons require more salient, immediate, and frequent consequences that must be managed. Ongoing management is required to stave off the inevitable problems surrounding their confusion about how to enact what they know at each point of performance. Managers are advised to use twice as many positives than negatives, change rewards frequently, and to take action rather than talk (Barkley, 2000).

Although as these forms of intervention are imposed, individuals are immediately deprived of the opportunity to develop autonomy and self-reliance. Here then is the inevitable key drawback of traditional intervention techniques, which in the long-run practically guarantees that ADHD will not be cured. Nothing will have been done to facilitate non-diagnostic functioning. Diagnosed children are clearly helped initially by the intervention, but they are also being trained towards complete dependence on external assistance. If diagnosed persons do not develop their own resources, and the elixir does not completely resolve ADHD responding, we suspect that they will have increasing problems as they spend time away from the managers who provided the directive assistance.

Traditionalists are adamant that poor prognosis and recidivism without medication and other traditional treatments relate to the nature of neurological ADHD, but it could alternatively be the nature of their training methods. The lack of generalization of treatment effects and patterns of dependency on the efforts of others (and medications) exhibited by many diagnosed persons could relate to the social training and interventions used to treat this heterogeneous aggregate. Most often, diagnosed persons are not exposed to conditioning that has a higher probability of shaping autonomous achievements. Recidivism may have less to do with ADHD being an intractable neurological condition, and more to do with the interventions that are deployed. If an individual operates constantly under orchestrated conditions and altered attentional states, it is not surprising that he or she returns to pre-treatment behavior if special support and enhancements are withdrawn.

It may be that removing the traditional interventions has changed circumstances such that the responses that had previously been conditioned are no longer elicited. Traditionalists insist that psychopharmacology, directives, and contingency management are the only proven ways to hold incurable ADHD in abeyance, but it is reasonable that people in general continue behaviors that have been conditioned early in life, and that traditional interventions would rarely lead to wholesale behavioral change if they were to be stopped.

A case could, moreover, be made that ADHD behavior is reinforced when traditional intervention is withdrawn. Subtracting the extras can compel the child to respond as if he or she is missing something, that it is no longer necessary to accommodate because there is no coercion, and/or that unwanted responsibility is being imposed. We anticipate that ADHD behaviors will quickly return when parents take steps to withdraw the extra compensations, pressures, and accommodations associated with the traditional intervention and reintroduce the expectation that the child contribute more.

It is in that context that our alternative approach can be utilized to help shape self-reliant/collaborative functioning. Diagnosed children are from the outset given responsibility that they can handle; they often participate in deriving solutions, and will also initiate the action to change. We anticipate too that behaviors evident during actions where the diagnosed person maintains discretionary authority are likely to repeat. Participants are encouraged to attend to each others' concerns, and reciprocity and success (rather than medication and managed rewards and punishments) stimulate greater coordination with others.

But the tradeoff, at least in the short-term, between adopting the learning vs. the traditional approach, is that loved ones will have a much harder job helping the diagnosed child learn greater autonomy, whereas the traditional intervention had previously provided greater ease and support for parents and caregivers. Stipulated tasks (such as schoolwork) will still expose diagnosed individuals to evaluation, disapproval, and loss of discretionary input, etc., so it will be an ongoing problem to help children respond less diagnostically to assigned situations and formal settings. It may also be necessary for teachers and parents to address numerous problems that occur in rapid succession, and to enact collaborative interacting consistently over long periods before significant behavioral changes are evident.

The first objective is to resolve problems related to diagnosed individuals carrying out *required activity* so that actions instructed by others are more palatable to them. For instance, if we want a diagnosed child (who likes sports) to read more, we encourage the child to read about sports figures and buy magazines related to her interest. The child may then by choice repeat what she has learned with typical school-related content as reading competency develops. Exposure to more reading may make the assignments seem less aversive to the diagnosed child who has spent more time reading.

However, there are many individuals who learn ADHD responding and who also have other functional problems that disallow their meeting age-appropriate expectations. So it is not surprising that they are likely to be reinforced to avoid or do other extreme behaviors that elicit reaction and concern. When such complicating problems interfere with normative learning, ADHD responses will be extremely difficult to extinguish even if attempts are initiated early. Children with complicating functional impairments will have more trouble meeting parental and societal expectations, and parents will also have greater difficulty shaping self-reliance and conciliatory responding. In these social circumstances the probability of reinforcing diagnostic patterning is greater.

Conditioning new behaviors and failure to achieve commendable results pushes many parents back again towards the recommendations of the traditional model. Many parents will accept the claim that their child cannot function adequately without the traditional compensatory measures of increasing coercion, directive assistance, and prescribing amphetamines, which indeed work exceedingly well in the short-term.

These parents bring their disruptive children to professionals because they have been upsetting and at times dominating family activity. Many of these children are on the verge of school failure; landlords might be threatening eviction due to noise; and many of these children will be placing themselves and others at risk when they behave outlandishly. Medication and contingency management usually work immediately to sedate ADHD disruptive behaviors and stimulate focused, productive, methodical responses and so has natural appeal. Moreover, if we accept that diagnosed persons will always be limited in their functioning, any psychological training to increase cooperation and autonomy becomes an unrealistic ideal that should not be expected or tried. The presumption is that everything possible is being done.

In the same way the traditional school recommendations of providing the diagnosed child with a permanently easier curriculum, as well as a personal assistant, also apparently hastens improvement in the school setting. Having an aide sit with the child to facilitate assignment completion, and simplifying and reducing assignments will usually produce rapid positive results. Giving the child stimulant medication, frequently cueing and monitoring him to write assignments, and/or prevent him from leaving school until he can demonstrate compliance with directives for homework, is likely to quickly change school behaviors.

Traditionalists will insist that diagnosed persons require this structure to offset the natural environment, but what if ADHD behaviors are *reinforced* behaviors rather than *delayed* behaviors? What if ADHD behaviors are inadvertently being conditioned when we attempt to withdraw the traditional treatment later, and that the recurrence of those behaviors reinforces others to reinstate the accommodations formerly provided? What if we are accidentally teaching diagnosed individuals to *only* complete schoolwork when sitting with someone else, or when functioning under the influence of an amphetamine? As these supplemental interventions are implemented they apparently become difficult to discard, and not everyone will want to give up this arrangement.

Traditional recommendations are also superficially consistent with what is familiar and customary for many people. The message that parents should control is very appealing, since many of us enjoy having others conform to our directives (i.e., we get our own way more often). For instance, Anastopoulos, Smith, and Wien (1998) implore parents to not treat a child's privileges as if they are rights. The authors advise parents to make access to resources contingent on compliance with parental dictums.

On the other hand, many parents find it difficult to behave in any way that would disappoint their child. They believe that being a good parent means that the child should be content, happy, and should not suffer—even when others are inordinately burdened. Some parents may have had troublesome childhoods that they do not wish to see repeated. They could ostensibly find it very difficult to facilitate self-reliance and collaborative interacting, and thus regard our alternative as not accommodating enough to adequately meet their child's needs.

We see that both extremes can be observed, and our aim is to shift parents to the middle ground—negotiation and autonomy—rather than either dominating or submitting. There are untold benefits to mutually-acceptable arrangements wherever possible. If, however, we always choose the quickest solution (i.e., to acquiesce or bully), other problematic consequences can and will most likely arise, especially over the long-term.

For example, the reliance of many diagnosed children on medication and tightened controls resembles the socialization process of military or institutional training. However, there are significant numbers of very conforming adults who have been consistently dominated by parents, and many have reported feeling discontentment in their personal lives; they indicate that they would like to be more assertive. The army-based approach might promote deference, but to what extent do we want deference in our family relationships?

Conversely, for individuals who imitate their parents' controlling and domineering behavioral patterns, we do not know how many individuals who interact with them on a daily basis (in particular, their spouses) are reacting negatively to their dominating patterns of behavior. We observe that individuals who care about these overbearing individuals would like to develop a compromising and conciliatory pattern to facilitate mutually-satisfying marital interactions.

There are many adults seeking outpatient therapy who want to learn how to interact in a less constrained and constricted way, and adults who struggle with loved ones' aggressive behaviors. Traditional methods might shape both of these patterns more frequently. We suggest that spouses and employers will often respond positively if individuals are proactive, assertive, committed, less bossy, and cooperative rather than either compliant or domineering.

Historical difficulties fostering self-management

Many barriers crop up when therapy is initiated for diagnosed persons. If professional assistance is unilaterally obtained by family members on behalf of a diagnosed person, it is not surprising if the individual does not participate enthusiastically, especially at the beginning. ADHD behavior is very likely to be cued when discretionary input has been dramatically undermined.

This problem may be a frequent mitigating factor when psychosocial intervention takes place with older disenfranchised diagnosed children, adolescents, and adults. If it is only the teachers, parents, spouses, and employers who are promoting behavioral change, success will not be achieved; it is crucial to reinforce diagnosed individuals' participation and initiative not only in situations and circumstances in the outside world, but also in the therapist's office. Unless there is at least some "buy in" from the diagnosed person, it becomes the sole responsibility of others to diminish ADHD responding.

Given that it is most often loved ones who initiate the action to change, we can inquire whether some of the failure of psychotherapy is due to ADHD being an incurable condition, or if it is actually very difficult to adjust behavior when individuals are defensive and unwilling. If diagnosed persons are non-participatory in therapy, and expecting to be blamed, the desire by others to accomplish anything of note is, in a word, futile.

However, the reluctance to give up atypical response patterns associated with long-term problematic consequences is not unique to the ADHD group. For example, it is extremely difficult to convince a parent to work fewer hours even if his or her family life may be suffering in response to those habits. If one considers this parallel, it is not that diagnosed persons are less able to recognize long-term complications of their response pattern when they are unenthusiastic about changing; it is that ADHD behaviors (like working long hours) continue to be reinforced.

It seems unreasonable to therefore infer that something must be biologically amiss when diagnosed persons are not eager during psychotherapy, and/or continue behaviors that correlate with maladjustment in life's major arenas of functioning. Diagnostic responding may still have many personal advantages: like the accolades for the workaholic who dedicates many extra hours to the office, but who is simultaneously also failing in marriage, family, and personal well-being.

Each of us takes numerous trials in order to reshape response patterns after having repeated an old pattern countless times (e.g., opening a kitchen drawer for silverware that is no longer kept there). Moreover, many of these conditioned responses continue to be reinforced despite escalating correlated problems. For instance, persons who spend much time cleaning may be doing reinforced behavior, in that they had learned at a very young age that "good children do not leave messes." Cleaning is also one of the few activities that provides reasonable discretionary authority for individuals who report feeling powerless in other aspects of their lives. However, these individuals may have little time to interact with family members (which can also reinforce the behaviors) throughout the time that they are relentless cleaners. While the frequent cleaning can heighten family tension, the observance of an immaculate house and compliments given about it (and numerous other reinforcing events associated with frequent cleaning) continues to condition the fastidiousness.

Similarly, how rapidly does a critical wife or husband alter behavior in response to the spouse's insistence to speak kindly? How quickly or effortlessly do parents stop yelling at their children, even though they recognize that over time many other problems occur in relation to yelling? How easily can an under-assertive individual, who continuously misses out, or is resentful and unhappy, enact more assertive patterns?

It seems to be a human condition that until particular actions sequence with changed results over a variety of conditions, we remain unaware of the extent to which those new sequences are distinct or pervasive. It is in this sense that extinguishing diagnostic responding and reinforcing give and take with others usually takes a relatively long period of time. Rarely does anyone quickly relinquish habits. For example, even though it might be safer to confide in a spouse, an adult may nonetheless continue to withhold if she has been conditioned to remain silent in the primary family. When understood in that light, saying that ADHD signs and symptoms are reinforced does not mean that diagnosed children *plan* to respond unacceptably or can easily behave differently. Nor does it mean that they or others know *why* they are doing ADHD responding, or are aware that they are doing the behaviors.

We anticipate that it is possible to identify event sequences that have reinforced less acceptable ADHD responses rather than considerate, appeasing, precautious, and conventional behaviors, but we do not presuppose that subjects are cognizant of what has reinforced them. It is only that the probability of particular responses is raised in particular situations in relation to a derived history. First person knowledge of particular histories of reinforcement that might account for the ADHD signs and symptoms is not required or presumed within this conceptual framework. It need not be necessary moreover that diagnosed persons or their parents agree with the interpretation that ADHD symptoms are reinforced (rather than chaotic) behavior. These individuals (like many of us) may be unable to identify the contingencies that increase the probability of their actions.

As mentioned above, even though these individuals are characterized as doing ADHD, there is no implication that they choose to enact the behaviors, that they enjoy the behaviors, that it is easy for them to change, or that they are manipulating others in a premeditative fashion. The model only proposes that diagnosed persons have learned a particular social patterning over time and that this patterning can be coherently understood in terms of a functional analysis that coordinates the frequencies of ADHD behaviors with particular sequences of situations and circumstances.

However, given the intricacies of shaping new behaviors, the utility of this approach (as with all psychological interventions) depends entirely on the resources of the participants, including the intervening professionals. When compared to other kinds of circumscribed and less complex presenting problems that respond better to psychotherapeutic intervention (e.g., recently occurring argumentativeness/defiance between parent and child, or adjustment reactions, etc.), we confirm that ADHD patterns may be harder to diminish.

For example, curriculums requiring diagnosed children to do self-directed speech about alternative acceptable actions when encountering particular situations may not lead to helpful results in many instances. Barkley (1998a, 30) notes that some investigators have posited that these cognitive behavioral strategies will help "guide" and "generate" better solutions when the child reacts to problem situations, but it could also be asserted that the requirement to do self-talk may only be helpful in very limited circumstances.

Those responses might only be advantageous when individuals first learn to change what they do, but not be particularly helpful over the longer term. How many times each day do any of us stop and think before we act? While occasionally the child can benefit from pausing and responding non-vocal verbally before acting publicly in order to minimize mistakes, it is unlikely that the child will be socially effective if instructed to repeat that behavior permanently. Such a procedure is burdensome and discouraging unless the child also learns when the sequencing will help rather than hinder.

Moreover, if it is presumed that non-diagnosed individuals do *not* do preliminary self-talk immediately before many instances of acceptable observable responding, it is unclear as to why this topic is discussed in the first place. Perhaps it is more often the case that acceptable responses can be conditioned whether one pauses or not to do antecedent self-talk. Furthermore, if ADHD behaviors also continue to be reinforced, it seems that these kinds of programs will not have satisfactorily induced behavioral changes. Instead, it looks as if the program is merely reinforcing the new behavior patterns.

Cunningham and Cunningham (1998) claim that the diagnosed child's problems with self-regulation will limit the application of conflict resolution skills learned in self-management programs, but the current alternative view offers a different account for those apparent failures. It is not that the rest of us typically regulate and then apply skills before we overtly respond to social conflicts: we simply emit the sequence of actions that has been reinforced within particular conditions.

If that presumption is adopted, traditionalists' explication for the unacceptable behavior of diagnosed children during social conflict is on shaky ground. Not only would the posited regulatory sequence of actions be unwieldy, cumbersome, and impractical to do, but it has never been demonstrated that individuals doing socially acceptable behaviors during conflicts actually undergo an antecedent regulatory sequence of responses when they carry out appropriate, correct, and typical conflict resolution interactions. While there will be circumstances when individuals rehearse or engage in preliminary action (including non-vocal verbal responding) before a subsequent public response, where people do respond acceptably, on most occasions they do not report having done mental preparation.

In a related concern, Milich and Kramer (1985) also note that task impulsivity and social impulsivity appear to be different constructs: that teaching diagnosed children to do certain kinds of antecedent behaviors in order to reduce social impulsivity will not very likely help them solve task-oriented problems increasingly effectively. According to Milich and Kramer, it is improbable that a program designed to train socially appropriate social responses will correlate with improvements in academic functioning or vice versa.

However, we speculate that self-management programs could be valuable if curricula were designed to help diagnosed persons respond effectively in conditions they typically encounter *without* also imposing the requirement that certain antecedent mental responses must be enacted. Hall (1980) raises a similar concern when he also notes that there are times when it is preferable to react without first going through a series of steps. He emphasizes that prescribed problem solving approaches are unlikely to be very helpful across settings and content.

Nonetheless, those diagnosed with ADHD have typically been subjected to training models that prescribe reflective problem-solving strategies. The hope is that what is learned will translate into acceptable behavior when particular situations and circumstances arise. These interventions purport to teach particular skills or procedures that diagnosed persons must follow to reduce ADHD responding. While behaviors learned within these programs might sometimes help diagnosed persons operate in acceptable ways for the specific tasks or social situations practiced and included in the training, it has not been consistently shown that these programs are generally beneficial, or that participants are reinforced to respond in *new* ways within a broader social matrix.

For example, Abikoff (1987) reports limited positive laboratory effects when diagnosed individuals are trained to self-manage, and that only some encouraging treatment results have been demonstrated at follow up. He surmises that these interventions have not met the "expectation that the development of internalized self-regulation skills would facilitate generalization and maintenance . . ." (p. 210) of the behaviors that are taught to the ADHD group. He claims that even though "youngsters can be taught social problem solving skills, there is little indication that they use these skills to mediate their social behavior in vivo" (p. 209).

By and large, it does not seem that either cognitive behavioral or social skills training has produced impressive results for diagnosed persons, or led to an adequate generalization of the behaviors that have been instructed (Abikoff and Gittelman, 1985; Bloomquist, August, and Ostrander, 1991; Braswell et al., 1997; Robin, 1998; Barkley, 2000; Pfiffner, Barkley, and DuPaul, 2006). Abikoff (1987) also emphasizes that many of these programs are too short to produce lasting behavior change, and many have not taken individual differences into account. That is, children might have very different reasons for their behavioral problems and academic failures, and a one-size-fits-all approach may not be sufficient to adequately help them.

In consideration of these matters, rather than require diagnosed persons to participate in a pre-established curriculum, or learn social skills training scripts, and follow the directive to do certain patterns of self-speech, the current model attempts to increase the probability of non-diagnostic responding by first determining what behaviors participants would like to change (i.e., define the problem, identify concerns). In contrast to classroom learning or administering psychological tests where a specific agenda is imposed, shaping self-management can start to resemble psychotherapy, where an agenda is rarely scripted to the same degree. Rather than altogether abandon attempts to increase self-governing for diagnosed persons, it might be more reasonable to increase self-reliant/collaborative interacting with diagnosed persons when figuring out ways to effectively manage their behavior over time.

Additionally, other problems with traditionally designed self-management programs arise when contingency management is presumed to be necessary. For example, Douglas (1980a, 1980b) insists that contingency management during self-management programs must be implemented to increase the probability that the person will enact the required behaviors. However, there is little concern about possible side effects when undertaking that procedure—even though it is now standard practice to monitor and reward diagnosed children when they comply with program requirements (Abikoff, 1987). For example, it is noteworthy that the frequency rate of the desired behaviors can often decrease when contingency management is withdrawn. Unless the prescribed behaviors are reinforced apart from the auspices of the program and the added contingencies, it is improbable that the preferred behaviors will continue when the program ends.

Consequently, while these programs have not resulted in a continuum of acceptable behaviors, we argue here that teaching diagnosed persons acceptable social behavior is also likely to fail if interventions are predicated on contingency management, and increasing self-talk and conformity in accordance with a pre-designed curriculum or imposed agenda. It matters not whether the teaching occurs informally, in the laboratory, in therapy, or during a formal self-management skills building program, since diagnosed persons continue to respond to external direction of actions and assistance that is unlikely to be influential as these individuals make decisions away from their overseers. Moreover, there is also the danger that the promised rewards offered by these programs send a tacit message that the behaviors are undesirable without the additional enticements, and that the behaviors are simply what others want, expect, and demand. In other words, if these behaviors are so advantageous, why is it necessary to offer extra incentives in order to compel individuals to enact them?

Hence when making inferences about our past efforts to teach self-management to diagnosed persons, we suggest that neurological ADHD is not preventing the acquisition of self-management behavior; but rather that the conditions of skill building interventions are limiting the probability of effective outcomes. The discretionary authority of the child is too restricted and the curriculum does not reinforce acceptable behaviors within *in vivo* conditions. If others stipulate required behaviors and impose extras to induce new skills, the frequency rates of new behaviors will plummet when the child functions independently. If the child is not a collaborative participant in the learning process towards behaving more autonomously, it is not surprising that he or she will *not* perform what is learned when *unsupervised*.

When we conceptualize ADHD behaviors in this alternative fashion, we recognize that traditional intervention does not rectify neurological delay. Symptomatic responses are seen here as different rather than delayed, and reinforced rather than disabled. ADHD behaviors are understood within the purview of psychology, and we suggest that they can be changed by formatting a different history of reinforcement.

Chapter 2

The Traditional Intervention Regime

The traditional disability model and intervention, which essentially parallels that of residential care, has become the exclusive form of treatment for those diagnosed with ADHD. Other ways of changing behaviors and conceptualizing the problem are not being given much credibility or consideration by most professionals who intervene with this diagnostic group.

Rather than posit that competency will be impaired when ADHD behaviors are learned, or that individuals with particular problems are likely to learn ADHD behaviors, traditionalists invariably assert a delayed biological/mental inhibitory apparatus as the seminal cause of the majority of unacceptable behaviors of diagnosed individuals. For traditionalists, ADHD is a biological problem, and social problems occur to varying degrees depending on how the external world reacts to that bodily delay. Learning over time is never understood as germane for ADHD diagnosed individuals.

Barkley (2000) moreover asserts that ADHD is *inherited* even to a greater extent than a person's height. Heritability studies of cohorts living together (or apart) purport to show that the ADHD diagnosis is congruent with genetic prediction models. Wilens, Spencer, and Biederman, (1998) echo those claims and note that adoption studies also indicate "genetic risk" factors.

Since ADHD "runs in families," is ameliorated by medication, and because many diagnosed individuals show specific bodily correlates, the common conclusion is that the condition resembles a medical problem rather than a psychosocial pattern of behavior. The inference is that one's genes *cause* the severity and frequency of ADHD behavior. This delayed neurobiological condition is the reason for the high heritability quotients, the correlated biological substrates, and the fact that medication has to date outperformed all psychotherapeutic intervention.

The result of this data compilation is that there is less emphasis on the investigation and identification of the functionality of ADHD behavior, and/or possible ways in which ADHD behaviors may be reinforced and shaped within the diagnosed individual's personal social world. In that the kinds of psychosocial variables studied thus far have not predicted the occurrence of the disorder, the traditional view is that the behaviors are primarily biologically-induced (rather than learned). It is claimed that less than 20% of the variance is attributable to environmental factors when twin studies are analyzed (Barkley, 1998a).

Traditionalists note that a small number of diagnosed persons seem to acquire the biological problem through adverse early occurring conditions, but for a majority of cases, ADHD has a genetic origin. For example, Barkley (2001) reports that maternal smoking may influence only 10-15% of diagnosed cases, and post-natal injury may account for only 3-5% of the cases. However, regardless of its etiology, the condition is emphatically regarded as a neurological inhibitory problem.

Even though most traditionalists no longer endorse the characterization of the brain-injured child (Strauss and Lehtinen, 1947), or the phraseology of "minimal brain dysfunction," in that diagnostic persons typically do not show defective characteristics, the accepted view is that the developmental delay occurs due to inherited biology (Acosta, Arcos-Burgos, and Muenke, 2004). Each of us will show disinhibition in varying degrees (as we also are diverse in height and intelligence), but traditionalists reckon that diagnosed persons function at the lower end of a normalized curve that measures one's capacity to sustain attention and subdue hyperactivity and impulsivity. These behavioral categories become the primary ways in which lack of self-control becomes evident. While treatment can help to manage inhibitory delay, the underlying biological disability is invariably recognized as permanent (Pfiffner and Barkley, 1998).

Professionals are mainly ascribing to the belief that ADHD is neurological and genetic rather than influenced by environmental factors (Barkley, 1998a). Experts assert that ADHD patterning is caused by lack of behavioral inhibition (Barkley, 1997; Schachar, Tannock, and Logan, 1993). The patterning becomes an inherent temperamental style which predisposes children to eventually show behaviors consistent with the diagnostic criteria (Anastopoulos, Rhoads, and Farley, 2006).

The Quay/Gray model (Quay, 1988) claims that the impulsiveness associated with ADHD comes from reduced activity in the brain's behavioral inhibition system (BIS). It is thought that biological behavioral inhibition is located in the orbital-frontal regions and the interconnections to the striatum. This system is understood to be "sensitive to signals of conditioned punishment . . ." which will raise activity in the BIS and inhibition of behavior when functioning correctly (Barkley, 1998f, 226). For those who subscribe to biological determinism, excessive frequencies of impulsive ADHD behaviors are always a result of neurological processes that are delayed or somehow deficient. Individuals frequently doing those behaviors have less capable inhibitory systems.

Traditionalists, however, do not want others to presume that ADHD connotes neurological malfunctioning, as their view claims that it identifies *delayed* functioning. While ADHD might be associated with a higher incidence of soft neurological signs that hint at neurological immaturity, these problems may also be found in other diagnostic groups such as those with learning impairments, psychosis, autism, and mental deficiency. Therefore, neurological immaturity should not to be used as a variable for diagnostic purposes (Barkley and Edwards, 1998).

While biologically-determined ADHD cannot be discerned from a typical neurological exam, which might or might not yield soft signs, it is nevertheless assumed to be operative whenever individuals behave in ways consistent with the diagnostic behavioral criteria. This is essentially the perspective utilized increasingly not only for ADHD, but also for a wide array of disorders. Traditionalists predict that medical science will continue to make advances, and more precisely uncover the definitive biological and genetic causes of ADHD. Traditionalists are adamant that ADHD typically originates in a person's molecular biology.

All treatment is designed to deal with a posited fixed and permanent lack of biological ability. Those attempting to help may merely ameliorate symptoms by administering medication that boosts the delayed system. Since that remedy alone may not always solve all problems, it is also advised that caretakers help to monitor the diagnosed person so that his or her behavior remains consensual and appropriate. It is presumed that the person is less able to function adequately without these external supports. Giving more discretionary authority to persons with less ability to self-control, and not treating them with medicine that counteracts their biological delay is equivalent to allowing a sick person to suffer needlessly, or allowing inmates to run the asylum.

The putative developmental delay makes it necessary for caretakers to remind, direct, and offer immediate rewards to offset motivational difficulties that decrease the probability that the diagnosed person will recognize the importance of particular responses. Immediacy of reinforcement, saliency, and increased physical representation are necessary, in that those conditions may counter the mental weakness of ability to effectively manage delays and larger blocks of time. While self-generated reinforcements are more frequently available to persons with adequate inhibitory systems, diagnosed persons may only show competency when situational demands require less reliance on the mental actions that traditionalists call "executive functions."

Even though diagnosed adults might eventually find a way to arrange, structure, and simplify their worlds by doing behaviors such as writing down requirements immediately and then referring back to these external cues, their limited ability to enact executive functioning will always impair their organization of behavior over time. Special precautions will always be necessary whenever diagnosed persons of any age must rely on their own sources of management. They are forever more dependent on outside help (including medication) no matter how many skills they are taught.

While this might not be pleasant for the diagnosed person, he or she will behave consistently with what is deemed acceptable when functioning under a system of tightened controls, simplification, amplification, and medication. Requirements are fulfilled only when others become more conscientious about managing the contingencies of their acts. For example, in an effort to promote safety, diagnosed adolescents might be pressured to take their medication by making driving privileges contingent on medication compliance (Barkley, 2000).

The diagnosed persons' environment must be fabricated at the point of each performance by appointed caretakers. Acceptable acts will only occur when under the supervision of a monitor and a stimulant drug. It is presumed that their condition negates the option of granting them the discretionary autonomy that might otherwise be afforded to individuals of similar age. Since diagnosed people are incurably less able to do necessary mental actions prior to motoric responding, increased management, and ingestion of medication are necessities, not the frivolous expenditure of available resources. Despite any and all previous reengineering, diagnosed persons will not behave acceptably at the point of performance. Attempts to reinforce autonomy and mutually-acceptable responding become increasingly irrelevant, or are forgotten as the time interval widens between past reinforcement of particular behaviors and present circumstances.

Developmental course

Barkley (1998b) describes ADHD as a relatively early onset condition that may not be reliably discriminated until the ages three or four. Apparently, many children younger than age three pattern too closely to the ADHD diagnostic category. The occurrence of significantly inattentive and overactive behavior for three- and four-year-olds does not guarantee a regularity of those behaviors later in childhood in at least 50-90% of those children (Barkley, 2006e). However, if the behaviors persist for several more years, the prediction is that the patterning will be severe and persistent (Barkley, Shelton, et al., 2002).

When there is a continuance of the behaviors over extended periods of time, Barkley (1998d) notes that there will be an increase in the likelihood of depressive patterning as well. It is estimated that 25% of ADHD adolescents will show depressive symptoms as they become discouraged about their limited prospects of future success. Many of these individuals may also reveal poor self-confidence and concerns about school completion. Barkley also reports that prognosis is not much better when diagnosed adolescents reach adulthood, as up to one-third who qualify for an ADHD diagnosis will also be diagnosed with Major Depressive Disorder.

ADHD responding also increases the probability of being diagnosed with Oppositional Defiant Disorder (ODD) for nearly two-thirds of the diagnosed population (Szatmari, Offord, and Boyle, 1989). Typically, the occurrence of those behaviors starts between ages five and seven (Barkley, 2000). Moreover, Taylor, Chadwick, Heptinstall, and Danckaerts (1996) have cautioned that individuals showing both ADHD and ODD are most at risk for significant adjustment problems.

Traditionalists emphasize that ADHD and ODD will most likely co-occur when the parent of the diagnosed individual also has an ADHD diagnosis, in that both individuals possess inhibitory deficits. Under these conditions it is believed that conflicts and inconsistent training will increase, disorganization within the home will also be more frequent, and emotionality will be typical. Altogether, these social patterns precipitate the occurrence of ODD behaviors (Barkley, 2000).

Whenever ADHD patterns persist, there is a greater likelihood of many different troublesome behaviors (including tics). For example, Faraone et al. (1997) have noted co-occurrences between ADHD and Antisocial Personality Disorder, substance dependence and abuse, and Conduct Disorder. Usually the more serious co-occurring problems will be most frequent when parents and relatives of diagnosed person also exhibit various psychiatric difficulties (Barkley, 1998d). Conversely, dire predictions are less ominous when ADHD is presumed to be mild, and comorbid conditions are not occurring. For example, Barkley (2000) predicts that diagnosed individuals with non-severe symptoms and no comorbid disorders will more probably outgrow their condition.

Consequently, and despite its reported genetic origins, not only is an ADHD diagnosis unreliable during early childhood, but early environmental exposures strongly influence the behaviors over time. A large proportion of individuals may learn to interact in non-diagnostic ways despite having initially behaved in ways consistent with the diagnostic category. Prognosis differs in relation to the complexities of the presenting problems, and the frequency rates of ADHD behaviors and other co-occurring problems may change depending on what transpires.

Most basically, we see that the ADHD debate revolves around accounting for frequency rates and the intensity of specific sets of behaviors that most children express in varying degrees. For traditionalists, ADHD children are differentiated from most other children by how intense (and how often) they do these behaviors. However, as will be demonstrated throughout this work, intensity and frequency of those and other ADHD behavioral issues can be interpreted without the invocation of biological determinism.

Instead, one might claim that traditionalists' data only shows that ADHD patterning may be easier to change when parents are well adjusted, and when the child does not express other complicating problems. Similarly, the finding that the ADHD pattern is often unresponsive to psychosocial intervention compared to other disruptive behaviors, may only indicate that ADHD patterning is related to instances of conditioning that are pervasive, subtle, and difficult to extinguish compared to other patterns (that began later in childhood). For example, sometimes simply changing who is in the room will alter diagnostic responding in significant ways (Draeger, Prior, and Sanson, 1986).

Nevertheless, when ADHD behaviors continue beyond the pre-school years, prognosis is dismal. Campbell (1990) indicates that if problems persist at that time, there is the increased likelihood of ADHD diagnosis *and* other conduct problems into early childhood. Once children meet the more rigorous criteria for diagnosis in this age group, as many as 80% persist with the condition into adolescence (Barkley, Fischer, et al., 1990). As ADHD patterning continues, it becomes difficult to diminish the behaviors and chances increase that other problems develop as well.

Although we could counter-argue that social problems generally intensify for most non-normative behavioral patterns the longer they persist, importantly, other explications such as continued reinforcement of behaviors in various contexts and circumstances, can reasonably account for persistent diagnostic actions. We also suggest that those with the fewest skills and most troubled psychosocial patterns may also be the *least* likely to change their problematic patterns.

In any case, those who study ADHD are keen to distinguish between neurological ADHD and other diagnostic categories commonly accepted as having social origins; this is particularly the case with aggressive and oppositional/defiant behavior, which highly correlates with an ADHD diagnosis (Loney, Langhorne, and Peternite, 1978; Loney and Milich, 1982). Researchers have pointed out that epidemiological findings indicate that ADHD is typically correlated with developmental delays and cognitive deficits, while conduct problems seem to be associated with psychosocial variables such as marital conflict and family dysfunction (Cunningham and Boyle, 2002; Szatmari, Offord, and Boyle, 1989; McGee, Williams, and Silva, 1984). For those reasons traditionalists see ADHD as a biological problem, whereas explicitly defiant behaviors are understood to be a consequence of particular kinds of social conditioning.

Traditionalists believe that neurologically caused ADHD behavior can be distinguished from psychologically caused behavior, and that ADHD can be considered as a unique set of neurologically induced problematic behaviors. In traditionalists' view, psychology has not adequately explained the occurrence of ADHD symptoms, while social parameters seem to explicate oppositional response patterns quite well (Barkley, 2000).

What is traditional ADHD?

In an attempt to promote consensual understanding, the Diagnostic and Statistical Manual of Mental Disorders (2000, 85) defines ADHD as an ongoing pattern of hyperactivity, impulsivity, and inattention that is more frequent and severe than typically observed in individuals at a comparable level of development. According to the criteria, the impairment must occur to some extent before age seven, and in more than one setting. Developmentally-appropriate social, academic, or occupational functioning must be observed to be disrupted. In order to qualify for an ADHD diagnosis, it should not be possible to better account for the behavioral symptoms by another diagnostic category such as mood disorder, anxiety disorder, dissociative disorder, or personality disorder. While the precise etiology of ADHD is unknown, it seems to run in families, and may occur in a context of various biopsychosocial risk factors.

In an attempt to promote standard usage, the editors also provide a detailed explanation of how ADHD behavior is to be identified. To warrant a diagnosis of ADHD, individuals must have at least six of nine specified instances of inattention, and six of nine hyperactive/impulsive symptoms over the course of at least six months.

The *inattentive* symptoms within the DSM IV-TR note that the individual: (1) often fails to give close attention to details or makes careless mistakes in schoolwork, work, or other activities; (2) often has difficulty sustaining attention in tasks or play activities; (3) often does not seem to listen when spoken to directly; (4) often does not follow through on instructions and fails to finish schoolwork, chores, or duties in the workplace (not due to oppositional behavior or failure to understand instructions); (5) often has difficulty organizing tasks and activities; (6) often avoids, dislikes or is reluctant to engage in tasks that require sustained mental effort (such as schoolwork or homework); (7) often loses things necessary for tasks or activities (e.g., toys, school assignments, pencils, books, or tools); (8) is often easily distracted by extraneous stimuli, (9) is often forgetful when doing daily activities.

When doing the *hyperactive* symptoms, the individual: (1) often fidgets with hands or feet or squirms in seat; (2) often leaves seat in classroom, or doesn't remain seated in situations where remaining seated is expected; (3) often runs around excessively in situations in which it is inappropriate (in adolescents or adults, these acts may manifest in subjective feelings of restlessness); (4) often has difficulty playing or engaging in leisure activities quietly; (5) is often "on the go" or often acts as if "driven by a motor;" (6) often talks excessively. Finally, the *impulsive* symptoms include: (1) blurting out answers before questions have been completed; (2) having difficulty awaiting turn; (3) interrupting or intruding on others (e.g., butts into conversations or games).

Although ADHD has been discussed as if it is a singular disorder or syndrome (Rutter, 1977; 1989), the editors of the DSM-IV-TR indicate that ADHD is a *heterogeneous* disorder; diagnosed individuals present a diversity of related psychiatric symptoms, family backgrounds, developmental courses, and responses to treatments. While some diagnosed persons show a pure ADHD diagnosis with no other significant problems, others show many different co-occurring problems including documented brain injuries. Diagnosed persons may vary extensively in their problematic behaviors relative to each other, and show incongruities in the ways they express ADHD behaviors. One may be non-responsive to one's parents, and highly reactive to one's peers, and the same neural biological delay may be invoked to account for both very opposite response patterns that can occur moments apart. Traditionalists reject the notion that ADHD is simply an aggregate of different kinds of troublesome behaviors despite the marked variations that occur.

Due to the disorder itself, it has also been noted that diagnosed individuals *on average* will show lower scoring (from 7-15 points) on standardized measures of intelligence (Barkley, 2006c). However, the use of this average score data obscures the diversity of the scores for the population of diagnosed individuals, as there is usually a wide distribution of intelligence scores within this diagnostic group. Given traditionalists' views, we would have to presume that even "gifted" diagnosed persons would be more brilliant if it were not for their ADHD.

It is emphasized that ADHD seems more adequately explained by a medical model. To see the problem in any other light would neglect the studies that show a relationship between diagnosis and biological relatedness, and the correlations that have been found between molecular biology, biological structure and function, and behaving in ways that are consistent with behavioral criteria. It is *claimed* that the disorder has an organic or endogenous origin, and there is no current way to remove a person's bodily limitation.

In that view, ADHD patterning may create stress during interpersonal functioning. Unreliable, disinhibited children, can be difficult for most people to manage, particularly when the parent also responds with ADHD patterns. Generally, parents report that it is extremely difficult to socialize a child who does not follow through with required tasks, shows poor self-help skills, and often becomes distracted when asked to carry out simple directives. More extreme social conflict is anticipated under those conditions.

Consequently, while both ADHD and oppositional/defiant behaviors are considered as socially disruptive patterns, and both may occur in a pure form without the existence of the other, traditionalists identify the two patterns as having very different etiologies. Oppositional behavior can be explained socially while ADHD cannot, and has not yet been adequately explained in that way.

Traditionalists emphasize that persons diagnosed as ADHD will have more difficulty relative to others maintaining attention, sustaining effort, and staying motivated in consistent ways (Pfiffner and Barkley, 1998). These problems will become more apparent when consequences of behaviors are less explicit. The diagnosis is not a result of family stress or mental illness (Barkley and Edwards, 1998). ADHD has been described by Douglas (1980b) as an inability to stop, look, listen, and think.

The individual's delayed biological functioning will purportedly hinder success whenever suppression of behavior is required. As a result of this bodily weakness, individuals will have difficulty persisting and maintaining concentration when it is important not to allow extraneous stimuli to disrupt performance, including being able to reengage after distraction without difficulty (i.e., inter-ference control). They are also likely to have problems when receiving the feed-back to shift to a new behavioral sequence because conditions have altered. The construction of the "inhibitory deficit" is imposed to account for a rapid loss of attention, as well as times when the individual is overly rigid and non-reactive to essential environmental cues. Persons with inhibitory deficits will have more problems than most in achieving long-term goals.

It is therefore expected that sometimes diagnosed persons become im-mersed or absorbed, and that it will be exceedingly difficult to distract them from what they are doing. The explanation for this concentration is that an ex-ceedingly focused response *also* represents a lack of behavioral control (as long as diagnostic criteria are met), in that shifting to more appropriate, expected, or correct responses also requires a competent inhibitory system. The overriding problem is that diagnosed individuals show difficulty sustaining participation when it is important, as well as difficulty shifting from what they are doing when it could be advantageous to respond to new environmental parameters. They are both *more* distractible and *less* distractible, depending on the particular conditions under which they operate.

Diagnosed persons have been told that their condition is similar to not hav-ing enough brake fluid in a car, thus interfering with the ability to stop (Robin, 2006). Impulsivity and hyperactivity typically co-occur early in development, and usually are more prevalent than inattentiveness in younger children. Males are typically more hyperactive and impulsive compared to females, who fre-quently qualify for the inattentive type of ADHD (Crawford, 2003). However, problems with inhibition seem to persist for both genders throughout life.

Incidentally, regarding gender differences, some traditionalists are con-cerned that the behavioral criteria overlook how ADHD is expressed in the fe-male population. Some ask whether it is reasonable to impose different diagnostic criteria for each gender (Barkley, 2000; Crawford, 2003).

Our counterclaim is that these changes in diagnostic criteria might make it easier for females to obtain a diagnosis, but it is unclear whether there is a neu-rological justification for introducing discrepant criteria, or whether this is sim-ply a way to compensate for the fact that females less frequently do the behaviors subsumed by the ADHD diagnostic category. If diagnosed females are not showing the same kinds of neurological delay or functional impairment as their male counterparts, it is unreasonable to implement this strategy.

Furthermore, if we alter criteria for females, are we willing to alter criteria for other subgroups that also show differing diagnostic base rates? If the diag-nostic category purportedly identifies individuals with a certain kind of underly-ing neurological delay, to what extent does the introduction of differential criteria also coincide with that notion? Moreover, in that females seem to be patterning similarly to males, especially when one considers the recent rise of aggressiveness and delinquency in the female population at this time, the rates of diagnosis for females could change even *without* altering diagnostic criteria.

Nevertheless, as children of both genders grow older, we expect that problems related to motoric action will diminish and inattentiveness and "cognitive impulsivity" will become apparent and troublesome. This anticipated shift will take place when the child (male or female) is expected to organize behavior over longer periods of time, and solve complex problems requiring mental preparation. However, whether symptoms are motoric and/or mental, the overall effect is that the individual will have a sense of futility over the management of his or her life.

That is why diagnosed persons are described as having an "intentional disorder," or in more popular vernacular, of not doing what they are supposed to do (Barkley, 2000). It is expected that there will be a shift from problems inhibiting motoric behaviors, to problems accessing and sustaining mind behaviors such as non-vocal verbal rehearsals, imaginings, memories, and ideas about the future, etc. A weakness in executive skill will eventually become apparent, because years of inhibitory failures will have prevented the non-observable mental actions from being practiced.

These private mental responses are thought to be derived from responses which have historically been public, and have, little by little, become private and indiscernible to others (Barkley, 1998f). Executive responses are understood as necessary for behavioral control to occur; they permit the individual to anticipate change and future possibilities before committing to other responses. Without medication and directive environmental management, diagnosed persons function with a less-than-competent neurological system that limits their ability to utilize "will power" or "free will" (Barkley, 1995).

When an individual has adequate executive functioning, there is greater arousal, and one can maintain and experience ideation that increases the desire to achieve in the absence of instant reinforcement (Barkley, 1998f). Diagnosed persons cannot achieve this very well, and that is why they rely on external and explicit cues, and are hamstrung without them. The upshot is that they are less likely to persist unless changes are made to kindle responses that otherwise do not occur.

The ADHD condition results in behavior that is less influenced by precursor mental actions. Significant others must correct for this problem by making information concrete. Everyone involved must assume that diagnosed persons are limited in their ability to control and sustain actions that have a future relevant form. Diagnosed persons are delayed in their ability to do prolonged mental reasoning, and when they do respond accordingly, the responses are often too feeble to yield information with the power to adequately change their future choices. The belief is that diagnosed persons have less access to mental representations to guide and enable them to control future events (Barkley, 1998f; 2000).

Because of the underlying neurological limitation, it is very difficult, say conventional practitioners, for individuals to persist when activities become monotonous. Problems become apparent when activities such as chores and schoolwork are encountered (Barkley, 1998b); diagnosed persons have trouble functioning adequately in these circumstances, since they typically do not inhibit reactions long enough to make socially-preferred decisions rather than ones that offer an immediate payoff. They might abandon the task rather than cue themselves about the reasons for persevering, and are less likely to try when activities are not very stimulating. Therefore, the diagnosed person seems at a disadvantage—not only when activities require more sophisticated planning and anticipating—but also when tasks are routine and boring.

School-related problems are the most frequent reason that parents consult with professionals. In the traditional view, schoolwork challenges the child's ability to sit still, attend, obey, organize actions, and follow through with instructions. ADHD deficits will also impair interpersonal functioning at school by disrupting the child's ability to share and play cooperatively with other children. Given the impairments inflicted on the child by ADHD, it is not surprising that as many as 90% of diagnosed individuals show poor school performance and a 30%-40% school dropout rate (Barkley, 2002).

Overall, the consequences of having ADHD will generally take its toll on family relationships in significant ways. When children respond with ADHD patterns and have difficulties in school, caretakers must often work extraordinarily hard to obtain even minimal compliance. Limits might not be kept, and the child has to be monitored extensively to increase compliance with expectations. It becomes more and more difficult to protect the child, in that he or she is not often adequately responding to advisements, warnings, and stipulations. Under these social conditions, parents can experience difficulty relaxing and attending to what they might prefer, since the child is often increasing the probability of significant risk to self and others.

It is commonly noted that these overworked parents become resentful, stressed, negative, and impatient. Family relationships become strained and unhappy. While temper tantrums can be common for many preschoolers, their frequency and intensity amplifies and worsens in an ADHD child (Barkley, 1998e). Traditionalists infer that a form of neurological delay causes extreme responses, and the parent is seen as *reacting* to the disorder rather than *shaping* it.

Given the traditional conceptualization, it is apparently permissible to describe non-diagnosed persons as selfish, insecure, egocentric, and self-promoting. Psychosocial categories may be imposed to account for their indulgences and atypical behaviors. Although once an ADHD diagnosis is applied, a disability is imposed to account for many of the unacceptable behaviors that occur. ADHD becomes an explanation for the disruptive patterning rather than a descriptor of particular social behaviors such as labeling a person as untrustworthy, insecure, passive-resistive, or exploitative. It is presumed that the individual has a separate problem that thwarts acceptable responding.

Once qualifying for diagnosis, behaviors consistent with hyperactivity, impulsivity, and inattentiveness are subsequently seen to be caused to some (unspecified) extent by a discrepant biology that delays inhibitory functioning. This

is *assumed* even though the presenting individual may have nothing biologically
in common with group prototypes or averages. Because these individuals meet
enough of the heterogeneous behavioral criteria, it is presumed that their behavior emanates from the underlying delaying problem. All behavioral events subsumed within a symptom check list are understood to be caused by ADHD (a
separate entity or process), and all these inferences occur because of the frequency rates of particular behavioral acts.

In those biologically determined explications, an ADHD individual's misuse of drugs, alcohol, and/or cigarette smoking (Whalen et al., 2002) is also interpreted as the person's way of coping with an inherent disorder. Evaluators
often proceed as if these individuals have no problems other than their ADHD.
Clinicians holding firmly to that view often encourage diagnosed persons to
derive solace from the knowledge that their behavior is a way to self-medicate,
and/or an attempt to soothe their ADHD or patterns of mental restlessness (Murphy, 2006). In that view, it is not that some people learn to do avoidance behaviors such as ADHD and substance abuse, but that ADHD creates the anguish
that instigates the escape reactions, and/or hinders persons from remembering
the long-term consequences of substance abuse (Aviram, Rhum, and Levin,
2001).

Because the traditional model assumes ADHD to be a condition of bodily
deficiency that causes symptoms, personal liability is therefore dramatically
reduced. Different from diagnoses that are socially pejorative (e.g., limited intelligence), a diagnosis of ADHD can actually validate ADHD diagnosed persons.
They no longer act out of self-interest, but suffer from a biological limitation; in
fact, Crawford (2003) worries that there is a bias against women for *under-
diagnosing* ADHD. She argues that females with ADHD have been neglected by
researchers.

Thus a diagnosis of ADHD is a socially acceptable reason for disruptive
behavioral patterning. The individual need no longer consider him or herself as
narcissistic, defensive, indolent, inconsiderate, or indulgent. Robin (1998) has
cautioned that individuals who live with diagnosed persons should not think of
them as malicious due to their biological problems.

Interestingly, this perspective is also gradually being extended to individuals who consume excessive amounts of alcohol; the current view is that alcohol-
ism is a disease or inherited condition that puts limitations on the individual.
Although this approach correctly seems to help relieve the excessive alcohol
drinker of shame, the characterization is also problematic, in that it allows individuals to blame their drinking on something which is beyond their control. Individuals are reinforced to present as passive victims who exist apart from their
own body's addiction.

Moreover, while Pfiffner and Barkley (1998) note that a diagnosis of
ADHD is not an immediate qualification for financial compensation, when there
are marked school problems current legislation exists to help individuals obtain
special services and assistance. For example, if Social Security criteria are also

met, diagnosed persons can qualify for this aid. Since access to educational and other helpful services may be based on awarding or denying a diagnosis of ADHD, clinicians are advised to be extremely careful when making a diagnosis (Barkley and Edwards, 1998); if they too easily assign diagnosis, those not in need of benefits will receive unwarranted advantages and support (Murphy and Gordon, 1998).

However, ultimately the view is adopted that molecular biology creates a neurological delay that causes the patterning. This view is held despite that diagnosis is *based solely* on observations of frequency rates of behaviors that we all perform to a certain extent. There are now thousands of published articles that reflect this perspective (Barkley, 2000); the traditional belief is that diagnosed persons would *not* do an ADHD pattern if only it were neurologically possible for them to function better.

For those who follow diagnosed persons over time, it is noted that they also show an increased risk of cardiovascular problems, shorter life spans, motor vehicle risks, money problems, early pregnancies, and an 8% higher incidence of requiring residential treatment (Barkley, 2002). Many diagnosed adults will have marital problems, poor job performance, and significant underachievement throughout their lives despite being intellectually competent (Weiss and Hechman, 1986). Up to one-half of the diagnosed population is predicted to also show gross and/or fine motor problems and various language problems, particularly those relative to organizing and performing intricate sequencing (Barkley, 2000). However, we must emphasize here that no explanation is given for the observation that approximately one-half of all diagnosed persons do *not* show these difficulties, yet are still presumed to have the same biologically-based delay.

We observe that there are many different combinations of symptoms and settings in which ADHD responses will or will not occur. Individuals who behave markedly differently may still qualify for the identical diagnosis. Diagnosed persons with histories of biological trauma may indeed function very differently from other diagnosed persons, but their underlying ADHD is considered to be the same. While significant numbers of diagnosed persons also show learning, motor, and various intellectual and encoding deficiencies, many diagnosed persons do not show any such complications. Yet despite the heterogeneity of behaviors and presenting problems, the presumption is that a unique biological delay invariably accounts for diagnostic responding, and is clustered with other correlated functional problems regarded as consequences of this neurological condition.

Again, each ADHD sign or symptom is understood to be caused by inhibitory failure. The supposed neurological delay results in a reduced ability to control actions when it would be more beneficial to do a different response. The diagnosed person always risks drifting off task, losing concentration, or failing to sustain advantageous behaviors. When it is necessary to maintain mental acuity, they need help from others, as they lack control over their mental actions.

Despite that these same individuals also show many instances of *attentive* responses that do not deviate from typical patterning, their higher frequency of diagnostic behaviors results in their being classified as meeting the criteria for a posited neural biological delay. In other words, indices of atypical frequency rates lead to a medical explanation, and it is presumed that this frequency would not be apparent, were it not for the person's inferior biological substrate.

There is also a biological explanation to account for why males show a higher incidence of ADHD compared to females (i.e., a 3-to-1 ratio) (Barkley, 1998b). It is claimed that females have a higher genetic threshold than males for the disorder to be expressed (Barkley, 2006d). It is also asserted that males apparently encounter more neurological risk than females, in that maleness occurs after femaleness during ontogenetic development. Also, males are more likely to become brain damaged during their lifetimes than females, which may also add to the disproportionate rates of occurrence for males (Barkley, 2000).

However, if that presumption were tenable, we would expect different behavioral patterns other than ADHD as a function of the particular kind, locus, and age of that injury, and we would also seek to catalogue the different observations of brain functioning (e.g., MRI data) for the different individuals. Additionally, since traditionalists posit that ADHD mostly represents inherited neurological delay rather than damaged biology, this explanation is extremely limited in the consideration of the majority of cases. Moreover, Braun et al. (2006) found that ADHD increased more for daughters than sons when examining the subgroup of mothers who continued to smoke despite being pregnant.

While traditionalists nevertheless introduce biological explanations when interpreting data, it may be that the higher ratio of males diagnosed as ADHD is due to how a greater numbers of males tend to pattern in situations (i.e., slapstick humor, physical risk-taking, less eager to request directions, less concerned with politeness, less picking up after themselves, etc.). Higher rates may also be attributable to different psychosocial patterns that tend to occur between mothers and daughters compared to mothers and sons, and related to patterns that tend to occur between males and females, even though these factors are considered by traditionalists to be incidental. For example, it has been found that mothers are more emotional and acrimonious with their diagnosed sons compared to their daughters (Barkley, 1989), and they give more commands and rewards to their sons (Buhrmester et al., 1992). Such differences, however, are not seen as germane when accounting for the large proportion of males who meet diagnostic criteria.

Conversely, when invoking a psychologically-based explanation, we speculate that girls may show less ADHD responding because girls are often more restricted than boys in socio-cultural groups. Girls are expected to help mothers manage the household and boys are often pampered and indulged (but nevertheless expected to provide as adults), *especially* when mother is compensating the boy for father's absence (or some other deficiency). It might also be difficult for opposite genders to understand each other, and mothers can find it difficult to identify common interests to share and enjoy with sons compared to daughters. It is premature, we think, to discount the possibility that these parameters may increase the probability that boys (in general) will learn diagnostic responses with greater frequency.

If the son's father or the mother's father has had a problematic relationship with the mother, or if the mother is faulted for discarding the father, the mother's relationship with the son could also have an antagonistic foundation that fosters diagnostic patterning as well. For instance, there might be an increased incidence of mother nitpicking, distancing, catering, complaining, worrying, clinging, domineering, or disparaging. Any and all of those patterns of social exchange could markedly influence the probability that diagnostic responding will be reinforced.

In contrast to the damsel in distress theme, we also recognize that, historically, females have pleaded with males to be less impulsive, and have then cared for them in the aftermath; this behavioral theme is reminiscent of ADHD. Similarly, there is also a long history whereby females over-accommodate males in order not to upset them, and thus preserve the relationship. This social pattern may also increase the probability that males are reinforced when acting ADHD-diagnostically.

We are not saying that any of these patterns are causing ADHD, and/or that the same patterns would not also increase the probability that girls learn diagnostic responding with either mother or father. However, there may be social patterns that (presently) correlate with the male gender, and the ways in which mothers and sons and males and females relate (from a cultural standpoint) that contribute to the higher ratio of males in the diagnostic population. Traditionalists discount the importance of psychosocial influences, but their apparent lack of a detailed analysis of psychosocial patterns does not rule out their influence.

In total, rather than professing biological determinism to account for the high frequency of diagnosed males, we claim that interactions occurring more frequently between males and females (as compared to same gender interactions) may more often condition ADHD patterns for males. Additionally, in our social group, it has also been more acceptable to medicate males (Pisecco, Huzinec, and Curtis, 2001). However, in order to make an assessment based on situation and context, we can investigate whether girls are just as likely to behave diagnostically as boys when they function in similar circumstances as boys. We can also remind ourselves that singular parameters (biological or social) are unlikely to yield impressive results that apply to the majority of cases.

Traditional recommendations

Despite the possibility of alternative ways to account for the data, traditionalists emphatically claim that even if a child's socialization has been exemplary, individuals inflicted with ADHD are unlikely to enjoy success in life's major arenas. Diagnosed persons are less likely to initiate helpful actions, or coordinate effectively with others, and behaviors will be emitted too quickly for socially appropriate or mature behavior to occur.

By understanding ADHD as a purely medical problem, the message is that health providers will improve the quality of the diagnosed person's life. It is undoubtedly deeply comforting for the diagnosed person to know that his or her difficulties have a legitimate explanation based on "neurogenetics" rather than "attributions to poor character" (Murphy and Gordon, 1998, 346). Diagnosed persons will eventually become aware that they are victims of their own bodies and should be treated like those who are inflicted with chronic medical conditions.

The selected treatment for the presumed biological delay— that is ADHD— is prescription medicine. Medicinal treatment most powerfully induces behavioral change, particularly by increasing attention span and reducing improper and impulsive behaviors (DuPaul, Barkley, and Connor, 1998). However, this intervention does not always produce complete remission of symptoms (and at times cannot be used); therefore, psychosocial interventions are often necessary to augment pharmacology and prevent other secondary problems from occurring. For example, diagnosed persons will be asked to manipulate an object rather than imagine the object. Or they might benefit from having a timer placed in front of them rather than having to rely on their unreliable perception of time. Often they will function well when materials are color coded and explicitly grouped and outlined, instead of depending on working memory and other executive functions to perform those operations.

Diagnosed persons must recognize that they will have to depend on written materials and behavioral charts to concretize and quicken the relationship between environmental requirements and desired normative responses. It is presumed that they will have difficulty when they must suspend taking action or organize behavior over time, in that their personal resources are insufficient to maintain behavioral appropriateness. Because an unmanaged natural environment is often too difficult and complex for them, events and problems that occur over extended time frames must be simplified, and artificial end points should be imposed.

The individual is encouraged to write down rules, procedures, or outcomes on cards, and use the cards to cue themselves about important things. Distant future events are unlikely to influence their behavior without the ever-present tangible signs. Diagnosed people must externalize their thoughts whenever possible: an act that traditionalists maintain will help them resolve many of their problems or dilemmas. They might "doodle on a pad," or "free-associate publicly" while a topic is discussed, and increase their creativity by reducing content to "slips of paper" and then "randomly reshuffle" the pieces in order to realize new possibilities (Barkley, 1998f, 255).

As much as possible it is important for diagnosed persons to assemble things into an observable form so they can do future-oriented activity. They will continue to struggle if they depend on their own cueing. Diagnosed persons are urged to place external props in their immediate environment, talk out loud about a reason for participating and working hard on a task, and rely as little as possible on less observable actions.

While many people will agree that verbalizing an idea out loud or writing the idea on paper can be helpful (e.g., attending psychotherapy and journal writing), it is deemed essential for the diagnosed person. These procedures are invaluable whenever it is crucial to anticipate consequences, when solutions require interdependent steps, and when preparatory activity may increase the likelihood of successful outcomes. Since diagnosed persons have greater difficulty doing these activities in mental form (i.e., thinking, imagining the future, etc.), their observable responses are often inadequate.

The external environment must organize and break things down into smaller and manageable units for them. Immediate contingencies for behaviors have to be imposed. We anticipate that the diagnosed person will less likely notice the relationships between events and consequences whenever larger temporal gaps are present (Barkley, 2000). Because of their internal delays, it is recommended that other people should "tighten up those consequences" so that accountability can be immediate. Point of performance interventions is needed in the natural ecology of the person's life where the problems occur (Barkley, 2006f, 327). These interventions will make consequences instantaneous, increase their frequency, and ensure that they are given in salient form. This supportive care (along with medication) has been shown to be the best way to offset the ever-present underlying delay. Trainers must make the individual accountable to others as often as possible (Barkley, 2000).

As an aside, despite that these recommendations are widely confirmed and verified, we remain unconvinced that traditionalists have proven that these approaches work more effectively with diagnosed persons compared to non-diagnosed persons who have problems on certain tasks. Given the presumption that diagnosed persons' primary difficulty is a failure to prepare mentally, we think that diagnosed persons should show the greatest changes in functioning when they overtly do preparatory behaviors. However, this comparison data has not yet been provided.

Moreover, there have been anecdotal reports from diagnosed children who say that they function better when allowed to do their math work "in their head." Often these claims occur in the context of complaints about their teacher's urging to write out each step when doing assignments. Furthermore, in many instances it is just as difficult to persuade diagnosed persons to speak their ideas out loud during problem solving as it is to convince them to accommodate to any other instruction. Moreover, the ideas that they say out loud often do not help them function any more competently, because they *still* do not seem to know what to do. Sometimes long silences occur without any response whatsoever when they are asked to "think out loud."

In addition, many diagnosed individuals become very tense and uncertain during instructional interactions, in that they seem to associate instruction with failure, disapproval, coercion, and intolerance. Given these reactions, we cannot be sure whether diagnosed persons' primary problem is a failure to do antecedent actions that would otherwise help them function acceptably, or whether some other different response patterns impede their learning. Traditionalists regard their explanations and interventions as ironclad, but there are many unresolved questions and concerns.

In any event, following a diagnosis of ADHD, the first component of the traditional intervention is to indoctrinate the individual into the biological (or medical) perspective. This intervention alone represents one of the most important steps of the treatment (Barkley, 2000). Diagnosed individuals are informed about the many support groups available to help them deal with their condition (e.g., CHADD, etc.). They are also instructed that medication and increased directive management are necessary in order to treat their disability. Since it has been determined that the identified person has an incurable condition, families are catalysts for acceptance of this special treatment, and accommodations are recommended at school or work as compensatory measures. Because the diagnosed individual has a recognized disability, there is ample justification to allocate extensive resources.

When adolescents attend initial treatment sessions, they might be told that having ADHD is nobody's fault (Robin, 1998). They are likely to be informed that their diagnostic behavior results from a "chemical imbalance" that makes them less able to stop and think before they act, and/or that neurotransmitter chemicals that provide the signals for self-control are not working up to par. They might be led to believe that their neurological delay will, on average, leave them at least 30% behind their peer group in social skills and behavioral organization (Pfiffner and Barkley, 1998), and they are likely to remain delayed in that sense (Barkley, 2006f).

While some diagnosed individuals and their parents are appropriately reluctant to risk potential medication side effects, and/or subjugate themselves to this form of intervention for other reasons such as fear of substance abuse, etc., we observe that many diagnosed persons nevertheless eventually agree to medication; this intervention becomes even more enticing when previous psychotherapy has not produced impressive effects. One of the benefits of the traditional model is that it helps ease the reluctance to ingest various medications. Most often, this intervention is reinforced when change is induced relatively quickly. The drugs (in the short-term) show an extremely high success rate in reducing troubling symptoms (sometimes without significant side effects).

However, we can also speculate that some of the rapid improvements reported by traditionalists after diagnosis potentially relate to a decrease of coercion and social blame. That is, when discovering that their child qualifies for ADHD, parents might act kindlier, as they now "realize" that the problem is beyond their child's control. Such responses can, interestingly, reduce the frequency of ADHD actions because relationships have become more harmonious.

Prescribing medication can also help the parent function less obstructively, as the medication (rather than the parent) is controlling the child for them. Some parents will also interact with the child in encouraging ways to increase the probability that the medications will have a positive effect. Positive effects will help them feel less personal blame for previous family and school difficulties, and reinforce that they were correct to advocate medication.

Interestingly, Conners et al. (1996) found that an intervention as simple as having diagnosed adults wear nicotine patches for two days reduced ADHD symptoms in appreciable ways. Much like having an ever-present parent, the drug exerts continuous influence and can provide quick relief. The traditionalists are unconcerned about possible chemical reliance; they argue that diagnosis does mean that one is forever dependent on special conditions and chemical remedies.

Conventional practitioners have thus far negated the efficacy and utility of behavioral techniques employed to help diagnosed persons; they deem them insignificant and of limited value compared to medication (Abikoff and Gittelman, 1984; Gittelman et al., 1980). Moreover, when the behavioral interventions are stopped any gains made have not persisted (Abikoff, 1991). Even worse, Braswell et al. (1997) found no treatment effects at any point in a year-long study using primarily cognitive-behavioral treatment with diagnosed individuals, and Shelton et al. (2000) found that after a two-year interval, there were no discernible benefits from training parents of hyperactive-aggressive children for a full year.

Psychotherapeutic interventions for adult ADHD individuals have not fared much better. For example, Ratey et al. (1992) report that insight-oriented therapy has not been helpful for diagnosed adults, and it is generally concluded that medication should form the basis of any reasonable treatment protocol. However, on a more positive note, Safren et al. (2005) report at least some benefits from a cognitive therapy approach they have developed in conjunction with medication for individuals who had previously not been treatment responsive.

Nevertheless, these less than impressive outcomes from psychological interventions are discouraging compared to the highly successful reports of those who utilize stimulants. As pointed out by Taylor (1986) only 10% to 20% of children taking stimulant medications fail to show clinically significant improvements in their primary ADHD symptoms. While medication response rates are lower for adults compared to children (e.g., as low as 25% found by Mattes et al., 1984), others indicate that up to 78% of adults have benefited from this intervention (Spencer et al., 1995).

Given these remarkable effects, there is little doubt that the psychotherapeutic interventions tried thus far pale in comparison to administering drugs for both children and adults. Stimulant medication seems to be the only reliable treatment intervention to produce significant positive results for symptoms specific to

ADHD. Parents and teachers regularly report rapid improvement in the reduction of task-irrelevant activity, compliance, attention span, concentration, and working memory.

Those advocating the use of medication note that CNS stimulants raise the activity, arousal and alertness of the central nervous system (DuPaul, Barkley, and Connor, 1998), an organic adjustment that allegedly rectifies the underlying biologically-determined delay. Consistent with this view, Gualtieri, Hicks, and Mayo (1983) claim that stimulant medication stabilizes variability and fluctuation in arousal, attention, and CNS reactivity, and permits better cortical inhibition and increased persistence on tasks. Haenlein and Caul (1987) also note that stimulants seem to decrease the amount of reinforcement required, in that they enhance the CNS behavioral activation system from which people experience rewards. Traditionalists emphasize that at this time medication therapy is currently the most effective way to increase situational involvement and responsiveness, and help make tasks seem more positive and reinforcing for anyone suffering with ADHD.

It is also pointed out that while the "potential iatrogenic effects" of amphetamines have not been carefully studied, follow-up studies of "substantial duration" have not found "significant" problems related to longer term stimulant use (DuPaul, Barkley, and Connor, 1998, 525). On these grounds traditionalists recommend using stimulant medications as a first-line treatment intervention. They advise offering prescriptions relatively early in treatment unless there are insurmountable mitigating factors, and emphasize that the more inattentive the child, the more likely stimulant medications will be helpful.

Those advocating for the use of stimulant medications to treat ADHD also claim that the stimulants currently being used are the "safest" of all psychiatric medications (Barkley, 2000), and the most well studied (Barkley, 2006a). Typically, side effects only include decreased appetite in one-third of cases, problems sleeping and stomach aches in one-fourth of the individuals, headaches, sadness and increased activity in 10% of the cases, and a very small percentage of individuals developing motor tics or twitches (Robin, 1998). When used with adults, Wilens and Biederman (1992) also report the same kinds of non-extreme side effects.

With the side effects being reported for both adults and children, the decision that these drugs are "safest" does not guarantee that they are totally benign. However, stimulants continue to be prescribed most often, and diagnosed persons are typically told that long-term use of stimulants is unlikely to disrupt their health; much effort is expended to reduce unease about drug therapy. For example, DuPaul et al. (1996), in an odd attempt to quell concerns about side effects, point out that when feedback is requested, children ages 9 through 15 tend to report more side effects than either teachers or parents.

Moreover, a recent large-scale study called the Multi-site Multi-modal Treatment Study of Children with Attention Deficit Disorder has also been interpreted by traditionalists as yielding data that seem consistent with a biological account and the importance of medicinal therapy. For six different sites with 592 total subjects, the findings were that psychosocial intervention is far less effective in treating the symptoms of ADHD compared to medication. Data from that study also seem to show that combining psychotherapeutic intervention with medication added no improvement in relieving the basic symptoms of ADHD (Barkley, 2000). Although in a recent analysis of those same data, Arnold et al. (2003) have reported that behavioral treatments were efficacious when treating lower socioeconomic minority groups with numerous presenting problems.

Overall, it is asserted that studies assessing the benefits of medication generally show that 50-60% of individuals taking medication become "normal" in their behavior if they abide by their prescriptions, and 75-92% show improvement (Barkley, 1998f). For children (ages 5-12) it has been estimated that from 70-95% show at least some benefits (Pelham, Greenslade, et al., 1990), and for clinic-referred adolescents (a more difficult population) the positive response drops slightly to 60-75% (Wilens and Spencer, 2000). These positive statistics contrast with the report that at most only 39% of the placebo subjects showed improvement when approximately 120 medication studies were taken into account (Barkley, 1977).

Amen (2001) has also demonstrated that normalization occurs both behaviorally and biologically when SPECT brain scans are performed on medicated diagnosed children. While traditionalists do not always specify what normalization means, or under what circumstances particular diagnosed persons function more acceptably, more problematically, for what length of time, for what particular behaviors, and with what consistency, it is espoused that medication has consistently outperformed all other known forms of treatment, both biologically and behaviorally.

Since medicinal treatment works, it is further argued that problem behaviors must result from a particular kind of bodily functioning. In that a high percentage of diagnosed individuals taking stimulant medication begin to function similar to non-diagnosed people (some of the time, for some behaviors, under some conditions, at the cost of a variety of known and possibly unknown side-effects), ADHD behaviors *must* have a biological etiology. The medicines are seen as rectifying a particular chemical irregularity. Traditionalists conclude that because the stimulant medication somehow affects the neurotransmitter dopamine, the observed developmental delay is likely to relate to chemical processes that involve dopamine.

Murphy (1998) asserts that the best hope for anyone advocating psychotherapeutic intervention is that someone will develop an approach that may prove more useful than what is currently available. For now medication is touted as a primary treatment option for those who manifest ADHD behavior. Trials with different medications and varying dosage levels that elicit satisfactory clinical outcomes could also increase the proportion of positive responders. DuPaul, Barkley, and Connor (1998) further emphasize that children who have not responded positively when very young may still show a more positive response to medication if it is given after age six.

Various laboratory studies have also reported that stimulants reduce impulsive reactions, increase vigilance and reaction time, and even improve fine-motor coordination (Knights and Viets, 1975; Rapport and Kelly, 1991). Stimulant medications have also been known to help diagnosed persons improve self-language, which is considered essential if a person is to effectively control the future (Barkley, 2000). There has even been enhancement of short-term memory as measured during laboratory experiments when taking medication (Bergman, Winters, and Cornblatt, 1991).

Teachers have also reported positive interaction with diagnosed children (Whalen, Henker, and Dotemoto, 1980), and the medication has also had similar beneficial effects on defiant symptoms (Barkley, 2000). Improvements in restlessness have been observed, and medication has consistently yielded superior results for increasing attentiveness and persistence of effort when individuals do various assigned tasks (Barkley, 1977; Barkley and Cunningham, 1979; Bergman, Winters, and Cornblatt, 1991; Elia et al., 1991; Milich et al., 1991). Investigators also note that many medicated diagnosed persons will begin to function like non-diagnosed persons when doing class work (e.g., Abikoff and Gittelman, 1984; DuPaul and Rapport, 1993; Pelham and Milich, 1991; Rapport et al., 1994).

A further claim is that in a relatively short time frame (several weeks) stimulant medication has been found to induce at least minimal improvement in academic grade level achievement (Barkley, 1977; Barkley and Cunningham, 1978; Gittelman, Klein, and Feingold, 1983). These medications quickly help to induce better productivity, more positive teacher ratings or school performance, and in some cases, better accuracy during completion of assignments (DuPaul, Barkley, and McMurray, 1994; Pelham and Milich, 1991; Rapport and Kelly, 1991). In that stimulant drugs have allowed for diagnosed individuals to orient positively at school, many anticipate (although it is not yet empirically established) that academic grades are likely to increase over longer time frames as a result of this intervention (Ballinger, Varley, and Nolen, 1984; Pelham, 1985; Pelham and Bender, 1986; Rapport et al., 1986; Sebrechts et al., 1986; Stephens, Pelham, and Skinner, 1984).

Diagnosed children taking stimulant medications can also show improvements during sports activities (Pelham, McBurnett, et al., 1990); many show less aggressive behavior, unruliness, and improved responsiveness to authority figures (Barkley, Fischer, et al., 1988; Hinshaw, 1991; Hinshaw, Henker, et al., 1989; Murphy, Pelham, and Lang, 1992; Rapport, et al., 1986; Rapport and Kelly, 1991; Connor et al., 2002). It has become less necessary to monitor, chastise, and punish diagnosed children when functioning under a medicated state in a wide range of situations and circumstances.

It is claimed that this benefit can greatly enhance interpersonal adjustment as well (DuPaul, Barkley, and Connor, 1998). Barkley points out that medicated children seem to be better liked and are more often accepted by their peers (2001). Moreover, stimulants have also been found to not only increase compliance to parental commands, but also to enhance responsiveness in social interactions (Barkley and Cunningham, 1979; Barkley, Karlsson, et al., 1985; Humphries, Kinsbourne, and Swanson, 1978).

However, Whalen et al. (1987) caution that increased social acceptance relates to a decrease in negativity and aggressiveness rather than to an increase in positive social behavior. For these reasons, traditionalists cautiously acknowledge that while medication might reduce the frequency rates of some negative behaviors, this treatment will not automatically compel the individual to behave in positive ways. Consequently, it is always advisable to help diagnosed persons learn acceptable alternative behaviors during any pharmacological treatment intervention. Focusing solely on preventing negative behavior and not teaching them appropriate social patterning will often result in children replacing one problem behavior with another (Pfiffner and Barkley, 1998).

Despite the usual accolades, Safer (1992), Solanto (1991), and Swanson (1989) have all expressed concerns that higher dosages of stimulants might adversely influence learning, and be associated with over-focusing and constricting attention. Similarly, Dyme et al. (1982) have voiced concerns that stimulants could also reduce flexibility in problem solving.

However, in reaction to those concerns, traditionalists do not agree that undesirable problem solving behaviors are occurring in significant ways (Fiedler and Ullman, 1993). Their endorsement of stimulant medication remains unequivocal; for example, Douglas et al. (1995) indicate that constriction or inflexibility in problem solving has not been found in dosages elevating up to 0.9 mg/kg. Thus when stimulants are used within the typical therapeutic range, there is no association with reduced flexibility and creativity during problem solving.

Traditionalists also refute the concern that the diagnosed person's self-esteem may be adversely affected by medication by citing a number of relevant studies. For example, it has been posited that diagnosed individuals will feel better if their success is attributed to their own efforts rather than the drugs (Whalen, Henker, Hinshaw, et al., 1991), but empirical inquiry by Carlson et al. (1993), DuPaul et al. (1996), and Ialongo et al. (1994) has not found this to be the case in the short-term. Moreover, Pelham et al. (1992) report that boys treated on stimulant medications liked themselves *even more* when on medication compared to boys treated with a placebo.

However, the Pelham findings should be approached with caution. First, it is not clear in what ways diagnosed boys are concerned about how others see them. According to the traditional view, diagnosed persons' self-reports are regarded as unreliable when asked whether they qualify for diagnosis. If it is accepted that diagnosed individuals are generally less self-aware and less attentive to others' opinions, then it is also not surprising that they are unfazed by the failure to function adequately without the added boost of medication.

Second, for individuals already oriented to reliance on external sources, it might not be uncomfortable, inconsistent, or disheartening to take medication in order to function adequately. Third, to the extent that a diagnosed person accepts a disability formulation, it would seem less likely that self-esteem is threatened when drugs are taken. Since they are told that medication is necessary to counter a medical problem, they are not being pressured or given the message that they should be better at functioning *without* the drugs.

Finally, the Pelham et al. study could also be interpreted as a drug-induced effect; many individuals report greater self confidence when under the influence of stimulant medication where work-related activity is often less daunting, overwhelming and more reinforcing. The finding that they like themselves more when in this state is anticipated.

At any rate, traditional researchers remain unconcerned about the adverse effects of their treatments. For example, while "rebounding" effects can occur with stimulant medication, they claim that these effects occur for only approximately one-third of the individuals (Johnston et al., 1988). Only 10% of diagnosed children show crying and/or irritability during the "washout" phase (Barkley, 2000). Moreover, given the availability of longer acting and time-released stimulant medications, these adverse effects are assumed to become even less pronounced in the future. In fact, most have begun to prescribe these longer acting medications as the first treatment option (Connor and Steingard, 2004).

Furthermore, even though many were initially concerned that stimulant medication might stunt height and weight gain (Safer, Allen and Barr, 1972; Safer and Allen, 1973), it is now believed that, for the overwhelming majority, this is not the case over time (Mattes and Gittelman, 1983; Zeiner, 1995). There is also the suggestion that smallness of stature correlates with having the condition, as diagnosed persons tend to be smaller than their peers before puberty (Spencer, Beiderman, and Harking, et al., 1996).

However, before we assume that this correlation is solely a biological phenomenon, we can investigate whether there are psychosocial consequences (particularly for boys) when smallest of stature occurs (such as insecurity about acceptability, etc.), which influence social adjustment such that a purely biological account is questionable. Having a small stature may simply increase the probability that a child will learn ADHD behaviors.

Traditionalists also suspect that ADHD neurological delay rather than medication is causing some of the reported sleep difficulties observed within the diagnosed population; they are quick to point out that sleep difficulties are apparent before medicinal treatments are initiated (Fine and Johnston, 1993; Ahmann et al., 1993; Ball, Tiernan, Janusz, and Furr, 1997). However, like shortness in stature, a more psychosocially-based account for sleep difficulty within the ADHD group is reasonable: children who have learned ADHD patterns may react to the requirement to go to sleep as an attempt by the parent to banish or reject them. There may also be unresolved problems related to giving up playtime to go to bed, staying up late to have uninterrupted personal time, and/or staying up late to have undivided time with a parent.

There continues to be firm endorsement of medicinal treatments. If or when side-effects occur, they are managed with additional medications. For example, if motor tics, delayed sleep onset or other sleep disturbance occurs from the use of stimulant medication, other medications such as Clonidine can be added (Spencer, Biederman, Wilens, et al., 1996; Tourette's Syndrome Study Group, 2002). Drugs such as Clonidine have sedating properties that can help decrease behavioral problems not always eliminated by stimulants. However, in the case of Clonidine, side effects can be severe compared to stimulant medication (Popper, 1995), so this medication is not recommended as a primary treatment option.

As a consequence of the view that a majority of the troublesome behaviors can be decreased with drug treatment, and that side effects can be effectively addressed with a drug solution, there was, from 1994 to 1997, a seven-fold increase in the number of children taking *both* stimulant and antidepressant medication (Bhatara et al., 2000). Consistent with that trend, Harris (2006) reported that 28% of the 3½ million children taking ADHD medications in 2005 were prescribed drug combinations despite a lack of empirical support for such treatments. Very similarly, in a study of ADHD adults taking Tricyclic medications, Wilens et al. (1995) reported that over 80% of these adults also took other psychoactive medication, and nearly 60% of these individuals took stimulants in addition to an antidepressant. While these adults might not be following a characteristic pattern of substance abuse (because they abide by their physician's recommendation), we observe that individuals on a psychotropic intervention may become increasingly medicated over time.

When we analyze the overall effects of ADHD medication, we observe that these substances may improve some problems, but can also potentially produce troubling side effects that worsen or create other problems. The medication may also cease working or otherwise affect the person differently after he/she has become accustomed to its influence. Although we acknowledge that when there are residual problems and side effects the medication type and/or dosage can usually be altered, it is now, worryingly, acceptable practice to change, add, and mix various drugs until the desired effect is reached. For example, if stimulants produce a lowering of the seizure threshold for children with epilepsy, their seizure medication can be increased (DuPaul, Barkley, and Connor, 1998).

Rather than quit medication when outcomes are not optimal, it is typical to experiment with medicines as long as the problem is presumed to be inherent and immediate relief can be obtained. Moreover, Connor (1998) recommends that, as long as a medication or combination thereof can be scientifically and/or empirically justified, it is reasonable to proceed—even if FDA approval has not been obtained for the drug or drug combination being prescribed. The end result, we fear, is that practitioners will prescribe medication combinations without sufficient guidance from empirical data.

Medication therapy is so highly regarded that "drug vacations" are no longer recommended when social demands are at a minimum (e.g., school vacations or weekends). Since stimulant medication has been the only treatment to date that helps normalize the core symptoms of ADHD, many are urging that diagnosed persons ingest these medications regularly without interruption. The tacit claim is that stimulant medications can always help maximize the concurrent effects of ongoing psychosocial and educational interventions. For that reason, DuPaul, Barkley, and Connor (1998) find no medical reason to stop pharmacological treatment at any time.

This belief is so strongly held that when religious groups and pseudo-libertarian groups in the late 1980s tried to discourage the use of stimulant medication for children, counter arguments insisted that failure to initiate medication would be a disservice to those who have been inflicted. DuPaul, Barkley, and Connor (1998) asserted that many of these children might have derived benefits from this treatment intervention had these groups not promoted their own biased views.

Although despite the firm entrenchment of medicinal treatment, some professionals caution that diagnosis of ADHD does not automatically require the use of medication. Some traditionalists have developed a list of mitigating factors. These include evaluating whether other therapies have been tried, the age of the child, the severity of symptoms, ability to afford the cost, the extent of supervision, attitudes towards medication, substance abuse in the household, a history of tics, psychosis, thought disorder, the capability of the physician to monitor, child's reaction to taking medication, whether the child cannot take medication due to competitive sport restrictions, and whether the individual plans to join the military (Barkley, 1981; DuPaul, Barkley, and Connor, 1998). However, while extenuating circumstances are noted, it is unclear as to how many diagnosed persons are taking stimulant medication without considering the aforementioned criteria.

Given the lack of immediate positive results from other interventions, many conventional practitioners are less inclined to resist giving the diagnosed person the benefit of what appears to work quite well, especially in the short-term. Although when families proceed with a medicinal regime, they will often stop their psychotherapy intervention as soon as the medication has altered the child's behavior, and complaints from the school have subsided. For example, 15 years ago, it was reported that up to 80% of diagnosed adolescents had tried stimulant medication, while only one-half had participated in psychotherapy (Barkley, DuPaul, and McMurray, 1990). Similarly, it is also reported that the length of stimulant treatment is typically much longer than psychotherapeutic treatment (Barkley, Fischer, et al., 1990).

Given those trends, we are concerned that medicinal treatment removes the urgency of the presenting problems, but neither child nor parents learn to function without reliance on the chemical inducements. Often it appears that families attend only enough psychotherapy to allay their physician's concern that the family does not rely completely on medication to address problems. If the medicine eventually becomes ineffective, limiting, or troublesome we recognize that significant time invested in other treatments has been lost.

However, for those *not* relying on medication, it is essential to exercise patience, since preferred learned behaviors are shaped over time and are less likely to occur initially without medication. Often the effects of shaping new behavior will not be evident until conditions recur later. Not all participants will obtain the same results; some benefits will be evident over time for only some families, although this shortcoming is evident for medication as well.

For instance, children purportedly show improvement while on medication when they also have a good relationship with their mother, who gives positive reinforcement in addition to medication (DuPaul, Barkley, and Connor, 1998; Cunningham and Barkley, 1979). DuPaul, Barkley, and Connor also note that it is the younger, relatively inattentive, hyperactive, uncoordinated, and less intellectually delayed child (whose parents engage in reasonable discipline and care) who will show the best response to stimulant medication.

When considering these outcomes we would assess the extent to which social relationships contribute to medication outcomes, and design a study that involves only the positive medication responders. Only individuals with the most intact family relationships would be included in the study. The benefits of medications could then be compared to various psychosocial treatments, including those that enhance self-reliance and collaborative interacting for the select group already demonstrating skillful relating. If it can be shown that a treatment intervention not including medication can produce similar (or better) results over time for some people, then it is worthwhile to avoid (or at least delay) using medication.

However, it is unlikely that traditionalists will endorse this approach even in relatively positive family interactions, because traditional beliefs necessarily require the effects of medication to compensate for neurological delays. Moreover, in their assertion that the preponderance of scientific evidence is consistent with using medication, they would argue that it is nonsensical to introduce greater unpredictability into the treatment activity and make people wait before providing the "best" treatment option.

Concerns have been raised about over medicating diagnosed children, but here too traditionalists present data suggesting that only a small proportion of diagnosed individuals are participating in a medication treatment regime. In a response to apprehension about stimulant drugs being over prescribed, Barkley (2000) noted that only 15% to 32% of diagnosed individuals were medicated at any one point in time.

Conventional practitioners maintain that those who protest about the possible future dangers of medication needlessly alarm some parents and professionals and create unwarranted hysteria. Moreover, they emphasize, medicinal treatment can always be combined with behavioral intervention in order to assure that diagnosed persons are not being deprived of multifaceted care.

Even though there is no empirical confirmation that stimulant medication leads to long-term success (DuPaul, Barkley, and Connor, 1998), and despite the controversy surrounding psychotropic drugs being given to children (Angold, Erkanli, Egger, and Costello, 2000), loved ones and teachers nevertheless report many difficulties, and that their disruptive behavior also influences classmates. Such occurrences support the view that medication is not a luxury, but a requisite. The firm recommendation continues to be that medications are likely to reduce negative interpersonal exchanges and unproductive behaviors which would otherwise have harmful social, academic, and biological consequences for the diagnosed person.

Finally, some individuals have hoped to wean themselves off medication once the problems have stabilized, but this approach has also not been fruitful. They speculate that they might profit not only from the immediate effects of the medication, but will also more easily learn new ways of living while under the influence of the medication and then stop the treatments. Not only would they obtain the benefits of medicinal therapy, but they would also avoid problems with side effects from ingesting stimulant medications over extended periods of time.

However, this view of short-term treatment regime has not worked very well in the past. Barkley (2000) notes that removing medication simply puts diagnosed persons back into their delayed biological state with all of its pitfalls and problems. Since ADHD is characterized as a disorder that limits the enacting of actions that they once knew, traditionalists do not see ADHD-related problems as potentially solved by skill acquisition. The finding that behaviors enacted while on medication do not repeat when individuals no longer take it (to address their inherent biological delay) is therefore not a surprising outcome. No behavioral treatment or management approach alters the underlying inherited deficits, according to Barkley (1998f); such interventions simply stop or limit the expression of the condition. Gittelman-Klien et al. (1976) identified this pattern of recidivism associated with the use and stoppage of ADHD medication over 30 years ago.

Reluctance to develop autonomy and collaboration

That diagnosed persons do not reflect enough, and are too impulsive and disorganized, prevents them from benefiting from interventions that promote autonomy (Pfiffner and Barkley, 1998). The researchers emphasize that past attempts to increase self-monitoring have essentially been fruitless, since they have less self-control due to their biological condition. The biological determinist presumes that methods to promote increased self-directedness and discretionary input are inadvisable, especially for younger individuals.

Even though Hallowell and Ratey (1995, 138) recognize the importance of introducing negotiation in family management at an early age, they also agree that with "younger children it is often not desirable." They insist that younger children "need structure and limits." The tacit belief is that young children require coercion to be socialized properly.

Hallowell and Ratey also note that parents of diagnosed children must guard against the child's "proclivity" to use negotiation to test their parents, shift the negotiation into an argument, and/or defend against their desire to obtain the "stimulation" that they "love." They endorse the claim that the discipline recommended here is less possible as well as inappropriate for younger diagnosed children. Hallowell and Ratey blame the neurological condition called ADD rather than problematic conditioning for difficulties shown by some diagnosed individuals during attempts to negotiate under some conditions.

In that same tradition, Robin (1998) is a proponent of problem solving by communicating with diagnosed adolescents, which includes contingency management and point of performance directing. However, he does not support the democratic problem solving intervention for pre-adolescent ADHD children. He also warns that many 12 to 14 year old adolescents may not adequately engage more collaboratively (Robin, 2006). Robin basically thinks that younger diagnosed children will probably not benefit from approaches requiring more discretionary input from the child.

Nevertheless, Robin asserts that, because the adolescent is becoming more independent, it is necessary to shift gradually from an authoritarian approach to a democratic pattern of discipline for this age group. He claims that while younger children require more controlling management, authoritarian control will not work as well with diagnosed adolescents. Robin encourages the use of a Socratic method when talking with adolescents about their medication concerns, and during scheduled family meetings, diagnosed teens are permitted discretionary input.

During these family meetings, we observe, interestingly, that a number of Robin's (1998) recommendations are completely compatible with our methodology of self-reliant/collaborative interacting. For example, he advises redirection rather than correction when negative interactions arise. He encourages family members to evaluate incidents in terms of their impact on the relationships between participants, and he recommends that parents monitor the adolescent's whereabouts without being heavily intrusive. In many ways our alternative intervention complements Robin's intervention; however, we begin the process with adolescents and younger children in order to enact the methods consistently across contexts, situations, and circumstances, and we also use less contingency management, point of performance directing, and medication.

Traditional intervention also dovetails with our approach when traditionalists "coach" adults who voluntarily seek professional help. For example, adults who self-refer are usually advised to obtain the services of a coach with whom they establish an ongoing relationship. The diagnosed adult is encouraged to use "a process of inquiry and personal discovery," which will eventually help them assume a higher level of responsibility (Murphy, 1998, 590). A coach offers encouragement, support, and structure to the diagnosed individual and they work collaboratively to identify goals and strategies as well as enact what is decided. The coach holds the diagnosed individual accountable through gentle confrontation, but there is no imperative to employ contingency management, nor is the coach required to unilaterally control resources or function as the individual's keeper, protector, or warden. In a more benign fashion, the coach assists the diagnosed person to take charge of his or her life and help them manage by encouraging the setting of reasonable goals that can be met, thus reducing instances of failure. Diagnosed persons learn ways to stay on task and intervention is done in a hopeful and compassionate atmosphere.

Anastopoulos, Smith, and Wien (1998) also recommend greater collaborative interacting when parents seek help for their diagnosed children. For example, during these parent training sessions, they recommend that therapists not lecture parents. Instead, the therapist is advised to allow the parents to ask questions and discuss expectations as well as mutually agree on a final clinical disposition. Similar to Leary and Miller (1986) and Meichenbaum and Turk (1987), these authors claim that positive results can be obtained if parents feel that they have derived solutions through their own efforts; this approach may help increase the parent's self-esteem and reduce their reliance on the clinician. They anticipate that treatment gains will repeat in various situations, even if they were not explicitly covered during treatment. By achieving greater independence, benefits are likely to persist after the program ends.

We suggest that if these social exchanges help reduce instances of ADHD behaviors for adults, it could be beneficial to also use the same approach for children (as much as possible), rather than use coercive/dependent forms of discipline currently recommended by traditionalists. Although when traditionalists utilize collaborative methods, it often seems that the theme of mutuality is abandoned or lost. For instance, while Robin (1998) recommends collaborative exchange during family discussions or therapy sessions, he also believes that collaboration must be supported by coercions in order to be effective. While he endorses greater mutuality in the family, he never abandons contingency management and directive cueing for any age group, and invariably recommends forced compliance discipline for the prepubescent diagnosed child.

Traditionalists are unwilling to reduce directive management with diagnosed children, despite our observance that their recommended interactions may become more relaxed and reciprocal during the very circumscribed time called "special individual attention." During these exclusive moments, parents are encouraged towards positive attending and are urged to ignore negative behaviors in order to build a positive rapport. Children are encouraged to think about the qualities of their most favorite and least favorite supervisor hoping to copy that behavior. Parents are advised to be less directive, corrective, coercive, and unpleasant, as such interactions are thought to increase problematic behavior. Children are often allowed discretionary input during these special occasions. Parents are advised to ask fewer questions and allow the child to take the lead in suggesting play. Any discussion about problems should be done positively, and parents are advised to ignore mildly unacceptable behaviors (Anastopoulos, Smith, and Wien, 1998; Anastopoulos, Rhoads, and Farley, 2006).

Given these kinds of recommendations, we see the rationale for advising a similar format of interaction in many more contexts and situations as a way to shape non-diagnostic responding. If traditionalists were to repeat similar strategies (where feasible), differences between the two intervention models would diminish; that is, both interventions would be weaving these less directive, non-critical, non-coercive encounters into the fabric of family life.

We acknowledge that it is necessary in many instances to be more directive than during "special individual attention," because it is often necessary to adhere to schedules, accomplish particular tasks, conform to non-negotiable limitations, and coordinate with the expectations of others, but we advocate the incorporation of special individual attention into ongoing patterning as a modus operandi. This recommendation includes focus on enjoying time with the child, rather than buying things, and/or frequently evaluating the adequacy of the child's actions.

Moreover, it is not known to what extent traditionalists have explored the effects of mixing collaborative and coercive approaches, as the coercion and directive cueing recommended outside family meetings could certainly interfere with or (counteract) the self-reliance and collaboration being facilitated during family gatherings. All side effects that correlate with the use of coercion during socialization may ignite when a reversion to forced compliance methods is put in place.

For example, in Robin's (1998) view, after the rules have been specified and consequences decided, parents are implored to take action rather than merely talk. They are instructed to prompt the teen to perform the specified rules, give reinforcements when they complete tasks, and punish when there is failure to comply. Parents should also expect to maintain supervisory tactics for a longer time period than most estimates at present.

Although when parents are advised to use punishment to handle adolescent transgressions (e.g., groundings, loss of privileges, etc.), it becomes increasingly unclear how that recommendation will promote social patterns that facilitate his ultimate goal of effective family communication. Interestingly, short-term studies of Robin's program compared with the usual forms of intervention have not shown any distinct advantages, and there have also been reports of increased family conflict for some (Barkley, Guevremont, et al., 1992; Barkely, Edwards, et al., 2001).

Rather than interpret those outcomes as consistent with the view that ADHD is immune to psychotherapeutic intervention because the behaviors are indicative of biological delay, we argue that Robin's rendition of a collaborative intervention may not be particularly effective in extinguishing ADHD behaviors. It might also be concluded that changing ADHD through psychosocial intervention (that includes stringent contingency management) is complex and difficult to manage, and people are unlikely to change significantly in the short-term.

However, traditionalists remain adamant that diagnosed persons are less able to behave reliably and they refuse to abandon that presumption. Thus their intervention remains consistent with such a view. Although they clearly seem to recognize the importance of collaboration, they wait too long to begin shaping the behaviors, and revert to coercion too quickly and frequently.

Very interestingly, Robin (1998, 456) has noted that the distinguishing factor between successful and unsuccessful treatment in the families studied was the "overall degree of warmth and caring" exhibited by the family, as well as its ability to "experience empathy and understanding of another's social perspective." Based on Robin's remarks here, we see the advantage of mutually-reinforcing behaviors for diagnosed children as the focal point of intervention as early (and as often) as possible.

Moreover, we also suspect that intervening with collaborative interacting *before* the parent's influence on the child wanes during adolescence will be utterly beneficial. For example, Braaten and Rosen (2000) report that diagnosed boys typically show less empathy than controls even though they also show more sadness, anger, and guilt. At present we can only speculate as to whether consistent and early collaborative interacting can diminish those patterns.

If a more collaborative intervention is not taken until well into the second decade of the diagnosed person's life, he or she will have had far less practice doing the behaviors when reaching chronological maturity. By the time mutuality is encouraged as a way of family life, there is greater risk that diagnosed persons will be much more familiar with unilateral problem solving, the behaviors that had most often been role modeled and enacted. The behaviors that Robin, in particular, has found to be therapeutically most important in his work (e.g., caring, warmth, empathy, perspective taking, etc.), thus may have scant influence on the social patterns of older diagnosed children.

It is also important to note that Anastopoulos, Smith, and Wien (1998, 373) report that many parents exhibit personal difficulties such as "sadness, frustration, guilt, stress, and marital strains" *as a consequence* of living with a child diagnosed with ADHD. And because of the difficulty managing children, parents often indicate low self-esteem (Mash and Johnson, 1983), and score higher on scales of depression (Cunningham, Benness, and Siegel, 1988). Many of these parents also feel that their diagnosed child's troublesome behavior is caused by something outside of their child's ability to control (Johnston and Freeman, 1997), and traditionalists are agreeing with these intuitions and lay assessments.

Conventional practitioners very clearly convey to parents that they are not the source of their child's ADHD actions; it is actually the difficult behavior of the diagnosed person that adversely affects the relationships within the home (Cunningham and Barkley, 1979; Mash and Johnston, 1982; Campbell, Endman, and Bernfield, 1977; Whalen, Henker, and Dotemoto, 1980). Even when prior family stress is observed in diagnosed families, it is seen as potentially worsening the functioning of the diagnosed person; it is never understood as its origin.

Cunningham and Boyle (2002) go so far as to reckon that the diagnosed person has created the sometimes critical and frustrated interacting between family members. It is argued that parents and teachers become less negative when diagnosed individuals take medication and show improvement in their functioning (Danforth, Barkley, and Stokes, 1991; Goodman and Stevenson, 1989). Because the social environment changes positively in response to the diagnosed person's improvements, the assumption is that the problems must have been entirely caused by the delayed functioning of the identified disruptors.

Some families come to treatment with problems that further complicate the treatment of diagnosed individuals, including parental depression (Cunningham et al., 1988), social isolation (Wahler, 1980), marital conflict, or other family dysfunction which amplifies negativity towards the diagnosed individual (Greist, Wells, and Forehand, 1979; Webster-Stratton and Hammond, 1988); but these problems are never seen as the cause of the high frequency rates of inattention, impulsivity, and hyperactivity. Environmental adversity is important to address only to the extent that it creates obstacles against effective intervention.

Although it is understandable why parents might appreciate the traditional message, it is just as reasonable that it is neither parents nor children who cause ADHD, but that they participate, and together they precipitate whether (or not) the behaviors get reinforced or extinguished. To extrapolate, we could say that it is unlikely that the spouse of an alcoholic would be held accountable for marital problems—simply because the partner's drinking stopped after the "enabling" behaviors were curtailed. Despite that the non-drinker's behavior changed first, and seemed to instigate subsequent changes in the alcoholic's patterning (including positive responding to spouse), we would not hold the non-drinker accountable for the troublesome marital relationship or the excessive drinking. Similarly, when a parent responds positively to a medicated child, it is equally untenable to argue that it was the child all along who created the difficulties, problems, and diagnostic responses.

It is thus reasonable to investigate whether diagnostic patterns are likely to be reinforced when parents withdraw, or engage in frequent relenting, defeated, infantilizing, apprehensive, impatient, or aggrieved interactions with the child. More children socialized in these conditions may learn to provoke, entertain, intrude, disengage, doubt their acceptability, or believe that their parent's misery is due to their own failings. Given the possibility of greater insecurity, dependency, and disappointment in the household, and problems coordinating and developing comfortable routines when parents are depressed, children could more often learn ADHD behavior.

Current empiricism has not ruled out that some patterns of social exchange can potentially reinforce ADHD actions and reactions more than others. Therefore, when Hoza et al. (2000) found that mothers in their sample of diagnosed children showed lower self-esteem, reduced parenting efficacy, and a more acute external locus of control compared to fathers, perhaps it is the case that when mothers (or fathers) show those characteristics in more extreme form, the probability of the child learning ADHD is increased. These parental influences can, moreover, be subtle and start very early. For example, O'Connor et al. (2002) found that a mother's reported emotional distress during pregnancy correlated with increased hyperactivity and inattentiveness in sons, and conduct and emotional problems in daughters when the children were assessed at age four.

However, Barkley (2000) speculates on a genetic link between parental depression and ADHD. Anastopoulos, Smith, and Wien (1998) argue that diagnosed children foster disharmony in the family by remarking that many parents of diagnosed children are quite effective with *other* children in the family. So when relationships are negative and too strict with ADHD children, ensuing problems are not due to parents' faulty behaviors. Parents are consistently reassured that the root cause of their relationship problems with their diagnosed child relates to the child's neurological ADHD delay.

The attempt to allay parental distress by discussing how difficult it is to manage a diagnosed child effectively diverts attention away from the fact that the same parenting behaviors that work with some individuals do not work equally well with others; moreover, socializing a child with a developmental delay presents a unique set of problems that are difficult for every parent. Some parents will not be as positive and/or effective with some children for many various reasons, including problems that can be ascribed to the parent.

There are numerous ways to account for problematic relations between parent and one child but not another. For example, from the perspective of a family systems approach, when a particular relationship is evolving between parent and child, it is often the case that the next child develops a very different pattern with the parent as a way to "stake out" his or her own territory, avoid competition, and obtain importance through doing different types of behavior. Similarly, siblings will frequently reverse patterns of behavior when one child changes. Therefore, as a means of intervention, it would be helpful to not only consider patterns between parent and child, but also sibling and extended family relationships as well. For example, having a sibling in the family who is close in age and very proficient can sometimes make it difficult for the other child to recognize personal competence.

Incidentally, there is apparently no heritability data for ADHD analyzing whether there are differing rates of ADHD for siblings adjacent in the birth order compared to siblings in general, and whether diagnosed siblings adjacent in birth order do very discrepant psychosocial patterns despite that both siblings qualify for the DSM-IV-TR criteria. This analysis would be reasonable to undertake. For example, Goodman and Stevenson (1989) found that fraternal twins did not show patterns of concordance consistent with a genetic argument, and Sherman, McGue, and Iacono (1997) found that there was a 0% rate of concordance for dizygotic twins. Both studies indicate that patterns of family relationships may significantly influence the occurrence of diagnostic behaviors. However, further investigations can consider age differences between siblings, and whether the diagnosed sibling is older or younger, because social patterning might be influenced by those variations (in addition to many other factors).

Our current state of affairs

Most professionals agree that ADHD can be a serious long-term problem. It had previously been believed that many diagnosed persons would "out grow" their condition; but this is no longer presumed. For example, it is now reported that, by using parent report (and a rigorous 98% criteria for diagnosis), as many as two-thirds of diagnosed children will continue the disorder in adulthood (Barkley, 2002). Silver (2000) also notes that 30-70% of diagnosed children will continue ADHD patterns into adulthood. Others have also reported similar statistics, but to a slightly lower extent. For example, some (Weiss and Hechtman, 1986; Mannuzza et al., 1993) report that approximately one-half of diagnosed children will continue ADHD into adulthood. Traditionalists highlight these findings, because they undermine the notion that ADHD is simply a childhood disorder that will stop as the child matures.

While these findings suggest that the disorder can be highly persistent over time, we might also ask what is different about the diagnosed persons who have stopped showing the delay, and how it has been possible for them to no longer have ADHD problems when the delays are purported to be *neurologically caused.* However, in response to this concern, traditionalists contend that many individuals are outgrowing the criteria of the disorder rather than the disorder itself, because the designated criteria are consistent with childhood patterning rather than adult behaviors (Barkley, 2000).

As a response to this shortcoming, it is recommended that different criteria be imposed to better capture adults who still show delays in their inhibitory functioning as that problem gets expressed by older persons (Barkley, 2000). For example, Murphy and Gordon (2006) point out that the older diagnosed individual may still endure significant problems relative to the cognitive signs of impulsive behaviors despite that these symptoms are usually difficult to uncover. The problems may include general disorganization and inattentiveness, which is not as easily observed as their patterns of impulsiveness had been: running into traffic or jumping from high places. Adult diagnosed individuals often complain of restlessness, distractibility, and forgetfulness (Biederman, 1998).

Older diagnosed persons will also frequently report that they have numerous intrusions (i.e., mental and external) impinging upon them, and/or difficulty preventing the intrusions from interfering with expected accomplishments. As a result of a lack of functional stability, it is difficult for them to maintain agreements and complete tasks requiring sustained effort, concentration, or consistency over time. To others they will appear to be highly unreliable and erratic.

However, since not all situations tax the inhibitory system to the same extent, the only way to give a person an accurate diagnosis is to observe his or her behavior across situations, and over an extended time period. It is claimed that this way of approaching diagnosis permits observations of the individual's behavior in relation to "time;" ADHD delays allegedly destroy a person's ability to organize behavior over time. It is on these grounds that diagnosis relies (largely) on observations of parents, spouses, and teachers who interact with the diagnosed person over the course of many days.

Because the disability manifests in this way, Barkley (1998f, 250) claims that *time* is the definitive yet almost "invisible disability" that troubles a diagnosed person. An ADHD functional deficit will "cleave thought from action, knowledge from performance, past and future from the moment, and the sense of time from the rest of behavior more generally." ADHD becomes a condition where the person has more difficulty enacting what he or she knows even if he or she has had the necessary training to know what to do. It is a disorder of "performance more than a disorder of skill" (Barkley, 2006f, 324).

However, we do not yet know how this characterization is distinct from other diagnostic categories—where we observe people who are aware that their actions will cause or exacerbate problems, yet they continue the same behavior. People in the general population will sometimes demonstrate that they know how to behave, and yet will not stop problematic patterns—that is, they are not markedly different from an ADHD-diagnosed individual who will not adhere to a schedule. For example, people know that ingesting steroids and not exercising is unhealthy, but some will continue to behave in this way, and *not* enact what they know.

Often we are aware that our actions are disliked by others, but we nevertheless continue those behaviors. Popular examples of this problem occur when children are told not to bite fingernails, crack their joints, and/or to not snack before meals. Children are often cognizant of problems associated with these acts, yet many do not follow the sound advice of concerned others. In the same vein, we observe the constant repetition of what children *know* to be dangerous behavior (darting into the street) and the highly disadvantageous tendency (of never completing schoolwork). However, when those kinds of actions continue unrelentingly, a child will eventually receive an ADHD diagnosis.

Failure to promote behavioral change by making people aware of problems associated with their actions does not mean that an incurable deficiency prevents their responsiveness to specific training. Negative treatment results may also mean that old behaviors are still reinforced in the contexts and circumstances in which they occur, despite attempts to inform.

It is exceedingly rare that behavioral change is induced simply by giving new information. For example, informing overweight people that eating too much will result in weight gain, teaching adolescents about the dangers of unprotected sex, and the use of illicit drugs, or telling a cigarette smoker that she will get cancer, will often not result in significant behavioral changes. Imparting new information can increase the probability of new learning, but that new information may not alter the reinforced behaviors when particular situations and circumstances recur in an individual's social matrix. Negative results could indicate that reinforced responses are not yet extinguished by the utilized intervention.

Nevertheless, traditionalists are convinced that diagnosed children must have a stringently managed environment in order to counter internal insufficiencies, and loved ones are urged to provide the diagnosed person with plenty of directive assistance. When diagnosed persons and their families get involved with child management programs, generally these programs encourage parents to use positive reinforcement, withholding of available resources (i.e., response cost), and/or time-out strategies. These interventions do not cure ADHD, but they are thought to increase parental understanding of the diagnosis, introduce changes in the child's ADHD behavior (Bor and Markie-Dadds, 2002), lead to a reduction in the parental stress level, and improve self-esteem and the quality of the parent/child relationship (Anastopoulos, Smith, and Wien, 1998; Anastopoulos, Rhoads, and Farley, 2006).

It is also currently believed that parent training has at least *some* efficacy in the treatment of childhood ADHD (Chronis et al., 2004). More recent findings from the Multimodal Treatment of ADHD Study (MTA) also indicate that a combination of stimulant medication and psychosocial treatment (including parent training) is superior to drug therapy alone when evaluated against outcome measures such as improvements in family functioning, working with oppositional behaviors, teacher rated social skills and academics, childhood anxiety problems, and when assisting lower socioeconomic families (Jensen, 2002; Anastopoulos, Rhoads, and Farley, 2006). These outcomes are rekindling interest in earlier reports that propound the benefits of combined treatments (Gadow, 1985), and more recent claims that different treatments may have unique and specific influences (Smith, Barkley, and Shapiro, 2006).

However, conventional practitioners have been the first to caution that even though modest effects have been noted when parent training is used alone to treat ADHD, when this treatment is evaluated in relation to prescribing drugs, very little positive influence is observed. It is maintained that these interventions generally seem most suited for diagnosed persons who also show co-morbid problems such as oppositional behavior, which can be adequately resolved with behavioral modification strategies. While parent training interventions may augment medication therapy, raise the acceptance and tolerance level among family members, and improve family life, medication continues to be the cornerstone of treatment (Anastopoulos, Smith, and Wien, 1998). Moreover, Smith, Barkley, and Shapiro (2006) note that it has not been firmly established that psychosocial intervention introduces any benefits at all for children who are adequately responsive to stimulant medication.

Furthermore, they say that even when gains occur within the family as a result of psychosocial training, it has not yet been established that diagnosed children generalize behavioral improvements in school functioning (McNeil et al., 1991; Smith, Barkley, and Shapiro, 2006). The continuance of school problems indicates that the school situation is still reinforcing diagnostic responding (even if parents are learning ways to shape alternative behaviors at home); but conventional thinkers nevertheless conclude that neurological delay must be preventing the diagnosed child from functioning adequately in school despite progress at home. Consistent with that interpretation is the finding that improvements can also occur in school with school-based interventions, but they do not generalize well in the home environment (Sheldon et al., 2000).

The failure of treatment gains to generalize remains an important issue, since problematic school functioning is the primary concern for most parents seeking treatment for ADHD. Traditionalists recommend monitoring school functioning as much as possible as a way to address this issue. They advise school personnel to do stringent behavioral management within the classroom. Practitioners are asked to design elaborate programs to enable the teacher to increase the accountability of the diagnosed person's behavior.

While Pfiffner and Barkley (1998) acknowledge attempts to compel the diagnosed student towards self-monitoring, and request that contingencies be made less frequently and be less discernable, traditionalists still doubt that diagnosed persons can ever be fully accomplished, given their perspective on the nature of neurological ADHD. Without the external support of medication, cueing, reminding, and explicit rewards and punishments, the diagnosed person is unlikely to meet the demands and requirements of conformity at school. Regression is anticipated if they were to try to manage the task without those particular forms of remediation.

Nevertheless, and most importantly for our analysis here, many families do request psychotherapy at one time or another to help them with ongoing behavioral problems. It is now being reported that parent satisfaction with behavioral treatments can sometimes supercede what is evident when subjects are in medication-only treatments (MTA Cooperative Group, 1999).

Recent reports from the MTA study also indicate that medication doses may be kept lower by instituting a behavioral intervention throughout a course of treatment (MTA Cooperative Group, 2004). Other studies show that children are less inattentive and over-active when parents improve their parenting skills (Anastopoulos et al., 1993; Dubey, O'Leary, and Kaufman, 1983; Freeman, Phillips, and Johnston, 1992) both in the short and long-term (McMahon, 1994). Thus, Sinha (2005) emphasizes that non-medicinal therapy can be a viable treatment option; he claims that unpublished data from the two-year MTA follow up—children treated with behavioral therapy, school intervention, and summer camp —functioned as well as children on high doses of medication.

It may therefore be advantageous to institute non-medicinal care and not completely abandon psychological intervention. This also seems very important for brain-injured diagnosed persons who respond positively to medication therapy only 50% of the time, as well as for younger diagnosed persons. More specifically, while success rates as high as 90% occur for older children, it is estimated that only 30% of 2- to 3-year-olds respond positively to medication.

Similarly, while 50% of 3- to 5-year-olds might respond well, the best benefits do not show until the frontal lobes are more fully developed for 5- to 7-year-olds (Barkley, 2000). Connor (2006) asserts that stimulants should not be the initial treatment for the very young child. He notes that preschoolers tend to suffer more side effects than older children (2002). While there is a diverse arsenal of medication available, many continue to strongly emphasize that little is known about the safety of these medications for preschoolers (Greenhill et al., 2003).

Consequently, even enthusiasts of a medically-based treatment regime hold that psychologically-based treatment could be of value. For example, Murphy (1998) recommends psychosocial intervention for adults in addition to medication therapy. He indicates that such interventions may lessen the emotional consequences and co-occurring problems. Similarly, Campbell (1976) indicates that medication has had little impact on the molar characteristics of cognitive ability (i.e., reasoning, problem solving, and learning) for diagnosed persons. While medicinal treatment has helped school productivity and diminished disruptive behavior in the classroom, it has not helped improve interpersonal skills (Pelham and Bender, 1982), or helped diagnosed persons do appropriate responses when others ruffle them (Hinshaw, Henker, and Whalen, 1984a; Hinshaw, Buhrmester, and Heller, 1989). Given the shortcomings of medicinal-only treatment discussed here, we recognize that psychotherapy certainly has utility and value in the process of helping ADHD diagnosed children lead better lives.

Chapter 3

Raising Questions about Traditional Claims and Formulations

We have discussed in Chapter 2 some of the positive immediate outcomes reported by those who have chosen to take medication, but there are also significant problems with the treatment. The decision to prescribe medication brings to the fore concerns about administering drugs when treatment has just started, despite that delaying medication deprives the individual of the instantaneous benefits that can occur when taking medication. We support the idea in this chapter that the decision to refrain from medicinal therapy at the outset of treatment (especially for young people) could be essential to long-term behavioral change. However, we also recognize that each situation is unique and that, indeed, there will be situations where prescribing medication appears to be the only practical option. Moreover, just as there are biological risks to taking medication, there are also biological risks to not taking them, in that continuous conflict, failure, and negativity may adversely influence one's biology as well.

Stimulant medication has always been a potent short-term way to reduce diagnostic responding, but some families nevertheless undertake alternative treatments. Alternative treatment decisions will depend on the urgency of the presenting problem and will require much more time and effort from all involved. Although for parents who choose a cautious approach, in cases where medication has apparently not produced impressive long-term benefits, and in circumstances where medicinal and psychosocial intervention seems like the best approach, alternative psychological interventions may be fruitful.

Reverting too quickly to medicinal treatments

Despite the known and suspected risks of taking stimulant medication, the number of prescriptions has been rising at an alarming rate. For example, it was reported five years ago that Ritalin prescriptions had increased 700% since 1990, and that Adderall prescriptions had increased "fivefold since 1996" (Sinha, 2001, 48). More recently, Mathews (2005) has noted that approximately 7.8 million prescriptions were dispensed in the U.S. last year for Concerta, and 2.5 million for Methylphenidate, based on IMS Health data. Those numbers may be compared with estimates that only 4 million children took stimulant medications in 1998 (Diller, 2000), and that only 1.5 million children or only 3% of the school-age population were being treated annually with stimulant medication approximately 10 years ago (Safer, Zito, and Fine, 1996). Interestingly, Bridges (2006) notes that spending on ADHD drugs in general has rocketed from $3.1 million in 2000 to $759 million in 2004.

Consistent with these prescribing trends, Tyre (2005) reports a burgeoning in the numbers of children currently taking psychiatric drugs for all diagnostic categories. She states that 15% of parents with children between the ages of 5 and 18 are now giving their children psychoactive medication on a daily basis. She further emphasizes that these frequency rates have persisted, even though approximately 28% of parents who give their children medication deem the treatment to be either somewhat unhelpful or extremely unhelpful. Similarly, Whitaker (2005) reports that in the United States, one in five children or 9 million schoolchildren are ingesting psychiatric medications of one type or another. She estimates that if current rates were to continue, 80% of the children in the U.S. will be taking a psychotropic drug within the next decade. Therefore, even if more pronounced side effects are not presently evident for ADHD stimulants, it is necessary to continue to study the potential adverse side effects and the limitations of traditional intervention before continuing to encourage millions of children and adults to comply with those treatments.

We need only remember that the many different medicines that have demonstrated remarkable short-term efficacy are now beginning to show longer term problems as new data becomes available (e.g., Cylert, Vioxx, etc.). The numbers of diagnosed persons have been increasing at such a rapid pace that a Health Maintenance Organization recently reported that one-third of all children referred for outpatient treatment were given a diagnosis of ADHD (Beacon Health Strategies, Summer Providers Meeting, 2003). There have been more than 200 controlled studies of stimulant medications for children (Connor and Steingard, 2004; Spencer, Biederman, Wilens, et al., 1996), longitudinal studies lasting up to 30 years, and usage in the military dating back to 1937 (Barkley, 2000), but there is always the risk (no matter how small) of noteworthy side effects, since higher numbers of *very* young children are now taking the medications.

There are, however, conventional practitioners who caution against medication therapy until it is confirmed that reasonable psychosocial intervention has been lacking. Others encourage that medication be used in conjunction with behavioral intervention (Pelham and Milich, 1991). However, we also observe that many families still initiate medicinal intervention immediately when a diagnosis is made, and vast numbers of diagnosed individuals do not participate in any *non-medicinal* intervention whatsoever.

As a consequence of that practice, and after taking stimulants for a long interval, many individuals eventually believe that they must continue to take the drug(s) in order to function adequately. Some also blame their unacceptable behavior on medication failures or missed dosages. Reliance on medication can worsen a pattern of externalizing blame and dependency. Therefore, from our vantage point of being wary of the high use of medication, despite its efficacy at first, we do not yet know how the medicinal approach affects the development of a self-reliant pattern over time.

A major empirical quandary arises too, when we observe positive behavioral changes after medication has been given. A person will typically believe that he or she could not have changed without the medication. If a child has taken medicinal treatments for many years, parents will also be reluctant to cease administering it, even if the child is currently failing in school. They remember the initial positive effects when the drugs were first given, and believe that those effects are still influential despite the notable continuance of dysfunctional behaviors. Moreover, to abandon medication once it is prescribed means that the individual has little opportunity to learn alternative behaviors without it; stasis may be disrupted by their elimination; and the individual may not believe that future improvement is possible without drug therapy. There is now an acquired dependency and reliance on the medication, and to consider giving it up can be disquieting and anxiety-provoking for all involved.

However, rapid behavioral change sometimes occurs with or without medicinal treatment, so medication may not always be responsible for the immediately satisfying results in some scenarios. For example, sometimes ADHD behaviors subside rapidly when the child has more opportunities to play outdoors with friends. Similarly, notable improvements have been observed when there is a change in custody, a positive male figure becomes more available, a negative male figure leaves the home, a promise is made to a dying grandparent to achieve in school, and/or when the child has had contact with the natural environment—hiking, camping, swimming, etc., as reported by Louv (2005).

Other short-term gains not ascribable directly to medication have also been identified by DuPaul, Barkley and Connor (1998); they note that practice effects may account for better scores on behavioral rating scales between the first and second administration of the questionnaire. Given the occurrence of those short-term effects, they advise that the second administration of a behavioral rating scale should be used as a baseline when assessing the medicinal impact on behavior.

However, despite the obvious advantages seen in delaying medicinal treatment, there is also the financial factor, which is also associated with a recommendation to administer medication early in the treatment. If a drug is sanctioned as the treatment for a particular disorder, and large profit margins are the result, pharmaceutical companies are poised to underwrite the empirical inquiry that elicits data to corroborate the efficacy of the posited helping agent. Conversely, there is substantially less financial gain to be recognized with non-medical interventions, and it is thus much more difficult to obtain the necessary funding to underwrite non-medically based work that could establish an empirical basis on which to recommend alternative therapies.

Financial concerns must also be considered when insurance companies pay for treatment, or when an establishment has a stake in obtaining quick results for the elimination of troublesome behaviors. Most medications for ADHD induce rapid favorable change when compared to psychotherapeutic interventions, so the traditional approach is generally advocated and encouraged by most underwriters and institutions.

Under such constraints, we observe that traditionalist presumptions and questions posed are consistent with the promotion of medicinal remedies. Anomalies arising from research as well as problems associated with ingesting medication are not responsibly and routinely explored. A recent example occurred when *Consumer Reports* (2004) noted that unfavorable trial results regarding adolescents and antidepressant medications were not being published. Not all trials can be discredited of course; the accomplishments of medicinal interventions are vast, but we acknowledge the influential component of financial pressure, and the fact that it is merely financially easier to promote a biological account. Although one only need remember that while antidepressants were unequivocally recommended for children and adolescents, many now question the use of antidepressants with these age groups as new data becomes available (Chase, 2004). The FDA now warns about their use with younger persons (Neergaard, 2004).

Nevertheless, psychosocial interventions are generally at a distinct disadvantage compared to medicinal treatments when attempting to establish efficacy. For example, medication can be monitored extensively for overall consistency. In contrast to therapists, each dosage is likely to be similar to the others, whereas therapists, despite having common perspectives, will differ from one another. Medical models seem to have the greater possibility of limiting individual variation when compared to psychosocial interventions during empirical studies.

Dosages can be precisely measured, so a medicine regime for ADHD diagnosed individuals can be relatively consistent compared to social exchange during behavioral therapy. While there are learning curves regarding the regulation of side effects, correct dosages, and correct target population, those parameters are generally easier to manage in comparison with helping therapists learn to instill self-reliance and self-confidence in ADHD children. Some therapists may learn to implement the recommended treatments quite well and produce positive outcomes, while others will show an opposite trend.

It is also generally the case that the kind of therapy recommended in the traditional approach is easier to control than a model based on establishing collaboration and self-reliance. Behavioral modification based on contingency management is clearly specified, compared to the complexity of identifying factors that contribute to effective psychotherapeutic intervention. When using psychosocial means to shape self-reliance and tact, for example, the therapist must figure out what is hindering mutually-acceptable patterns of interaction, what is impeding self-sufficiency, and what is reinforcing intrusiveness or non-participation. Often these discriminations are complicated and subtle, and it is likely moreover, that therapists vary considerably in their formulations. It is not surprising that conventional practitioners tend to dispute the psychotherapeutic approaches on these grounds, and observe very few positive effects.

Parents too will have difficulty implementing our approach, because it will require that they be less permissive, less over protective, and less insistent on compliance: compared to the traditional compliance model which advocates that they should be in control; generally, this will be unappealing and difficult to implement.

With the countless possibilities and parameters to consider, it is not clear whether any therapeutic model can provide adequate prepackaged guidance for optimal and consistent use. We suspect that some therapists, parents, and teachers would effectively enact the approach recommended here, and successfully discriminate patterns of reinforcement and/or benefits to the ADHD behaviors. Other parents and educators meanwhile, would be unable to resist thinking that the non-preferred pattern of behavior arises from an uncontrollable neurology. Still others would regard the suggested treatment intervention as antithetical to their own upbringing (i.e., use of forced compliance). These individuals will not have had experience using the language forms which promote compromise, camaraderie, and self-reliance in social exchanges.

However, we genuinely think that the one-size-fits-all system used by traditionalists prevents a number of individuals who would benefit from an alternative approach from trying to address ADHD behavior by a different method. Traditional interventions (medication and contingency management) will always permit greater control over sources of variance than our current model, and easily recognized treatment effects (especially in the short-term), but we also suspect that *rigidity* introduces its own set of problems. That is, while medication and coercion might help in some individuals' lives, that same approach can also hinder effectiveness when circumstances change, thus impairing desirable responses.

A relatively inflexible model of therapy creates problems whenever there is insufficient accommodation to the unique circumstances of each individual. Anastopoulos, Smith, and Wien (1998) warn against the "cookbook" approach, even though they typically prescribe contingency management therapies. This problem becomes apparent after the first few sessions, as more subtleties regarding the presenting problems become evident, and unique complications begin to occur. We observe that even within traditional intervention, professionals are encouraged to tailor their recommendations to the needs of the presenting family.

In any case, while medication therapies are showing the best short-term treatment effects, we also notice that the superiority of medication over other forms of treatment is being exaggerated due to the ways in which treatment outcomes are measured. Treatment effects in conventional practice are usually assessed in time intervals of up to 1-½ years (Barkley, 2000). This places nonmedicinal treatment interventions at a disadvantage, since it generally takes longer to change interpersonal patterning. Given this time fixture, we have not yet had the opportunity to know what transpires over extended time frames for individuals who persist and maintain participation in the outpatient psychotherapy recommended here.

Consistent with this view, *Consumer Reports* magazine (1995) published results from their large-scale study of readers who participated in outpatient therapy for a wide range of presenting problems. Positive treatment outcomes were reported by those who remained in therapy for at least six months. When evaluated over this extended time frame, the only added effect for those also taking medication was the experience of some medication-induced side effects. Interestingly, in other words, there was no extra advantage to prescription medication when we examine treatment effects over a fairly long time frame.

More recently (2004), *Consumer Reports* reviewed the effects of medication and talk therapy for the treatment of depression. It was found that while medication worked the fastest, those effects were tempered by significant side effects, a leveling off and then a decrease in improvement; meanwhile talk therapy produced increasing benefits, especially when at least 13 therapy sessions were attended. We therefore acknowledge that the success of psychotherapy depends on relatively long-term involvement from clients; a commitment to participation and learning is critical.

Moreover, in some scenarios the effects of medications may be exaggerated. For example, it is likely that individuals who receive medication *also* receive some psychosocial intervention. We observe with regularity that most psychiatrists and physicians dispensing medications also attempt to establish a rapport, frame the medication within a positive context of usage, address psychological problems, and deal with obstacles. Thus, individuals may be receiving more psychotherapeutic help than would otherwise be suspected when medication comprises the core of the treatment.

In that sense a "medication only" condition is a misnomer. This second level of help might lead to greater treatment outcomes and encourage continuous contact with a treating provider, but the drugs are the catalyst. Conversely, individuals who do *not* take medication often drop out of care completely when they become discouraged by a lack of immediate results from psychotherapy.

Numerous authors have discussed the barriers that many diagnosed families experience when trying to access psychotherapeutic help within clinic-based training programs (Cunningham, Bremner, and Boyle, 1995; Kazdin, Holland, and Crowley, 1997). Generally, it is reported that many parents do not participate or comply optimally with treatment recommendations. As Breggin (2001) points out when examining attendance rates for the MTA study, very few psychotherapeutic sessions took place for any of the enrollees. In particular, Smith, Barkley, and Shapiro (2006) note that by the fourteenth month, sessions had been reduced to a schedule of one per month or were eliminated completely. It is therefore important that, whenever psychotherapeutic effects are evaluated, to assess patterns of attendance, type of therapies, kinds of clients seen, and intensity and longevity of psychosocial treatments.

For example, the MTA study (Arnold, 1998) included a large sampling of clients and therapists, and yielded outcomes that seemed consistent with traditional views, but the sampling was limited to clinic populations. Moreover, the extent to which interventions included in the analysis identified the concerns advocated by the current model, such as promoting self-reliant patterns and collaborative social interactions, or the attempt to understand ADHD as reinforced behavior that may be shaped and extinguished was not at all outlined in the aforementioned study. As noted above, generalizations about the effectiveness of psychotherapy drawn from this large-scale study (compared to medication) are limited to the therapies and populations being tested, the amount of psychotherapy given, and to other variables such as the competency of therapists on staff at clinics, and other non-random sources of variance that were not controlled.

Along these lines, Breggin (2003) points out that the behavioral treatments in the MTA study were based primarily on those developed by Russell Barkley. Breggin claims that Barkley's behavioral approach is "doomed to fail because it treats the child as a defective object suitable for control by parents and teachers rather than a sentient being in conflict with adults and teachers." According to Breggin, Barkley's methods "ignore everything that is known about family systems and the necessity of changing the overall patterns of relationships in the family."

Breggin also claims that the non-medicinal treatment in the MTA study tapered off substantially over the course of the intervention, thus perhaps significantly influencing its effectiveness. He also concluded that the available data did not indicate drug-induced improvements for several important measures, which is something not always sufficiently highlighted by traditionalist reporters. In Breggin's analysis, subjects did not perceive themselves as any better; blind raters of classroom behaviors did not find differences favoring medications; social skills were not enhanced by medicinal treatments; and measures of academic performance did not favor that group.

He also noted that the study was not placebo-controlled, parents were exposed to pro-medication propaganda, adverse drug effects may not have been rigorously examined, and the sample size and selection of the medication group seemed exceptionally small and non-random.

If we consider Breggin's critique of the MTA study, traditionalists are neither demonstrating short nor long-term data to meet acceptable standards. Consistent with that assertion, Smith, Barkley, and Shapiro (2006) note that when considering all of the (traditional) treatments used in the MTA study, each showed declining effectiveness at the two-year follow up. This decline in effectiveness occurred despite that the medication group was carefully monitored and matched with the medicinal treatment that seemed to work best for each individual.

Moreover, when considering medicinal treatments in general, it is also worth noting that even for those studies using a double-blind design for assessing a medication's effectiveness, it is important to assess efficacy when "active," rather than inert, placebos are used. For example, empirical studies assessing the drug Prozac (Kirsch and Lynn, 1999) have found that people react to bodily changes; they seem to know whether or not they are taking an active agent. When studies include the use of active placebos (i.e., giving a person a drug that might produce bodily change, but has nothing to do with treating the presenting problem), treatment effects for the active placebos are observed to occur so often that they come extremely close to duplicating that which is obtained with the drug being tested.

However, it has always been more common to use "inert" placebos in studies assessing stimulant medications (Barkley, 2000). It is therefore possible that the effectiveness of stimulant medication is not as extensive as it appears from the many studies being conducted. As Kirsch and Lynn caution, the effects of *suggestibility*, including thinking that the active placebo is the drug being tested, can be quite pronounced.

Psychotherapeutic interventions can also be at a disadvantage, in that some individuals who do not experience bodily changes may also feel discouraged after recognizing that they were assigned to the non-medication group with or without concurrent psychotherapy, due to the widespread publicity about the positive effects of stimulant medication. This could have a significant impact on what transpires for many people; for those who are hopeful to obtain relief from their symptoms through medication, it could be disappointing to have been relegated to the non-medication group.

Moreover, instead of thinking that "the drug" is helping to control the child's behavior, some parents could revert to old patterns of establishing control, thus potentially limiting outcomes for the inert placebo group. Given the current level of public awareness, one could argue that it is problematic to carry out any treatment intervention for ADHD that does not include medication or active placebos, since the trend is to accept that diagnosed persons have a biologically-based problem.

Furthermore, it is essential for studies showing the efficacy of medication therapy compared to psychotherapeutic to clearly identify how they handle the problem of dropouts; this factor can significantly impact on inferences drawn from the data. People quit for many different reasons, including non-positive outcomes, intolerable side effects, and altering of previously acceptable behaviors. Dropouts represent a treatment failure, and it is therefore reasonable to treat them as anomalies and include them as such in the data analysis.

Biological shortcomings of medicinal treatments

A large subgroup however, prefers the medication intervention compared to the cumbersome less predictable psychotherapeutic approach, but the decision to ignore possible alternative formulations and treatments looks far less sensible as more shortcomings of traditional intervention are exposed. Despite the accumulation of impressive statistical outcomes using the traditional intervention, it is not without its problems.

For example, it is reported that as many as half the diagnosed adults do not respond to stimulant medication, have too many side effects to tolerate their use, and/or have other comorbid problems that are exacerbated by the medication (Taylor et al., 1987; Biederman et al., 1993). Because medication therapy for adults seems to have significant limitations, Wilens, Spencer, and Biederman (1998) emphasize that pharmacotherapy should comprise only one component of a treatment plan for adults, and moreover, should not be used exclusively. The recommendation is sound, because the reduced effectiveness of stimulants could become a serious problem for diagnosed children when they grow up having fully relied on stimulants—without any other therapy having taken place.

DuPaul, Barkley, and Connor (1998) also note that 20% to 30% of children do not exhibit a favorable response to pharmacological treatment; some show a deterioration of behavior, and some show improvement on some measures of learning, but experience either no reaction or adverse responses on other measures. Spencer et al. (1996) also report that up to 30% of diagnosed individuals show no positive response, or have difficulty with side effects when placed on stimulant medications. Not all children will therefore respond positively or similarly to this treatment intervention.

Ingesting stimulant medications can also impact on brain development and operation. For example, Redman and Zametkin (1991) note an increase in brain metabolic activity in the bilateral orbital-frontal and in the left sensorimotor and parietal areas, and less activity in the left temporal region when examining seven adults with emission tomography while taking methylphenidate. These results suggest that brain activity is altered in subtle yet important ways, and that the drugs influence more than one brain region. Here then is another example of potentially deleterious effects as a consequence of ingesting drugs over extended periods. As DuPaul, Barkley and Connor (1998, 512) indicate, the brain is a very "complex organ." Inducing changes in one area of the brain can lead to unanticipated consequences and changes in activity in other regions.

Furthermore, even though it is now generally accepted that stimulant medication will not significantly affect eventual skeletal height, some remain cautious about this potential side effect. For example, Klein and Mannuzza (1988) indicate that group data does not rule out the possibility that individual children will have their skeletal growth adversely affected. Similarly, in the two-year MTA follow up study, it is noted that children taking stimulant medications continued to show a slower growth curve when compared to others (MTA Cooperative Group, 2004).

But in response to concerns about stimulants and lower growth curves, Reeve and Garfinkel (1991, 298) maintain that these changes should only concern us if there is a "persistent loss of height velocity," or if the child's height levels off and does not conform to the "newly-established growth curve." Hence, while some downplay this potentially serious side effect, apparently there is still the risk of growth impairment for some children. In this regard, Reeve and Garfinkel caution that "a more thorough endocrinologic investigation including thyroid function tests, growth hormone, and bone age may then be warranted . . ." (p. 298) if problems with height are evident.

Stimulants can also increase heart rate, systolic and diastolic blood pressure. While these side effects are usually quite mild and benign, Brown and Sexson (1989) caution that African-American adolescents may be at greater risk compared to Caucasians for evolving a serious diastolic blood pressure increase that requires intensive monitoring. Likewise, individuals with tics, Tourette's Disorder, or psychosis must also be monitored very closely, since stimulant medication can worsen these conditions in some instances. These potential side effects are noteworthy; in that Spencer, Biederman, and Wilens (1998) indicate that more than 30% of ADHD diagnosed children show chronic tics or Tourette syndrome according to recent studies. Moreover, if a child already has a tic, then 13% of the time stimulants will exacerbate these symptoms (Caine et al., 1984).

Sallee et al. (1989) also report that stimulants may increase the probability of choreiform movements, behaviors such as the licking and biting of the lips, and/or picking at the finger tips. Due to these side effects, it is not surprising that DuPaul, Barkley, and Connor (1998) caution that diagnosed children with anxiety may not respond positively to stimulant medication, although more recently, some researchers question that conclusion (Abikoff et al., 2005). In any case, when given in high dosages, DuPaul, Barkley, and Connor emphasize that stimulants may cause temporary symptoms of psychosis, and not surprisingly, they encourage a reevaluation of dosage after a period of six months, as well as a monthly appraisal of side effects such as depressed mood, weight loss, tics, and so on.

Similarly, while Tricyclic Antidepressants have also produced positive results in reducing ADHD symptoms with no consistently demonstrated adverse serious long-term effects, or negative impact on tics or Tourette syndrome, these medications have correlated with other adverse side effects. For example, Spencer, Biederman, and Wilens, (1998) note that anticholinergic effects may occur, and at times these medications can lead to increased tooth decay, blurred vision, and constipation. Tricyclic Antidepressants may also be associated with adverse cardiovascular effects, depending on serum TCA levels. They recommend using these medications only as a second-tier treatment for most juveniles without other complicating problems, and only after a careful risk/benefit analysis.

We recognize that there is always the risk of side effects when psychopharmacology is employed with any group. For example, Mathews and Abboud (2005) report that the FDA plans to issue new labels for popular ADHD stimulant medications that outline adverse effects, including hallucinations, suicidal ideation, psychotic behavior, and aggressive or violent behavior. The FDA will also explore possible adverse cardiovascular side effects, as well as problems with hypertension, chest pain, arrhythmias, and tachycardia, although the general claim is that those problems usually disappear—even if initially evident (Zeiner, 1995)—or are generally not a problem for otherwise healthy diagnosed persons (Rapport and Moffitt, 2002).

Of greater concern is DuPaul, Barkley, and Connor's (1998) mention of serious medical consequences from ingesting stimulant medications. They note the remote possibility that less than 1% of children might develop a Tourette's Disorder, which is not reversible. They point out that some practitioners have also worried about "bone marrow suppression and neutropenia thrombocytopervia anemia . . ." (p. 525) occurring as well.

There is no denying the inherent risk in treating any atypical behavioral pattern with psychopharmacology, and the subtle long-term effects of ingesting these drugs over many years have not been fully determined. So it remains to be seen whether these substances will lead to lasting unwanted biological changes when taken continuously starting at a very young age.

Although suffering can also occur as a result of not taking medication, this must be weighed against the consequences of taking it, including the extent to which it interferes with the desire to function adequately *without* it. Moreover, even if a diagnosed person obtains significant short-term benefit from stimulants to treat ADHD, the outcomes over time using alternative treatment approaches to manage effectively without reliance on medication have not been fully assessed.

Concerns have also been raised that the therapeutic value of many different medications has been shown to wear off as the person builds psychological and physiological tolerance. Tyre (2005) notes that many children experience an outgrowing effect after taking a stimulant medication for several years, and as cited earlier, this decrease in efficacy is observed with antidepressant medications as well (Consumer Reports, 2004).

Barkley (2000) similarly acknowledges that, after only 2 to 3 months, there can be a period of decreased effectiveness with drugs such as Ritalin. When this occurs, the usefulness of the drug is cast into doubt, and it becomes necessary on occasion to change dosage or introduce a new medication. He points out that this pattern of reduced medication effectiveness was observed in the MTA study after several months of treatment. Moreover, longer term follow up during the second year of that study also indicates a greater deterioration of efficacy compared to other treatment modalities, but authors of the study speculate that this was probably due to patterns of attrition rather than to ineffective medication (MTA Cooperative Group, 2004).

Consistent with that view, Charach, Ickowicz, and Schachar (2004) found that when three groups of children (approximately 15 per group) were studied over five years, the group of children who tolerated and adhered to medication did relatively well on teacher reports even at the final follow up. However, before concluding that long-term use of stimulant medication does not lead to a depreciating outcome, it is noteworthy that the positive responders also tended to be the most impaired. Regression to the mean alone might account for the *appearance* of greater improvement for those individuals at the five-year follow up, even if the drug was gradually losing its effectiveness.

However, given the current quality of the ADHD empiricism, we have yet to verify via longitudinal studies whether stimulant drugs are useful and safe over long spans of time. Connor (2006) emphasizes that, with the exception of several studies, most are short-term (less than 4 months). He indicates that long-term studies are crucial in order to truly know whether stimulants are safe and effective in the long-run.

If diminished effectiveness does occur, perhaps it relates to the psychological and physiological novelty of the drug state wearing off. Perhaps as new learning takes place under the influence of the medication, the former ADHD pattern may once again be conditioned to occur. Consistent with this view, Lawlis (2004) claims that ADHD medication loses its effectiveness over time and becomes almost completely ineffective by the teenage years when individuals continue to rely solely on medicinal treatment.

Further, Doherty et al. (2000) have also found that 50% of diagnosed preteens and adolescents would prefer to stop taking their medications. Moline and Frankenberger (2001) have reported that one-third of their adolescent sample would like to cease their medications right away, while another 23% were undecided. These teens recognized that people seemed to like them better on their medication, but they reported the usual side effects, and did not think that medication helped them with academic achievement.

But in an attempt to rescue biological determinism, DuPaul, Barkley, and Connor (1998) claim that medications may seem to lose their effectiveness because parents change their own expectations. Rather than ascribe the recurrence of problems to drug failure, the notion is put forward that parents might be forgetting their child's initial baseline functioning. The authors claim that tolerance to stimulants has not been substantiated by empirical work, and that only anecdotal reports suggest that this can occur.

While at first glance this account might seem reasonable, it is mysterious as to why parents would complain about their children's behavior if the child complied. Moreover, since traditionalists see ADHD as emanating outward from the diagnosed person, it is contradictory to assert that parents are behaving in ways that recreate problems. They cannot reasonably insist that parents are only reacting to the disinhibited child, are contributing little to nothing to the frequency rates of ADHD behaviors, and *then* claim that parents fail to respond positively to the improved behavior.

Similar to what usually happens during "scientific" inquiry, data is often interpreted to maintain an existing and preferred paradigm until such time when the anomalies become so abundant that the old model is reconstituted, reconfigured, or changed altogether. Therefore, when parents show positive behavior in response to the medicated child, the child, according to the traditional view, has been the culprit in the difficult relationship. On the other hand, when the child is on medication, and an increase in ADHD behavior is reported after a short period of time, it is the *parent* who now has too many expectations. Because medication is presumed to be reparative, it must be the parents who are mistaken.

They also stress that it is important to ensure that the individual is taking the medication regularly, as this can also influence the drug's efficacy. Similarly, individuals might gain weight and become larger, and other environmental variations can occur that thwart the medicated diagnosed child's ability to show stabilization of symptoms after many years. The view that ADHD causes family disruption and that medication is the panacea for the biologically-based delay is continuously promoted and maintained.

Therefore, most conventional practitioners are skeptical of the view that stimulant medication loses its effectiveness over time, but some do acknowledge that since dopamine receptors are complex, the number of receptor sites may change and compensate for the longer term use (DuPaul, Barkley, and Conner, 1998; Connor, 2006). Of great concern is the fact that those assertions are made without the provision of data indicating whether the changes in dopamine receptors are permanent or temporary. In this regard, Mechan-Mayne et al. (2005) are reporting that amphetamine treatments used with the diagnosed population seem to be damaging the dopaminergic nerve endings in the striatum of adult non-human primates in very significant ways.

If permanent changes or damage of some kind is occurring, this is a grave problem. We are concerned that the brain is being irreparably altered as a consequence of the medication, and wonder if regular use of these medications early in life increases the probability that the recipient will be physiologically (and psychologically) dependent on the drugs. Even though some psychiatrists tell their clients that stimulant medication might "fix" the brain such that their use may no longer be needed (i.e., anecdotal report), our utmost concern is that if the posited alteration *is* imprecise and the brain *is* changed (or damaged), some functioning may be permanently worsened.

We do not exclude the possibility that altered brain and bodily functioning can occur as a result of taking stimulant medications over long periods of time. Reports that eating patterns seem to be altered in response to ingesting stimulant medications also poses the question as to whether a long-term disruption of eating patterns will develop as well. For example, parents are sometimes instructed to coerce eating between dosages or feed the child before bed, and sometimes children overeat when the drug is washing out of their systems.

The requirement for further study is crucial, since there is evidence that more serious side effects are occurring for some persons. For example, Anand (2005) reported that the drug Adderall XR (which nearly 750,000 Americans are ingesting) was temporarily removed from the market in Canada due to a small number of deaths and strokes that were apparently linked to that medication. Anand also noted that the drug Strattera (a non-stimulant also used to treat ADHD) has been potentially linked to serious liver damage in a small number of cases.

Concerns about liver damage have prompted the FDA to issue a warning to appear on all Strattera prescription labels (Beacon Health Strategies, 2005). While the Canadian government eventually reinstated Adderall after six months, further reports of potential cardiovascular risks have also led the FDA to request its Drug Safety and Risk Management Committee to scrutinize the long-term adverse effects of all ADHD stimulant drugs (Bridges, 2006).

When considering these negative press releases, we see the need to investigate gross side effects as well as the subtle aversive changes in functioning that correlate with the use of the typically prescribed ADHD medication. We must discover the behavioral and bodily side effects of these medications, especially when medicinal therapy is initiated with very young children whose brains and bodies change and develop rapidly.

In a related matter, it was reported in the *Worcester Telegram and Gazette* (2004) that the first high-resolution MRI study of individuals with a history of Methamphetamine abuse shows that "a forest fire of brain damage" was created in the limbic system and hippocampus as a result of ingesting that stimulant. While we do not know if this has relevance for the *prescribed* use of the much more benign Methylphenidate, the article states, "With chronic use, the brains that over-stimulate dopamine and another brain chemical serotonin, are permanently compromised." We ask then how much the continued use of any stimulant is completely safe. As pointed out in the article, "We expected some brain changes, but did not expect so much tissue to be destroyed."

Of additional concern, Schlozman (2005) reports that chromosomal abnormalities (seen in some forms of cancer) were found in children who took Methylphenidate for several months. He also indicates that rat pups that were given stimulants seem to become passive and helpless when observed as adults. However, since these disconcerting findings are not widespread in the population of long-term users of stimulant medications, Schlozman is not yet prepared to abandon their use, especially when they may make a difference in whether the child completes homework.

Adverse behavioral effects of traditional interventions

Regardless of the apparent shortcomings of medicinal therapies, primary care physicians are now diagnosing ADHD and prescribing medicines increasingly frequently; many children are moreover given the ADHD label *without* the assessment of a mental health professional. After receiving an ADHD diagnosis based on DSM-IV-TR behavioral criteria, there is a *rite of passage* to the prescription, which is viewed as a panacea for a presumed medical problem. For example, Diller (2005, 72) states, "These days, it isn't just the power and big money of Big Pharma setting the agenda: it's also our own professional culture, which seems more and more enthralled by the biochemical fix."

A corollary of this perspective is that when symptom relapse occurs after a reduction or removal of medication, it is taken to mean that the person cannot function without the medication rather than an indication that going on and off a drug poses its own problems. Rather than understand the return of the former behavioral pattern as an indication that the individual is reinforced by old behaviors when not in a drug-induced state, or that the individual has not *yet* learned to behave acceptably without the medication, the behavioral change is highlighted as proof that the person *must* have the medication to offset a posited chemical imperfection. Likewise, when combined help from family members, therapists, and/or school personnel produces improvements, those changes are attributed to the interventions rather than the diagnosed person's competence.

Since traditional treatments require diagnosed persons to become habituated to rely on others to help them change through cueing, directing and managing resources, or require them to function in a continuous drug-induced state, we should not be surprised then, that if assistance and medication becomes unavailable or is removed, the effective responses and actions do not occur. The individual has not learned to rely on his or her own cues and directives, or learned to enact certain behaviors without the stimulants.

In an analogy, the traditional treatment regime is like offering a person a crutch or wheelchair when she has difficulty walking, as it is presumed that independent walking is not possible. The device allows the person to be able to travel quickly and easily compared to moving on wobbly legs, and in many ways the supportive device solves the problem reasonably well. Once she is resigned to the fact that she will never walk independently, this approach makes more sense than enrolling in a rehabilitation program focused on exercise to shape behaviors that purportedly cannot be learned. In the same way, if the traditional disability model is regarded as tenable, most efforts to shape self-reliance and initiative will be abandoned.

However, there are problems weaning off medications, regardless of the etiology of the problem. Parrott (1999) illustrates the example of individuals who try to stop using nicotine. Continuation of a smoking pattern not only offsets the adverse effects of nicotine withdrawal, but also reveals the difficulty of learning (reinforcing) substitute behaviors to replace the habit. The individual has learned to smoke in response to particular events, emotional states, bodily discomforts, or other problems, therefore recidivism is very high when the individual tries to quit smoking. This pattern occurs for many drugs, as the individual has become habituated to respond to various conditions by producing a particular drug-induced state.

Smokers often undergo a period of adjustment after quitting; they gain weight, and have difficulty coping, even after physiological withdrawal has passed. They report having felt more at ease when they smoked, and many begin smoking again. The essential point is that learning to live in the world in a new way takes time, and to stop using any drug (or medication) requires a long period of readjustment.

Therefore, the failure to produce positive effects upon withdrawal of medicinal treatment could be a side effect of using that strategy rather than a consequence of a posited delay. Medication therapy is unlikely to produce persistent effects for any atypical behavioral pattern; this limitation is not exclusive to ADHD. For example, Begley (2004), in a review of therapies for treating depression, noted that research now shows that patients who complete a course of psychotherapy without medication will relapse far less often.

Moreover, and in addition to concerns about adverse biological effects, positive behavioral outcomes have not always been evident when taking stimulant medications. For example, some studies indicate that stimulant medications have not helped to induce improvements in school over long-term. Investigators caution that grades ultimately have not been elevated to the extent that had been envisaged during the positive short-term improvements in productivity and compliance with the school curriculum (Rie et al., 1976a, 1976b; Whalen and Henker, 1991). Similarly, Connor (2006) notes that it is still not known whether drug-induced short-term improvements in school functioning translate into long-term scholastic achievement, and Conners (2002) states that the effects of medication have been less pronounced when looking at the outcome of relieving academic deficits.

Moreover, we suspect that some of the short-term treatment effects regarding school functioning might be exaggerated in some instances, as teachers could overstate the effects of medication when it is first administered as a way to encourage the child. For example, the diagnosed child may immediately become student of the month, even though other students are outperforming that individual; teachers are often thankful that now the child is no longer as disruptive and does more work.

Medication effects can also initially be augmented as parents become affirming and available to help the diagnosed child with schoolwork. The medication is producing immediate behavioral change, therefore it is more enjoyable to work with a child who is compliant and engaged. Parents will also be less irritable and more relaxed when their son or daughter has completed homework, and when news from the teacher is positive. Psychological factors may therefore be amplifying the reported medicinal outcomes.

Given the available data, medication is no panacea for long-term school achievement despite short-term reports of efficacy. For example, there has been concern that certain dosages of stimulant medications help behavior but simultaneously impede learning (Spague and Sleator, 1977). Similarly, DuPaul, Barkley, and Connor (1998) note that a higher percentage of diagnosed children show improvement in classroom behavior, but that approximately 50% of children do not show advancement in *academic functioning* at the higher dosage ranges. What the statistics indicate is that the influence on academic performance is related more to work productivity rather than work accuracy, and that medication does not help children comprehend complex academic material.

Rapport et al. (1987) also warn against the many different response patterns to stimulants. Some individuals will show increasing improvement with higher doses, while others will reach a plateau where there is no advantage to raising dosage levels. Some worsen when dosages are raised too high, and others will show inconsistent reactions to dosage changes. Some children show improvements in behavior, but no change or even a worsening of academic functioning. Even the same individual can be differentially influenced over time by the effects of a particular drug (Rapport et al., 1994).

Sinha (2001, 50) is worried that stimulant medications might "hyperfocus the child on solitary activities," and inadvertently disrupt long-term social adjustment. Others studying this problem also caution that methylphenidate may have the side effect of social withdrawal (McBurnett, Lahey, and Swanson, 1991). Moreover, Stambor (2006, 16) is concerned that stimulants will increase "delusional ideation or suspiciousness" over time because they increase the release of cortisol, which has been associated with symptom severity in schizophrenia.

As noted by DuPaul, Barkley, and Connor (1998), medication does not teach children skills; it only increases the probability that children will emit a competent behavior already in their repertoire. They also emphasize that there are few methodologically sound studies that have assessed the long-term value of the most efficacious ADHD medications. In their view, when studies have attempted to address concerns about long-term efficacy, children on medications did not show any improvements when taken off their medications during follow up.

Moreover, Pelham (1985) and Weiss and Hechtman (1993) see no remarkable benefit to using medication compared with *not* using medication when evaluated over time. Likewise, Abikoff (1987, 172) asserted 20 years ago, "There is little evidence that long-term stimulant treatment substantially alters the eventual outcome for these children, because deficient social and learning skills and poor academic performance are still present in adolescence and young adulthood." Even when traditional treatments yield initial benefits, many will show poor outcomes when assessed as adults (Gittelman, Mannuzza, and Shenker, 1985).

More recently, Diller (2005, 59), author of *Running on Ritalin* (1998) and *Should I Medicate My Child?* (2002), maintained the view that medicinal therapies have not demonstrated long-term advantages. He notes that "after nearly seven decades of prescribing Ritalin, Adderall, and similar stimulants for millions of children, we still don't know whether these drugs boost kids' chances for success later in life." He adds, "Given the critical importance of this issue, why are we still so steeped in ignorance?"

If one considers these cautious reports, it does not seem as if stimulant medication has produced enduring effects that would permit individuals to stop taking them. There is also nothing that unequivocally indicates that over extended periods medication treatment produces any significant advantage whatsoever, including academic success. When framed in such a light, we might then ask, how many families do not participate in psychotherapy because they were initially given the medication option, and then realized what *seemed* to be remarkable immediate changes in diagnostic behaviors. How many end up with poor long-term outcomes simply because medicinal treatment was encouraged at the outset?

A critique of the traditional evaluative process

It seems that the majority of Americans understands and frames diagnostic behavior using the now-popular ADHD vernacular. Given that the condition is also popularly accepted as *inherited*, any presenting individual who says that a family member also shows similar behavior is under greater suspicion of having this presumed genetically-transmitted neurological condition. The evaluative process has apparently become a self-fulfilling prophecy. Our presumptions and expectations increase the likelihood that diagnosis will conform to a familiar patterning, and that alternative ways of investigating the presenting problem are ignored.

Interestingly, Barkley (1998e) describes an opposite pattern for self-reporting adults who do not actively seek treatment. He claims that they seldom describe their behavior in ways that would qualify them for diagnosis, even though loved ones might disagree. Under these circumstances, to report symptoms could increase blame or social pressure to alter their behavior. As with most individuals, diagnosed persons will be less likely to endorse statements that reveal their own shortcomings; they will tend to underestimate the effects of their disruptive behavior, be inured to their ADHD symptoms, or deny having any symptoms whatsoever. These circumstances are in contrast with times when adults self-refer to clinics expecting to reduce their discomfort.

Not only do traditionalists characterize diagnosed adults who disavow ADHD as in denial, but they also posit that they lack awareness of their behavior due to ADHD. Instead of entertaining the possibility that many of these adults may actually recognize a functionality or utility to their response patterns, or that they behave differently when apart from their parents, the traditional presumption is that they label themselves inaccurately, because other *family members* proclaim an ADHD pattern.

Similarly, when Prince et al. (2006) notice non-symptomatic interview behavior from self-referred diagnosed adults, they also suspect that these persons have developed various strategies to enable them to compensate for their deficiencies. When data conflict with the traditional understanding of the disorder, the validity or accounting for the individual's actions is altered to coincide with the views of biological determinism.

This problem is even more pronounced when parents bring their adolescents to treatment. In these circumstances adolescents will often deny that anything is wrong with them. Robin (1998) indicates that many teens oppose taking medication or participating in any intervention. However, it is not clear whether therapists typically investigate whether some of these diagnosed adolescents are ADHD responding to painful or arduous family patterns of behavior, or are objecting to being identified as the cause of problematic relationships. The conclusion is that ADHD makes these individuals behave unacceptably.

Robin thinks that many teens contest diagnosis because developmental changes during adolescence make them less likely to affirm their unremitting functional problem. He posits that teens want to identify with peers, and that medication will eliminate wild and exciting behavior. In these situations it is the therapist's job to *educate* the adolescent about his or her genetic, incurable, neurological disorder, and to recognize the necessity for medication. When teens are brought to treatment by family members, their reports almost invariably carry the most weight. If under-productivity at school is relevant, diagnosis is even more probable with corroborating information from family members.

Similarly, Murphy and Gordon (1998) note that when parents of an adult who actively seeks treatment are interviewed, it is not unusual for parents to confirm fewer DSM-IV ADHD symptoms, either current or past, than might their sons or daughters who have initiated the therapy. The implication is that parents will have forgotten what happened long ago, or perhaps have their own psychopathology. The authors also speculate that parents are not keen to admit inadequacy as a caregiver when their child was younger. Some will feel guilty, others will deny the severity of the problem, and some will report that the individual was not as troubled as another sibling. Parents will be reluctant to think that their offspring are anything other than normal. In these instances, however, the self-report of the diagnosed person is seen as more credible than that of loved ones (Murphy and Gordon, 2006).

Moreover, even without ancillary data, traditionalists often agree that information given by an adult seeking treatment is permissible for diagnostic and treatment purposes. Similar to most other disorders, they say that the presenting adults are appropriate reporters of their own functional difficulties (Wilens,

Spencer, and Biederman, 1998). Given these clear contradictions, we do not know whose report to consider as tenable, which particular data is essential for ascribing the ADHD label, and on what grounds are self-reports accepted or rejected. Furthermore, we do not yet know why diagnosed individuals are regarded as credible when admitting problems, compared to those diagnosed persons who vehemently oppose an ADHD diagnosis, especially when it is difficult to determine whether ADHD difficulties have occurred early enough or consistently enough to meet diagnostic requirements.

Despite attempts to accumulate independent evidence of impairment, without a coherent explanation, diagnosed persons will either be accurate or inaccurate reporters. For example, while it is claimed that diagnosed persons are not fully self-aware to credibly disavow having ADHD (when their parents say they indeed have the condition), they are nevertheless surprisingly accurate reporters when identifying their own children's ADHD (Faraone et al., 2003).

With these problems in mind, and because individuals will self-refer for various reasons (as well as sometimes fabricate), it is therefore incumbent on the *clinician* to determine whether an ADHD diagnosis is reasonable. In this regard, Murphy and Gordon (1998, 363) find it more believable when the self-report contains a particular "heaviness" pertaining to the impairments experienced; sincerity must accompany the self-report in order for it to be credible. Examples include bouts of tears, regret, problems with self-esteem, and learned helplessness. Individuals report that they have problems finishing tasks, and note frustrations in school and work; they seem to know and demonstrate firsthand what it means to live with ADHD. They often report losing and misplacing items, or explain that these problems have carried on for as long as they can remember. According to Murphy and Gordon, these kinds of presentations highlight the probability of having the condition; the more one describes behaviors consistent with traditional views, the more frequently an ADHD diagnosis will be assigned. These presentations stand in contrast with self-reports related to obtaining a drug to enhance performance, as in the recent trend of sexually healthy males who request Viagra (Olivero, 2004).

That approach does, however, seem incompatible with the assertions of Wheeler, Stuss, and Tulving (1997): that ADHD individuals are relatively limited in their ability to show autonoetic awareness (i.e., they fail to recognize how their behavior is rule-consistent or deviant, and how it compares and contrasts with other behavior). They elaborate that individuals with this awareness have a sophisticated working memory which permits their analysis of behavior over extended time frames. Since the argument that ADHD interferes with autonoetic awareness is a robust one, a diagnosed person's appraisals of their own actions are thus not particularly credible. This argument is used to account for the high frequency of adults (not actively seeking treatment) who, when interviewed, report no longer having the condition.

Once again, given traditional assertions that diagnosed persons have limited autonoetic awareness, it is baffling as to why self-referred (very emotional) diagnosed persons are regarded as accurate reporters when they make discriminations about their own behavior over time; meanwhile, those who are brought to treatment are thought to have a severe autonoetic delay which discounts their report of having no symptoms. One could argue that adults who actively seek treatment are more self-aware (and their reports are typically consistent with hard data) than adults who do not seek treatment, but the criteria for making diagnostic decisions is *not* well defined. For reasons that are not fully explicated, diagnosed persons sometimes have less difficulty being aware of symptoms and reporting them.

It would therefore seem prudent for clinicians to observe that, rather than sincerity as proof for a medical diagnosis, it could be that some persons seek help, and/or are look for permission to take a drug that will help them achieve. They may be searching for someone to confirm a socially acceptable reason for their lapses, or are hoping to obtain special accommodation from their social group that would otherwise not occur. From this vantage point it does not matter whether individuals are profoundly sincere, whether they report symptoms to which others agree, or whether they are dissatisfied with their current patterning: self-reports neither confirm nor deny the presence of a coherent neurological condition.

The traditional view is also inconsistent when they say that diagnosed children (i.e., not self-referred) do not have enough self-awareness to be reliable reporters about their own ADHD behavior, but they *do* have enough autonoetic awareness to report accurately about behavior disruptive only to themselves. In other words, these children cannot be trusted to report on categories of action that suggest they are behaving in a socially disruptive fashion, but they *can* be trusted to report about categories related to anxiety or depression that is personally uncomfortable rather than disruptive to others. For example, Barkley and Edwards (1998, 276) note that a child's report of his or her "internalizing symptoms" (i.e., anxiety and depression) is reliable, and that examiners should use those reports when diagnosing for those problems. Hinshaw (1994) also proffered this argument.

However, it remains unclear as to why it is so very difficult to be self-aware of ADHD behaviors, such as high activity levels, provocation, and non-participation/non-conformity to instruction; whereas the recognition that one feels anxious, nervous, or depressed is easy to identify. Nowhere has it been established that the one class of behaviors requires a more complex set of discriminations than the other.

In pursuing this matter further, it would seem that for individuals to recognize that they are doing ADHD, anxiety, and/or depression, they must be able to compare between self and others, or have someone else make these discriminations. Because loved ones inevitably comment on ADHD behaviors, we can assume that diagnosed individuals overhear that they are frequently acting in antisocial ways by being overactive, inattentive, or some other unacceptable behavior. In the same way, they will hear comments that they are more anxious or depressed than other children, as this condition would be discussed by loved ones as well.

Our stance is that the inconsistencies between self-reports of ADHD individuals and reports of observers is related to the benefits (in particular situations) of either admitting or denying socially unacceptable behavior. The presumption that ADHD diagnosed persons' neurological delay prevents them from accurately describing their ADHD behavior, but does not hinder their perception of other behavioral patterns, is utterly baffling.

Before we reach any conclusion that diagnosed persons lack self-awareness because of a biological limitation, it is essential to investigate whether diagnosed individuals differ from a normative sample when they are asked to report about their socially disruptive acts. How common is it that any of us shows awareness of the impact of our difficult behavior on others? Are many of us oblivious to these "wrongful" acts? During the interview we can also inquire into whether diagnosed person are equally unaware of their *acceptable* behaviors.

Although remarking from a very different framework, when discussing the unreliability of a child's report during the initial interview, Barkley and Edwards (1998) assert that decreased self-awareness and lack of impulse control in defiant diagnosed children makes it difficult to obtain dependable information. They add that children with ODD and ADHD will often not reflect long enough when the examiner asks questions. Many children will lie and distort information in order to satisfy themselves.

Such appraisals seem consistent with the traditional perspective, but inconsistencies are nevertheless present in that account as well. For instance, when an ADHD individual distorts or lies about behavior, we suggest that control over the future is taking place, and that there is awareness of behavioral consequences. In other words, it is preferable to *not* be seen in a negative light by "blurting" out or acting impulsively—which could lead the diagnosed person into social difficulty—a frequent problem of diagnosed individuals. However, if that is true, then the self-aware response is not very consistent with the characterizations often ascribed to ADHD individuals.

Further, if impulsivity accounts for diagnosed individuals' dismissal of the examiners questions, why are they sometimes not too impulsive to provide answers that are seen by the examiner in a positive light? Why do they sometimes show enough impulse control to withhold or lie in order to not suffer indictment, when the easiest (or more impulsive) response would be to tell the truth? The construct of disinhibition therefore does not provide a coherent or consistent means of accounting for the variations in initial interview behaviors, or the variations of behavior in general within the diagnosed population.

However, in response to our portrayal, traditionalists would likely argue that the prepotent responses are different when the various interactions occur, and/or that other external factors influence symptom expression, such as the saliency of being evaluated, and the importance of not self-incriminating. They might hold that when deception is displayed, or when they are impulsive, each situation taxes the inhibition system differently. They might insist that some interactions make deception more prepotent than any other response; or they may even go so far as to posit that it is the nature of the disorder to be inconsistent in its expression, and that variation in interview behavior is expected.

Of course this is mere circular thinking, and until the parameters are specified *prior* to the behavior, the paradigm is essentially flawed. For example, when giving a self-report about behavior, when is it prepotent to tell the truth, to accurately report being depressed or anxious, to construct a lie, or to avoid self-incrimination? When is it prepotent to answer questions and please the examiner, or not answer questions and displease the examiner? Since the diagnosed person does all of these behaviors within the initial interview, there must be some way to predict symptom expression beforehand; otherwise the explanation is always post hoc. ADHD is always presumed to exist because post hoc explanations permit the initial premises to remain intact whenever there are exceptions to the baseline rules.

The counter argument is of course that diagnosed individuals are doing behaviors that have thus far been reinforced in their lifetime. Personal history can be invoked to account for their particular acts and reactions. We suggest that this kind of personal data more adequately accounts for their situational lying, deception, consensual, and/or non-consensual responses when reacting to individuals who evaluate them.

This distinction is critical, in that the inference in the traditional explanation is that the inability to be self-aware is a function of neurological problems, while the argument in our alternative view is to examine the particular learning history of the presenting individual. In our approach, we first determine the extent that lying or not acknowledging disruptive behavior results from reinforcement: such as avoidance of punishment and disapproval, and then we predict these behaviors when similar conditions recur. If they lie, they are not delayed; they are reinforced to lie in specifiable conditions.

Other problems are apparent as well when traditionalists attempt to address the credibility gap during the initial interview by recommending that data should be accumulated from more than one source. By doing so, it is claimed that diagnosis can be more accurately assigned. As a way to safeguard against giving a diagnosis based on only one perspective, limited information, or problems within one setting, the subject must offer evidence that the condition has occurred over an expanded time frame, from multiple sources, and in at least two spheres of life. Corroborating evidence (i.e., hard data) such as school records should also be presented. Although in order to not unnecessarily limit a diagnosis, persons may receive diagnosis as long as problems exist in two of life's major contexts at any time during the person's development. When following that recommendation, diagnosticians are urged to combine symptoms from different settings so as not to omit from diagnosis someone who is experiencing impairment and needs assistance (Barkley, 1998e).

Despite attempts at introducing consistency into the diagnostic process, reports about symptoms vary extensively; diagnosed individuals behave in diverse ways across contexts, situations, and circumstances despite attempts to label them in a definitive way. Often diagnosed persons will behave quite differently with particular people in an interaction, and respond differently with regard to subject matter being discussed. Individuals who interact with a prospective diagnosed person will differ in topics they consider problematic or acceptable. For example, one father was told by his wife, "If you fill out the questionnaire that way, they won't give him the Ritalin." In many ways, it seems that unreliability of an evaluation is much more prevalent than under such conditions as frontal lobe injury or diabetes.

This problem has often been discussed in terms of "goodness of fit," which proposes that a relationship is likely to be positive if involved individuals share similar preferences about behavior (Buss and Plomin, 1984; Gunnar et al., 1989; Thomas and Chess, 1980). Similarly, Scantling (1998) points out that when different types of people pair with each other, very different problems and benefits occur for different combinations of individuals.

For instance, an infant who does not regain composure easily can pose a threat or scare certain parents, or inspire feelings of inadequacy, exploitation, and rejection from others. When mismatches in "goodness of fit" occur, interactions are potentially difficult, irritating, and aversive for all involved. However, the patterns are not *caused* unilaterally by either parent or infant, as some parents would more easily learn soothing responses to alter interactions in positive ways with the same type of infant.

In the same way, highly active behaviors can also be troubling for sedate parents, or when loved ones are overwrought and do not have the resources and time to manage a motoric child who is prone to injury and overstepping bounds. With this mismatch, and when parents do not identify the events that entrench the commotion, the child's active behavior will often be described and responded to in a negative way. However, the same behaviors can also be understood in a positive light (e.g., curiosity, athleticism, creating fun and engagement, etc.), and be managed more effectively by another parent who raises a similar child in different circumstances.

Whalen and Henker (1980) also highlight the importance of the interaction between the child's capabilities and the environmental requirements imposed on the child. For example, even for infants showing negative temperament, prediction rates for an ADHD diagnosis are not very high when negative temperament is considered on its own. Barkley (1998e) points out that there is greater predictability when combining temperament variables with parent characteristics, especially those related to child management and possible psychiatric problems. Similarly, Anastopoulos, Smith, and Wien (1998, 377) note that before referring parents of diagnosed persons to training interventions, one must consider whether the parent can "tolerate" the child's atypical behavior. These comments indicate that much of what happens depends on the *relationships between—*

rather than merely internal factors of the child—that account for the relevant data outcomes.

ADHD behaviors: Reinforced or lacking in control?

Reports of powerlessness expressed by individuals in relation to ADHD behavior do not identify the etiology or source of the pattern, or confirm whether the description is tenable. Diagnosed persons are not necessarily less capable of altering their behavior than others. The fact is that they have been doing unacceptable behavior for a long time, and because it is more socially acceptable for their troublesome behaviors to be *out of their control*, they are generally reinforced to adopt a biological causal model of helplessness when evidence supports that belief.

However, this interpretation contrasts with the traditional inference that imposes credibility when these kinds of reports are made. For example, Murphy and Gordon (2006, 445) note that when diagnosed adults recall school-related problems, it is possible to discern that their "choice not to do homework was not usually deliberate." While this seems to be a critical discrimination within traditional beliefs, it is not clear how it is established other than through the framing of the event by the reporter. That is, how does the evaluator decide whether a behavior is or is not deliberate? Therefore, even though diagnosed individuals are believed to be less self-aware, traditionalists will nevertheless overlook the contradiction and, to fit the square peg into the round hole, accept the reports as valid; thus, a presentation of helplessness enhances the probability of a medical account.

Reports of incapability are believed because they coincide with the disability formulation of the traditional view. However, when giving these assessments, no mention is made whether the diagnosed person has engaged in sustained effort, concentrated, focused, or showed motivation in other activities (i.e., particularly when self-initiated, non-coerced, or associated with success) before accepting the premise that they are incapable.

Interestingly, Skinner (1953, 82) notes that individuals are often "unreliable and inconsistent . . ." when asked about the "pleasantness or satisfaction provided by stimuli." He holds that "we may not be able to report at all upon events which can be shown to be reinforcing to us or we may make a report which is in direct conflict with objective observations." He cites the examples of masochism and martyrdom to illustrate this problem. In Skinner's view, first person corroboration is not required for a learning paradigm to be tenable, and first person reports have no special veracity. Skinner maintains:

> The subject himself, of course, may be in an advantageous position in describing these variables because he has had an extended contact with his own behavior for many years. But his statement is not therefore in a different class from similar statements made by others who have observed his behavior upon fewer

occasions. He is simply making a plausible prediction in terms of his experiences with himself. Moreover, he may be wrong (p. 88).

For example, many inveterate house cleaners, shoppers, gamblers, and promiscuous individuals might report the same powerlessness, unhappiness, and sense of being externally controlled by their pattern as those who report ADHD symptoms. While it may seem impossible to change and/or not feel "out of control" after enacting many behaviors over many years, we do not suggest that these behavioral patterns are caused by a biological incapacity simply because the person reports feeling helpless. However, traditionalists are seemingly accepting these accounts in order to bolster a medical explanation of ADHD patterning—despite not operationally defining what distinguishes deliberate behavior conditioned over many years from non-deliberate behavior resultant from a delayed biology that victimizes the individual.

Of equal concern is that the traditional perspective permits offsetting parameters that allow one to achieve in exceptional ways and still be labeled with an ADHD delay. For example, Polis (a diagnosed teen who recently completed a book about having ADHD entitled "Only a Mother Could Love Him") indicated in his interview with Tarkan (2003) that he was able to finish his manuscript by working late at night when he was "too tired to be hyperactive." However, given that explication, treatment for diagnosed persons would presumably only entail that we require them to exercise on treadmills early in the day before attending work or school.

Similarly, Belkin (2004) interviewed a diagnosed male who said that he could achieve because he "turned on at night" when "all the distractions were gone." Rather than understand that improvement as possibly related to a situation of increased discretionary authority, less likelihood of missing out on other activities, and no evaluation or haranguing from others, functional improvement was instead relegated to the offsetting of a biological limitation. People in the general population will often report increased work productivity late at night, but these data are highlighted to illustrate the effects of a neurobiological delay.

When advocating for their perspective, traditionalists also seem to be confounding the mitigating conditions of saliency, interest, and immediacy of reinforcement with how the person responds. There is circularity to their thinking that prevents crediting the diagnosed person with having behaved competently. If diagnosed persons respond competently, the parameter must have been salient or immediately reinforcing. If the individual fails to respond to the stimulus in an acceptable fashion, the stimulus is deemed either not salient enough or not immediately reinforcing enough to offset the inherent delay. In our view, individuals are not responding attentively because stimuli are salient; we simply identify stimuli as "salient" when individuals show intrigued reactions. Whether or not they become engrossed with particular stimuli depends on their history of conditioning.

Although for those endorsing biological determinism, the individual can still be biologically incompetent and function adequately some of the time. A history of conditioning does not enter into the equation. It is presumed that they "have" a neurological delay simply because they repeat particular socially appropriate acts *less often* and complaints from others are noteworthy. But social impairment does not rule out that the behaviors are reinforced or that acceptable responses cannot be learned.

Moreover, while traditionalists generally insist on having found ways to reduce the consequences of ADHD delay, their interventions would make conformity and task performance easier for most of us (e.g., increase task importance, ingest stimulant medication, eliminate competing activities, add more rewards and punishments, provide external cues). Very similarly, Skinner (1953, 110) indicates that during daily activity people in general arrange conditions "in order to make sure that a future stimulus will have a given effect when it appears."

Since no evidence exists to the contrary, one could argue that both non-diagnosed and diagnosed persons benefit similarly from arranging conditions in the ways described by traditionalists when intervening with diagnosed persons. Most of us require novelty, immediacy, and saliency when we change reinforced behaviors entrenched over many years. For example, if an over-eater places a "do not eat" sign on the refrigerator to help lose weight, the sign loses its effectiveness if left for too long. If, for example, money is not intermittently found in the coin return of a public telephone, or there is no news forthcoming that others have found coins, individuals will eventually stop checking. However, if a person's financial situation takes a turn for the worse, or when in the company of certain individuals, or when rushing to a destination, such parameters (among others) will affect the frequency rates of checking for coins. Again, saliency and immediacy can be altered by circumstances in obvious and subtle ways. The fundamental argument is that different kinds of diagnostic responses can be understood as a function of differences in contexts and situations, and that those responses may be related to an individual's history of conditioning.

While traditionalists would most likely respond to these concerns by saying that they recognize that ADHD behaviors may be highly contextual and varied, they would also likely argue that what separates diagnosed individuals from others is the frequency and severity of their atypical behaviors. They would emphasize that no one is diagnosed because of isolated instances of symptomatic reactions, and indicate that ADHD problems must occur over time and be related to impairment in important areas of functioning. While the classification requires an arbitrary statistical cutoff point, they note that many diagnostic categories have to face these kinds of problems. Categorization, they say, is simply a way to designate a behavioral extreme of a dimension of behavior, and idiosyncratic influences are minimized by requiring the behaviors to occur in more than one setting with more than one evaluator. As their trump card they would accentuate that no one has yet identified environmental parameters that can account for the occurrence of the diagnostic patterning.

However, despite these arguments, traditionalists ignore the many behaviors seen within the diagnosed population that are contradictory to ADHD: they remain adamant that all exceptional behaviors may be incorporated into their biological determinist belief system. They contend that ADHD is a delay of performance not ability, and that one can always point to sporadic instances where reasonable enactment of normative ability occurs, in that sometimes people may be inordinately interested in particular achievements, etc. They might insist that what makes ADHD a problem is that these instances of non-delayed behavior are rare when compared to how most people function. Although when making such claims, it seems that the ADHD diagnosis is a condition of merely not being interested enough to achieve often enough in socially-preferred ways; this is hardly grounds for discarding a learning paradigm.

Moreover, when critiquing the traditional view another very important concern arises. While the diagnosis is based on a continuum where only extreme frequencies are labeled as diagnostic, a behavioral dichotomy is nevertheless tacitly asserted. Each instance of behavior is either of the sort where a prior inhibition did not occur (i.e., prepotent), or of the sort where an inhibition occurred with at least some executive functioning (i.e., non-prepotent).

For traditionalists, behaviors are differentiated in relation to the occurrence or non-occurrence of antecedents. Those who are diagnosed are not doing enough behaviors with prior antecedents. The view is maintained that ADHD behavior occurs because a *prior* biological process has not taken place, even though it is only the behavior's frequent repetition and social consequences that occur *after* it has been emitted (as determined by evaluators), which forms the basis of the labeling.

Traditionalists infer that diagnostic responses would less likely occur if those antecedents took place more often, but as far as we can ascertain, they have not demonstrated that *not doing antecedent mind actions predicts instances of doing the diagnostic responses* outlined in the DSM-IV-TR. For that reason alone, it is an overstatement for traditionalists to insist that they champion the nature of the condition. No one debates the existence and frequency of ADHD behaviors, but traditionalists have frankly not established that their own account predicts the frequency or severity of ADHD behaviors any better than a learning paradigm claiming that people are reinforced to do the behaviors.

At this point it might be helpful to conduct a detailed comparison between our psychological interpretation of ADHD and the traditional biological account. By utilizing Robin's (1990) illustration of a "chain of ADHD-related behaviors," differences between the two interpretations become even more apparent. In Robin's scenario a boy enters his home and carries out a sequence of behaviors that traditionalists identify as caused by the underlying biological delay:

> Bill may come home from school, race in the door like a human dynamo, get mud on the carpet, leave his wet coat on the sofa, leave the milk out and cookie crumbs on the counter after his snack, tease his little sister and pull the dog's

tail, leave the light in the bathroom on, and race upstairs with a pounding step to play Nintendo after telling his mother he has no homework and he doesn't remember what he did in school that day. Halfway up the steps, Bill may remember he promised to call his girlfriend, and come racing back down the steps, then grab the telephone without any explanation, putting his feet on the furniture and acting oblivious to his by now screaming mother (p. 493).

In Bill's case, his behavioral pattern can alternatively be named "Responsibility Deficit/ Look for a Reaction Disorder," because he fails to meet expectations and mobilizes the entire household in the process. If there is dysfunction to his patterning it is that others actively dislike it.

Traditionalists see this "chain" of events as caused by a medical problem or a reduced ability to inhibit. However, instead of asserting that Bill has trouble inhibiting and doing mind behaviors about consequences, it would be scientifically prudent for traditionalist researchers to provide data linking his actions to these behavioral failures. The traditional model has thus far been unable to establish which behaviors are caused by an incurable insufficiency, and which can be related to a history of living in the world.

Conversely, a learning paradigm would impose a very different account by addressing Bill's sequence of actions as reinforced behaviors in relation to context, situation, and circumstance. For example, we observe that Bill's chain of ADHD behavior permits him to maintain his own agenda rather than modulate to the preferences of others. He also shows the wherewithal to disavow homework rather than "blurt" a response that would impel his mother to intercede. In our view, Bill's pattern of coming home like a "dynamo" is a conditioned behavioral pattern rather than a neurologically uncontrolled set of responses.

Bill's behavior also illustrates another important problem with the traditional formulation, which posits a necessary precursor action called the inhibitory response. That is, when he seems to consider a broader time frame and remember that he has promised to call his girlfriend, it appears that his working memory is cued when he starts upstairs (possibly to his bedroom). However, it is uncertain how it is established that he first inhibited and then experienced that memory, as it could also be claimed that this memory is automatically cued in relation to external parameters such as proximity to his bedroom, the upstairs phone he uses to talk with his girlfriend, the staircase, or some other mental or observable behavior occurring just prior to the memory response. Again, his memory responses can be regarded as being situated in a sequence of behaviors that occur in relation to context, situation, and circumstance. One need not posit an intermediary inhibitory step for the behavioral sequences to unfold.

Of equal importance, given the description of Bill's actions, it appears that he has the memory *prior* to changing directions on the stairs, and that the posited mind activity occurs *before* (or in conjunction with) a change in motoric behavior rather than *after* an inhibition of motoric behavior. This is not an insignificant concern, since traditional theory of ADHD rests entirely on the premise that the inhibitory response precedes and stops behavior. In the traditional view, ADHD means that one must stall an action so that control over the future is permitted to subsequently occur.

Moreover, even if it were the case that an instance of inhibition did take place, what would account for its occurrence at *that* moment and no other in the chain of his disruptive behaviors? Wouldn't Bill also have to know before he inhibits that it is important to inhibit, and if that were the case, what posited agency would permit him to know how to function in that way? Succinctly put, *if one has to inhibit to know, how does one know when to inhibit?*

In summary, we propose here that the category of delay in the context of an ADHD diagnosis pertains only to a failure to meet a standard. While traditionalists claim that diagnosed persons fail to meet the standard because the more future-oriented pattern is too complicated to enact (i.e., it entails inhibiting and executive functioning), we observe that it has not been empirically established that non-diagnosed persons do those additional responses more often when they are not behaving diagnostically, and/or that diagnosed persons respond with ADHD patterns because they do fewer of the antecedent responses.

While diagnosed persons seem to operate in particular ways in response to the requirements, stipulations, and directives of others, it is not yet clear to what extent statements about them accurately describe circumstances when they enact non-coerced behaviors, or when they achieve on non-assigned tasks where social expectations and concerns about discretionary power and evaluation are low. Statements about disinhibition, executive deficits, insufficient planning, disorganization, lack of time management, persistence, and productivity might not accurately describe diagnosed persons when they enact their own agendas, compared to when they enact the agendas of others.

Traditionalists nevertheless assert that diagnosed persons have more difficulty functioning in the world, that they do not typically do the necessary preparatory activity to effectively meet expectations and coordinate differences of opinion. They maintain that these difficulties will become most apparent when it is necessary for them to control the future by imagining or remembering the past (hindsight), synthesizing, recombining, and/or analyzing variables before behaving in public: diagnosed persons are not making sensory representations to help them design adaptive long-term responses, nor are they remembering through covert audition or imagery in order to imitate past successful behaviors. They are allegedly too disinhibited to delay committing to a response long enough for mental mechanisms to help them solve their problems.

The inhibitory disability model has become fully entrenched as an explanation for ADHD patterns, but as Nigg (2001) warns, there has always been a lack of clarity when characterizing ADHD as a disorder of disinhibition. In the next chapter we will further outline our alternative model in a concerted return to psychology.

Chapter 4

A Return to Psychology

In our framework we define ADHD as a conditioned set of non-participatory, atypically paced, intrusive behaviors that evolve as a consequence of living in the world.

Instead of positing that a self-regulatory problem is the determining factor for the observed disruptive behaviors, ADHD behavioral patterns are the *actual* condition. Signs and symptoms are not seen as manifestations of a substandard neurobiology, but are instead reinforced behaviors whose frequency rates can be predicted by referencing history. The explication shifts from inherent disability to that which is learned when encountering conditions that have gradually become associated with various adversities or discomforts.

Despite the numerous inconsistencies in the traditional explication, individuals receiving an ADHD diagnosis are usually indoctrinated into the belief system that their ADHD responses are involuntary and due to their genetic coding. Traditionalists interpret diagnostic reactions as being "driven to distraction," and assert these notions as facts rather than as constructs of an imposed conceptual framework. Diagnosed persons moreover, are informed that there exist two kinds of behaviors: those that are under-controlled by executive guidance, and those that are controlled. These assertions occur even though an ADHD diagnosis is based entirely on the observation that some people respond at critical times with ADHD patterns more often than others. Apart from these observations of behavior, no independent discernment of the ADHD condition has been made. The controversy has always been about ways to account for (otherwise competent) individuals not doing necessary or acceptable acts that are within their behavioral repertoires at crucial times.

We recognize that ADHD does not coincide with other problems that are considered to be medically-based. Because no independent biological parameter or set of parameters exists, and since other functional limitations cannot thus far reliably predict who will or will not enact the behavioral pattern outlined in the DSM-IV-TR, the traditional construct of bodily anomaly is itself flawed. In our view, ADHD is merely a *descriptive* category of a particular set of heterogeneous behaviors as described in the DSM-IV-TR. The frequency and severity of ADHD behaviors are coordinated with patterns of event sequences.

A detailed presentation of this conceptual framework is available in Wiener (2007). Although we acknowledge that the individual's biology affects behavior, we do not support the premise that biological parameters are the root origin of ADHD. Instead, we suggest that a person's learning history can more adequately account for increased frequency rates of ADHD behaviors.

We agree that some diagnosed persons show particular (and consistent) limitations in functioning, which are unrelated to contingencies of reinforcement, however, we also strongly state that (to date) there are no specific limitations in functioning that can be ascribed to *each* diagnosed person; this is generally the case when a medical model is asserted. Medical problems relate to a particular limitation in functioning that occurs whenever a competency is required, but ADHD behaviors seem to occur in relation to context and circumstance without any discernable consistent limitation in functioning. If it were the case that ADHD behaviors are expressed indiscriminately in relation to conditions, and that frequency and severity of those behaviors do not change by altering subsequent event sequences, a learning paradigm would then *not* be a reasonable tool. However, empirical observations indicate that diagnostic responses *do* correspond with event sequences.

ADHD is characterized by a particular set of disruptive behaviors, and is discriminated from other socially disruptive patterns (such as oppositional behaviors), but we suggest that ADHD can nevertheless be understood as being shaped during socialization. ADHD is different only to the extent that it describes a unique pattern of social and task behaviors. A particular molecular biology and/or functional anomaly can increase the probability that ADHD behavior will be learned, however, again we emphasize that ADHD behaviors are conditioned independently beyond any biological or environmental parameter. For instance, while a subset of diagnosed individuals might have shown negative infant temperament, we propose that this condition merely increases the probability that ADHD behaviors will be environmentally reinforced. Our interpretation contrasts with the view that ADHD either causes the problem or occurs in tandem with particular functional problems due to non-random mating patterns.

Biological problems indeed contribute to an ADHD diagnosis, in that individuals with various functional difficulties or patterns will have a harder time meeting task and social expectations. As a consequence, these individuals are more likely to learn ADHD behavior, but they do not confirm that ADHD behaviors manifest because of neurological delay. For instance, a significant proportion of diagnosed persons show fine motor, encoding, and/or learning problems, but many diagnosed person do not; moreover, many *non-diagnosed* persons will have some of the aforementioned difficulties as well. Wide variations thus disallow a definitive judgment of genetic causality to be ascribed to ADHD.

In our view, early occurring problems might increase the chances of learning ADHD patterning in the same way that being attractive increases the probability of learning how to flirt. Sternberg, Grigorenko, and Kidd (2005) make a similar argument in relation to the finding that there is a statistically significant heritability coefficient for occupational status. They note:

> Clearly, there is no gene or set of genes for occupational status. How could it be heritable, then? Heritability can affect certain factors that in turn lead people to occupations of higher or lower status. Thus, if factors such as intelligence, personality, and interpersonal attractiveness are under some degree of genetic control, they may lead in turn to differences in occupational status (p. 53).

In considering the remarks above, even if it were found that certain bodily parameters could reliably predict the frequency rates of doing ADHD (e.g., particular forms of molecular biology), we can still claim that ADHD patterns are environmentally conditioned. An identified parameter is representative of an increased *probability* that one will *learn* ADHD when the biological characteristic is evident. For example, if a person is seven feet tall in our North American socio-cultural context, it is highly possible that he or she will be urged to or will want to learn to play basketball. The argument also seems to apply when accounting for similarities between identical twins and other related individuals, as their possibilities for learning can be similar.

Individuals who show functional delays and lower intelligence will often have more problems meeting family and/or socio-cultural expectations. They are likely to have their opportunities for socialization altered in relation to their problems. In a comparison with a sample of children who do *not* show these functional anomalies, they will more often learn to rely on the labors and efforts of others, learn numerous avoidance behaviors, and learn to monopolize social exchanges frequently and intensely. For instance, if a child is awkward and uncoordinated, silliness and giving up can become reinforced, in that this behavior permits avoidance of further criticism, failure, and humiliation (i.e., if I'm foolish or don't try, then I control their laughing).

When children are seen to suffer, are less competent, or have problems meeting basic expectations, they usually become the focal point of their parents' concerns, and in effect, proceed to learn a variety of extreme responses in order to elicit concern or promote avoidance. Loved ones will often act as cues: they might express impatience, indulgence, over-protectiveness, detachment, or will organize in relation to their child's struggles, perceived limitations, and greatest frequency of problems. A vicious cycle ensues in which the child's suspected incompetence compels others to reinforce ADHD behavior rather than shape age-consistent maturity and self-reliant behaviors.

Instead of positing that ADHD is a problem of not performing what one knows, we assert that not enacting what one knows becomes a matter of whether the acceptable behavior (within a person's repertoire) is that which has been reinforced for the conditions that are extant for that person; the *biopsychosocial* history is the basis for predicting that a particular behavior will occur. Past conditioning is the culprit for the observed changes in frequency rates of particular behaviors for both diagnostic and non-diagnostic responding in specific contexts and circumstances.

In this framework an individual's learning history comes to the fore when assigning meaning to behavior, which resembles the approach recommended by cultural anthropologists. Inquiry focuses on identifying parameters that reinforce diagnostic responses. While significant numbers of diagnosed individuals show problems that are endemic and consistently evident (i.e., documented brain injuries and impairments, pervasive functional delays, etc.), their ADHD behaviors will typically vary in appreciable ways with the recurrence of particular equivalent situations. We generally anticipate that diagnostic functioning will be *least* prevalent when diagnosed persons do actions associated with positive event sequences, while diagnostic behavior is likely to be prevalent in circumstances associated with negativity, denial, or adversity.

ADHD behaviors can be understood as reinforced, monopolizing and detaching responses instigated most often when the individual is *expected* to conform, achieve, and participate. For those who learn diagnostic responses, we anticipate that they will be most prevalent during times of social exclusion, when others verbally inundate, during imposed transitions, and when requirements are imposed by others; that is, unless those requirements are compatible with the diagnosed individual's preferences (e.g., "We have to stop so we can go to the mall; put your pencils down, it is time for recess," etc.). Cunningham (2006) claims that diagnosed children have trouble making transitions from one situation to another because they fail to anticipate their occurrence, but we suspect that transitions are problematic when they impinge on a diagnosed person's discretionary authority, and require him or her to submit to a less enjoyable change.

We observe that ADHD actions and reactions are most evident when others give directives, or when conditions are associated with disappointment, evaluation, deprivation, discomfort, limitation, badgering, and disapproval. The behavioral set depicts several behavioral extremes: individuals may be nonresponsive, react too quickly or slowly, or act garishly. Conflict arises when individuals behave in these extreme ways, because their actions are characteristic of behavior typical of younger people. Conversely, diagnostic responding is less evident with fewer obstructions, when a person is given amphetamines, is overtly threatened or enticed, or when task mastery has already been shaped.

In contrast to oppositional behaviors, a diagnosed child need not be irate or antagonistic to respond in an ADHD fashion. The child can say no indirectly simply through non-reaction. During these interactions, the parent is left with uncertainty; and it will be difficult to distinguish between whether the child is unaware of a request or is passively resisting.

Often it is easier to identify factors that reinforce hostile behaviors, because generally, the situations and circumstances that reinforce ADHD behaviors are less explicit. Moreover, even if parents make concerted efforts to extinguish ADHD behaviors, other family members can unwittingly continue to reinforce irresponsibility, intrusiveness, and infantile behavior, which is characteristic of ADHD individuals. For these reasons the behaviors are harder to change than oppositional behaviors; most will find it easier to help parents resolve family power struggles with less acrimony than reshape children towards courtesy and self-confidence in their interpersonal patterning.

There is no debate that diagnosed individuals frequently commit errors of commission that can be attributed to the time interval of the response (hyperactivity/impulsivity) and errors of omission (inattentiveness/distractibility) when interacting socially and during task completion situations. It is also indisputable that these errors are disruptive and difficult for everyone involved. However, we dispute the assertion that ADHD (a delayed process) is the trigger for these problems; these diagnostic responses are, we argue, conditioned over time as a means of coping with circumstances.

In our view, individuals are labeled ADHD when they learn to do the DSM-IV-TR behavioral set more frequently and severely than others in patterns that eventuate into significant disruptions in family, school, and/or work. However, it is not that these individuals always behave in that fashion, or are permanently relegated to do ADHD. We observe that contingencies of reinforcement can be identified that account for the atypical rates of occurrence of ADHD patterns, and that traditionalists' explications do not comprise a consistent account for the vicissitudes of diagnostic responding across situations.

In response we propose a *learning paradigm* as an alternative way to analyze ADHD behaviors. That is, we think that many diagnosed persons have learned how to easily slip into behavior in which they disengage, instigate, overreact, and/or vary the pacing of behavior. Conditioning (which of course includes biology), accounts for pattern recurrence, and ADHD responses are seen as a class of conditioned behaviors whose frequency rates can be altered by subsequent events. In this framework, ADHD resembles non-compliance, lack of confidence, and insecurity.

Lack of consideration, carelessness, selfishness, immaturity, reliance on environments to provide relief, disruptiveness, disorganization, and discontinuance of behaviors are conditioned responses in the context of an ADHD diagnosis. We test the learning model by observing changes in the frequency rates of ADHD behaviors when we alter the sequencing of contexts and circumstances that diagnosed persons encounter over time. Our procedure provides the grounds to infer that the behaviors are more *functional* than *under-controlled*. Instead of claiming, for example, that diagnosed persons make inappropriate comments because they lack the ability to inhibit, we investigate the ways in which such comments have been reinforced.

If one were to utilize traditional terminology, diagnosed persons can and do control future contingencies as well as generate their own intrinsic motivation, but not when it is deemed essential by parents and teachers. Diagnostic behavior is analogous to learning to apologize rather than asking for permission, and learning to avoid rather than fail. Their primary problem is that they have learned ADHD responses when stifled, slighted, pressured, or ignored, and that they have been reinforced to intrude or detach rather than conditioned over time to defer, share, and contribute.

We do not deny the existence in some diagnosed individuals of functional delays, or that having them increases the probability of learning ADHD responding. Nor do we discount that once the responses develop, these individuals are likely to encounter disappointing and disrupted social relationships, miss out on skill acquisition, and fail to complete tasks competently. However, we interpret the diagnostic patterning as being reinforced while living in the world, and, by perceiving that it is malleable, we orient to alter ADHD patterns by changing the contingencies of reinforcement.

Conditioned ADHD responding is more probable with children who have negative temperaments, asthma, brain injuries, learning problems, depressed mothers, and so on, but these same persons can function in non-diagnostic ways if circumstances are secure and comfortable. To illustrate, one can envision the behavioral differences evident when we control the television with the remote compared to enduring someone else having the remote: behavior will depend on context and situation.

A number of traditionalists agree that diagnosed persons sometimes demonstrate competencies, and insist that an ADHD diagnosis be imposed only when individuals show problematic behaviors in utterly consistent ways, but here too it is unreasonable to presume a neurological delay, even when those criteria are met. In other words, if a person consistently responds with ADHD patterns, that data still does not tell us whether they have merely not yet learned to function less diagnostically, whether problem behaviors have been ubiquitously reinforced, or whether they are permanently less able in a biological sense to do less ADHD.

We suggest that learning can entrench a pattern of being fidgety, over active, distracted, and easily bothered by failures. Moreover, while changes from an established baseline of functioning that occur after a documented bodily insult or debilitating condition (e.g., senility) can reasonably be ascribed to biological attenuation, this kind of source data is typically unavailable during an ADHD diagnosis. Traditionalists usually infer biological limitation because problems are frequent and long standing.

Therefore, in this view, even if it is confirmed that diagnosed persons coordinate their actions with future contingencies less competently in all instances compared to other people, one could still posit that they have not yet been conditioned to function adeptly, because learning ADHD responding impedes the development of the acceptable future-oriented responses.

We emphasize that current functioning does not establish inability. For example, Klingberg et al. (2005) report that diagnosed children learn through practice to increase their working memory during task completion. The success of this training has also resulted in many of these children showing less ADHD responding in the ensuing months. This case indicates that deficits and delays present in the diagnosed population may not be as fixed as is implied by the disability model.

We can reasonably presume that ADHD behaviors develop precisely the same as most other social behaviors, that is, as correlates of their unique societal experiences when mastering behaviors handed down by parents, sociological status, ethnic origin, and socio-economic status. However, as noted, most professionals doing empirical investigation have failed to study the learning histories, contexts, situations, and circumstances of ADHD diagnosed individuals to inquire whether they are reinforcing diagnostic responding and making the unwanted behaviors resistant to extinction.

While Barkley and Edwards (2006, 360) indicate that ADHD often co-occurs with "motor in-coordination, enuresis, encopresis, allergies, otitis media, and greater somatic complaints in general," this does not necessarily mean that ADHD results from a lesser functioning body. One can reasonably claim that diagnostic responding initially is conditioned at the time when the child has greater physical or emotional needs.

For example, in the case where ADHD diagnosed children suffer with otitis media, they may not be normatively responsive to the initiations of others due to language delays and difficulties communicating related to hearing loss, and relationships become problematic in multiple settings. Since these children have difficulty hearing, they can therefore behave more loudly, be less responsive to instruction and feedback, rely on repetition more than their peers, and evolve a social pattern of less participation and greater reliance on others to problem solve. Obstructive interactions may also become frequent when parents set limits to protect the child's health, and physical discomfort may increase the child's irritability. The co-occurrence of otitis media with ADHD can indicate that this biological problem increases the probability that ADHD behaviors will be learned.

Similarly, although some children with a pattern of ADHD may have been inordinately motoric early on, it is not invariably the case that all children receiving diagnosis exhibited highly motoric (or thrill-seeking) patterns as toddlers. It seems that exceptionally motoric individuals will also learn sports, ride bikes, hike, compete in gymnastics, exercise vigorously, dance, and/or seek adventurous employment, and *not* learn any of the hyperactive/impulsive/inattentive patterns of behavior included in the DSM-IV-TR behavioral set. Rather than interpret parental reports about toddler high activity rates as a sign of burgeoning ADHD, neurological delay, and thus the need for managed restriction, the development of ADHD patterning for highly active toddlers is a function of contingencies of reinforcement that manifest over time in myriad situations and circumstances. The initial adjustment to sedentary activity will be difficult and uncomfortable for active individuals, but many will nevertheless be able to change over time.

In an analogy, some people gain weight easily in relation to the amount of food they eat, but they are not *predestined* to become fat. In fact, weight loss success stories are numerous because people learn to adjust and change. ADHD correlated bodily and environmental parameters are understood in the same way. The parameters identified by traditionalists represent the probability of learning ADHD behaviors, but equally, one can learn to *not* do ADHD when adopting a very different narrative of socialization. ADHD behaviors can be seen as a continuation of behaviors common in young children; having not yet learned basic social skills they are less competent, and tend towards irresponsibility and intrusiveness. However, socialization for all of us is a matter of developing less reliance on others to protect and direct, and gradually shaping the behaviors which assist others as we grow into adulthood.

A new way to proceed

Traditional practitioners use a genetic model that is based on an individual's molecular biology and the probability of doing ADHD behavior. However, even with the current finding of high genetic loading for ADHD, it is worthwhile to explore possible ways in which environments influence the severity and frequency of behaviors. We think useful empirical data will emerge from a specification of environmental changes that are seen to shape new behavioral patterns and extinguish ADHD responses. Not all identical twins, for example, are concordant for ADHD, so it is logical and prudent to regard environment as influential.

Our account aims to make these environmental influences explicit. Interventions encourage participants to alter their responses to ADHD behaviors in systematic ways so that extinction of ADHD behaviors can occur. We anticipate that the introduced variations in socialization will significantly alter what transpires, alter reported heritability quotients, and change how the neurobiology of diagnosed persons develops and functions.

There is a possibility that many diagnosed persons will begin to show changes in their brain functioning as they learn to do less ADHD responding, in that brain function (rather than being antecedent and causal) is co-occurring with behavior. We know that biological structures are formed early during ontological development, but there is no way to know a priori what behavioral and biological changes are possible over time as new conditions or patterns of rein-forcement are introduced. More specifically, the brain does not cause behavior; brain operation is a function of what is being done. If you change the way a person responds, you change the way the brain responds. This assertion is consistent with the views of McClintock on this subject in her interview with Angier (1995). ADHD empiricism, in our view, does not tell us the extent to which patterns of neurobiology are the consequences of having biological ADHD, whether those occurrences increase the probability of learning ADHD, and/or whether they are the consequences of having learned ADHD.

Studies pertaining to genetics and ADHD do not establish a dominance of nature over nurture; what evolves over time is always a function of a confluence of parameters that operate *with* each other as events transpire. One's biology might change the probability that certain behaviors will be learned given the occurrence of particular kinds of environments, and the learning of particular behaviors might also shape biology in certain ways.

Therefore, high heritability quotients do not inform us about the extent to which a behavioral pattern might be malleable. Establishing that ADHD is accounted for by a biological genetic model only tells us about possible temporal origins given a particular assemblage of environments. The model does not tell us about causes; different temporal sequences can occur as conditions are altered.

Traditional genetic models also do not inform us about possible unrecognized environmental influences that contribute to the frequency rates of the behavioral pattern amongst relatives; often it is the case that relatives encounter analogous environments. Moreover, if there has been a dearth of environmental variation for individuals showing particular bodily anomalies (i.e., people respond in predictable ways to individuals showing negative infant temperaments, coordination problems, and speech problems, etc.), then individuals showing those characteristics are likely to encounter similar environments and learn similar behaviors. It is therefore not surprising that individuals with analogous biological substrates show a greater probability of learning similar behaviors.

Thus, it is understandable that the correlated parameters identified by traditionalists to establish biological determinism do not show strong predictive value. Instead, the diagnosis is given frequently, regardless of the presence of atypical bodily characteristics or functional irregularities, including particular genes, patterns of dopamine, statements about brain structure and function, and executive functioning competency. Again, other than behavioral criteria, traditionalists have not produced any discrete biological parameters that reliably co-occur with the diagnostic label. The more medically-based explications have neither confirmed the cause of ADHD nor been astute at predicting diagnosis.

However, if we explore environmental influences, we also see that singular variables add little predictive utility, and that a wide variety of atypical circumstances and interactional patterns can contribute to the increasing frequency rates of ADHD patterning. For example, in some cases we find that ADHD patterning is conditioned when the family goes to great lengths to satiate and please the child. At other times we find that ADHD patterns increase when parents respond to the child's unacceptable actions as personal failures, when parents excessively direct and protect the child in order to avoid hardships or mishaps, and/or when parents try to rectify significant losses the child may have sustained, such as parental desertion. Parents who express separation anxiety may also often reinforce many of the behaviors included in the diagnostic category, although in other instances we find that estrangement from the child also correlates with patterns that reinforce diagnostic responding.

We doubt that only one pattern correlates with the majority of diagnosed persons. For example, socialization that is neglectful or extremely indulgent may compel children to monopolize, not wait for others, or not participate or contribute. We suspect that a wide array of conditions will be seen to increase the learning of diagnostic behaviors, and that an individual's response to environments will differ as a function of each individual being dissimilar. In that sense no one's *Umwelten* is the same, even when conditions of socialization and training are indistinguishable.

Moreover, it seems impossible (even for monozygotic twins) to have exactly the same environments (e.g., one might be cared for more by one parent; they might learn complimentary patterns when interacting with each other, etc.), and the evolving differences between us (biological and environmental) alter the probabilities of what we will learn in similar environments. In that we become different transducers, no one's environment is identical to another's, and ostensibly similar environments might correlate with very different outcomes in relation to who is responding.

Rather than assert environmental causality, we merely claim that biopsychosocial conditions increase the probability that ADHD patterns will be learned. Generalized environmental parameters such as identifying the parent's personality, frequency of criticism, marital problems, etc., have not helped account for the occurrence of a diagnosis, and formulations regarding "attachment deficits" (Ladnier and Massanari, 2000) require more rigorous analysis. However, the expectation is that contingencies of reinforcement for ADHD behaviors can be identified, and that they coherently account for the patterns of actions and reactions in the diagnosed population.

An essential first step when developing this learning paradigm is to identify interactional patterns that reinforce diagnostic responses for a particular individual. For example, ADHD responding may be reinforced for some individuals when a negative evaluation is imminent, when having to endure patronizing behavior, when social importance is diminished, and/or when individuals encounter irrelevance, or comprehension difficulty. Because such events often take place when others expect conformity, the behaviors can have a great impact on the extent to which a person fulfills societal requirements and establishes positive relationships.

When pursuing learning explanations, we can for example, observe diagnostic patterning in a public waiting area, and ask the diagnosed child what he or she was told about an upcoming appointment. The child's reactions to the imposed agenda are pivotal when accounting for an occurrence *or* non-occurrence of ADHD behavior in that particular waiting room in that circumstance. Furthermore, an investigation into the past when acting out in similar public places, or when the child entertains and/or embarrasses the parent in an immature rambunctious fashion in other contexts and circumstances, can yield insights. Diagnostic responding may be cued as soon as the parent speaks to another person, or starts reading a magazine; the individual's history is the vehicle to predict ADHD actions and reactions.

However, in a very different set of presumptions, Hallowell and Ratey (1995, 139) claim that the "attentional delay" of diagnosed persons prevents them from not "dealing with frustration by blowing it off, or by reaching closure too quickly." Their comments contradict the assertion that we say people are ADHD when they do those behaviors more frequently and severely than others. We are thus left in the dark by not knowing what is added when the authors insist that the behaviors are caused by "attentional delay" when such a delay has not been reliably identified for those in the diagnostic category.

In the same tradition, Anastopoulos, Smith, and Wien (1998, 373) claim that "because of their inattention difficulties . . ." many diagnosed children fail to listen vigilantly to parents' instructions. These children will miss information crucial to task completion. Their condition makes them "unable" to stay seated through dinner, or prevent themselves from jumping onto furniture, breaking up conversations, or blurting out improper comments. These explanatory statements suggest that ADHD has the antecedent status of acting on and rendering the individual incapable of behaving differently. However, no parameter of any sort that coincides with the behavioral criteria is of any clinical value, so we begin by asking what all diagnosed persons have in common besides their qualification for the highly disjunctive set of behavioral criteria listed in the DSM-IV-TR.

Therefore, in our view biology and environment are presumed to conjointly factor into which behaviors get reinforced; this is what we mean by the term "biopsychosocial matrix." We propose an interactive model that has the "bio" category embedded in each and every social exchange and behavior. Biology does not *create* diagnostic responding; but rather ADHD diagnostic responding is conditioned over time. Emitted behaviors are a function of a constellation of parameters that mutually influence each other.

Individuals will differ in the rates at which they learn new behaviors, but the particular behaviors that occur more routinely in particular situations may be related to events in the past. We take the view that, although biology contours which behaviors will be learned, behavior also influences biology: behavior and biology are entwined. Rather than an antecedent causal factor, biology becomes a parameter that influences what can be learned.

In our conceptualization the repetition of particular diagnostic behaviors in particular conditions is accounted for through conducting an historical analysis, which includes a malleable neurobiology. Biology is involved in all of our reactions (e.g., the speed of response, sensations, reflexes, etc.), but a biological account cannot explain changes in frequency rates of ADHD behaviors when particular situations recur.

Variations in learning will account for those changing patterns more consistently, and will, as a consequence, better predict instances of diagnostic responding. We adopt a learning model on these grounds, and acknowledge that ADHD behaviors are reinforced only in certain contexts and situations. For example, frequently occurring hyperactive behaviors are significantly less apparent when diagnosed individuals are occupied with a non-assigned activity, satiated, and/or initiating behaviors to please others.

Giving up biological causality

A larger problem for those who subscribe to the notion of flawed neurobiology is illustrated when parents ask whether forgetfulness and failure to conform to instructions are instances of disobedience that require punishment, or failures caused by delayed biology that should be pardoned. Robin (1990, 491) replies that it is "usually impossible to determine the truth." But he goes on to advise parents to assume that neurologically caused ADHD is factoring into the adolescent's behavior, and that the parent should still hold the adolescent accountable.

Given Robin's response, it seems that traditionalists recognize the impossibility of distinguishing between a person being victimized by ADHD and one who competently enacts a non-acceptable behavior. The point is crucial, in that their account depends on the assertion that ADHD behaviors result from neurological delays that prevent persons from behaving acceptably. Hence, it seems that even supporters of traditionalist views recognize that their dual-category system is indeterminate; their construct adds nothing to our understanding of the behaviors being enacted. Very similarly, while Aviram, Rhum, and Levin, (2001) attempt to differentiate ADHD incapacity (e.g., distractibility) from functional behavior (e.g., avoidance) during therapy sessions, other than therapist assertion, the authors provide no independent basis on which to make that determination.

In a similar vein, Barkley (2000) insists that ADHD interferes with persistence and ability to complete an activity, but we assert that the seemingly "uncontrolled" pattern of quitting particular tasks will seem more functional than delayed when the observer becomes aware of what has previously occurred when the individual encountered equivalent conditions in the past. For example, if an individual has learned that criticism is forthcoming or associated with completing certain tasks, the closer he or she is to finishing, the more germane is the concern, and the more reinforcing it is to give up.

Leaving tasks undone may be conditioned whenever such reactions decrease the probability of dissatisfaction. With the completion of each step, the individual is brought closer to the adverse condition of evaluation, potential disappointment, or surrender to those who make the demands. Moreover, in that work can also become more detailed and cumbersome as completion nears, difficulty and fear of failure or discomfort, rather than neurological inability may be a viable alternative way to account for the behaviors. In other words, quitting relates to history rather than ability to control behavior. The apparent *intentional delays* of diagnosed persons make sense when events become known about previous follow through under similar conditions. An individual's history becomes the vehicle for understanding the exhibited behavioral acts.

Biological determinists also argue that ADHD diagnosed individuals require novelty, and that they have an excessive desire for environmental stimulation and instant gratification. According to Barkley (2000), novelty helps to counteract disinhibitions because the delayed individual requires frequent change and stimulation to offset endogenous under-arousal, especially when tasks are "tedious, boring, repetitive, painful, unrewarding, and effortful." Zentall (1985) has also noted that ADHD children are often positively influenced by the degree of stimulation in a task. Traditionalists generally claim that, due to motivational deficits, diagnosed persons rely on the outside world for motivation.

Conversely, external variations rather than internal deficits can, we argue, be helpful in the sense that requirements may seem less coercive, restrictive, or limiting when new content is introduced. Novelty is reinforcing in that conditions are less constraining where diversity is evident. Frequent repetitions may often cue the same responses that often occur when social exchanges, for example, comprise redundant and long-winded lectures. Moreover, we argue that if diagnosed persons need more novelty because of a neurological delay, why do they not invariably respond favorably to *transitions* that, by definition, introduce novel conditions?

We also contend that the favorable response of diagnosed persons to novelty may be due to their being reinforced to rely on environmental change in general, rather than use their own resources to solve problems or reduce discomfort. Improved responsiveness to novelty is consistent with their increased reliance on parental efforts in general (or the television set in particular). They seem to achieve less often when there is less involvement from other sources.

In contrast, instead of complaining of boredom or relying on others to "fix the problem," non-diagnosed persons will usually initiate an action to make a situation tolerable (its being novel or different notwithstanding). Non-diagnosed persons will likely introduce novelty by using their own resources, but diagnosed persons will have learned to avoid, escape, or seek an outside source in order to brighten events; they will usually become more responsive when others do things for them. Their attraction to novelty may be understood as a repetition of their social patterning whereby they rely on others to lessen hardship or to indulge them.

However, in what seems to be a contradiction, while ADHD behavior can become more frequent in redundant situations, this is not always the case. At times the same individuals will engage in highly repetitious forms of play, and not do any ADHD behaviors during the *self-imposed* repetitions. For example, a diagnosed child can repeat the same song or phrase throughout the day, incessantly watch the clock during school, frequently nag a parent about the same content for long periods of time, and overreact when parents change the accepted routines, unless of course the change includes a trip to the toy store. When noting that few symptoms occur during actions that diagnosed persons initiate and enjoy (with or without novel situations), we see once again that ADHD relates to situation and circumstance rather than to traditional categories.

Additional problems with the traditional view arise when Murphy and Gordon (2006, 437) report that many diagnosed children have "relatively normal early developmental histories." They recommend that it is best not to give too much credence to developmental history when determining a diagnosis of ADHD. Such assertions are meant to protect traditional beliefs, but their claim also supports the learning paradigm. That is, if "relatively normal early development" can still result in diagnosis, the source of the problem cannot reasonably be presumed to be inherent, and/or occurring independently from living in the world categories.

Moreover, since some traditionalists assign diagnosis as late as adolescence (Applegate et al., 1997), it is sometimes permissible to presume that a person has a developmental problem, even though that individual has lived to 12 years thus far symptom-free. These children will, under this presumption, eventually qualify for diagnosis despite the fact that their parents described them as unproblematic during infancy and early childhood (Barkley, 2000).

Certainly many behaviors will have become reinforced during childhood to increase the probability of eventually qualifying for the behavioral criteria. Conventional practitioners will explain that the preteen's delayed neural biology has finally been sufficiently "taxed" to the breaking point, or that a latent developmental delay has, unfortunately, blossomed. But they will neglect to specify what precisely has sufficiently taxed these persons at age 12, given the fact that they had functioned non-diagnostically until then.

Again, these rationalizations are imposed *after the fact*, and are not independently verified or rigorously demonstrated in a scientific manner. In other words, when persons begin doing ADHD after having shown normative adjustment, it must be that environmental demands now exceed their ability to self-control. However, all we know is that some individuals are ADHD responding relatively late in childhood, and we still have no established criteria that permits us to measure the significance of having a "taxed" inhibitory system.

Meanwhile, the mystery of why significant numbers of diagnosed individuals stop doing diagnostic behaviors remains unresolved, despite that situations become increasingly demanding as one grows older (Barkley, Fischer, et al., 2002). The fact that some people stop doing troublesome ADHD patterning refutes the traditional notion that diagnosis emerges later in life because environments have become sufficiently challenging.

Troublesome behaviors can be reinforced

An extreme variant of the hyperactive pattern occurs when the child behaves so incredibly silly and outlandishly as to seem deranged. At first glance, this psychosocial pattern looks "out of control" and crazed. Typically, these individuals crash into things, engage in slapstick humor, roll on the floor, put foreign objects in their mouths, and/or lean back in chairs with legs raised as when infants and toddlers are being diapered. When entering a new setting they will often immediately locate whatever is fragile or dangerous. Parental reactions and concerns about "what others might think" seem to escalate the frequency rates of the extreme and inappropriate behavior.

However, since the behaviors so consistently affect others (and promote physical contact), it is difficult to think that the patterns are concomitants of thoughtlessness about consequences. Why wouldn't these children touch items in the room that would sequence with less reactivity and panic, and/or more haphazardly stumble upon the more problematic objects—*if* movement and novelty were the only reinforcements? The behaviors are *too functional* in mobilizing others and increasing drama to be understood as functionally delayed. Moreover, if the actions are so "out of control," why is it often possible to get these children to stop abruptly when a dominant figure enters the scene, or are able to change incrementally in response to systematic training? We therefore characterize the behaviors as those which are challenging, intrusive, and/or inciteful, rather than "disinhibited."

An ADHD child's emotional reactions may also be loud and extreme. Like a child of a younger chronological age, events are hated or loved, depending on whether events unfold in ways that the child enjoys. The smallest success might yield a stiff immature handclap, arms might flap when excited, and the first disappointment can often result in complaining, whining and giving up. Behavioral extremes occur with such frequency that it becomes very difficult to forget the child's presence in the home.

Many diagnosed children will accuse the parent of giving preferential treatment to siblings or insist that the parent "never" does what he or she wants. The child might describe the parent as "mean," or denigrate them for not spending enough time together, and/or admonish them for spending money too selfishly. When such over reactions and pressure tactics sequence with others giving in and/or compensating, the less acceptable over reactive ADHD responses can easily be understood as reinforced.

It seems that children expressing a diverse range of characteristics and co-occurring problems will learn ADHD behavior (i.e., finish quickly and carelessly, act in extremes, and escape). Given the complexity of the behavioral set, it is not surprising that ADHD behavior has been less responsive to psychotherapeutic intervention than other disruptive behavioral patterns. The behaviors are less likely to be correlated with a circumscribed set of more obvious conditions (more often the case with overt defiance). Often the behaviors continue to be reinforced within an individual's world in many subtle ways, and it is usually the case that the behaviors have occurred since early childhood.

Moreover, many interventions designed to reduce the frequency of unwanted patterns can inadvertently exacerbate their occurrence; for example, parents can impose solutions and discriminate possibilities for the diagnosed child that appear to be helpful, and which orchestrate and direct the child's actions, but these interactions may actually have little effect in reinforcing non-diagnostic responding. This is true especially when compared to interactions that encourage independence and greater contribution from the child. The parental intervention is an attempt to help, yet it does little to extinguish behaviors consistent with the ADHD diagnosis. The doggedness and resilience of the behavioral pattern will potentially convince parents that the patterning is caused by an impinging force that is impervious to environmental influence.

Our learning model characterization of ADHD patterns is a clear departure from commonly held beliefs, but in some instances that portrayal corresponds with traditional accounts. For example, Barkley (1998b, 59) notes that when diagnosed persons are encouraged to delay gratification and work for long-term goals and larger rewards, "they often opt for immediate, smaller reward that requires less work to achieve." He claims that diagnosed persons are well-known for "taking shortcuts" when completing work, and exert the least effort in the least amount of time when doing tasks they "find boring or aversive" (Barkley, 2006b, 80).

In the traditional view it is only possible for individuals with access to their executive functioning capacity to organize for the future. When these functions are scarcely used, they do not develop consistent with one's age group. Since the behaviors occur before puberty, the presumption is that the child has a developmental anomaly, and if one does not consistently show a preference for long-term larger rewards compared to short-term smaller rewards, they are presumed to have no self-control (Barkley, 1998f). Adequately self-regulated children will have a capacity for reasoning and not be influenced by momentary whims; being more future-oriented will turn their behavior away from the influence brought to bear by immediate contingencies (Barkley, 2006f).

Although if diagnosed persons "opt" for an unusual choice when they are busy, this departs markedly from a characterization of ADHD in which a person might be "driven to distraction." We suggest instead that these non-preferred behaviors are reinforced in relation to quickly stopping an uncomfortable activity.

Moreover, despite Barkley's assertion about self-control, other interpretations are also reasonable, including having enormous difficulty meeting expectations, and encountering obstacles and discomforts continuously when relating to others. Having such histories as these will mean that persistence does not often pay off.

He or she does not learn long-term behavior, because previous results of these patterns have been unsatisfactory. The child is increasingly reinforced to be impatient, and to seek smaller, predictable, and immediate rewards, since deferring has in the past led to regret. Similarly, if a child often loses what has been accumulated, either through punishment or frequent upheavals, working for long-term event sequences will rarely be reinforced; the consequences of diligence and postponement of gratification typically go unrewarded, particularly if unpredictability or threatening treatment is routine in some families.

ADHD persons learn that behavior towards enhancing long-term rewards is futile and can rarely be achieved due to ineptitude or obstacles outside their discretionary authority (e.g., poverty, inconsistent/remote family patterns, dispute, unending criticism from others, and so on). The smaller rewards will be taken as remedies for current suffering, because future events have less relevance, probability, or priority when compared to current hardship and distress. Uncovering their history of reinforcement will reveal critically important incidents that have conditioned the aforementioned type of "short-term gratification" behavior pattern.

In the same way, if problems arising from short-term indulgences can be rectified by throwing tantrums, becoming volatile or insistent, and/or by acting the victim, there will be no incentive towards self-reliance and future-oriented responding. Individuals are reinforced to be myopic; waiting and persevering are not being shaped because others will hurry to accommodate them whenever there is deprivation. They do not learn to manage their environments without ongoing compensation from others and their self-indulgence has positive rather than negative consequences. Others will give immediate assistance when a diagnosed person concedes or runs into difficulty, and he or she will get what is wanted even though there is minimal work or effort.

Many children in this scenario are indulged with toys, have their rooms cleaned for them, and receive help getting dressed; activities they could learn to do for themselves. When loved ones provide assistance in finding missing belongings (e.g., books, toys, keys, etc.), relieve distress immediately as discomfort appears, and tell the child what to do rather than encourage her to figure out a course of action autonomously, the development of mature response patterns is neglected. In an analogous example, whoever pays the electric bill will be most concerned about conserving electricity by turning off lights, and most aware that long-term consequences are relevant. The bill payer is conditioned to notice that a light is on in an empty room—much like the diagnosed child who seldom forgets to remind a parent about a promised trip to an arcade.

Comparably, people who rent homes can be careless about damaging property compared to owners; this presumption is the basis for the security deposit designed to protect property. Security deposits prevent people from destructiveness and help them factor in long-term consequences. Therefore, rather than highlight biological determinism, we argue that in the context of an ADHD diagnosis, individuals are reinforced to be intolerant of delays, and are thus conditioned towards individual rather than social welfare.

Generally, the aforementioned accommodating social patterns will occur when the parent presumes the child to be incompetent or needy, when for example, they compensate for parental absences, when they atone for past indiscretions, when they attempt to prevent the child from becoming like another family member, and/or when parent protects child against another frightening accident, etc. A disproportionately managed or frequently rescued child will learn to act for short-term rewards; if long-term troublesome scenarios arise, loved ones will inevitably intervene to mend the damage.

Although many practitioners currently believe that ADHD time blindness causes the short-term smaller reward pattern, we suggest that reinforcement patterns can create a narrowing of one's time horizon. For example, there will be instances where diagnosed children do little work in school and nevertheless pass to the next grade. Often in a last minute flurry, the child is given extra help, especially when adults worry about harmful consequences to the child's self-esteem if the child were to suffer the consequences of his irresponsible behavior during the school year.

As a way to further illustrate that one need not be delayed in order to exhibit behavior that results in long-term problems, we turn to the many adults who clean house or read for long periods of time at the expense of greater involvement with their children. Relationship problems could result from these behaviors, but should we believe that these people have inhibitory problems that prevent them from stopping reading or cleaning—despite potentially damaging consequences? Traditionalists would insist that our example does not show a pervasive developmental problem, but we argue that behavior in early childhood which is enacted frequently does not guarantee the existence of a delayed neurology. The patterning has been conditioned early and generalized in pervasive ways despite the problems which appear later. Moreover, individuals who manifest problematic behaviors can know full well that long-term negative consequences will result, yet they will continue the behavior anyway. For example, some people will abandon personal achievements because they are beholden to others; therefore, knowingly—and at their own expense—they will forfeit their own goals.

Moreover, one can also argue the case that caution and forethought are not always the best chosen behaviors. Sometimes it is better to act without prior rehearsal and regard for long-term consequences or social propriety. Quick reactions are necessary in, for example, a lunge forward to grab someone who trips on the pavement, or doesn't notice an oncoming car. Similarly, there will be occasions when individuals change initial responses to incorrect ones, and then lament afterwards that they had thought too much about the problem. When these event sequences occur, individuals are disappointed that they didn't abide by their initial intuition or idea. Conversely, if individuals commit an egregious error when acting decisively without prior rumination, they might also regret their response and wonder why they reacted so "impulsively."

We observe that acceptable or preferred behaviors are contingent upon context and outcomes: not antecedents. While rapidly-paced behaviors can at times correlate with mistakes, those behaviors may also correlate with success, depending on timing, context and consequence. For example, grabbing a toy first when there is limited playtime reduces the probability of missing out, but grabbing a toy and bumping into another child in the process can be seen as a troublesome impulsive act.

Interestingly, we recognize the opposite situation in which many individuals attend psychotherapy with the expressed goal of learning how to enjoy the present; they report little satisfaction in their daily lives, due to an overemphasis on delayed gratification. People also admit during psychotherapy that they would like to become less fearful about the perspectives and reactions of others. They often feel cheated and anxious when responding to the world in highly constrained ways. Their basic problem relates to delaying gratification too frequently, being overly austere, or "opting" for long-term larger rewards in most instances. These individuals are dedicated towards greater self-indulgence and spontaneity in order to recognize life's daily pleasures as therapeutic goals.

Are we to therefore presume that the people mentioned above have advanced inhibitory systems and over-use their executive functioning? Do they require medical intervention to create disinhibition, or can we accept that the behavior of these individuals has been conditioned? If we are willing to characterize these patterns as learned social acts rather than resultant from a stringent inhibitory system that prevents prepotent responses from being expressed, we think it is disingenuous to accept a disinhibition explanation for the opposite ADHD behavior patterns of behavior.

Therefore, before presuming disability, it is essential to first determine whether a diagnosed person is reinforced to coordinate behavior with particular socially preferred long-term event sequences. Diagnosed persons may be reinforced to precipitate the occurrence of other event sequences; for example, their actions can be organized around achieving the highest level on a video game, or evading disappointment that occurs in the attempt to meet expectations.

Moreover, when Barkley (2006e, 252) observes, in contradistinction from the notion of disinhibition, that diagnosed children can be "persistent in their wants," and often "insatiable in their curiosity of their environments," a neurological delay that prevents persistence and sustained uninterrupted action is incongruous with those assertions. Comparable problems also arise when

Hallowell and Ratey (1995, 177) claim that diagnosed individuals can some-times "hyperfocus" when their minds are "engaged." Their account leads us to the conclusion that diagnosed persons can be "driven to distraction" as well as driven to concentration.

Emphasizing context

When pursuing a learning model we identify the situations associated with either attentive or non-attentive responses. For example, diagnostic behaviors may be reinforced when they sequence with notoriety, since adults grow con-cerned whenever a child is floundering, wasting time, or creating unacceptable infringement or risk. The failure to stay focused or act appropriately will result in more rescuing, less discomfort and insecurity, and more discretionary author-ity.

We neither suggest that parents are teaching their children ADHD behav-iors, nor do we claim that the child rehearses or preplans those responses. We merely assert that the responses become entrenched based on past equivalent event sequences. The consequences of maintaining discretionary influence, di-minishing adversity, and provoking help and concern are useful categories that help us predict ADHD frequency rates more successfully than the mentalist bio-logical categories invoked by conventional practitioners. But this does not mean that the enactor of the behavioral acts is aware of the contingencies of rein-forcement at the point of performance.

In our view, non-diagnosed individuals do not have the extra advantage of a supervisory function operating outside a determinist model or stimulus/response paradigm (Barkley, 2006f); instead we claim that executive responses are learned just like any other action or reaction. Non-diagnosed persons are not imbued with more "free will" than diagnosed people; they are simply condi-tioned differently.

Thus, if non-diagnosed persons report undertaking mental actions more than diagnosed persons, mental actions can also be understood as cued by situation, and accounted for precisely as more public responses. Mental actions per se are simply private conditioned responses, and those private actions can be rein-forced like motoric behaviors. In this view, mental responses can influence fre-quency rates of subsequent motoric and mental responses the same as what occurs when motoric responses influence frequency rates of subsequent motoric or mental responses.

For example, when I learn to imagine the outcomes of possible chess moves, I might become more effective in my game; that sequence of events will reinforce those behaviors when equivalent situations recur. Similarly, when I put my appointments on the calendar and check it each morning, I am more likely to keep my appointments, and those motoric sequences will be reinforced as well. However, when understanding behavior in this fashion, it is not always *neces-*

sary for a person to engage in antecedent musings to function non-diagnostically. The observation that behavior relates to an *outcome* rather than to mental antecedents and inner actions distinguishes "intentional behaviors" from other classes of response in our conceptual framework.

Skinner (1953, 116) points out that once we begin to discriminate "variables that are responsible" for our actions, "we are likely to drop the notion of responsibility altogether and with it the doctrine of free will as an inner causal agent." He adds:

> In the present analysis we cannot distinguish between involuntary and voluntary behavior by raising the issue of who is in control. It does not matter whether behavior is due to a willing individual or a psychic usurper if we dismiss all inner agents of whatever sort. Nor can we make the distinction on the basis of control or lack of control, since we assume that no behavior is free (p. 111).

We suggest that "free will" refers to our failure to adequately predict what a person will do. However, as we continue to identify contingencies of reinforcement that account for the recurrence of particular behaviors in particular situations (including predictions about the occurrence of certain mental actions) many of our responses could become less surprising or less "free." In this understanding, people are not imbued with "free will." The more we coordinate past with present, the less *freedom* we all seem to have. For example, spouses become skilled at predicting the behaviors (including non-vocal verbal responses) of their partners in numerous circumstances.

Skinner (1953, 112) also notes, "It is natural that the 'will' as an inner explanation of behavior should have survived longer in the study of operant behavior, where the control exercised by the environment is more subtle and indirect." In that "we ordinarily lack anything like adequate knowledge of all these variables, it is simpler to assume that the behavior is determined by the guest's will" (p. 113). Since "the current strength of behavior . . ." relates to events "which have occurred in the past history of the organism . . ." those events "are not observed at the moment their effect is felt." We are left with the impression that a free acting agent is determining what to do. However, once we identify a particular stimulus that "has an effect upon the probability of a response . . ." we recognize that "the present environment is indeed relevant," although it is "not easy to prove the inevitability of the control without an adequate account of the history of reinforcement" (p. 112). In light of these assertions, all of our behavior may be understood as reactive and based on a stimulus/response learning paradigm.

In our view traditional intervention is reinforcing acceptable participation, response pacing, and less provocative behavior, in that enticements for acceptable behavior are increased, and the consequences of failure to conform are made pertinent and vital. However, most of us follow the instructions of others, and work conscientiously when such conditions are present. It is therefore unclear how the diagnosed population represents a unique sample, or that endogenous delays are rectified by traditional interventions. Moreover, Barkley, Edwards et al. (2001) found that diagnosed adolescents did not differ from controls when given the choice to take less money now or more money later, as long as the size of the future reward was large enough. With that empiricism in mind, our approach aims to condition acceptable responses instead of orienting to compensate for a posited neurological incapacity that expresses itself incoherently.

In our approach, for example, we might recommend that a parent play a game that requires counting objects at varying speeds. Parents can hand the child objects at varying rates so that the diagnosed child learns to accommodate his counting to the pace set by the parent. Social interactions throughout the day can be contoured so that diagnosed persons increasingly accommodate their actions to the initiatives of others. The expectation is that the child will learn to coordinate acceptably by shaping those responses.

Other problems arise, however, when Whalen and Henker (1985) posit that diagnosed children know the socially acceptable behavior, but they miss social cues, misinterpret what others are doing, and become overly intrusive. We, in contrast, argue that they attend to *different* cues and make different interpretations, and that they are abiding by past learning. Whalen and Henker have not definitively established that these individuals are incapable of the two-step process of stopping and identifying content that prevents one from missing cues. They have only established that diagnosed persons respond differently.

In the general population many of us are prone to overreact and lash out towards others if we believe that they will exclude, disappoint, dislike, or blame us. Once our reinforcement history is derived, the unusual responses seem much less pathological. We argue that when rejection and disapproval are so common to their social history, they characterize others as hateful and judgmental. Having been excluded themselves, they might learn to act outlandishly and annoy in order to be noticed, and then turn the tables to avoid further vulnerability (i.e., they control the rejection). However, importantly, diagnosed individuals do not *decide* to do ADHD any more than an under-assertive person selects/chooses to be exploited. Entrenched behaviors are usually difficult to stop (e.g., thumb sucking, answering the phone in a certain way).

Situations associated with adversity require a great deal of desensitization in order for participatory behaviors to occur (similar to attention required to quell phobias and anxieties). Not surprisingly, rapid success in school settings (where immersion is crucial) is difficult to achieve for diagnosed persons without inducing attentiveness with stimulant medication. However, a period of reconditioning is necessary whether one is diagnosed or not. Some mothers, for example, report that frequent interruptions by their children make it difficult for them to relax and read even when they have the time to do so.

In Pepper's root metaphor terminology (1966), the learning model represents a metaphor shift from Mechanism (i.e., traditional view) to what he refers to as Contextualism (i.e., our learning paradigm). The traditionalist mechanistic metaphor states that we have a mental mechanism that permits us to inhibit and control responses by doing other mental actions called executive functions. These mechanistic action sequences must occur for us to behave in non-diagnostic ways.

In juxtaposition, a contextual metaphor posits that the occurrence of particular behaviors may be explicated by a confluence of parameters that influence each other in a simultaneous or reciprocal fashion. The metaphor does not invoke a temporal sequencing of events to account for infrequent ADHD responding, and does not presuppose that one must first inhibit and then behave mentally in order to then behave acceptably outwardly.

When understanding ADHD within a contextual matrix, a causal locus or directionality to the problem is not assigned, and the influence of any one parameter changes depending on the other parameters that are involved. The environment influences the individual, and the individual influences the environment.

Traditionalists recognize a degree of interaction between the diagnosed person and others, but their basic premise is that problems associated with ADHD emanate (in a mechanistic fashion) from fixed insufficiencies within the diagnosed person outward. They believe that viable interventions must always *offset* inherent delays by providing the diagnosed person with conditions that also have inherent qualities (e.g., saliency, interest, and immediate reinforcing influence). These *compensatory* conditions will then (mechanistically) operate on the individual and temporarily remedy their internal deficiencies.

However, we counter those claims by asserting that while the responses that occur pertain to the transducer (i.e., the individual) who gives the event its representation, events are not inherently reinforcing or boring. There is no attempt to locate the reinforcement, saliency etc. within the content of the activity. What occurs is interesting, boring or important only to the extent that the person reacts accordingly. Normative data accumulated for various activities as a means of producing a scale or rank ordering for "what most people find interesting or boring" under particular sets of conditions, does not confirm imminence in an activity to make it enjoyable, boring, negative, or problematic.

Even were a majority of individuals to respond similarly, it is the individual's reaction to an activity that determines "what it is." As noted in the previous chapter, statements about saliency and reinforcement always refer to the respondent, and both normative and less typical responses may be learned. For example, after finding coins while walking, persons are more likely to notice similar objects under foot. Traditionalists are not rectifying delays when they present stimuli that are responded to as interesting; they merely identify conditions that reinforce non-diagnostic responding (including giving stimulant medication to induce task immersion).

Moreover, in our view, intellectually competent people (diagnosed or not) may learn to coordinate in acceptable ways with the future, and it is not necessary to presuppose that inhibition and other mental actions immediately preceded that behavior. While the traditional account presumes that a mechanistic sequencing of steps is necessary for persons to effectively coordinate action with the future, the learning model presumes that the assessment of the behavioral act in a circumstance (not antecedent precursors) determines whether an action is organized, anticipated, creative, intelligent, impulsive, and so on. For example, if a verbalization is deemed socially inappropriate and leads to negative social consequences, we will identify that action as "blurting out." We apply the characterization without knowledge about whether particular antecedent mind actions and inhibitions had or had not previously occurred.

To further illustrate, when I act with consideration for future events, we say that I have anticipated. I have not inhibited and carried out other mental actions and then behaved; I have simply behaved in that particularly effective way (e.g., eating over the table so that food will not fall on the floor). Similarly, when a song on an album is ending, I can imagine hearing the next song before it actually starts to play; the completion of the prior song cues the "anticipatory reaction." However, the imagining "is" the anticipatory (working memory) response, and the situation triggers the competency.

Likewise, if a child becomes excited when a parent enters a room with a baseball glove, it is not that the child first inhibited in order to access working memory to know what follows. Instead, we assert that the presence of parent and the glove *automatically* cues the response that a game of catch is to happen. Moreover, and very importantly, these seemingly instantaneous reactions can possibly occur whether the cued future event will take place in an immediate or distant future time horizon; there need not be a relationship between the amount of time doing mind behaviors and the breadth of the time horizon. For example, a person might watch a baseball game and something takes place to cue ideation about a basketball game scheduled for the autumn. Such responses can then cue other thoughts and actions pertaining to other distant or short-term future events, and so on.

In sum, we may learn to behave in particular ways (e.g., hesitate, proceed, quit, blurt, defer, remember current or remote events, anticipate, imagine, show diligence, exuberance or apathy, verbalize both vocally and non-vocally, etc.), and history of reinforcement may be invoked to account for what particular response occurs more frequently. When certain responses occur more often with the reintroduction of equivalent conditions, we say that that person has learned.

A learning paradigm does not discount biology; it asserts only that ADHD responses are reinforced by the environment. The increased repetition of ADHD responses in situations is explicated by a recounting of the past rather than understanding those reactions as less controlled bodily happenings. However, the fact that some people emit more ADHD behaviors does not establish that they cannot learn alternatives.

If we alter conditions to increase mutually-acceptable interactions (essential for older diagnosed persons), and increase instances of success through the gradual weaning of assistance from others (pertinent for younger diagnosed persons), non-diagnostic patterning can thus be developed. A learning intervention orients to increase non-diagnostic responding with less medication and fewer unilateral forms of management, and is designed to circumvent problems that occur as the child ages and is expected to function increasingly independently with less supervision. In the next chapter we provide discussion on how to implement the learning model.

Chapter 5

Getting Started

We know that all forms of socialization are coercive to some extent because of limits imposed by society on the individual. However, the aim of the learning model presented here is to shape acceptable behaviors in relation to mutually-acceptable arrangements; in so doing, exchanges where individuals arbitrarily limit access to resources to induce acceptable socio-cultural behaviors are kept to an absolute minimum. Our methodology shifts the locus of attention away from coercion by encouraging interactions based on compassion and a mutual recognition that participants are having a difficult time; both children and parents learn behaviors that subsequently reinforce an increased willingness to be co-reliant.

Another aim is to accentuate acceptable responding that is more autonomous. This is accomplished in two ways: first, loved ones are advised to observe and identify possible ways that ADHD behaviors are reinforced within the individual's social matrix; they are then advised to alter the sequence of events that apparently perpetuate unwanted acts. Second, loved ones are urged to use less coercion and less reliance on external cues or directives in order to socialize diagnosed persons to meet socio-cultural expectations. For example, the parent can *show* the child the strategy of retracing steps rather than find missing objects for the child.

Rather than frame the problem as one of less inhibitory control, diagnostic behaviors are understood in relation to the ongoing sequencing of events that correspond with unwanted behaviors. For parents to gain insight into this process, they will be urged to solve problems related to their child's integration with others (e.g., high failure rates, diminished social importance, and difficulty meeting expectations). For example, when addressing the acting out that occurs while the parent talks on the telephone, it may become evident that the child is jealous that the parent behaves in a kinder and more effusive way with the friend than what usually happens with him or her. These relational problems are the focal point of our approach. The act of identifying which behaviors parents want their child to change, as well as those that the child wants the *parent* to change is vital to collaboration, a cornerstone of our intervention.

When embarking on this endeavor it is helpful to ask whose agenda is it to do the behavior, whose agenda is it to be in a particular setting, and/or who is initiating the instruction to behave in a certain way. ADHD behaviors typically occur more often in response to circumstances initiated and imposed by others. Parents can address the unwanted responses by incorporating the child's viewpoint as regularly as possible; this approach is designed to foster more amicable ways to resolve the problem of *who accommodates to whom* during social exchange.

For example, a parent can say, "If we go to that store, is it alright with you if we only window shop today?" instead of saying, "Don't ask me to buy you anything." Similarly, a parent might ask, "When we have to leave in five minutes, will you quickly shut the game off and come with me?" instead of demanding immediate compliance at the last moment without considering the child's frame of reference.

We expect that affinity, mutual care, and compromise arising during collaborative interacting will reinforce the child to enact a mutually-acceptable sequence of behaviors. There will always be times when consensus is not reached, and the parent must solve problems unilaterally in order to end an activity, for example, if the child is disrupting others; but instances of coercion will be the exception rather than the rule. The parental role shifts from forging the trail to helping the diagnosed child find his or her own way, much like riding a bike with "training wheels" and then riding independently.

By taking our recommended precautions, the probability of enacting the discussed behaviors will increase without the necessity for point-of-performance management. Because everyone who is involved is re-conditioned to enact behaviors with less pressure or reliance on external directives, we suspect that preferred behavior will over time come to the fore as other, undesirable behavior recedes. In our view, if the child has been constantly reminded at each point of performance, we would not expect that she will learn to self-cue necessary actions or to manage time effectively.

Behaviors that jeopardize mutuality are extinguished by helping participants learn to coordinate in ways that result in less difficulty for each other. Diagnosed persons with sufficient language development learn to discuss problems as an alternative to doing ADHD. All involved learn that self-reliance is advantageous, and that mutuality is preferable to domination.

When adopting the self-reliant learning approach, we presume that many or most diagnosed persons will show radically different patterns of persistence, concentration, and problem solving when completing activities associated with success, compared to their behavior when increased social restriction, segregation, disappointment, irrelevance, disapproval, evaluation, and/or other discomforts pertaining to high failure rates and negative social exchanges have been the norm.

ADHD responses are much more likely to be reinforced when diagnosed persons are given assignments that can cue *negative* responses such as a probability of failure, disapproving or tense parental verbalizations, and/or the requirement to wait and watch others enjoy themselves. However, it is not that diagnosed persons have difficulty adequately inhibiting behavior and talking themselves out of doing ADHD misdeeds, but rather that they have been reinforced to monopolize, respond too quickly or slowly, and/or not participate as expected.

As stated throughout, our particular biopsychosocial circumstances indicate that some of us are more likely to learn ADHD behaviors, but conditions of socialization can over time help to configure more synchronized responding. In our intervention to change ADHD patterning, we focus on what happens when diagnosed persons relinquish, instigate, or react carelessly when they are confronted with obstacles and problems. These event sequences, along with circumstances that occur when competing interests are present, are significant in our observations, and crucial in accounting for the frequency rates of diagnostic responding.

Context rather than deficiency (proposed by traditional biological determinism) are used to explicate ADHD patterns. Our formulation is reasonably consistent with Hyde's (2005) recent meta-analysis of gender similarities and differences. She reports that "context" rather than inherent differences between males and females much more often account for variations in response patterns.

For example, it might be found that diagnostic responding occurs frequently for some or many when the teacher presents material to the entire class, and/or when there is less opportunity for assistance in the classroom. ADHD responding might be rampant when parents or teachers speak about content pertaining to what the diagnosed person "needs" to do, and/or what he has been doing wrong or "should" do differently. Diagnostic responding might occur frequently for some diagnosed persons when specific directives are imposed, when attention from others is diverted, and/or when parents solicit conformity if the child is doing a self-initiated task.

Not all diagnosed persons always have the same difficulty adapting to social and task requirements, but the particular behaviors we identify as ADHD occur increasingly in relation to certain conditions as the child's behavioral repertoire widens. In this framework it is important to assess how, when we change context and situation, diagnostic responding is influenced. For example, in what ways does altering the source of instruction, manner of presentation, content of the instructions, and/or setting where interactions take place affect patterns of carelessness, discontinuity of behavior, or extent of participation and responsiveness?

Environmental influences can be identified through this method. Subtle effects pertaining to ongoing behavior patterns will be noted during social exchanges; it is important to first evaluate these before wondering whether a problem stems from a functional limitation. For example, we can ask why it is neurologically easier or less taxing on the inhibitory system to listen attentively to a rap song, decipher the exact wording, and comprehend meaning, compared to listening to a teacher in the classroom.

The view taken here is that diagnosed persons can be effectively socialized without presuming that intervention must add to what is inherently lacking. As we obtain information through observation of behaviors in contexts, we will gradually become better qualified to alter the situations that diagnosed persons encounter, thereby reducing ADHD responses. The first rule of thumb is to allow diagnosed persons to use their own resources to some extent before interrupting (even if they ask for help quickly). Another recommendation would be to encourage them to voice concerns and grievances when they encounter problems, rather than direct their actions.

Parents are encouraged to avoid pressuring the child to do specific behavioral acts wherever it is feasible. They might ask the child what she would like to accomplish; what she thinks is best for her; and what she can do to accomplish a goal. Parents and diagnosed children decide together how to change a typical sequence of events in order to be less obstructive to each other. Parents are role models who set the example of the behaviors they *want* their children to enact. A coercive response is used only to protect the child and/or stop infringements that escalate to the point of a stalemate. Parents are encouraged to be explicit about what they will do to protect themselves and others if problems recur, as well as indicate the changes that will be necessary before they reengage in a specific activity with the child.

If, after having discussed various actions to stop problem behaviors, the diagnosed child continues her inconsiderate behavior, a firm decision may be necessary. For example, parents can allow fewer dishes to be available to the diagnosed person if kitchen utensils are piling up in the child's room. The parent is in this case reducing filth that is problematic to the household, as well as alleviating family annoyance by making utensils available to family members.

Parents "turn off the faucet" of inconsiderate behavior. However, parents are urged to not cause suffering in order "to teach a lesson." After a defensive intervention taken by the parent to deal with a child's lack of concern for others, the child may begin to enact a more acceptable pattern in the new circumstance. Coercive management is used less often, but parents are certainly advised to act in order to eliminate misuse and self obsession that disturbs everyone. However, displeasing parental actions only occur until a more mutually agreeable arrangement can be sculpted, and the child need not be miserable for a predetermined period of time in order to learn acceptable responding.

When the child does not participate in the search for an acceptable solution, it will be necessary to take unilateral actions to resolve the problem, since the child's lack of contribution and inflexibility essentially forces others to take control. For example, it is unpleasant to live with someone who rarely washes. The diagnosed person might not want to alter his lapse in hygiene, and such behavior impacts on everyone. If he rejects attempts to find mutually satisfying solutions, he will have to accept what others decide. It will sometimes, for example, be necessary to ostracize the non-hygienic child rather than take him out to public places.

We do not condone punishing the child into changing behavior; but it is unreasonable for others to be oppressed by a malodorous family member. *Any* family member with a lack of hygiene would be subjected to the same defensive response. The child is included whenever he undertakes a reasonable level of hygiene, problems with self-esteem are addressed, and the child is neither mocked nor criticized. Parental consistency lets the child know the importance of resolving a particular problem without further delay, but they emphasize that they much prefer to solve the problem without coercion. The parent may say, "Let's see if we can solve this together" before imposing discomfort, and they are willing to rescind the disagreeable solution if and when a mutually agreed solution is reached.

Our recommended approach is designed to dismantle extreme self-centered behavior. Diagnosed children do not, in the long-run, benefit from fettering adults in order to "get their own way" at the expense of others; nor should parents give children tacit permission to impinge on family members and monopolize. Focus is on what works best for the child, but the child is not given authority to dictate or exploit others. For example, at any time the parent can say, "I don't think that arrangement is good for us," and take action to immediately curtail the activity.

Reducing the focus on unilateral parental management

Since many problems occur when diagnosed children vacillate between unproductive extremes, the traditional advisements that parents should be consistent, intolerant of exploitation, and providers of positive discipline, are indeed reasonable. However, when traditionalists *also* recommend solutions that result in diagnosed children becoming unduly reliant on parental directives, medication, use of additional managed rewards and punishments, and emphasis is placed on compliance rather than cooperation, traditional advice loses its effectiveness. While the traditional approach shifts diagnosed persons from a non-accommodating response pattern to a more conforming response pattern, the current alternative approach shifts them to a midpoint where it is mutually acceptable to everyone.

Instead of professing that goods and services equate with privilege and freedom, we suggest a very different tactic: less withholding of access to civil liberties, and more help to identify both personal and relational benefits recognized through cooperation and mutual recognition. When we identify certain behaviors and resources as privileges, the implicit message is that the parent owns all the resources and sources of enjoyment, and that all discretionary authority within the household belongs to the parent as well.

We would be concerned in this case that traditional methods, for example, correlate with a problem sharing money at other times (e.g., in marriage). Individuals trained thusly will understand money as individually owned and synonymous with power, rather than as a pooled family resource. Most therapists working with couples will attest that sharing money is a recurrent problem in marriages, in that the wage earner often presumes the "privilege" of getting his or her own way. If many diagnosed persons already have problems taking turns and sharing, we suspect that the introduction of this discipline will only exacerbate the troublesome behaviors.

Parents might instead help their younger children identify the "return" for the investment in cooperation. For example, a parent might say, "If we find a better way to tidy the house early in the day, we will have more time later on to play." Or, "If we go upstairs now, we will have more time for stories before it gets too late," or, "If you bring me back the change, I can keep giving you extra money so you will be sure to have enough." If the child can grasp a generalized statement, rather than demand a specific reward for a specific act, the parent can also say, "If we find a way to get along better in public, we can go to more places," or, "If you are more responsive to me, we can figure out a solution that will be more comfortable for us both."

Such interplay can facilitate the repetition of cooperative acts in a range of situations and draw attention to the benefits of working together. For example, if the diagnosed person returns what is borrowed, others will be likely to loan possessions in the future. If he is polite, others will likely be considerate and extend invitations in return. Again, mutually acceptable patterning is fundamental to behavioral shifts, rather than coercion, externalizing blame, "pulling rank" or emphatic negativity. For example, instead of saying, "You didn't put the games away last time so you cannot play with them today," a parent can reply, "Last time you left the games on the floor. If we take the games out today, can I count on you to put them away?"

Even though unilateral pronouncements may seem necessary sometimes, regular use of coercion can be fraught with correlated side effects. For instance, coercion can interfere with sharing and compromising, but also increase the probability that the child will learn how to protect his discretionary authority. Self-protective behaviors will increase in response to external pressure. Thus, when a child functions "under the thumb" of others he may also learn effective ways to elude other imposed limitations.

Anastopoulos, Rhoads, and Farley (2006) note that the long-term benefits of building positive relationships within families should not be underestimated, and we think that vastly improved relationships can be developed by departing from the well-worn path trod by most traditionalists. Perhaps traditional approaches produce some relational benefits, in that parents become less blameworthy and learn more positive attending, but we suspect that over the long term, some of the more coercive aspects of traditional parent training intervention will impede progress that could otherwise be attained. For example, instead of commanding a diagnosed child to comply, we recommend that attempts to shape cooperative responding be made much sooner in the child's life than traditionalists recommend. The extra time taken to practice collaborative social skills can, in the long run, lead to a significant reduction in ADHD responding that might not otherwise occur.

Additionally, although extra rewards offered to the child will initially please her because more is being offered for actions that were formally required without enhancement, problems will quickly appear when rewards are not earned. The failure to receive the rewards may very well be perceived as an outright denial. The parent may also then be regarded as unsympathetic, mean, unfair, and insensitive, especially if the child declares that extenuating circumstances have interfered with her ability to fulfill expectations.

Even if the parent does not explicitly punish the child when withholding and/or denying access, many disruptions in psychosocial patterning can occur when disciplining in the traditional manner. The child may regard the parent as an adversary, and refrain from sharing information in order to avoid possible reprisal. Problems can become significant despite traditionalists' certitude that training for compliance is the best and only feasible means of socializing persons who have the ADHD neurobiological delay.

There is therefore a strong likelihood that managed contingency systems (even those based on enticement) can be as disruptive to relational patterns as those which incorporate punishment. Additionally, biddable responses may only occur for the duration that the reward is withheld; it is not unusual for parents to report that their child no longer behaves in a helpful manner after obtaining a promised remuneration. Moreover, children can also learn to conform only to *minimum* standards in order to obtain rewards and avoid reprisals, and not accommodate to others, as the objective is to receive the reward rather than promote care and intimacy. Traditionalists claim that these problems can be resolved, but managed systems are not devoid of these side effects; many participants stop using these systems over the course of intervention, and even more so when therapy stops. If the systems work so well, we wonder why so many people abandon their elaborate behavioral charts over the long term.

Not surprisingly, many adults are skeptical about giving rewards to diagnosed children when they behave problematically (especially parents who are unwilling to accept that their child has an inherent disability). They worry that their child is getting reinforced towards unruly, unreliable, and uncooperative behavior, which allows them to exercise greater monopoly over family resources. Such children essentially force their parents to give more because they do not cooperate easily. The child is therefore inadvertently reinforced to respond in diagnostic patterns.

Given the frequency of these kinds of problems, many cease using the contingency management systems endorsed by traditionalists after a short period of time, even if they notice behavioral improvement at the outset when those systems were first introduced (including some reports of relationship improvement as well). It seems that while many children initially respond to the behavioral charts as opportunities to get "something extra," they later recognize that parents maintain unilateral control over their resources, particularly when rewards are withheld. Many children soon revert to the troubling behaviors and, in many instances when following a traditional course of treatment, families end up relying solely on medications to reduce the frequency rates of ADHD responding.

We know that shaping self-reliant/collaborative interacting is time consuming, requires parents to learn unfamiliar behaviors, is slower to yield results, and can be perceived as a loss of discretionary authority for parents and caregivers. But we anticipate that the child will progressively learn satisfactory responding over time with fewer side effects, greater consistency of expression of learned behaviors, and increased initiative, ambition, philanthropy, and ingenuity.

Moreover, if it is true that immediate short-term compliance is *not* imperative due to the limiting nature of ADHD, we see no necessity for coercion, subjugation, fostering dependency, and/or threatening behavior when it is possible to achieve acceptable behaviors in a mutually-dignifying way that also shapes more autonomy over time. For example, instead of saying, "Don't touch that" and then threaten to punish, parents might say, "Before you touch anything on that desk, please talk with me first."

Consistent with this view are the findings of Latham, Erez, and Locke (1988), who report that if a goal is assigned tersely and is not fully explained, performance is often lower than if the goal is set in a more participatory fashion. Similarly, Locke, Alavi, and Wagner (1997) note that an important benefit to participatory decision making is that it promotes information exchange to help people identify strategies and improve self-efficacy, and potentially increase achievement as well.

Despite the unfamiliarity of our recommendations here, the learning model is not requesting that parents change established limits or behaviors they prefer that their children enact (e.g., responsibility for belongings and personal care, meet deadlines, maintain safety, not exploit others), nor are we urging parents to excessively please the child, which may already be the case for many parents. Shifting to a less coercive, more self-reliant social patterning does not endorse ill-defined liberalism; it is simply a different way to discipline, and a new way to extinguish ADHD behaviors. For example, instead of rigidly coercing the child to eat a prepared meal, or cooking a different meal for a demanding child, parents might wrap up the food and extend an offer for the child to eat the meal at some other time. It may at times also be reasonable for the child to make an alternative meal, as long as a mess is not created in the process.

Problems implementing collaborative/self-reliant interacting

We recognize that our model departs markedly from the forced compliance approach that thus far predominates our understanding of ADHD. As with all new approaches, it is difficult to gain everyone's acceptance after previous investment in some other now familiar conceptualization, but our primary aim is always to establish greater mutual respect via agreeable interacting.

At first it will seem like a strange and unworkable idea. The socialization process can be unfamiliar and contrary to the child-rearing methods used by parents in the past. Some parents will quickly accommodate or rescue their ADHD diagnosed child, thus preventing her from learning about behavioral consequences on her own. Other parents report that they *want* to change the controlling or neglectful patterns that occurred in their primary families, and so will too often indulge and acquiesce to their own children. Still others are too directive and coercive, and do not encourage the child towards autonomy and assertiveness. Because many of us are socialized to either dominate or submit in our relations with others, an alternative approach will therefore be time consuming.

The act of compromise, for example, requires that parents talk in ways that depart from the usual; many parents have not been exposed to language designed to promote effective diplomacy. A shift from remarks such as "I let you," "you must," "you need to," "you have to," and "you should," to: "do you want to," "will you," "would you like to," "we prefer that you," and/or "you get to," can indeed shape mutual relational patterns.

For many parents any solution that is inconsistent with forced compliance is perceived as permissive. But this approach is *not* equivalent to granting the child impunity or permission to behave with disregard for others. For example, the diagnosed child is not given the option to play with his mother's pocketbook. Nor does this approach grant them immunity from consequences of their behavior. A collaborative approach does not mean that unacceptable risks must be introduced, or that parents must acquiesce if the child protests. These techniques do not require that parents suffer endlessly while the child moves willy-nilly through unreasonable behaviors. There will necessarily be instances (whether the child agrees or not) when the parent has to make unilateral decisions or take action to which the child will strongly disagree. In dangerous and intransigent situations, the child's opinion will be irrelevant.

For example, when emphasizing a bottom line, parents can communicate that they are willing to invite the child's friends over only if there is a reasonable way to deal with the mess afterwards. If the child is uninterested in solving the problem, the parent can reply, "I guess it's alright with you if we figure out a solution without your input," and/or, "Let's wait to invite your friends over after we have figured this out."

Similarly, if a child refuses to wear a seat belt in the car, or if a young child wants to roam unattended around a building, it is unreasonable to *not* protect and enforce limits. Not driving the car until the seat beat is buckled, and restraining the child from roaming a building are necessary unilateral maneuvers (requiring compliance); this is preferable to other options when attempts to persuade the child fail. The collaborative basis for interacting is advised to maintain the child's discretionary input whenever it is deemed sensible, feasible, or practical by parents. But parents are not asked to idly sit by without addressing problems.

When attempting to strike a balance between the interests of the diagnosed person and those of others, participants are advised to acknowledge multiple perspectives, but not accommodate simply to mollify. Parents are asked to avoid highlighting relatively innocuous annoying behaviors and to not overreact to instigating. They are urged to talk non-critically with the child about problems, and encouraged to not please the child at the expense of others.

During collaborative exchanges parents are also asked to direct the child towards the possible rather than emphasize what the child *cannot* do, as well as calmly divert the child to positive content when they express negative responses. If the child stifles collaboration, the parent can say, "I can hear you better if you speak calmly and quietly." Similarly, the parent can remark, "If we stay calm we can problem solve better," or "If you talk with me patiently we can try to work it out." By keeping one's composure, parents do not convey the impression that the child is disliked; and subversive diagnostic behavior that prevents others from establishing authority is less likely to be evoked.

Greater coordination among family members can be developed, for example, when instead of establishing a routine in which the adult exits the car when picking up the child at a friend's house, a routine can be established whereby the child looks out the window at an arranged time so that, when the adult arrives, the child is ready to leave. By establishing this new routine, the child learns how to be considerate of others, or in the ADHD vernacular, he can control the future effectively.

As a way to develop collaborative interacting, parents are also encouraged to discuss concerns *prior* to engaging in a potentially troubling situation. For example, the parent might say, "I'm going to be busy with a guest, what do you want to do while the company is here?" The parent might also communicate that it is sometimes difficult to immediately stop a conversation in order to help the child learn how to occupy himself when others are occupied elsewhere.

As described by Kvols (1998), the parent can also affectionately acknowledge the child by touching him on the shoulder when he wants attention, but also continue talking so that intrusiveness as such is not reinforced. Helping diagnosed children to understand the intricacies of a situation will eventually result in less invasiveness; he or she will also not feel rejected or diminished. For example, mutual respect is maintained when the parent says to the child, "What if we signaled to each other rather than barge in?"

Some parents will be more effective than others, but we presume that parents and children can learn to be self-aware of the contingencies that reinforce their behavior. For example, when a child exaggerates disappointment by saying, "You never let me have fun," parents can emphasize that the child's overreaction will not convince them to agree. They are saying no because they love and respect the child and therefore want to avoid problems that would occur if they said yes. Parents in this case can distinguish that they neither want to deny the child nor do they mistrust the child. Moreover, they are saying no in this particular circumstance, but at other times it will be reasonable to say yes. Parents can then explicitly identify the conditions under which saying yes is probable so that the child learns about the complexities of decision making.

Some parents will nevertheless prefer autocratic methods, because they believe that children should do as they are told. But such methods do not guarantee that children will learn to integrate and identify multiple perspectives as effectively as will collaborative forms of socialization. Some adults will react to learning model procedures as if they give too much control to the child, but many who choose to implement these methods will discover that they are being *more assertive* using the learning approach.

For those who remain suspicious that collaborative methods are too liberal, we emphasize that there is no injunction stating that parents must always give the child additional chances before imposing unilateral problem solving, especially in risk situations. However, in collaborative interacting parents can communicate this limitation prior to the event as a way to mitigate relational side effects, by saying for example, "I'm willing to try it this way only one time," or "We will have to leave if there is any rough play so that we can show courtesy to others." Similarly, a parent might say, "If you don't come when we call, it will be necessary to start dinner without you."

However, a word of caution: on numerous occasions, less coercion and fewer instances of directing the child's actions can correlate with an *initial* worsening of problems. Children with a long history of functioning within forced compliance arrangements (e.g., grades for privileges, groundings for misdeeds) often respond poorly when less coercive alternative interventions are first introduced. Children can possibly initially react as if they now have ultimate freedom, that others do not care about them as they had in the past, and/or that problems are insurmountable without the parent always being available.

When initial deterioration of performance occurs, parents are reinforced to *revert* to their old pattern of medicating, excessive helping, and coercion to quickly save the day. Parents will often be desperate to alleviate the burgeoning problems. They might regret having tried to shape self-reliant/collaborative functioning (particularly if the child's grades begin to drop). Some parents will become even more convinced that the child cannot function outside of a highly supervised arrangement without parental inducement and stimulant medication, as for example, when diagnosed children respond unfavorably (at first) to the parent's reluctance to find lost objects, remind them about appointments, and/or cue them to do personal hygiene.

Moreover, when fully utilizing these alternative approaches, behavioral change relating to specific interventions may not become evident until far into the future when equivalent conditions are repeated. Until that time, parents are left hanging with the sense that they have simply let the child "get away" with inappropriate behavior. Immediate problems and a concomitant sense of urgency will distract the parent from recognizing that they can effectively extinguish particular behaviors over longer spans of time by stopping indulgences, dispassionately redirecting, ignoring, or letting events play out rather than use coercion methods.

We recognize that ultimately diagnosed children have learned a variety of non-normative behaviors to protect themselves from loss or humiliation. Frequent whining, complaining, faulting others, and myriad histrionics when others are slow to accommodate or when encountering situations that threaten their adequacy are commonplace in ADHD diagnosed children. Individuals who witness these displays will often conform to the child's unacceptable responses simply to get them to stop. Some feel sorry for the struggling child who behaves as if the world is ending. However, each of these social reactions may only entrench the behaviors more.

Additionally, when first implementing our learning model, if the diagnosed person is asked to figure out a solution she might respond as if being mistreated or unreasonably pressured. Others will refuse to follow the instruction to try, and worry that their decision making will expose them to negative scrutiny. Many diagnosed children will only put forth a cursory effort, give up quickly, accuse the parent of indifference, or respond in order to escape when parents initially institute these alternative approaches.

However, we must keep in mind that diagnosed children have excellent memory capacity, can freely contribute, and will often express ideas in other circumstances with other content they enjoy. Therefore, we need not assume that initial difficulties stem from an inherent limitation of "having" ADHD. Participants may feel discouraged about shaping collaborative patterns, and parents may at times too quickly apply coercive methods to get at least something accomplished, but these initial bumps do not mean that success with this approach is unattainable.

Addressing the diagnosed person's initial reluctance

Generally, diagnosed individuals tend to make fewer agreements because it implies restriction; a vicious cycle of evading responsibility is created when they make agreements and are punished for breaking them. An analogous problem occurs when parents learn that promises made to children can lead to problems because children do not always grasp the concept of extenuating circumstances. The diagnosed child will often equate the failure to keep promises with lying, meanness, or indifference. In much the same fashion, diagnosed persons might learn that making an agreement will increase the likelihood of blame, failure to meet expectations, and reprisal if something goes wrong. Many diagnosed children are also conditioned that it is safer when policy is derived by others, in that if something does go wrong, it is the fault of the originator of the idea.

For these reasons it can be very difficult to learn effective collaboration, and learning curves among parents will differ markedly. However, subtle facial cues and voice tones during interactions is one way to distinguish participatory behaviors from avoidant actions. Sometimes what is unsaid tells us whether follow-through will occur even though the diagnosed person says all the correct things. For example, "Kind of" or "I guess," and "Whatever" are lackluster affirmations which allow the verbal exchange to end sooner, and enable the child to avoid prolonged debate. But rarely do such responses signify that acceptable behavioral change will occur later.

We advise a detailed analysis of social interaction, and some parents (and therapists) will initially be more skilled than others. For example, while at times diagnosed persons do not "know" what to do, in some scenarios the remark "I don't know" can mean: "Do it for me," "You are controlling or interfering by asking," "Get off my back," or "I'm afraid to make a mistake." With this response we realize that they have not yet learned how to resolve conflicts of interest, nor have they learned how to meet expectations; thus a defensive stature is maintained.

Many parents will complain that they have tried to promote self-management and collaborative problem solving with their diagnosed child to no avail, but the crux of the problem is to change reinforcement history rather than override a functional limitation. The process will require greater perseverance.

It is therefore necessary for parents to take the lead in instances where only the parent seems amenable to change; he or she can delve further to identify what prevents the child from showing curiosity to conjointly problem solve. Any notable reluctance on the child's part to work together is important to understand and resolve, as that reaction can signify other unsolved problems in the relationship which hinder attempts to build positive rapport.

Often the parent's first task is to encourage contribution and rectify problems that impede negotiation and courteous behavior. For example, the parent can say, "Your input is important to us if you would like to share your ideas," as well as ask, "Is something else bothering you?" The parent acknowledges the importance of the child's perspective, gives her respect, and maintains her dignity at all times; without that accommodation little will become generalized when the parent is not available as overseer. Pressure tactics can meanwhile be imposed anytime, but they carry the significant long-term cost of sabotaging the whole process of interdependence.

Parents can also ask, "What do you like about that solution and what problems might arise if we behaved in that way?" By giving the child an opportunity to think, more acceptable self-management skills can be forged. Traditionalists claim that diagnosed children must be told what to do, but we might discover that they are more capable than we think if we provide them with chances to practice figuring out pragmatic, achievable, and mutually acceptable solutions.

In sum, loved ones role model perspective-taking by exploring what the diagnosed person says. The learning intervention is designed to reassure the child about his or her importance in the family and to create conditions to increase the child's opportunity for success. Participants are advised to keep it simple, express it concisely, and orient to be less obstructive with one another. As they work towards consensus, diagnosed children gradually learn to recombine, organize, and reassemble words to make new sequences and possibilities.

However, since a lack of contribution can sometimes result in loved ones going to great lengths to elicit even minimal participation, it is often helpful for parents to avoid over accommodating the child if and when responses are not forthcoming. Rather than revert to antagonistic behavior, the facilitator can either shift to other content or solve the problem in a way that does not require the child's contribution. By following such a procedure, the child does not gain discretionary authority or social importance when others are solicitous. The child might then feel as if he is missing out when not voicing concerns, and regret his lack of reciprocity.

Facilitating self-reliance

In situations where parents have quickly come to the aid of their diagnosed children, they are asked instead to refrain from filling in the gaps when diagnosed persons speak, including when the child forgets what he was saying or loses his train of thought. Instead of immediately correcting the mistakes, parents can ask questions that encourage the child to reconsider the initial statement. It becomes increasingly incumbent on the diagnosed child to maintain continuity and clarity of ideation whenever he is loquacious. Parents are urged in this case to indicate when they do not understand what has been said (in a non-critical way) rather than speculate or immediately reconfigure the child's speech to make it easily understandable.

When assisting diagnosed persons to reduce the frequency of losing their train of thought, loved ones can wait for the diagnosed person to identify what has been said before giving assistance; this waiting time may help facilitate the child's own use of resources rather than highlight reliance on others to maintain the focus of the exchange. Parents are advised to impart strategies to help diagnosed children organize their ideas during instructional periods at other times, but not to reinforce immature reliance.

We anticipate that, as the child becomes less conditioned to expect answers to be provided, that this alternative form of socializing will incrementally help diagnosed persons become fluent with language. With long-term practice, moreover, such socializing will allow the diagnosed child to engage in complex verbal problem solving without help. Parents are asked, however, to *not* permit their children to talk incomprehensibly without coming to their aid or making it clear that communication is not occurring.

When problems are encountered that can be solved independently by the child, parents are advised to promote those achievements. For example, if a child asks why there is a sign indicating "speed bump," instead of providing the answer, parent can say, "What do you think it warns people to do?" so that the child is stimulated to think. Brain storming is encouraged, and there is an emphasis on fostering the child's curiosity to understand the world.

As noted previously, when loved ones consistently provide relief or resolve what appears to be reckless inept behavior, orienting for long-term outcomes may have little advantage, since errors and problems are borne by others. If excessive compensatory social responses take place it is difficult to extinguish what are classified as impulsive behaviors. Traditionalists tend to undervalue the possible effectiveness of various natural consequences of events, scenarios, contexts, and the like, but they also neglect to provide data showing how frequently parents or loved ones allow natural consequences to influence the actions of diagnosed children. Nor do they calculate the extent to which significant individuals take definitive steps to stop behaviors that seem to be increasing the frequency of ADHD patterning.

It is always necessary to prevent diagnosed persons from harming themselves or others, but there are numerous instances where nothing dangerous will happen by allowing the usual sequence of situations and circumstances to play out without leaping in to rescue; such responding may help to extinguish the self-pampering or short-sighted behavior of many diagnosed persons. Given the current ADHD empiricism, we still do not know how much coordination with broader spans of time can be exhibited if the child is not reinforced to behave heedlessly. Traditionalists do, however, recognize that most individuals seem to achieve better when goals are self-set (Barkley, 2000), but traditional presumptions about ADHD can actually sabotage the process towards self-reliance by not affording the opportunity to function autonomously, especially at a younger age.

When facilitating self-reliance, we can, for example, extinguish the frequent pattern of diagnosed children to ask questions before attempting to derive solutions independently. For many of these children, questioning is associated with eliciting contact from others or diverting social exchange rather than to learning something new. Responding to the diagnosed individual's accomplishments can also reduce diagnostic patterning. Instead of designing social interactions so that the diagnosed person *reacts* to what others specify, they can learn to identify solutions by making the first move; the goal is to increase instances where the diagnosed person formulates ideas, initiates, and suggests alternatives.

Therapists, parents, and teachers can also sensitively withhold from offering suggestions (even if it relates to their own experience), until the diagnosed person has had ample opportunity to initiate an idea; facilitators would then be in the position to respond to the diagnosed person. If he or she does not recognize possible benefits and problems associated with behavior, facilitators are requested to intervene to the least possible degree. For example, instead of identifying benefits, the parent might ask, "Do you think it will work better for you if you talked with the teacher after class rather than answer her back when you are furious?" or "What positive things might happen for you if you carried out the teacher's request?"

Starting early with younger diagnosed children

Regardless of one's conceptual framework, most agree that early, rather than later, intervention is preferable. ADHD is a persistent condition that is likely to entrench as years pass; the more severe are symptoms or co-morbid problems, the less likely is the chance for remission or improvement. In the vernacular of the current model, the more complex the presenting problem and the more the behaviors repeat and are reinforced, the more difficult it is to change or extinguish those patterns. Not surprisingly, when the child is ready to attend school, the pattern will be implanted and resistant to change, thus confirming the high failure rate of psychotherapeutic intervention when children initially present for treatment. We know that it is crucial to abide by a child's developmental level, but our recommendation of early intervention coincides with Martens and Hiralall's (1997) approach, which induced noteworthy behavioral changes for preschoolers by having teachers embed social reinforcers into ongoing classroom interactions rather than design coercive token economies.

Interestingly, when parents and teachers facilitate self-reliance in a variety of settings, they express concern about whether it is advisable to approach a child when he or she is achieving independently, or if they should not interrupt the child's autonomy and allow events, within reason, to unfold. Anastopoulos, Rhoads, and Farley (2006) note that it can be helpful to move toward a child during independent play, but one could argue that parents *not* distract the child from independent accomplishments. Specifically, when approaching a child who is functioning independently, the parent avoids talking to the child until there is an interval.

Additionally, if parents are worried about overreacting to minimal accomplishments, they can encourage more age-consistent patterns of social exchange and shape accomplishments that *add* to diagnosed children's behavioral repertoire instead of repeatedly embellishing minimal deeds. Overreactions to trivial feats can inadvertently condition the child towards lower levels of achievement. The child will learn that he need not do much to gain notoriety. Exaggerated responses can, in the case of minimal accomplishments, also infantilize diagnosed children even further by making a "big deal" out of insignificant acts. Conditioning the child to anticipate extraordinary accolades for minor accomplishments can also result in feelings of deprivation when the parent stops being impressed. Teachers moreover, are less likely to indulge the child, so these patterns of social exchange can hinder the child's adjustment to an unfamiliar, less enthusiastic audience.

Some children will also react *negatively* when parents are over-exuberant when they do meet expectations. They respond as if the parent is manipulating conformity by being inordinately happy about particular achievements; conversely other children are offended by their parents' low expectations. Some children will curtail particular achievements when they get angry with the parent, in that non-achievement is a way to punish the parent who seems so (evaluative) and sensitive to each and every success or failure. While we do not advise parents to stop complimenting the child, we do recommend that parents attend to these concerns and recognize the subtlety of the problem of effectively encouraging a child. For instance, a rave review can dissuade a child, in that he becomes apprehensive about possibly failing when trying to duplicate the previous success.

In our approach a positive attitude works best, such as when parents enjoy, admire, and appreciate their child's accomplishments instead of criticizing or making comparisons. For example, the parent can say, "Thank you for doing that" or "I'm impressed by what you did." Adult responses are more effective than an immature clapping with stiffened fingers or telling the child, "I told you that you could do it!" which does not always sound complimentary. Similarly, parents might reconsider such comments as, "We know you would get excellent grades if you would only try or behave more positively" and ask themselves whether their remarks are likely to increase achievement. Rather than hit their target, those reassurances can actually backfire and intensify avoidance behaviors that elicit those remarks. Many children, for example, may not want to risk of jeopardizing the belief that they "have potential."

Instead, parents can focus on what the child has achieved independently and note those accomplishments with other people when it is fitting to do so. Parents might do this in a fashion that conveys the message that the parent is not at all surprised by the child's competence and acts of kindness. The child's proficiency and consideration for others are highlighted more often, and social importance is established in relation to valued actions.

Problems when reducing medication

Shifting now to an entirely different concern when intervention is initiated, we observe that parents are often unsure whether it is best to medicate or intervene without stimulants. Our approach here regards this as a practical problem that depends on how quickly change is required, the resources of the participants, and concerns about side effects. Effective treatment may be psychosocial in nature, and thus administered with or without medication. The decision to prescribe can be based on benefit/risk analysis for each diagnosed person, depending on the presenting problem, the wherewithal of those involved, the surrounding conditions, and the urgency of obtaining immediate behavioral change.

In specific cases medication and contingency management will be the only efficacious ways to proceed.

And despite the apparent differences between our psychosocial "learning
paradigm" approach and traditional intervention, in limited ways it may be possible to blend the approaches for practical reasons or enact the interventions se-
quentially. For example, it is always possible for an individual to take medication, and at the same time take steps to increase instances of self-reliance and
collaborative interacting. By blending medication with the reinforcement of self-
reliance and collaborative interacting, diagnosed individuals may obtain the immediate benefits of medication, show progress on lower dosages, and simultaneously derive the long-term benefits from developing personal resources and
cooperative patterning. Individuals can then gradually wean themselves off
medication as they learn to interact collaboratively and autonomously.

Parents might also feel uncomfortable with our alternative approach if they
have not had the opportunity to enact the traditional intervention for a suitable
period of time. They further believe that their child will eventually learn to initiate and enjoy actions that have heretofore been coerced. These parents will emphasize that some people have indeed benefited from military-type training, and
even continue the routines learned in the armed forces throughout their lives. In
their opinion, one must at first subjugate in order to be successful at developing
a more congenial self-reliant pattern.

However, despite that some behaviors learned under coercive conditions
will become generalized; our approach provides a way for diagnosed individuals
to achieve greater autonomous competence *at an earlier age*. The intervention
could also diminish the risk (often significant) that behaviors learned under coercive conditions and medication will *not* repeat when coercion and medication
are withdrawn. The acting out, which is often evident during freshman year
when many young adults leave restrictive and over-protective households to
attend college, or the behavior of many people who travel to Las Vegas, are such
examples.

Any attempt, moreover, to reduce medication should be taken cautiously
and with professional advice from a physician. Behavioral regression (at home
and school) may be significant if stimulant medication is suddenly stopped. An
individual may not yet have learned to behave acceptably without medication,
and behaviors that have not occurred while medicated have not yet been extinguished. We expect that there will be many cases where family members have
not learned to effectively deal with high activity levels and less responsiveness
to directives that is typical when stimulant medication is withdrawn.

Therefore, it is prudent to remove the child's medication only after psychosocial patterns are agreeable to participants, and when the child shows acceptable age-consistent self-reliance during assigned work periods. It is usually
better to wait until the school year ends before deciding to stop the medication
(Connor, 2006), or allow the child to slowly outgrow the dose in order to ameliorate any adjustment problems the diagnosed person may experience. Compli-

cations like these are reason enough to avoid introducing medication in the first place, as readjustments can be arduous for everyone.

While there are no significant medical reasons to wean persons off stimulant medication slowly, titrating medications in this fashion could reduce the flood of new learning required when medication is removed. A strategy of reducing medication doses incrementally and gradually (as with other psychiatric medications) could temper readjustment problems and lessen reports of sadness and fatigue (Prince et al., 2006).

Generally, waiting until the summer months before weaning the child off medication is the most conservative approach; much relearning can be accomplished during that period even though many families tend to reduce the frequency of psychotherapy when school is out of session. However, because the child spends so much time away from scheduling and group participation during the summer, it is advisable to maintain the child in a routine (e.g., day camp) in order that acclimation to school will be less extreme by September.

The use of an active placebo (administered in a double blind fashion) may also help ease the diagnosed person into a non-medicated behavioral pattern. Diagnosed persons could also delay their initial dose if they normally function better in the morning (Dane, Schachar, and Tannock, 2000), or increase the amount of time spent before taking their initial dose in order to learn to function adequately for longer periods of time without feeling medicated. Skipping or lowering a dose when the day has fewer demands, or staggering non-medication days can be tried in some scenarios, however, the inconsistencies introduced by these procedures could mitigate their effectiveness.

Regardless of the technique used to reduce medication, we expect that diagnosed individuals will obtain at least incremental success with less medication, and gradually learn to function acceptably without the pharmacological stimulus as time passes. Traditionalists are more reluctant to withdraw medication, but we consider this option under a wide range of conditions when participants express interest in taking this step. Withdrawing medication, in our view, opens the opportunity to shape acceptable functioning without medicinal side effects.

Diagnosed individuals who are interested in stopping medicinal treatments might find it helpful to explicitly identify the successful behaviors that have occurred without medication. Intervention may then help these individuals replicate the competent behaviors that are already occurring in some situations when not in a medicated state. If they declare that they cannot or, alternatively, have not performed competent acts without medication, then conjointly noting the exceptions to this claim could help to dispel their entrenched notion that certain competent behaviors are beyond their capability without a stimulant.

If they sometimes exceed their claimed disability and show proficiency that is supposedly delayed, in what sense are they *less able*? Facilitators will refer to these acceptable responses when establishing a benchmark relative to what an individual is "able" to do, even though learning to respond with non-diagnostic patterns in situations that previously cued those behaviors will require additional learning. One possible example would be for the diagnosed person to imitate problem-solving strategies used when playing a hand-held video machine or when operating a computer which requires a great deal of organizational skill.

In that same vein, we might also inquire whether the diagnosed child sometimes brushes teeth without being cued or reminded, or whether the child sometimes initiates and completes chores, homework, and follows routines independently. We can investigate whether the child wears a watch under certain conditions, sometimes returns home for meals without being called, and sometimes wakes up on time without fuss or assistance. We can inquire into whether the child keeps a collection of prized objects organized, or whether the child performs certain activities consistently so that achievement occurs over time (e.g., playing a musical instrument, progressing through a complex video game, etc.). By identifying the ways that particular diagnosed persons function non-diagnostically without compensatory measures, we establish a starting point and then proceed to shape the repetition of non-diagnostic responses.

Generally, it will be worthwhile to investigate whether there is increased continuance of treatment effects when using a collaborative/self-reliant model with and without medication, compared to interventions that advocate compliance, dependency on the resources of others, and contingency management with and without medication. These inquiries will eventually allow for the identification of greater numbers of global (or generalized) effects for the different methods of intervention, and differing effects for some therapists and client populations when considering the various combinations. If the usual pattern repeats, however, it seems probable that outcomes will differ in relation to particular subsets of clients and treating professionals.

Helping the child in a different way

Despite the potential of this alternative intervention for subgroups of clients and therapists, many parents might continue to be reinforced (and report less anxiety) when they rescue their children from their trials and tribulations. It is often easier to do for our children than for them to do for themselves. An example of this parental dilemma occurs when the diagnosed child functions poorly in school due to video gaming instead of studying. The traditional solution is to take away the video system until grades improve, offer to pay for higher grades, require the child to take a stimulant, and have the teacher send home daily school reports. If higher achievement occurs, parents are recommended to continue to use the removal of the video system as a contingency for academic success.

This approach will, in the short term, yield improvement in grades, but we notice that the child does very little self-management, and is being trained to be highly reliant on continuous parental involvement (as well as stimulant medication). The child does not enact solutions that he or she has helped to derive, and is not being conditioned to say no to excessive playing without coercion or a drug to induce thoughtfulness.

There will thus be a greater probability that the child will return to the earlier pattern of excessive playing as soon as parental decision making and medication are removed. Since the child has not endorsed the solutions to the problem, not helped to consider the advantages of one solution compared to another, or learned to do the expected behaviors without medication and parental involvement, the child's resources are not being developed adequately to allow the support system to be withdrawn.

When ADHD is characterized as a disability, there is the risk that individuals will see themselves as forever limited. Diagnosed individuals could believe that they have this condition even if they function well in numerous situations. Interestingly, persons with physical "handicaps" have been alert to the possible adverse effects of labeling, and prefer to identify themselves as "physically challenged" rather than accept a label that connotes a comprehensive limitation.

The concern that individuals are reinforced to behave consistently with their labels (i.e., the Pygmalian Effect) has been discussed for years in the psychological literature (Rosenthal and Jacobson, 1968; Snyder, Tanke, and Berscheid, 1977). After having been identified as having ADHD, the effect of the influences discussed above can add another barrier to diagnosed persons' development of self-reliance. The label can reinforce the perpetuation of symptom behaviors, as well as the belief that interventions cannot succeed unless they rectify an inherent ineptitude (e.g., medication and/or compensatory management).

We are concerned too that constant assessments and punishments during contingency management will impede goal accomplishment in many instances. For example, Dweck (1996) claims that people are more likely to attain goals when their intentions are categorized in terms of what they might *learn* rather than when focused on performance, which can elicit fears of inadequacy and thus hinder goal achievement. Additionally, Higgins (1997) indicates that individuals are more likely to achieve goals when they are characterized in positive terms.

In an attempt to incorporate this empirical work, this current alternative model also orients to permit input from the trainee, and places emphasis on what is gained when certain behaviors are enacted. Negativity is usually avoided. Diagnosed persons are requested to specify actions they will take to solve particular problems. Their involvement in deriving plans of action reinforces the later occurrence of the behaviors in lieu of extra management from others. They learn that their ADHD responses are functional, malleable, and are the consequence of conditioning. Those benefits outweigh any "relief" experienced by blaming one's own body.

Given anecdotal observations of numerous diagnosed individuals (and traditionalists' own reports), we recognize that there are often great disparities in the frequency rates of diagnostic responding, depending on whether the action is what the diagnosed person "wants" to do or "has" to do. We observe that parameters related to the *history* of the person with content, activity, and social circumstance (including others involved) will more adequately account for diagnostic responding when compared with the categories imposed by the proffered biological determinist model.

In our view, diagnosed persons are likely to behave markedly differently depending on who retains discretionary authority. Investigators might note instances where discretionary authority is interrupted or perpetuated as a way to measure the influence of this parameter on the frequency of diagnostic responses. Conditions that cue non-diagnostic responses can be recorded and reconstructed in order to better understand the functionality of diagnostic responding.

Repetition of non-diagnostic responding can also be facilitated by helping diagnosed persons identify the closest equivalent behaviors already being competently enacted and encourage them to repeat those actions in other situations. For example, this will help them show similar concentration and attentiveness in Biology and English class that is shown during History class, repeat the same intensity of focus while reading a school book as when reading a strategy guide for a video game, and demonstrate the same flexibility when parents change plans to go to a hardware store as when parents change plans to get ice cream. Parents might ask, "What if you tried to be noticed at school by being friendly just like when you showed your sister how to play that board game?" Competencies evident in situations will likely recur as diagnosed persons recognize previous successes with similar requirements and circumstances. Intervention orients to make assigned and non-assigned circumstances similar.

Additionally, once it is determined that diagnosed persons are amenable to changing their actions (which might also require solving other problems that reinforce a reluctance to change), the aim is to assist each individual in identifying what behaviors under particular sets of conditions achieve the specified result. For example, does tuning out a parent, get that parent to "hound" them less often, or does such a cavalier tactic result in parents treating them as caring, trustworthy, and competent? Do they *really* want the family dog to go without eating when they are upset with their parents for "nagging" them? Similarly, while poor performance at school may spitefully punish others, avoid the discomfort associated with trying and failing, and provoke worry and concern, the child *also* fails in the process. It is therefore reasonable to ask them if they are certain that they want to continue to endure such a negative side effect.

Solutions to reducing ADHD responding could also include certain hesitation and preliminary "mental" consideration during the outlined sequence of behaviors as highlighted in traditional view. Although whatever the solution, we think that the probability of enacting the specified behavioral sequence will increase by encouraging diagnosed persons to indicate (beforehand) the conditions under which they will emit those (mental or observable) responses. We expect that if they designate or visualize the action sequence prior to point of performance, they are likely to initiate the action sequence *at* the point of performance much like the benefits that occur when individuals rehearse for a play.

Diagnosed persons can also be asked how they could help themselves remember certain behaviors. For example, what would they do to remember to take their backpack with them in the morning when leaving the car (e.g., put the backpack near the car door so they will see it when exiting the car). While it might be necessary to have these new verbal exchanges near to the actual enactment of a behavior when children are young, we suspect that these interactions occur further away in time from point of performance as the child learns a sophisticated behavioral repertoire, and begins to make subtle and intricate associations between events.

Interestingly, we observe that traditionalists are recommending a similar approach when they urge parents to discuss ahead of time with the diagnosed child what is likely to occur during family outings. Traditionalists do not advise parents to consider or integrate the diagnosed person's perspective into social patterning, but rather their recommendations acknowledge that discussion about the future can be beneficial. For example, Anastopoulos, Rhoads, and Farley (2006) encourage parents to inform the child before entering stores what will happen, and parents are instructed to be clear about expectations and consequences prior to the event.

However, rather than condition the child to be concerned about parental coercions and retributions, if it is the case that the child continues to behave unreasonably during family outings, proactive collaborative interactions might help participants identify what reinforces the responses and clarify problems. Discussion can focus on better ways for individuals to take care of themselves as well as coordinate with others. For example, cooperation during family outings will permit family members to complete errands both to the hardware store, and on other occasions, to the toy store as well.

When the diagnosed child understands the benefits and detriments to diagnostic responding, more informed decision making can take place. For example, a diagnosed child might initiate the action to build a particular object and give up quickly; this behavior results in a sibling or parent stopping their activity in order to give him assistance. While he might have been thriving without their help, his "giving up" successfully pulled them away from their activity, and thus he was no longer excluded. As always, the understanding of context, situation, and circumstance is our most precise method of predicting ADHD responses for individuals who have learned those patterns, and we strive to make diagnosed persons more aware of what either diagnostic or non-diagnostic responding will accomplish.

Furthermore, to stop reinforcing diagnostic responding, parents are encouraged to curtail the incidental chat about the child's diagnostic responses in front of the child. Stop remarking about the outlandish behavior that the child will "probably" do. Stop treating the child as if he or she were chronologically younger or incompetent. Stop emitting intense reactions to instances of provocation, jeopardy, or risk-taking. Stop criticizing when the child fails to meet expectations. Stop enacting patterns of behavior that potentially increase the likelihood of separation problems. Parents can also anticipate problem situations and take steps to prevent them from happening. For example, parent might say, "I noticed that there are problems when I talk on the phone; would you like to work together to find a way to make it better for both of us?"

Parents are, metaphorically, leading children to water, and rather to force them to drink, the children's drinking will eventually happen. Over time, we anticipate that the child will behave in more socially acceptable and independent ways with less participation from others, even though greater parental involvement is required at the *outset* when new learning takes place. For example, the parent can at first cue a behavior and participate more frequently, then wait and see if the child starts to behave accordingly on his or her own with fewer cues and participation when those conditions recur later.

Self-reliance is shaped incrementally so that aimless floundering is unlikely to occur. Complaints of boredom are not indulged, as intervention orients to develop the child's resources. If it is the case that the child is struggling, then more hints, suggestions, and thought provoking questions can always be introduced in order for the child to continue to make progress. The intervention orients to help children do for themselves, and to cooperate with others, but if results do not meet practical concerns in a timely fashion, interventions corresponding with traditional methods can always be imposed as a last resort. The immediate power of traditional discipline may always be harnessed.

In summary, rather than explicate ADHD patterning using neurological categories, we alternatively presume that ADHD behavior is related to a history of reinforcement. For example, in our view, not interrupting or cutting others off requires no more inhibition than waiting for others. People can learn to stand by while others leave without having to do particular antecedent mind responses to convince them to do x, y, z when for instance the elevator door opens. Action depends on what reaction has been conditioned for a situation or circumstance. One can avoid an ADHD diagnosis simply by learning acceptable and polite routines.

On the other hand, there might be numerous situations when interrupting is reinforced for particular diagnosed children. Such responses might be conditioned by an ensuing drama or when the behavior prevents others from excluding them. Those consequences can increase the frequencies of the intrusive actions despite their social unacceptability and the awareness that the behaviors are unacceptable.

In our view, at times people are either so insecure (or entitled) in their social patterning (given their reinforcement history), that they learn patterns of action consistent with ADHD. As noted by Gerrard and Anastopoulos (2005), diagnosed children seem to show less secure attachment in parental bonding when compared to controls. That problem alone may account for many of their diagnostic patterns (Ladnier and Massanari, 2000).

A delay model is not required to account for differences in the frequency and severity of ADHD behaviors within our population. The behaviors may be understood as contextual, situational, and circumstantial. It is not that diagnosed persons are less able to restrain themselves, but that behaviors such as "interrupting," not "awaiting one's turn," or "blurting out" are conditioned.

Both diagnostic and more polite responses may be immediately reinforced by what transpires afterwards; that is, blurting and interfering will occur not because of the failure to do antecedents, but because those actions have been reinforced by what followed in particular milieus. Persons who "await their turn" and seldom vocalize in unacceptable ways are not necessarily inhibiting and then enacting the behaviors called "executive functioning" more than individuals who interrupt and blurt. Non-diagnostic responses are also cued by particular *conditions* rather than the presence or absence of precursor mental/ neurological antecedents.

Although if it is true that we have precursor mental/neurological antecedents, diagnosed individuals may nevertheless also be shaped towards socially preferred patterns (as with intellectually competent persons) simply by changing the sequencing of situations and circumstances they encounter over time. However, the onus rests on parents to decide whether or not to use medication, as well as consider the problems and advantages associated with using our alternative learning intervention. Parents must live with the consequences of the decisions they make on their children's behalf.

Consequences of problem behaviors and exploitation will, over the long run, range from very overt and extreme (e.g., lost wages for having to leave work, removal from mainstream classes, etc.) to the subtle (e.g., not closing the back door, leaving food out to spoil, neglecting to pick up hazardous small objects). It seems unfair to try to convince parents to adopt an intervention that generally takes longer to be effective. Moreover, we acknowledge that coercive urging will not necessarily result in follow-through when the parent leaves the therapist's office, no matter how compelling the presentation may have been.

For the above reasons, traditional methods are enticing for many parents who seek help for their ADHD diagnosed children. Justified as purportedly the only scientifically-proven method of treating ADHD behaviors, the traditional approach is often seen by parents as the *only* reasonable choice. Given these attitudes about the traditional approach, advocates of the self-reliant /collaborative model can help parents reach the goals they deem important, and inform them about problems and complications attending to forced compliance discipline and medication. Therapists can also help parents conduct a benefit/risk analysis pertaining to which behaviors are worthwhile to coerce, and what side effects correlate with which solutions. It is difficult to extinguish ADHD patterns after many years of living with patterns of troublesome behaviors, but perhaps an intervention that fosters self-reliance and collaborative interacting will yield treatment benefits for many diagnosed families.

Chapter 6

A Comparison of Interventions

The learning approach recommends that child and loved ones start to recognize event sequences that reinforce ADHD behaviors. Commands and coercion may be less effective in helping diagnosed children learn about the consequences of their actions when compared to a self-reliant/collaborative intervention. Adults and family members are advised to role-model courtesy, mutual respect, and compromise, and also help facilitate self-reliance within ADHD diagnosed children. By so doing, they will be less conditioned to outmaneuver, sneak, retaliate, lie, and suffer silently about unresolved problems.

The failure to address conflict can have a negative influence on future social patterning similar to when people go to bed with nagging problems on their mind, which results in disruptive dreams. Even if conflict does not become overt and the child concedes, there is no definitive evidence showing that traditional discipline has helped diagnosed children learn valuable social skills, such as caring for others, kindness, and altruism. The use of compliance thus far empirically demonstrated is touted as a short-term success, but we doubt the efficacy of traditional remedies over the long term, especially with regard to the aim of shaping values of self-reliance, dignity, and civility.

The problem of contingency management seems particularly evident, for example, when a manager responds negatively in response to the child's failure to please. When this happens, the interaction centers on the child's failure to carry out the manager's instructions. Rather than focus on what has reinforced the diagnosed person to respond in a particular way, and help the diagnosed person and loved ones coordinate in mutually-advantageous ways, a negative response fills the gap.

The intervention model proposed here attempts to avoid such problems. Parents of course must delineate limits to facilitate protection, as well as develop mutually-reinforcing social patterns rather than use their authority to establish dominance. Rather than risk having the child react to the parental initiative to protect as a sign of mistrust or presumption of incompetence, it is important to help the child distinguish between caring and suspecting something negative. Parents are encouraged first to ascertain whether the child is already aware of certain risks, and then talk calmly and non-critically when figuring out how to protect him so that he will not act defensively about "being treated like a baby." We claim that ADHD behaviors can be effectively extinguished by transforming situations and circumstances into cooperative ventures whenever and wherever possible. Diagnosed persons can be shaped to participate as well as become less capricious and irksome. To implement this new conditioning, parents are advised to address and resolve adversity as it arises.

In a related matter, Locke and Latham (2002, 708) report that "leaders can raise the self-efficacy of their subordinates . . ." by "ensuring adequate training to increase mastery that provides success experiences." Leaders can role-model desired behaviors, and practice "persuasive communication that expresses confidence that the person can obtain the goal." Our alternative is designed to implement such patterns of management. As long as the new behaviors continue to be reinforced by success, they will repeat even without extra contingency management and other coercions recommended by traditionalists.

Despite that a diagnosed person's actions are not considered to be advantageous within traditional view, after deriving a reinforcement history for that individual, we recognize that both diagnostic and non-diagnostic responses can be understood as being influenced by environment. We recognize that intermittent schedules of reinforcement can be vigorous, as some event sequences may continue to reinforce particular behaviors even if not all the events transpiring in relation to the behaviors are positive (e.g., gambling, studying, not exercising).

Lack of punctuality in response to schedules and limits within the family is a good example of how event sequences reinforce behavior, as the individual no longer has to wait for others, and others will often accommodate despite complaints and resentment. It is in this sense that ADHD patterning can correlate with significant social problems, but still not be extinguished. Similarly, procrastination can lower grades, but procrastination also keeps discomfort at bay, intensifies the excitement of work completion, and mobilizes others in substantial ways as a deadline approaches. As with most behaviors, there are pros and cons related to those actions.

Since ADHD behaviors have typically been reinforced over long periods of time, it is often the case that persons patterning thusly continue "protracted responding" even when attempts at extinction are being made (Skinner, 1953, 70). Many conditioned behavioral acts might appear to be unrelated to the consequences of living in the world, and yet be highly related to learning that has occurred long before observations were initiated.

According to Skinner (1953, 69), "operant extinction takes place much more slowly than operant conditioning," and many behaviors may be maintained insidiously by various schedules of reinforcement. Since behavioral extinction is often difficult to achieve until we gain the necessary experience to differentiate particular conditions and suitable responses, it is not surprising that effective psychological intervention has been difficult to accomplish. For example, some people will learn to eat only when hungry; many others when quite young will also learn to eat as a way to reward themselves or to relax; they may also eat when angry, sad, avoidant, anxious, bored, and so on. Repetition of these behaviors often has the extreme consequence of obesity, although the eating behaviors themselves resist extinction.

In the same way, diagnosed individuals continue to be reinforced when doing ADHD despite their recognition that the entire family is unhappy. We observe that children are brought to therapy by loved ones when school difficulties arise, and/or when increasing disruption within the family makes life with the diagnosed person less tolerable. Barkley (2000) also emphasizes that a large percentage of adults come to therapy because of a spousal and/or employer complaint.

Traditionalists think that diagnosed persons lack the adequate neurological ability to recognize the necessity for change, but when they plead ignorance of the problem (true or not), or an "inability to stop," diagnosed persons evade the injunctions of others to change, and it becomes difficult for others to blame them as well. In this regard, many diagnosed adults will under-report symptoms, thus further impeding the pressure to change.

Similarly, many diagnosed individuals (especially teens) resist the demand to take medication, even if it initially helps them meet standards of behavior. While a number of peers might be keen to buy stimulants, diagnosed teens respond to the requirement to medicate as a method of suppression or control (Robin, 2006). In this type of situation it is also not surprising that problematic behaviors coincide with the elimination of the medication, as the teen's decision to stop medication already indicates that the teen is averse to the expectations of others.

However, it is also the case that many people refuse to admit wrongdoings, and many of us will remain reinforced to behave in ways that others find intolerable. Before accepting the premise that ADHD responding is not retractable due to biological delay, we must incorporate the influence of social training. People can learn to repeat avoidance behaviors: to procrastinate, rush, incite, intrude, and/or give up when encountering adversity (i.e., "You can't fire me, I quit!").

To counteract negative learning, parents can demonstrate non-diagnostic patterns while interacting with the entire family. As emphasized earlier, the technique of acting as role-model will give diagnosed children regular opportunities to learn acceptable ways to coordinate action and resolve conflicts of interest. As parents reliably follow through with their statements, as they determinedly stop the child's exploitative behaviors, and when they consistently integrate the child's perspective into social patterning, greater receptiveness to differing perspectives will develop. The new conditioning increases coordination with others over time, in that less disappointment will occur.

Diagnosed persons change as loved ones alter their own actions because it is easier to change one's own behavior than force others to behave in particular ways. Compared with the traditional approach, which highlights pressuring diagnosed persons to do particular behaviors, our approach changes ADHD patterning by altering how others respond to the diagnosed individual. Caregivers learn ways to react differently so that unwanted behaviors are not reinforced; solutions are formulated so that family members are not exploited regardless of whether or not the child changes. A parent can, for example, assert a firm, yet guiding hand by saying "I'll be glad to work with you as long as it is before supper."

However, unbeknownst to parents is that in many instances their behavior actually exacerbates diagnostic responding. Sometimes even a slight facial reaction or eye contact may be all that is necessary to condition a response. At other times more explicit reinforcements—including excessive parental guilt after mishandling a situation, or when accommodating after diagnostic responding—will prevent non-diagnostic actions and reactions from developing.

Moreover, parental response patterns that reinforce diagnostic responding may have been occurring prior to the child's birth, and then reignited with intensity afterwards. There are numerous personal background scenarios; some parents have difficulty with assertiveness, and have experienced great anxiety when not able to please others (including birth parents). Others have had problems handling anger and over reactions directed at them. Some become excessively anxious in response to risk and danger; and others overreact to disapproval or innuendo suggesting that they are bad parents. Some parents have had a long history of disappointment establishing intimacy, and therefore, currently employ avoidance behaviors. However, others will show the opposite pattern and worry overly about separation and thus inadvertently encourage dependency. Diverse patterns of response can heighten the probability of reinforcing ADHD rather than help extinguish the behaviors, and particular interactive patterns can, for numerous reasons, develop with one child rather than another.

ADHD behaviors, for example, have a greater probability of being reinforced when parents withdraw from the child, are excessively preoccupied or troubled for long periods of time, or when another adult or child in the home role-models those behaviors. A high probability also exists that diagnostic patterning will be reinforced when parents are at first indulgent with the child and then cease to do those behaviors. ADHD responses can increase in frequency when a parent feels overwhelmed by responsibility, when over-compensating the child for a perceived deprivation, or when there is constant discontentment with other family members (including the child's grandparent) for either their interference or aloofness. ADHD can also be reinforced if a parent becomes critical when the child fails to show appreciation, and then becomes over accommodating after having been too harsh.

Traditionalists emphasize that no one has yet found parenting characteristics that account for significant numbers of children qualifying for diagnostic criteria, but within the learning model only certain interactional patterns will reinforce diagnostic responding. Traits ascribable to the parent will not cause an ADHD diagnosis, and since diverse interactional patterns increase the occurrence of those behaviors, it is not surprising that one pattern will not account for the majority of cases.

As we have discussed above, patterns of reinforcement will be subtle and require keen observation. For example, on some occasions a parent might smile when the child behaves diagnostically, establish physical contact, or pick up after the child when exhibiting a lack of responsibility or immaturity; but in other instances, the parent will blame excessively and express frustration when the child repeats the exact behaviors. Sometimes asking the child "Did you hear me?" will reinforce the child to have an ADHD justification for non-compliance. Traditionalists would declare that all these patterns are "consequences" of living with an ADHD-inflicted child, but we argue that particular interactive patterns may well increase the probability that various ADHD actions will be reinforced and repeated. Moreover, when ADHD patterning is conditioned inconsistently, and when the child is placed on an intermittent schedule of reinforcement, it is very likely that the behaviors will be even more resistant to extinction.

Ameliorating ADHD in a less dominating manner

Traditionalists argue that loved ones simply react to the difficult behaviors of diagnosed persons, but the alternative explication presumes that child and environmental characteristics determine the pattern of "symptoms." ADHD behaviors do not originate within the diagnosed person or emanate from loved ones; they manifest through interactions over the long-term in various contexts. Limited attention span with toys and other objects, intense and demanding early response patterns, and/or numerous health problems and functional delays need not eventuate into an ADHD diagnosis, but probabilities are increased.

As difficult as it is to change diagnosed children, it can be equally difficult to change the behavior of the adults responsible for training these individuals. Parents will have to learn how to redirect the child by nonchalantly changing the subject so that ADHD behaviors are no longer reinforced. They will often have to stop reacting critically and intensely, while simultaneously learning to shape achievement, politeness, and consideration for others by *noticing* when the child is obliging, conciliatory, and proficient. Sometimes no response is best, specifically when diagnostic responses do not present an imminent risk to self or others, and thus may effectively extinguish because others are not noticing. Parents can learn to stay calm when antagonized, like water off a duck's back.

In a related matter, parents are puzzled about why diagnosed children (who receive reasonable amounts of attention) compound the behavior that multiplies the attention they receive. Traditional practitioners hold that these children are less able to stop, or have less awareness of negative outcomes at the point of performance, but in our view, these children are conditioned to do ADHD in certain situations and circumstances irrespective of the amount of attention they receive.

Overreactions, reconciliations, and other interaction patterns occurring after diagnostic responding can increase rather than decrease the frequency rates of ADHD behaviors. For example, diagnosed children can indicate that they "hate" the parent, or that the parent "hurt their feelings" when parents have expressed aggravation about the child's impulsive misdeeds. Parents might then attempt reparation in order to make amends. By so doing, the social sequence can increase the repetition of the patterning. Similarly, after being chided, children remark in self-deprecating ways, which leads the parent towards conciliation and compliments (e.g., "you are not a terrible child"). Given that these exchanges occur so often, we observe that ADHD behaviors effectively increase parental accommodation and can reassure the child that he or she is valued by the parent.

If parent metaphorically "takes the bait" and reacts intensely to the child's provocation, we suspect that diagnostic responding will be conditioned. Often children are compensated for having been victimized by less positive parents who feel indebted to the child and are attempting to compensate. The incident might have been instigated by the child, but the interaction ends with the parent apologizing or appeasing for their inappropriate behavior, which leads to an outpouring of emotion resulting in parental guilt and placation.

If we compare the diagnosed child and parent to a domestic violence pattern, we observe the initial incitement and follow-up reconciliation. When these event sequences take place, contact with the child is prolonged and family members treat each other kindly and positively after the turmoil. Lingering problems can finally be discussed after the volatile episode has occurred.

Sometimes diagnosed children look at parents while simultaneously enacting an unappreciated behavior, knowing full well that they will inflame the parent and possibly receive punishment. The parental response seems to reinforce the behavior more than the punishment, especially when the child behaves explicitly vindictively (i.e., you upset me so I will upset you). Conflicts that ensue in which the child insists that he or she will "be good," or pleads with the parent to reverse the punishment, can also lead to reinforcement. In many instances if the parent rescinds the negative consequence, this further reassures the child that the parent cares enough to relieve suffering.

Various (annoying) tests of limits are reinforced in numerous ways. Antagonizing is reinforced when the child gains relief by displacing and releasing frustrations. Sometimes the other parent enters the scene to protect the child from the parent who overreacts. The recurring triangulation scenario reinforces the child to continue the diagnostic responding and hence will repeat the pattern with teachers at school. The behaviors consistent with ADHD are here associated with the notion of rescue, and thus reassure the child about his or her importance to the parent.

In other instances "pushing buttons" tests the tolerance of others and helps the child measure his or her acceptability (i.e., does this person *really* like me?). Diagnostic patterning also permits the child to reject others *first*, in that the child presumes that he or she is unwanted. Occasionally, conflicts are instigated as a way to avoid assigned work, as the child obtains justification to leave when the parent begins responding negatively to provocation.

Moreover, if the child is angry with the parent, those frustrated parental responses reinforce the diagnostic actions, as the child's provocations and intrusiveness are very effective ways to retaliate and disrupt the parent, much like the feuding between countries. The child may be reprimanded, but the adult is punished as well.

However, after heaping intense disapproval and coercion onto the child, do we really think that she will become more conciliatory when we ask her to respond in acceptable ways? Might she instead copy the behavior of an aggravated and intolerant role-model, since that is how others around her have frequently responded? For all of these reasons, we doubt the utility of negative discipline.

In our view, diagnostic behaviors, including impulsivity, are conditioned to occur if they effectively counteract limits, confinement, deprivation, and exclusion even if this means violating the personal space of others and creating a stir. Those behaviors can also alleviate discomfort and prevent others from denying access to resources (i.e., I will do it before they stop me). If waiting and conforming frequently result in missing out, then rapid inconsiderate behavior can be reinforced. Moreover, if the adult frequently interrupts the busy child, teases or provokes the child (even in jest), or seldom follows through with promises, it is not surprising that the child will *also* imitate those behavioral patterns. By and large, given the usual sequencing of events, how out-of-control is the child who expresses this patterning? We claim conversely, that the child is *taking* control or establishing discretionary authority rather than losing control during diagnostic responding.

Negative parental responses also reinforce inattentive symptoms, in that the child can effectively escape from the negativity when doing those behaviors. Since it is usually the case that a child is reprimanded numerous times for the same thing, we suspect that they are acutely aware that their behavior is unacceptable. When parents repeatedly admonish or lecture, the outcome of such parental interventions can unfortunately merely reinforce the child's distractibility, even if the child succumbs when the parent escalates.

It is within this context that one asks if sufficient positive attention is being given to the child or whether sufficient time is being spent on discovering collaborative solutions to recurring conflicts of interest. To what extent is the child participating in figuring out acceptable alternatives, and how do parents shape less diagnostic responding by changing their own reactions to those behaviors? It will be necessary to systematically address these concerns before diagnosed children can become less reinforced to impose on others or escape altogether.

When applying the learning strategy to commonly occurring problems such as handling and sharing money, rather than attempt to coerce the child to handle money in a manner that the parent finds most reasonable, a different approach might be tried. Instead of giving the child a specified sum of money for the completion of a particular chore, the parent can give the child "family money" to use at his or her own discretion apart from any particular helpful act (i.e., free money). This approach might diminish the potential effect that the child will be less likely to willingly help the family when a payment is not on offer. There is a shift away from inducing behaviors with contingency management.

Parents might also emphasize that family members all help to operate the household, assist each other in alleviating hardships, and that lack of contribution is not appreciated or acceptable for any family member. If the diagnosed child continues to balk, perhaps other problems in the relationship are impeding caring behaviors. However, as a last resort, the parent can always reduce the allotment given to the child, and justify that action by informing that "family money" is needed to hire someone or compensate another family member who must overextend due to the child's non-participation.

It might also be necessary in some instances to charge the child a fee when having to rectify uncaring actions that cost the family money, such as when the child destroys property. The parent may say, "We need your free money to help pay for the damage." However, if the parent can discover how to persuade the child to willingly reimburse the family, fewer adverse side effects will occur, and there is a greater likelihood that the child will not repeat the unwanted behavior in the future.

Parent might also point out that damaging family property reduces family assets, and all family members are likely to be affected by that outcome. These more benign responses may prove to be less disruptive to family relationships in the long-run, and may outperform coercive strategies, as they are more diplomatic than "iron fisted." From this perspective, the child learns to be less caustic and tyrannical, even when the family does not utilize coercive tactics to offset the tirades.

If parents revert quickly to negative solutions, there is a high risk that more harm than good will result from such disciplinary measures, in that negative coercive solutions sometimes yield unwanted side effects such as resentment, sulking, and revenge. Parents can benefit from identifying what might be reinforcing the child to not contribute or to react acerbically. A resolution of those problems leads to better results than withholding allowance and coercing reimbursements.

More often than not, the child's lack of helpfulness and other unappreciated behaviors signal that other unresolved problems are reinforcing the child to behave accordingly. For example, some children carelessly break household objects when angry with a parent who apparently cares more about material objects than spending time together with the child. Some children mimic parents who frequently take their belongings away when punishing. In other families, the child is so over-indulged that little reason exists for the child to safeguard possessions, or do even a modicum of work to please others. In other instances children will not help because they anticipate that the parent will be displeased by their efforts.

Some will contest that learning approach recommendations do not sufficiently teach the child the value of money, in that the child receives money without explicitly earning it. However, our emphasis is on conditioning diagnosed children to assist in the management of the family. In a global fashion children earn their keep, and are likely to learn the benefits of everyone's participation without counting each and every obliging deed. Tasks are identified as ways to assist the family in a wide-ranging fashion. Children are urged to take a leading role in helping the family operate effectively, and their contributions to family functioning are extolled.

Whereas traditionalists advocate that parents count out loud to a certain number in order to achieve the participation mentioned above, and then threaten the child for non-compliance, we do not endorse such an approach. Although counting initially produces an acceptable effect, it is also probable that the child will learn to wait until the final number, or learn to not respond until others threaten. If procrastination is already an entrenched problem, it may be disingenuous to implement a training strategy that reinforces those reactions.

Given our concerns, we instead orient to increase acceptable age-consistent responding by helping diagnosed persons obtain incremental successes autonomously, and by collaboratively helping them resolve obstacles related to meeting family and socio-cultural standards. Parents are urged to provide the rationale for their instructions and limits so that the child can understand the associated benefits or reasons for particular actions. Provision of this information helps the child accept instruction as well as learn about managing the future.

For example, if a child returns home from school with a report indicating he called out instead of raised his hand, talked excessively, grabbed a pencil from another student, or ran down the hall loudly on the way to recess, we recommend a collaborative exchange to resolve the problems. Traditionalists advocate imposing a managed consequence such as no television, but we recommend solving the problem conjointly.

After discovering what has happened, parents can encourage the child to talk (with them) about events at school. If he has been conditioned to be less apprehensive about managed consequences, we anticipate that he might share more information about the day's events rather than "plead the 5th amendment." If parent has consistently deigned to be helpful rather than punitive, including withholding possible extra rewards, he will be reinforced to consult with (rather than avoid) parent. The intervention is designed to reduce the child's concerns about retribution, and focus on solving a problem in an acceptable way to both himself and his parent.

Most importantly, he must not characterize the parent as enemy, judge or jury. Our aim is that the child sees the parent as facilitator who offers counsel and helps him towards independent thinking when problems appear. But this does not mean that parents remove negative consequences in relation to inappropriate social actions (i.e., the school can still take away the child's recess). Parents are merely not adding to consequences already in place. Intervention is meant to help the child be reinforced to succeed at school, irrespective of parental involvement.

Instead of seeing pencil-grabbing as a disinhibited act, a parent asks what has led to the transgression, which will certainly include investigating the child's ongoing relationship with his classmate. There is also a discussion about what the child imagines would happen after the event, such as possible revenge, or provocation of a seemingly non-empathic teacher. The parent asks the child if he would like to obtain different kinds of results, and when necessary, encourages the exploration of solutions that would enhance his best interests in school and when handling relational problems with peers and teachers. We anticipate that he will learn socially acceptable ways of dealing with peer and teacher conflicts by addressing problem solving in this manner. A non-threatening approach allows diagnosed children to be reinforced to discuss problems with loved ones, obtain beneficial guidance, and learn how to deal with similar situations in the future.

Perhaps these explorative discussions will also help participants understand so-called under-controlled or impulsive behaviors differently. For example, both the parent and the child will gain awareness that the "overreactive" and "thoughtless" pencil-grabbing during class was retaliation to being teased. Diagnosed children are not significantly different from the rest of us in this regard; many of us overreact and seek retribution when problem situations, such as bullying, repeat time and time again.

We may also observe that the child's relationship with a teacher is problematic, and when we delve into the issue, we discover that simple values are being undermined during some of their interactions. In our case here, for example, the child is angry and embarrassed about being criticized in front of his entire class, and that social history is influencing the frequency rates of his rule breaking. As a way to help, his parents can encourage him to voice his concerns assertively and calmly with the teacher instead of exaggerating his discontentment out in the hallway. The manifestation of negative feelings in physical form gradually evolves into an improved ability to verbally protect himself.

Similarly, if he is worried about being excluded or stifled by others, we can help him identify substitute responses that thwart the behavioral pattern of going to extremes and creating alienation. By intervening thusly, the child learns alternative ways of handling social difficulties. Importantly, the solution that eventually reduces the frequency of diagnostic responses will have little to do with whether the child pauses and does non-vocal verbal responding about future distant penalties associated with obstreperous behavior prior to an action (the traditional model).

Drawbacks to traditional child management recommendations

It is alleged that, because of their neurological delays, diagnosed persons need some kind of punishment in addition to rewards in order for them to be effectively socialized. Anastopoulos, Rhoads, and Farley (2006) claim that ignoring strategies and the giving of positive attention will often not be adequate to effectively manage diagnosed children. The now common assertion is that these children will more typically require tangible rewards, as well as the utilization of "response-cost" and "time out strategies" for misbehavior.

However, and unfortunately, if the social matrix is employing contingency management, diagnosed children may also learn to imitate coercive contingency management strategies during dealings with others. Bribery and manipulation of parents are commonplace behaviors among diagnosed children who receive traditional training; they, for example, may show reluctance to please unless an explicit payment is in the offing. In some instances children raise the price to induce parent to make additional payments (i.e., I will only comply if you pay me more), and these children can also learn to withhold what the parent enjoys in order to increase parental compliance with their own demands. This coincides with their role-model experiences: this is how their parents have behaved.

Coercive management socialization methods instigate other behaviors as well. A reluctance to inform those in charge that they enjoy an activity (secrecy) can avoid the problem of others taking that activity away when dissatisfaction arises. The failure to consider input from the child also creates resistance, in that conformity becomes equivalent to losing face or admitting inadequacy; the child concludes that others direct his actions because they think him to be incompetent. Moreover, by behaving in ways that others criticize, diagnosed persons may effectively control the occurrence of their parent's negative responses, even though the child is only gaining a false sense of dominance with this kind of patterning. Rather than conform, which would encourage the parent to repeat the coercive tactic, the child learns to resist.

While traditionalists might claim that diagnosed persons require contingency management to counter their delays, we suggest another interpretation—that giving rewards and punishments as the primary and preferred way to socialize diagnosed children can amplify unacceptable behaviors. For example, many diagnosed children will exacerbate problems by seeking revenge against those who have wronged them (i.e., you have made me suffer, so I will make you suffer). Like most ADHD responding, the child enters into a vicious cycle that worsens situations over time.

Traditionalists have always been adamant that more coercive interventions are essential with diagnosed persons, but it does not seem as if the possible side effects of those strategies have been adequately studied and identified. This issue is highlighted by Barkley who advised parents to use a procedure incorporating mild spanking as another type of secondary form of discipline as late as 1987 (Barkley and Edwards, 1998). One might ask why this approach, although no longer recommended, was part of an intervention program in 1987, given the well-known concerns about role-modeling aggressiveness during socializing (Weiss et al., 1992).

Kvols (1998) has apparently adopted a similar critical view of contingency management discipline when she claims that bribing individuals may risk increasing a "what's in it for me," or "what are you going to give me" attitude. Since behaviors pertaining to "what we can do for each other" are already infrequent for diagnosed persons, the traditional approach merely seems to exacerbate (or increase) the frequency rates of behaviors that are most important to *extinguish* within this diagnostic group.

Additionally, persons who are intimidated by authority not only learn clandestine tactics, but they may also refuse offers of assistance. Such reactions help them to avoid the difficulty of having to owe others and become more obligated to submit. Children will learn to spend less time with their parents, as that solution protects them from having their actions stifled and evaluated. This dynamic reduces the parent's opportunity to influence the child even more over the long term.

Overly stringent management of the child can also compel him to learn more sophisticated ways to outsmart attempts at being controlled. An illustration of this problem is the diagnosed child who learns to outfox his behavioral charts, despite a purported less ability to deal with the future. When this occurs parents are urged to continuously close "loopholes" in order to maintain coercive solutions.

Within the traditional scheme the presence of competition allows participants to learn countertactics in order to prevent others from dominating. Actions are taken only to the extent that they increase the frequency rates of obtaining a reward or prevent the removal of resources. The manager responds positively to the increased compliance, but we observe that other behaviors that reduce the manager's discretionary authority are simultaneously being conditioned. Moreover, there might be numerous occasions when individuals are reinforced to suffer (at times) negative extreme consequences (e.g., school failure) rather than permit others to maintain complete discretionary authority.

All too often socialization under a contingency scheme is more adversarial, and more like a "cat-and-mouse game" rather than a cooperative endeavor. Concealment is often maintained so that wrongdoing will not be discovered, and fearfulness and neuroticism may increase as well (Masserman, 1943). There is less discussion about preferences so that others cannot use that information against the managed party. In other situations, non-participation and disinterest allow the child to deflect disappointment, in that failure can be avoided, and pleasurable activities cannot be yanked away if the individual stays disengaged. Individuals may also have more difficulty enjoying activities when they have been coerced to partake.

Spite or self-deprivation also increase, as such responses prohibit others from dominating. Because the diagnosed child's achievement and wellbeing are essential to the contingency manager, resisting the manager's instruction is a very powerful weapon. These responses may occur in relation to any activity the diagnosed person reports enjoying (e.g., television, driving the family car, and playing video games). Giving up those pleasures can be more beneficial than allowing others to "pull their strings" or "buy them off."

Overall, when a system of managed rewards and punishments is introduced, individuals learn certain behaviors in relation to payments and penalties determined by the managing parties. Since discretionary authority is not shared, the manager invokes suffering or pleasure depending on whether or not the diagnosed person conforms. The weaker person learns various behaviors in order to contend with the unbalanced power arrangement. The outcome is often that relationships become more competitive (and negative), in that failure to please the manager results in a disagreeable outcome for the weaker individual.

Moreover, in Kohlberg's (1969) conceptualization of moral development, an act of kindness without remuneration is considered to be a "higher level" of functioning than an act performed for personal gain. If we want to (eventually) shape this kind of moral behavior for diagnosed individuals, we must ask ourselves if contingency management is the most effective method, since it focuses the child on egocentric concerns rather than altruism.

Traditionalists declare that problems correlated with coercive management can be adequately solved by fine-tuning the design of the contingency management systems, but we have observed that many people stop using those systems after a period of time, since successful outcomes are difficult to achieve through coercive means. Coercion has generally helped to induce compliance in the short term, made training consistent, and has excited children about receiving extras, but problems inevitably arise as soon as punishment or withholding takes place. Children often become disenchanted when they recognize that their parents still control their access to goods and services, and that they must continue to function as a subordinate with very little discretionary authority.

Moreover, even when parents escalate coercions, they do not necessarily gain compliance, and sometimes they suffer even more than the child when enforcing punishment. Some parents report that rather than sit in the "time out" chair, their child runs away. They comment too, that it is difficult to prevent a grounded child from escaping from the house. Others have recognized that their child steals withheld rewards. Traditionalists argue that, ultimately, the parent can "win out" by establishing ascendancy, but we are concerned that the child will also learn how to counter those efforts. Many parents report that it is as difficult to contain an older diagnosed child (particularly an adolescent) as it is to elicit cooperative behavior.

Compounding matters still further, traditional methods that isolate children can potentially condition an association between being alone and being unacceptable. Such associations might undermine the ability for these individuals to enjoy their own company, or tolerate intervals when others are unavailable. For any child, but especially diagnosed children, the side effect of increasing insecurity is not inconsequential.

Prescribed isolation can also have the effect that the child keeps unsolved problems to himself, thus further impeding him from discussing troubles with others. This is not a trivial matter if we presume that many relationships evaporate over the long term due to an unwillingness to address problems when they arise. Moreover, we are concerned that forcing a child to sit in a chair for a predetermined period of time might only further reinforce the behavior of "squirming" in one's seat (to escape), which is an ADHD sign or symptom, in that chair-sitting becomes associated with discomfort and restriction.

Restricted individuals may also tend to "take a mile" as soon as they are "given an inch," simply to counteract the ongoing deprivation and attempts to block particular behaviors. Rather than reduce diagnostic responding over the long-term, there is an increased probability that traditional coercive and confining strategies inadvertently aggravate many different unwanted (impulsive) response patterns evident in this group.

Given these concerns, the learning model intervention avoids such strategies such as "time out," even though we recognize that sometimes it can help defuse an escalating conflict. However, this recommendation largely contrasts with advice from Anastopoulos, Smith, and Wien (1998), who state that the child's chronological age in years should determine the minimum time in minutes of "time out." Interestingly, traditionalists seem to recognize that "time out" does not always produce the desired results (especially in classroom settings), because in reality, some students might want to avoid work or want to be left alone (Pfiffner and Barkley, 1998).

We regard "time out" as generally disruptive rather than helpful, even if the child capitulates. The intervention can result in children merely learning that powerful people get their way, and that it is acceptable to force others to relent through constraint when conflicts of interest arise. We doubt that the diagnosed person's isolation from others will help solve interpersonal problems effectively when compliance is gained through this dominating tactic.

Rather than use "time out" merely as punishment, advocates of collaborative forms of child rearing have reassessed this procedure in order to distinguish it from its punitive use. In the alternative vernacular, "time out" interventions become "self quieting times" (Kvols, 1998), or "cooling off periods" (Nelsen, 1987). When implemented in this way, children are encouraged to disengage until they are willing to interact collaboratively with the parent. The time apart is utilized to "calm down," and "think about alternatives." Reengagement is initiated by either parent or child when it becomes likely that compromise, negotiation, and mutually acceptable exchanges can occur.

The separation is neither an imposed fixed sentence nor is it meant to elicit submission; it is a method to increase discussion rather than recriminations, withdrawal, and isolation. When this procedure works well, individuals learn how to initiate this solution rather than have it imposed upon them. Gradually it becomes less necessary for parent to coax child to do "self-quieting."

There will be occasions, particularly in public places such as classrooms, church, and Boy Scouts, when an adult will have to discretely escort the child into a "self quieting" place in order to protect others from disruptive behaviors, but the procedure neither simulates incarceration nor embarrasses the child. Parents might initiate "calming down" by retreating to a quiet place first; this can effectively solve the problem, even if the child continues negative behavior. If the child attempts to follow and harangue, it may also be necessary for the parent to find a place that prevents the child from intruding. Over numerous trials, we anticipate that the child will imitate the parent and initiate "calming down" rather than merely react in unproductive and angry ways.

Additional problems and concerns when comparing methods

Let us keep in mind that diagnosed persons are conditioning *us* to behave in particular ways as much as we think we are conditioning *them*. If we stop embellishing, simplifying, and reducing expectations, they quickly return to doing ADHD, since that response results in the reestablishment of compensation, enticements, and greater parental vigilance. The child responds to the decrease in management and hovering as a reduction in social importance, or as an attempt to impose extra work.

When considering that sequence of events, ADHD patterns continue to be reinforced, in that behaving thusly often leads to receiving an influx of concern and compensation from outside sources. The ADHD behavior reverts once again to having fewer imposed requirements to be personally responsible, and the diagnosed person can monopolize family and school resources. Because traditionalists are increasingly concerned that some people endorse symptoms in order to obtain social benefits, these effects are a problem that biological determinists also recognize.

However, traditionalists continue to emphatically state that only medication and stringency are strong enough to manage the "disinhibited" diagnosed person, who is too neurologically delayed to work for long-term goals or sustain mutual coordination with others over broad time frames. They would also assert that diagnosed persons are least able to share, concur, understand the perspectives of others, remain patient long enough to effectively negotiate solutions, or enact mutually-acceptable patterns without external prompting. They would remind us that when it is time to perform those collaborations and self-reliant acts, their ADHD will interfere.

Instead of accepting the disability framework, we believe that in the case of intellectually competent diagnosed persons, their failures can be attributed to insufficient conditioning. Old disciplinary patterns can return very easily, and parents can quickly revert when problems thicken. We observe this sometimes even before the parents leave the therapist's office, when for example, a parent remarks, "say thank you" and "get your coat," which invariably continue the entrenched diagnostic patterns.

The learning approach is therefore unlikely to obtain results as quickly as coercion, but the all-important question is whether long-term outcomes might improve compared to what we see in longitudinal research when treating ADHD using contingency management. Some traditionalists allow for more collaboration during adolescence, but we recommend starting to socialize diagnosed children at a much earlier age, because empirical evidence shows that early learning is influential in later development, in both a biological and psychological sense. For example, the degree of hyperactivity one has in very early childhood will predict whether the behaviors will continue into adolescence (Campbell and Ewing, 1990), so stopping the patterning early would be preferable.

Even when encountering initial difficulties, parents are encouraged to continue collaborative problem solving with younger age groups. For example, when Plan A fails, conjointly figure out a Plan B, help the child learn about the benefits of working together to solve problems, and listen carefully when the child voices objections to proposed solutions. Parents might say, "If we tell each other what we want, we can make better arrangements." As pointed out by Greene (2001; 2005), parents must continuously decide whether it is more efficacious to ignore a problem, coerce the child, or work out a more mutually-satisfactory blending of concerns in various problem situations.

If safe resolutions cannot be found, coercion may be the only feasible way to reduce danger in some situations. Parents can explicitly tell the child, "We are stopping you because we like you." However, since the child might find a way to sneak or do some other dangerous behavior in response to these impositions, coercion is usually not productive over the long term. The child is not likely to be reinforced to implement safety policy without constant overseeing by adults if he continues to object.

We recognize that a child's negative responses are important to resolve when the child is calm and there is ample opportunity to discuss the child's concerns, and that it is reasonable at times for a parent to take assertive unilateral action to protect the child. Barkley (2000) points to research indicating that the *way* a command is given may account for over one-third of the variance in whether compliance occurs, but from the learning perspective, that result is less important than determining the extent to which self-reliance and cooperation are elicited from the parental initiative.

In this regard, Nelsen (1987) discusses the problem of understanding a child's goal when non-cooperative functioning is occurring. In her four category system, the child might be orienting for increased attention, operating to establish power, looking to obtain revenge, or presuming incompetence. When using Nelsen's category system, it is advised that interventions explore the possible reasons for the child's failure to interact positively with the parent. Nelsen suggests that, although her work is not directed specifically towards diagnosed individuals, by intervening in a kind and firm manner, it is often possible to obtain a socially acceptable response without resorting to forced compliance solutions or contingency management.

Nelsen (1987, 13) claims that the side effects of punishment may include *resentment*, whenever people interpret policies as unfair. Often these individuals will learn to orient in a distrustful way. Nelsen is also concerned that people are likely to seek *revenge* when disciplined coercively, in that children might learn to "get even" with those who are "winning now." She holds that punitive discipline may also increase instances where the child becomes more *rebellious,* and/or orients to do "just the opposite" to prove that they don't have to behave as others command. In Nelsen's view, *retreat* behaviors also become evident with punishment. She notes that children do more sneaking and clandestine behavior in order to avoid "getting caught the next time." Finally, Nelsen claims that punishment is likely to reduce self-esteem and correlates with the child believing that he or she is a "bad person." As a constructive way to address these reactions, Nelsen offers an alternative approach called *Positive Discipline* and discards the presumption that children must be punished to be adequately socialized.

If Nelsen's framework were to be applied here, the actions of diagnosed individuals can also be accounted for by identifying their goals or concerns, or in the current usage, what is reinforcing those particular responses in particular situations. Rather than approach diagnosed children as if they must be subdued or subjected to a fixed interval of suffering in order to learn, we recommend that parents strive to understand the circumstances that relate to children's failure to coordinate behavior in ways that the parent finds acceptable.

For example, consider when a parent immediately flops in a chair after returning home from work. In this scenario the child is conditioned to behave in a pattern that induces the parent to respond to him or her rather than permits parent to relax, read or watch television. The child's behavior may become rambunctious when parent fails to react. The child's behavior would be characterized by traditionalists as an inability to wait, or the result of being disinhibited, but we suggest that the child's actions frequently sequence with more involvement from the parent. As noted by Nelsen, understanding the child's goal can shed light on behavior that had initially seemed defective or unreasonable. That some children enact these responses more frequently and severely does not establish that the child is less able to behave differently.

If the parent often busies himself with other things when the child is calm and reasonable, the child might be conditioned towards behaviors that incite in order to get parent to be more responsive. Any unhinged reaction by parent conditions the child to repeat the behavior that had resulted in such a prominent effect. While the parent might yell, promise to play later, threaten, and/or bring the child to "time out," if the motive of the action is to increase involvement and fluster the parent, then the parental responses mentioned above will reinforce the provocation. In that sense ADHD behaviors are reinforced by myriad parental responses, including the frequently employed disciplinary measures.

As a way to avoid the above negative scenario, the parent can talk with the child prior to sitting down, depending on the age of the child. Parent and child can discuss the difficulties they are having with current behaviors, and identify alternatives that might be more satisfactory. For instance, the child might find it acceptable to do parallel activity with the parent while the parent takes time to relax and/or open the mail. Parent might indicate that he will be available to play after a specified time interval so that child is assured that the parent will be available. The expectation is that the mutually acceptable pattern will ultimately be more reinforcing than the old disjointed one.

When deciphering the psychology of diagnostic responding, ADHD behaviors seem to be conditioned when parents are frequently harried and hurrying to maintain schedules. In these circumstances parents frequently are impatient and exhausted, and numerous interactions can potentially reinforce the child to do ADHD. Since the parent therefore dictates the pace of activity (e.g., "come on," "hurry up," "slow down"), child will learn behaviors that thwart the parent's attempts to orchestrate (e.g., either speed up or dawdle).

To avoid conflicts that revolve around tight schedules, parents are urged to plan ahead and allocate more time to interact patiently and cooperatively with their children. This approach will, we think, reduce the probability that schedules become associated with discomfort, indenture, and ADHD responding. By encouraging parents to rearrange time, it is probable that they will successfully role-model non-diagnostic behaviors, including effective planning and time management. The parent will also feel satisfied by having an opportunity to allow the child to carry out actions autonomously rather than take over and complete actions for them in order to save time. A good example is to give the child time to tie shoes rather than tie her shoes for her to avoid being late. As with most interventions with children, adequate results often depend on the wise use of parental resources.

In another problematic situation, rather than relate the younger child's failure to maintain a bedtime routine—as well as the overreaction to bedtime limits as concomitant problems of ADHD disinhibition and/or a reduced ability to organize behavior over time—the behaviors are understood as conditioned responses. Such behavior may very well increase the probability that parent will extend the "free time" available before bed. However, the behaviors may also occur in reaction to a parent who has not been adequately available.

Solutions include spending more positive time with child prior to bedtime, as well as giving parents privacy at a certain point in the evening. The child might also video tape a television program instead of staying up late to watch the show, and/or complete school work at an earlier time so that he will have more time to relax during evening hours. The child could also carry out quiet activity in bed until he is ready to fall asleep. Our basic goal is to establish a routine the child will do without parental cue or coercion. Parents can facilitate that outcome by asking the child, "How will you know when it is time to get ready for bed?" and help the child identify cues that occur independently from parental actions.

Another example where it is important for participants to learn how to co-ordinate with less discomfort or submission is when loved ones discuss the importance for the child to inform the parent about her whereabouts. We recognize that the parent does not want to impart a message of mistrust or rigidity by in-voking a "curfew," but that the parent prefers to be informed about her location in order to stay coordinated, and to contact her if an urgent situation should arise. Parents encourage their children to inform them by telephone if plans change rather than convey feelings of anger, control, or inflexibility. Since the parent also informs the child about his or her location, the arrangement resem-bles the "buddy system": a way for family members to protect and care for each other, not to spy. In this approach, the child's mother comments, "Your father often calls me to stay in touch this very way."

Loved ones can also focus on increasing instances of encouragement and appreciation rather than "praise" during social patterning (Nelsen, 1987, 103). Valuing and thanking diagnosed children when they do acceptable acts gives the child affirmation, increases positive rapport, and promotes an internal locus of control, but praising children often runs the risk of communicating to the child the message that only parental expectations matter. This may negate the child and deflect away from the child's self-appraisal and satisfaction with what he or she is doing.

A child might also respond to a "proud" parent as an instance of conditional love, and react as if he is valued only to the extent that compliance with a par-enting standard is being met. He may also worry about failing to maintain the achievement, or that more will be expected in the future. These reactions can increase intimidation rather than encourage the child.

Parents can instead indicate that they are happy *for the child* when he or she is pleased about an achievement. While being proud seems to place greater em-phasis on conformity, being impressed places a greater emphasis on the child's personal accomplishment and elevated status. For example, the impressed parent says, "It was exciting to hear the news about you," "Congratulations," or "I'm glad it worked out so well for you."

Parents are urged to show pleasure when diagnosed children are enjoying their successes, and not focus on how children are meeting particular expecta-tions (i.e., encouragement vs. praise). Responding this way may help keep interactions geared towards how the child's achievements are advantageous to the child. Rather than achieve in order to make others happy (e.g., "be good for the teacher"), children learn to achieve to keep themselves happy and interested. Distinctions between praise and encouragement may seem trite to some, but these intricacies of communication are important when shaping collaborative interacting; subtle changes in communication patterns can be influential over long periods of time.

For instance, instead of holding the child's face to ensure eye contact, collaborative methods utilize the technique of talking kindly and positively in order to increase attentiveness. We presume that inattentiveness is more frequent when children are conditioned such that others will often say what they don't want to hear, or force them to do something they don't like. In the case of collaborative learning the child can eventually make eye contact without having to have his or her face held in a stationary position.

Similarly, instead of immediately grabbing an object when it is misused, or commanding the child to put an object down, whenever feasible the trainer intervenes with a concerned and caring voice. For example, the parent says "Maybe it is better that you play with something else," or kindly ask, "Would you play with that toy more carefully?" Even when it is imperative that the child comply due to imminent danger, the parent imparts a sense of urgency, not as controlling, angry, or critical. It is important in this instance to not allow the child to associate negativity with parental intervention; such associations can decrease responsiveness to feedback (i.e., an ADHD problem) rather than promote efficient and obliging reactions.

When children do mishandle objects, parent can also calmly indicate that continued banging of an object might result in breakage or injury. If the child does not respond acceptably, it is always possible to intervene firmly and remove the object that had been mishandled. However, these assertive actions can be conducted in a relatively benign fashion, and the object can be returned to the child relatively quickly as a gesture to develop trust. The younger child can also be gently guided towards a more acceptable activity as a way to minimize deprivation and sidestep conflict or power struggles. Parents might also allow the child the opportunity to find a suitable alternative activity, courteously ask what else he or she might like to do, or give the child a substitute object.

The response pattern of *not* touching the object is then more likely to recur without parental involvement, since the touching does not lead to a monopolizing drama, and conditioning from the outset is less dependent on parental actions to keep the child away from the object. Respectful behavior towards the child also increases the probability that the child will imitate the same behavior with other people.

A diagnosed child who "tests limits," or engages in other inappropriate behavior, might not require a coercive intervention or punishment for behavioral change to occur. The child will, however, require social training that requires competency, reinforces kindness, reciprocity, perspective taking, and self-reliance. By giving an object back to the child relatively quickly and asking if she would be "willing" to handle the object in an acceptable fashion, the child is treated as a reasonable and honorable person. This parental response of eliciting affirmation from the child will cue non-diagnostic functioning with fewer side effects over the long-term, compared to traditional intervention, even though the diagnosed behaviors may not cease as quickly.

In a similar vein, while it is reasonable to problem solve in order to reduce the recurrence of earlier difficult behaviors, it is certainly counterproductive for a parent to reignite a conflict by instituting reprisal or punishment for transgressions that had occurred hours or days earlier (e.g., "why should we take him to the mall after his behavior this morning!"). These responses only increase the likelihood that diagnosed children will copy the negativity, not forgive the parent's past transgressions, and become livid with the parent for continuing a conflict.

Because the child's discretionary input is essential for the learning intervention, the act of "asking for permission" is also handled differently. Instead of training children to request permission, trainers encourage the child to discuss whether it is reasonable to enact certain behaviors under particular sets of conditions. This strategy encourages the child to initiate a consultation with the parent to assess safety, explore alternatives, and address concerns about inconveniencing others. The interaction is designed to identify potential problems and benefits that can occur in relation to different courses of action. By increasing the frequency of integrated or joint decisions during daily functioning, diagnosed children will likely be reinforced to initiate contact with parents to better coordinate with them and achieve.

The same approach applies when behaviors such as sneaking and lying are observed. In these scenarios we do not presume that that behavior can be properly addressed by introducing punishment. It is unclear how punishment will condition the child to be more truthful, informative or trusting. If the parent also conveys that the child will be punished "double" for lying, the edict merely increases the probability that the child will avoid the parent even more, and perhaps become skilled at lying to avoid the escalating consequences.

Conversely, if clandestine actions and lying correlate with a failure to resolve problems with the help of a parent, it is incumbent on the participants to identify what interferes with truth telling. Lying and other avoidance responses are often cued when parents act suspicious towards the child when inquiring about events. Parents can reduce the frequency of lying simply by adopting a neutral vocal tone when asking the child to report about troublesome happenings.

As noted previously, when deceit is commonplace, it is often the case that other problems exist between parent and child that must first be unraveled. By resolving other problems we anticipate that diagnosed children will be conditioned to approach their parents more often and not be fearful of their wrath; we suspect that they will interact in genuine ways, and regard parents as providers of beneficial assistance. For example, parents can say to the child, "We can work together to resolve the situation if you tell us the truth" or encourage the child by saying, "Would it be better for you to trust us more and talk with us, rather than avoid us until problems become overwhelming?" In our approach, parents orient themselves so that the child feels comfortable telling the truth rather than fearful about penalties for lying and evasion.

Also when reinforcing a trusting and open relationship, parents first ask the child about reactions to a problem situation before assessing or offering their own appraisal; this approach permits the child to self-evaluate and shape the discussion. The child's concerns and ideation will gradually form the basis of the interaction. It will take much practice before parents can contour less directive verbal exchanges, and enable the locus of control to be mutual, but this alternative form of interaction can be learned like any other social pattern.

We acknowledge, however, that developing a mutually comfortable and trusting rapport is a very subtle endeavor. If the child is angry with the parent or excessively accommodated, he or she might refuse to do the smallest chore without complaint. Although we also assert that if coercion and punishment are such effective strategies, we think that fewer families with diagnosed children would seek professional help, since most of these families already incorporate strict disciplinary strategies.

Increasing participatory behavior for parents and children

Concerted effort by adults to help diagnosed persons resolve problems they choose to solve, and for adults too, to promote outcomes they want to occur is a valuable strategy. If diagnosed individuals, however, focus on changes they want *others* to make (common during therapy), they are asked if they prefer to be in a passive position, waiting for the other person to change. If they identify impossible, unlikely, or angry solutions such as going to school and punching someone, having the teacher fired, having another child removed from class, or having less work assigned, they are asked about the likelihood of those events, and whether they actually want to endure the negative consequences of behaving aggressively. However, as we noted above, if the child reacts in extreme ways, we suspect that other problematic events are affecting the child.

Rather than telling diagnosed families (or facilitating a self-fulfilling prophesy) that collaboration is not enough, the learning intervention assumes the opposite. Instead of telling them that self-management is beyond the child's capability, and that being kind to each other is insufficient, the family is given the message that it is worthwhile to facilitate the child's independence and to rely on the child to participate in a trusting relationship. It is presumed that diagnosed persons can function competently with less help from others as they learn new skills (or patterns of actions and reactions), and that they may be adequately reinforced by positive social exchanges to cooperate with less supervision.

Traditionalists, however, presume that greater direction from loved ones is a necessity, and that contingency management, typically used as a first option, is an invaluable tool. There is also equal willingness to impose coercions on parents of diagnosed children when it is believed that they transgress or digress from therapist directives. Socialization through coercion is presumed to be a "best practice" intervention for all participants.

For instance, Barkley (2000) recommends that parents be punished by having to give money to their least preferred organization when they do not comply with agreements established with the therapist. Rather than question whether therapy is helpful, whether renegotiating is reasonable, and inquiring about obstacles that still require resolution for "recalcitrant" parents, a failure to comply is treated as requiring punitive action. The therapist is encouraged to relate to the parent precisely as the parent should relate to the diagnosed child.

The same punitive recommendations are evident when traditionalists attempt to facilitate a negotiation or compromise, which in this view diminishes the likelihood that the alleged agreement will be mutually acceptable. For example, Robin has shifted from advising therapists to "push" parents to make agreements about consequences (Robin, 1998, 454) to "asking" parents to make such agreements (Robin, 2006, 542), but we suspect that therapists risk functioning outside the collaborative format with this behavior. Instead, the therapist can *ask* parents if they would *like* to make such agreements, and also ask them to indicate which obstacles they encounter when socializing their child. If the therapist directs the interactions to meet a particular requirement (e.g., they must make agreements), a collaborative tone is lost, and problems that could be interfering with cooperative parenting will not be adequately addressed. There is also concern that if parents intend to please the therapist, and by so doing do not adequately address their problems, they will be unlikely to carry out their statements after leaving the therapist's office.

In another example of the importance of parental *compliance* during traditional intervention, Anastopoulos, Smith, and Wien (1998, 381) suggest that therapists withhold treatment sessions in order to increase parental accord with therapist directives. Therapists institute a "breakage-fee system" where a sum of money is left with the therapist and returned to parents only when evidence of satisfactory conformity is observed. In this approach parents may also be "forced" to give money to a disliked political group when congruity with intervention is lacking.

Similar to children, coercion could initially increase compliant behaviors for both children and adults, but intervening in this fashion can also destroy the benefits that could have been achieved in a collaborative approach. Problems with limited generalization, avoidance, and increased dependence on the therapist can increase as well. Most importantly, by coercing the parents of diagnosed children, therapists are not taking advantage of the opportunity to role-model self-reliant/collaborative interacting when functioning *in vivo* with these families. Traditional forms of coercion may also relate to the increase in drop-out rates of some parents who avoid therapy in response to imposed punishments.

In closing, an ADHD diagnosed child's failure to follow through is not insurmountable in the learning model scenario. Continuing discussion allows parents to ask if the child has changed his or her mind, if something about the plan was unacceptable, or if an event or situation makes it difficult for the child to enact a previously discussed plan. Rather than characterize the failure of enactment as an inability to access working memory (or some other ADHD delay), the problem is understood as a matter of not yet being reinforced to enact the identified solution.

If diagnosed persons fail to enact what is discussed during collaboration, then modifications can be implemented to address problems. Unlike traditional implementation of collaborative models that advocate contingency management to ensure compliance with "agreements," the learning methodology investigates what might have interfered with follow through; additional collaboration takes place in order to incorporate the new information.

In this regard, Polivy and Herman (2002), in their extensive review of research on relapse with problematic behaviors such as weight loss, hypertension, smoking cessation, and so on, emphasize that most individuals who attempt to change behavior in a particular way will eventually experience a relapse. Diagnosed persons are not unique in their inability to change without some fallback to previous behavior. Their enactment of ADHD behaviors says nothing about the etiology of their problematic functioning or their ability to learn.

Polivy and Herman's findings suggest that it is highly likely that diagnosed persons will return to doing ADHD responding when functioning *in vivo*. Old behaviors can return even though individuals had seemed reinforced to change their actions at an earlier time during smooth-running collaborative interactions. This is particularly the case when old conditions recur, such as when parents again start to criticize, over accommodate, direct, and function as controllers of resources when pleasant discussion ends, or when the child encounters a succession of failures, deprivations, or losses.

However, in contrast to the traditional approach, because mutually satisfying interdependence is a difficult endeavor, we cannot emphasize enough the necessity for families with diagnosed persons *under age twelve* to engage thoroughly in self-reliant/collaborative interacting. Rather than react with an ultimatum, punishment, reprimand, or other negative response to unwanted behaviors, loved ones can talk with the child about problem behaviors when language becomes sufficiently developed, discuss the sequencing of events surrounding problem behavior and the desire to change or remain the same, and take action to minimize further difficulties.

Parents function as guardians, but also as mentors and facilitators in the learning alternative socializing process for their diagnosed children. Emphasis is on the reduction of the side effects linked to more authoritarian forms of management. Participants learn new ways to self-manage instead of blaming others or waiting for others to change first; this is a tenet of our learning model. Some assistance (e.g., posting reminders, hints, etc.) can help when the child is first learning to enact new patterning, but once routines have been established, we presume that it is possible to shape the occurrence of the behaviors without continuous prompting from others.

In this chapter we have discussed how ADHD is affected by the contingency management methods used by traditionalists. The learning paradigm can reasonably be applied in the event of unsatisfactory outcomes. Within this behavioral context we can begin to reinforce acceptable behaviors (observable or mental) in, ideally, ADHD children under the age of twelve, using less coercion (and less medication whenever feasible). Within our model, children learn acceptable behaviors through encountering the consequences of their actions with progressively less reliance on others to manage, and consistently engage in collaborative interacting with loved ones, teachers, and other caregivers.

Chapter 7

Additional Applications and Considerations

We presume that many different behaviors are conditioned over time in response to contentious events; it is therefore incumbent on therapists to identify the reinforcement contingencies that affect the higher frequencies of some response patterns but not others (i.e., including ADHD responding).

Different patterns of response may be conditioned, depending on events, even when individuals initially behave similarly. It is in this sense that the ADHD behavioral pattern is not situated within the individual, although specific biological and functional problems increase the likelihood that ADHD behaviors will be learned. In contrast to traditional understandings, ADHD behavior is perceived as solution behavior whereby the evaluator coordinates a history of reinforcement based on the frequency rates of ADHD behaviors. For example, individuals may not learn to save money if others give more and take less.

Because ADHD behavior disrupts families and leads to vexing problems, it is not surprising that most people think it ludicrous and insensitive to purport that conditioned behaviors correlate with extreme problems when these behaviors repeat in a variety of contexts and situations. For example, spiteful withholding may get a parent to approach and worry, but the same behavior with a spouse merely precludes the resolution of marital conflict in a congenial way. It is with this normative view in mind that we try to identify how ADHD behaviors are being reinforced.

Not working to obtain certain socially valued long-term goals or behaving courteously may also be reinforced in numerous ways. For example, we observe that there are diagnosed adults in relationships where others do a great deal for them. Loved ones often remind, rescue, anticipate, support, and clean up so that living in the world is easier and organized. Many of these diagnosed persons will be constantly reassured about their importance when others go to such lengths for their benefit (similar to life with parents). However, spouses of diagnosed persons are not satisfied to have the bulk of responsibility on their shoulders.

Some would argue that this pattern has evolved because the diagnosed person began showing delays and troublesome behaviors; however, these patterns could have been very different during their courtship. The same adults were likely accommodating, generous, and considerate at the start of their relationship. Traditionalists may claim that courtship was more salient and thus immediately reinforcing, but it is reasonable to assert that if diagnosed persons could function adequately and mutually during that initial period, it does not seem tenable to assert that their neural biology, at some arbitrary time, suddenly hinders their ability to behave pleasantly. We doubt that a frontal lobe-injured person would be equally able to impress a partner during the early courtship period.

Perhaps it was also less necessary to impress the partner after the initial courtship had taken place and they were now familiar with one another. If the non-diagnosed partner had also begun to accommodate the increased occurrence of ADHD patterning, asymmetries in the relationship will have also become greater. Conditioning can adequately account for these changes in the relational patterns without invoking the existence of an ever-present delay. The learning approach focuses on identifying possible ways in which ADHD behavior is reinforced as the individual interacts with his or her surroundings. Individuals engaged in ADHD behavior may fail in school, frustrate others, and be intrusive, but we assert that such behavioral patterns can be reinforced as other normative behaviors, given the individual's biopsychosocial circumstance.

Barkley (1998d, 143) states that diagnosed children are often "more talkative," "more negative and defiant," "more demanding of assistance," "less compliant and cooperative," and less able to function apart from their mothers. However, if those patterns of response effectively persuade the mother to acquiesce and/or help reduce adversity for the child (despite that the behaviors are socially undesirable), why would the child stop? While social practice in our approach is modified to appeal to the child, parents must nevertheless safeguard against mistreatment, intrusion, or danger, as society in its strongest form protects the weak.

Within this context we recommend two alterations in social patterning in order to reduce ADHD behavior. The first is to increase instances of collaboration whenever it is necessary for individuals to settle interpersonal differences; this is a means of easing conflict associated with establishing discretionary authority. The second is to reinforce self-reliance so that effort and success become more highly correlated; this is a means of increasing task persistence and contribution. When promoting these alternatives, parents help children learn to respond to their failures in more constructive ways, and scrutinize events that seem to reinforce risk taking, overreaction, and evasion.

While many diagnosed children more frequently focus on what they are not getting from others when there is talk about sharing, the learning intervention also orients so that diagnosed children focus more on what they can give. Children are invited to join in and help the family operate. When enacting this intervention, for example, individuals can develop a code system whereby participants non-critically signal each other or say a particular word when they notice the return of selfish or non-productive negative patterning. This is one way to develop increasingly affable interactions that direct us away from fault finding.

That the parent pay close attention to attributions, stereotypes, and generalizations made about the diagnosed child is absolutely crucial, as characterizations increase or decrease the frequency rates of target behaviors (Johnston and Freeman, 1997). For example, diagnostic functioning can increase when parents constantly say things like "He can't stop himself." "He is a handful, he never stops moving." "He has no fear." "She never studies." and: "I never know where he might go when I am shopping." "He'll never remember to take that with him." "He drives me crazy when he does that."

Sometimes diagnosed children are labeled as the cause of family hardship; that label also reinforces the disrupting and terrorizing of others as a reaction to criticism and rejection. Diagnosed children often overhear parents talk about how "out of control" they are, or are commanded to "calm down." Rather than ameliorating situations, those interactions only seem to rev up the child even further.

Conversely, in our learning model, parents reinforce mutually acceptable interacting through acting as role models for actions that are known to be preferred by the diagnosed child. An example of this patterning with adults occurs when couples report greater intimacy when the non-cooking partner prepares a meal without being asked. We anticipate that by changing conditions via role modeling, the child will copy the behaviors, and increasingly coordinate acceptable behavior with others. The parent can reinforce the child subtly, and these reinforcing interactions may be enacted without discussion beforehand, in that we guide the child towards courteous behavior. The child frequently gets the message that the parent is glad to see her.

We expect that incidental positive exchanges will negate an important contingency management side effect, which is to only behave acceptably when others threaten or promise extra rewards "up front." Our recommendation is in stark contrast to the traditional advice that contingencies should always be externally represented, salient, and immediate at the point of performance. The parent plans and initiates activities the diagnosed person enjoys, responds positively when he initiates contact to play together, and provides unsolicited favors for him. Acceptable responding is therefore role modeled, and ADHD behaviors are slowly extinguished by simultaneously and incidentally reinforcing the child to function similarly.

When behavioral change is first occurring, parents will notice that the child's old behavioral patterns reappear, or notice that they themselves have reverted to old behaviors. However, as further learning takes place, new behaviors become habitual or consistently reinforced in lieu of ADHD responding and contingency management discipline. Since children can learn the complexities of language without a formal contingency management program, we expect that they can learn other complex social behaviors in the same way.

Intervention becomes a matter of seeking to understand what might *extinguish* ADHD behavior as well as how to develop competence and cooperation. For example, the individual must learn to be more secure with others (e.g., "we like you better when you are not so silly or embellishing to be grandiose"), and adults must cease negative typecasting of the diagnosed child. Recommended approaches are not designed to remedy deficits, delays, defects, and/or disruptions in biology, but are implemented to change behavior reinforced over a lifetime. For example, if asking permission frequently results in dissatisfaction, then that behavior may not become reinforced.

We think it best to intercede *earlier* and maintain consistency in our approach; by so doing, the transition into adolescence and adulthood can be less problematic. If it is true that most of us repeat patterns of behavior learned early in life, our approach facilitates patterning which is consistent with how adults are expected to behave.

This method contrasts with authoritarian approaches that sanction caretakers to use pressure as a first option throughout childhood. However, we do not condone over-extending to please the child, which can often lead to resenting the child. Parents instead work to establish mutually-satisfying social arrangements. Early on, parents ask the child to consider how others might respond if he or she behaved in a particular way. Children would be asked to voice opinions and be given reasons for directives and requests. Children gradually learn about the benefits and problems associated with specific actions both in the short and long term. Parents can consistently solicit the child's opinion about family functioning, as well as ask how she would make improvements.

Parents are urged to incorporate the child's ideas and solutions into social patterning whenever possible. Even with younger diagnosed children, parents are advised to consider the child's preferences rather than use bribes or pressure. Coercive strategies can be implemented at any time to immediately stop an intolerable situation, but ADHD responses can only diminish over the long term by checking regularly if the child is receptive to the course of iterations. One way to facilitate positive changes, particularly with persistence and task immersion, is to make work seem much more like play.

When utilizing traditional remedial tactics, on the other hand, there is the increased probability that particular responses will be conditioned to occur only in conjunction with the medication and added rewards and punishments. Since there is less emphasis on conditioning non-diagnostic responding without medication or an assigned manager, we anticipate that the positive behaviors will likely extinguish when the medication or the manager is no longer influential to the trainee.

Moreover, one might declare that even if the behavior had been occurring frequently before the introduction of management, its removal is likely to reduce frequency rates below previous baselines. This problem has been deftly illustrated in Lepper, Greene, and Nisbett's (1973) study that identified the frequency with which pre-school children drew pictures in response to contingency management.

In the study, the pre-school children were randomly assigned into three groups. The first group functioned as a control group (i.e., no changes imposed). The second group was given rewards after drawing pictures; while the third group was informed before drawing that they would be given rewards if they drew pictures. After exposure to the three conditions, they observed how often the children drew pictures when they returned to unmanaged conditions. The results indicated that the control children (who were left alone) continued to draw in ways similar to patterns observed prior to the experiment. The group given rewards after drawing (but not told beforehand about the reward), still drew a significant amount, but somewhat less than before. However, the group that was told (prior to drawing) that rewards were contingent on drawing, ended up drawing very little when rewards were discontinued.

We can interpret these findings to mean that introducing contingency management reduces the frequency of particular behavioral acts when the management is withdrawn, often to levels below prior baselines. If contingency management is used as the primary way to socialize diagnosed persons (as traditionalists advise) we lower the probability that these children will repeat managed behaviors when surveillance and manipulation of contingencies are removed.

Therefore, rather than insist that diagnosed persons are less able to repeat what they learn because of their disorder, traditional interventions may in fact be largely ineffective at promoting desired responding when interventions are dismantled, and instead be contributing to continued medication dependency and reliance on the efforts of others evident in the ADHD population. Succinctly put, nothing has been done to shape the child to achieve autonomously.

Conversely, by addressing how children react to assignments, difficulties understanding, chores, directives, responsibilities, scrutiny, social exclusion, and other environmental hardships that cue diagnostic reactions, ADHD responding will have diminished without having added extra inducements. Whenever diagnostic responses are emitted, facilitators kindly redirect the child, react calmly so that the behaviors are not so powerful, and ignore behavior that is unlikely to escalate. By not relying on power and control to socialize the child, the hierarchy reversal that can occur during adolescence is mitigated as well.

In conjunction with these strategies, it will often be necessary to alter how the child responds to failure so that she will be willing to try again in the future. For example, she can be asked "What happens when you displease others?" Facilitators then help her explore the consequences of various actions in different situations, as well as identify assertive and reasonable responses. Exploring her concerns about "not being good enough," may counteract her sensitivity so that she will not *avoid* situations. A successful intervention will help a diagnosed child recognize that mistakes are expected in order for successes to occur. The child is asked, "How unhappy do you have to be before it is worthwhile for you to try?"

Starting early

When applying learning techniques to younger children we expect that it will often be necessary to specify options in more situations, as younger children are less skilled at generating possibilities. Verbal exchanges pertaining to the distant future are suitable for older diagnosed children who have developed the behavioral repertoire to comprehend greater complexity. It will also be necessary to show younger children what to do rather than merely discuss particular actions. However, by presenting requirements in an inviting fashion so that younger children have opportunities to affirm what is proposed, they will learn to respond enthusiastically when their cooperation is needed.

Parents still promote the development of the child's resources, but not by specifying each and every necessary action. For example, parents can indicate that it is time to leave, instead of telling the child to put on shoes, brush teeth, and so on. Similarly, parents can remark that it is cold outside instead of explicitly telling the child to put on a coat. They can also inform the child that their play is too loud, and wait to see if the child calms down before taking any action. Through repetition the child develops resources to self-manage beyond that which is expected when a directive approach is used. If intercession becomes necessary, at appropriate times, parents ask questions rather than give answers.

Younger children nevertheless require more demonstrations, exemplars, and immediate observable actions, physical representations of parameters, increased guidance, and protection. Younger diagnosed children also require more help identifying activity statements that correspond with nouns; for example, a bee is an insect, and it can also sting, etc. It is typically necessary to focus on the here-and-now with younger diagnosed children, rely less on verbal interacting, and more on *demonstration*: of courtesy, generosity, and trustworthiness in day-to-day functioning via role modeling of such behaviors.

For example, if we want a younger diagnosed child to clean his room more thoroughly, in addition to soliciting his input (e.g., Where would you like to put your toys?) we can explicitly *demonstrate* the sequence of identified actions whenever necessary. If we want children to form a line, we rehearse that activity rather than merely talk about it, and also address concerns that they might have regarding that procedure. By kindly showing younger diagnosed children what we would like them to do, and redirecting them to acceptable behaviors when problems occur, younger diagnosed children learn with less monitoring later on.

In that a significant percentage of diagnosed children may also show language and other functional delays, these kinds of explicit verbalizations, enactments, and demonstrations might also be necessary for longer periods of time within a more diverse range of situations in order to promote adequate learning. However, inadvertent prolonging of irresponsibility, unilateral power arrangements that inspire devious behavior, and the increased probability that a child will characterize others in negative ways, can be thwarted more often when enacting these courteous and demonstrative procedures.

In a related concern, Tarkan (2002) reports that success can be achieved by treating autistic children *as soon as* troublesome behaviors arise. Tarkan hypothesizes that early intervention with this population helps to alter neuropathways before they become fixed. We draw from those findings by proposing that alternative ADHD intervention will be most helpful (psychologically and biologically) for diagnosed persons if implemented sooner rather than later, and as often as is practical or feasible.

With that in mind, Robin (1998) lists "problem-solving communication skill deficits" as a significant problem between diagnosed persons and their families; therefore an intervention to help participants rectify those shortcomings as early as possible is necessary. He notes that when families communicate in an "accusatory, defensive, or sarcastic manner . . ." participants often become infuriated, and may respond with "hot emotions rather than cool logic," which tends to interfere with "rational problem solving" (p. 414). Perhaps ADHD correlated behavior such as impulsivity, over reactivity, and difficulty solving complex problems can be improved by following approaches similar to Robin's recommendation: early, often, and prior to adolescence.

Interestingly, the problem of changing behaviors that have been conditioned early is best illustrated in the example of couples who abstain from sex until marriage. On their wedding night individuals are urged to alter the sex avoidance patterning, but having sex confidently without concern for taboo is not easy for many people who are conditioned to behave otherwise throughout their entire lives until marriage. Similarly, some parents will have conditioned their children to be seen and not heard, but other adults and spouses will not appreciate such a non-communicative response pattern; moreover, we would argue that recipients of such training are also not typically content to have been uncommunicative, because loved ones will not necessarily be aware of what they enjoy. Conversely, if the learning approach recommended here can satisfactorily condition initiative and teamwork (highly valued in the workplace), this alternative will have proved effective in shaping the child in every significant way.

Consistent with the approach of shaping self-reliant/collaborative interacting prior to adolescence, Cunningham and Cunningham (1998; 2006) suggest implementing "student-mediated conflict resolution teams" for diagnosed students in elementary to middle-school grade levels. These programs have been touted as beneficial to diagnosed individuals while attending school. They are designed to assist students in conflict resolution, primarily in low supervision settings, but the general approach is consistent with building self-reliance and collaboration.

The authors note that fifth graders have benefited from these programs; many have learned to show less negative attributional bias towards others. Consistent with the recommendations provided here, effective mediation requires that participants maintain a neutral position, listen carefully, reflect on feelings, role play, discuss, and promote win/win solutions. Interestingly, Gentry and Benenson (1993) report that parents of children receiving mediation training at school also show a reduction in the frequency and intensity of conflicts with siblings in their households.

Although the traditional intervention has predominantly been based on additional monitoring, draconian tactics, increased management from others, and the permanent simplification of the diagnosed person's world, we acknowledge that self-reliant/collaborative functioning is *at times* encouraged by some investigators—usually in limited situations and for certain age groups. However, we suspect that more comprehensive effects can be developed earlier in childhood—not in the limited ways currently indicated in ADHD literature.

With younger diagnosed individuals as a target group, Kvols (1998) and Nelsen (1987) advocate training for self-reliance and less coercive interacting when socializing children at very early ages (e.g., self-dressing, win/win negotiating). Similarly, Shure (1994) asserts that the ICPS approach (i.e., I can problem solve) is applicable with children as young as age four. She helps children learn to identify a problem, appreciate how participants feel, conjointly derive solutions to solve the problem, and anticipate consequences of the solutions. Shure claims that the strategies can reduce both overly shy and impulsive behaviors when children do not get their own way. If that is the case, it is worthwhile to investigate whether Shure's approach reduces instances of diagnostic responding.

Given the frequent infantile, insecure, and demanding behaviors of many diagnosed children, it is difficult to understand why any autocratic approach is appropriate in principle, even for younger children. The promotion of the opposite type of patterning seems to be the most reasonable and essential choice. Traditionalists do, however, acknowledge that autocratic approaches will become significantly problematic as the child ages; therefore it is disingenuous to delay the development of the child's autonomy and collaborative interacting until late childhood or puberty—when parents have fewer opportunities to influence their behavior. Shaping behaviors that consider other perspectives, as well as cultivating greater self-reliance at an earlier age, will certainly pay dividends later on for ADHD diagnosed individuals and their loved ones. Below we will illustrate a number of likely behavior scenarios and suggest ways to address them.

Addressing ADHD behavior in the learning approach

If a diagnosed younger child is leaving personal belongings scattered throughout the house, and walks on top of them instead of putting them away, a parent can command the child to pick up the belongings, or simply take the things away when there is non-compliance. Conversely, the parent can calmly request that the child pick up the possessions, and then thank him if he cooperates. The parent can also talk in a non-disapproving way with him about caring for property and being considerate of others, and encourage him to offer an alternative acceptable solution in order to protect the objects from being broken and under foot.

If he continues to show carelessness with the belongings despite parental requests, the parent can indicate disappointment, but also again request (without escalating into negativity or coercion) that he be conscientious with the objects. The child has an additional opportunity to behave acceptably before the parent resorts to a unilateral solution. If results are still not forthcoming, the parent can take a more limiting action, but always be prepared to ease off coercion when the child shows a willingness to accommodate family concerns. Actions are taken to stop unwanted behaviors, but parents are urged to promote reconciliation, since it is more beneficial to "steady the ship" than impart discipline by using negative withholding strategies that keep him in "the doghouse."

However, it is also strongly advocated that parents *not* adopt an under-assertive or obsequious child-rearing style. For example, parents kindly and politely ask child to "please pick up the toys," and/or indicate that "it is time to pick up the toys." The parent less often commands or dogmatically informs the child that non-compliance will result in reprisal (e.g., if you don't put it away, I will not let you play with it for a week, or you will go to time out), but the parent is neither at the child's mercy, nor does the parent permit the child to exploit or control.

If the child continues to ignore the request to put possessions away, at any point in the sequence parents can resort to removing the toys or other articles. The coercive intervention is enacted *without* anger and incorporated only to prevent further exploitation. For example, the parent can put some of the belongings in temporary storage so that no one has the burden of caring for so many possessions, and return them to the child when he demonstrates the skill to manage them. However, when training children to routinely put away toys (or other belongings), parents can also inform the child that if objects are put away more regularly, it will be easier to find them later and they will last longer.

Parents can also help resolve problems (identified by the child) related to putting away toys, for example, by assisting her in figuring out a category system for storage. Parents can take note of and value her vigilant handling of the toys and other household articles, and inform her that it is now possible to buy additional things that she enjoys. She is made aware of the benefits that occur in relation to developing competency.

However, if problems related to care of personal belongings arise, it may be necessary to change some family behaviors that reinforce the unacceptable patterns. For example, sometimes children respond to parental complaints about household messes as a sign of rejection, or believe themselves to be a burden to the parent rather than a source of pleasure. Sometimes parents react to messes as if the child is ungrateful, which is interpreted by parents as utter disregard. Sometimes parents buy the child too many things and are inadvertently promoting carelessness with personal belongings. Sometimes parents complain, but continue to pick up after the child, and sometimes the messes are a vehicle for the child to keep the parent attentive. Problems like these are more important to resolve than to merely focus on a disheveled room.

In our approach parents as primary caregivers use their role to facilitate the development of considerate, competent, and caring behaviors in ways that diverge markedly from traditional forced compliance strategies. For example, instead of determining portion size for the child, parents ask the child to help determine portion size so everyone receives a share. On other occasions they ask if the child is *willing* to reduce an allotment so that others get a chance, or ask the child to help them decide what to do differently so that next time no one misses out. Instead of orienting to prevent diagnostic acts by specifying what to do and then impeding, the advantages of non-diagnostic functioning are made explicit so that the child has the opportunity to show autonomous acceptable behaviors with less pressure. The child is given more opportunity to learn from mistakes.

For instance, rather than repeatedly cue the diagnosed child to remove shoes when they are soiled, parents hand the child a dust pan and brush to clean the mess as a way to help extinguish negligent actions. Similarly, instead of invariably telling the child to say "thank you," parents talk with the child (at other times) about benefits that accrue from acknowledging others. For example, people are inclined to continue to please if they feel appreciated and informed that they are doing well. Parents also show appreciation when the child is polite without being told; this helps to develop courtesy without parental directive.

Similarly, when the child's lack of courtesy insults others, parents can ask the child if she would like to say "thank you" rather than immediately command her and negate her initiative to do gracious acts. When interventions are successful, the diagnosed child will act magnanimously rather than respond to an order to behave accordingly.

Therapists, parents, and other concerned persons are urged to take the facilitator's rather than director's role. Even if additional time is necessary for the diagnosed person to derive a plan of action, the results will differ markedly from a prescribed agenda that requires the ongoing participation of an appointed manager to ensure compliance during each point of performance. Diagnosed persons are encouraged to function as much as possible as the source of instruction to change ADHD actions. For example, it is more advantageous for them to indicate "wanting" to wear a watch or to keep an appointment book, instead of assigning or coercing those solutions. A reasonable intervention will initially focus on helping individuals resolve problems relating to their reluctance to conform to particular schedules and assignments, and then help them discern acceptable alternatives that work better from their point of view.

Implementation intentions

Gollwitzer (1999) argues that individuals learn to enact behaviors at later times without prior thinking or another person's directive at the point of performance. He holds that intentional behaviors are generally cued *instantaneously* by circumstances. Individuals, he says, do not have to hesitate and do particular mental actions in order to engage in time-organized behaviors throughout the day. Gollwitzer states that people may increase reliability of responding in a particular way by vocally (or non-vocally) specifying the behaviors that they will enact *before* encountering an anticipated future situation. He calls these plans of action "implementation intentions."

According to Gollwitzer, implementation intentions provide a sense of "commitment that obligates the individual to realize the goal" (p. 494). Implementation intentions "help people get started . . ." and "lead to heightened activation of specified situational cues" (p. 495). They are pronouncements that indicate when, where, and how a particular behavior will be enacted at a later time. He claims that when persons formulate implementation intentions, the specified behaviors are likely to be triggered *automatically* by situational cues. Persons will then not have to stop functioning, reassess, and continuously self-monitor; he emphasizes that the effects of implementation intentions will show stability even if "much time has passed between the formation of the implementation intention and the encounter of the critical situation" (p. 499).

Implementation intentions are antecedent to doing the actual behavior, much like the traditional executive functions and posited inhibitory responses. However, *unlike* executive functioning, they are stated plans of action specified prior to encountering the anticipated set of conditions, rather than after the posited inhibitory step when the individual is already functioning within a particular circumstance. In Gollwitzer's view, time-organized behaviors might be conditioned by doing implementation intentions much earlier in the behavioral sequence, and the probability of acceptable responses at the point of performance might increase without the inhibition and executive guidance mimetically expressed prior to the act.

When formulating implementation intentions people are asked to identify significant environmental cues ahead of time. This procedure is designed to elicit "the intended behavior in an automatic fashion once the critical cues are encountered" (p. 497). Persons then enact behaviors reliably over time by devising further behavioral plans. Increased attentiveness, operating carefully and methodically, considering the perspectives of others, working for long-term goals, and emitting calm behaviors can be reinforced to occur automatically by creating implementation intentions. Non-vocal verbal rehearsals and other mental preparatory behaviors and imaginings can also shift to automatic control and situational cue: a person can formulate implementation intentions to do those responses as with many other motoric actions.

Moreover, even if one decides that diagnosed persons have a delayed inhibitory mechanism that impedes executive guidance at crucial moments, it is nevertheless helpful for them to formulate implementation intentions. Because Gollwitzer argues that, by so doing, one increases the probability that particular actions will occur *automatically* at point of performance, this would potentially bypass problems caused by failures to inhibit and access executive functioning. Consistent with the view that implementation intentions are indeed helpful, Berk (1992) reports that overt private speech will often improve task competency when the task is next encountered.

Gollwitzer points out that it is often customary for us to implement our intentions by "passing the control . . ." of our "behavior on to the environment." He notes that by making these plans of action, "people can strategically switch from conscious and effortful control of their goal-directed behaviors . . ." to having their actions "automatically controlled by selected situational cues." For example, "people who have formed the goal intention to exercise regularly can furnish it with implementation intentions that specify when, where, and how they want to exercise" (p. 495).

If Gollwitzer's approach is effective, it might then become possible to intervene with diagnosed persons very differently than current traditional methods. By shaping diagnosed persons to formulate implementation intentions, they may eventually function less diagnostically without the extensive monitoring, coercion, and psychopharmacological intervention. Gollwitzer notes that these interventions have aided special populations that purportedly have "conscious control" difficulties (e.g., schizophrenics and frontal lobe-injured persons). This is particularly important, since traditionalists hold that ADHD persons share characteristics with individuals who have been documented with frontal lobe tissue damage.

In fact, Lengfelder and Gollwitzer (2001) found that frontal lobe-injured persons benefit even more than controls on neuropsychological tests (e.g., Tower of Hanoi) when they make implementation intentions. These plans of action allegedly transfer the correct responses to automatic control. The impaired individual need not rely on what is often called "conscious control" (i.e., autonomous problem solving while already in the problem situation) when making implementation intentions beforehand.

Even when ascribing to conventional views about ADHD, there is apparently no biological obstacle to prevent their making descriptive statements (out loud) about behaviors they will enact under specified future conditions. Therefore, we expect that commitment to furthering a behavioral sequence will be enhanced when children (and adults) formulate implementation intentions, including such examples as brushing teeth each night before bed, covering their mouths when coughing, turning off lights when leaving a room, putting keys only in one place, raising their hand before speaking out, playing after homework is complete, and listening intently when class starts in order not to miss out on important material.

Moreover, even if it is found that diagnosed persons do not enact their implementation intentions as often as non-diagnosed persons, rather than proclaim intentional disability, we can still pursue the idea that a failure to enact plans may be due to not extinguishing previously conditioned responses which are automatically cued in select situations. We can posit that more behavioral shaping is required, which might also include additional implementation intentions to help cue the new behaviors at designated times.

To increase the power of doing implementation intentions we encourage diagnosed persons to identify likely benefits when enacting them. For example, cleaning up after company might compel parents to invite guests to the house on other occasions. Taking out garbage the night before allows for extra sleep the next morning. Finishing homework early permits time with parents or friends after supper.

Data consistent with this recommendation reports that implementation intentions work best when a person expresses that the outcome is highly valued. For example, Stellar (1992) claims that effects of implementation intentions may be enhanced if persons also state that they strongly intend to follow the specified plan. In the same way, the influence of an implementation intention can also be improved by noting that the diagnosed person is already doing a comparable behavioral sequence with other content, in other contexts, and with other people. Framing the problem as an issue of repeating successful behavioral enactments will make task completion less insurmountable; it will reinforce continued effort, and draw attention to the benefits associated with positive behaviors.

Gollwitzer (1999, 494) emphasizes that "automatization of goal implementation through pre-deciding . . ." will help with the "swift seizing of good opportunities," as well as "help a person protect goal pursuit from tempting distractions, bad habits, or competing goals." In instances when persons know that they are likely to encounter difficult circumstances "the person would have to pre-decide only how to best escape these unwanted influences on behavior." For example, parent can ask the diagnosed child what she would do if another child kept teasing her, despite attempting to ignore the taunting, or ask her what she would do if a friend rang the doorbell during homework period.

According to Gollwitzer, implementation intentions may be as "effective in automatizing action initiation as the repeated and consistent practice implied in habits." While he claims that some implementation intentions may be more effective than others, and that it is important for a person to be committed to an implementation intention, formulating plans of action help to "create instant habits" (p. 499).

Similarly, Kirsch and Lynn (1999) also encourage the use of implementation intentions to increase the frequency rates of certain behaviors under particular sets of conditions. They help individuals derive the action plans in highly specific ways. While the younger child's behavioral repertoire may be significantly limited compared to that of most adults, these techniques can be adapted to younger children as well. For example, Kirch and Lynn state that

> Rather than merely specifying behavior in general terms (e.g., being assertive), actual behavioral responses and their environmental cues should be specified. Also, because response sets can be strengthened by repetition, imaginative and behavioral rehearsal (e.g., role playing) can help promote the activation of adaptive responses. The key is to have clients practice the actual words and behaviors they intend to use in the real-life situation, rather than merely talking about what they might do (p. 512).

Role playing and other rehearsals help children learn effectively, so Kirsch and Lynn's approaches may be well-suited for younger age groups as well, especially if adjustments are made for language and intellectual competence. As emphasized throughout, if the child derives the behavioral plan, it might resemble other non-coerced time-organized enactments that the child already demonstrates in, for example, remembering to search for a small toy that dropped in the driveway when he got out of the car the previous day.

Changing entrenched patterning

The effect of routines on behavior is evident whenever we experience problems if our routines are interrupted. Examples include being side-tracked while starting the car, and then attempting to start it again despite that the engine is already running, failing to remember usual morning routines, or not knowing the day of the week while on vacation. Rather than presume that inappropriate sets of behaviors are always more automatic (prepotent) than satisfactory acts, we presume that a person automatically behaves in ways consistent with socially acceptable criteria as long as those routines are established.

In our posited framework, otherwise competent diagnosed persons have bad habits rather than neurological delay; they are conditioned to continue irresponsible or careless behaviors. Treatment for ADHD is a question of making the completion of homework, for example, become reinforced exactly like other habitually-enacted behavioral sequences, under the condition of returning home from school.

However, when altering established routines, discussions about change will be more effective when they occur close in time to the behavioral event when learning is first taking place. Although as the child becomes more proficient in understanding discussion about the not-here and not-now, these verbal exchanges can occur further in time from the point of performance. For example, when the child is agreeable to talk earlier in the day, parent and child together can identify alternative behaviors that both will do when parent is busy with housework during the afternoon hours; this allows for less intruding and antagonizing by the child. The parent can also give the child an approximation of how long the work will take, prior to becoming immersed in the activity, as this also reassures child that the parent is considering his perspective. Parent and child can also figure out what the child might do while the parent completes housework. For instance, the child can help or otherwise find an activity in the same room in order to remain in the parent's company.

In many ways increasing the child's input and self-reliance is consistent with empirical findings indicating that people generally achieve goals more often when they vocalize a desire to change as well as anticipate success. Hollenbeck, Williams, and Klein (1989) note that public commitment to particular goals often increases the probability of doing behaviors that promote attainment of goals, and the authors claim that this relates to concern about personal integrity.

Similarly, Locke and Latham (2002, 707) report "two key factors that make goal attainment important to people." These include "the importance of the outcomes that they expect as a result of working to attain the goal," and the person's "belief that they can attain a goal (self-efficacy)." According to these authors, persistence and goal attainment are more probable when the enactor identifies the outcomes she wants to accomplish (i.e., discretionary input), and has a history of success with required particular behaviors (i.e., self-efficacy).

Frayne and Latham (1987), in a similar venue, asked government employees to formulate specific goals for attendance, and keep track of how environment helped or hindered attainment of their goals. Employees were asked to self-manage contingencies that help them achieve. This strategy was found to increase their self-efficacy, and helped many employees deal effectively with personal and social obstacles related to job attendance. The findings indicate that when enactors maintain discretionary authority and are conditioned to anticipate reasonable success, achievements are enhanced.

With that in mind, parents can encourage teeth brushing, for example, by complimenting the child when they exhibit competency. Instead of coercing or cueing teeth brushing, the parent can say, "If you want to protect your teeth, you might want to brush them in the morning and at night." Prior discussion of the problem of teeth brushing will, of course, have been necessary. Intervention orients to help diagnosed children brush teeth to better protect themselves, and therefore require less dental work (never pleasant). Children will be reinforced when others notice their healthy smile, and remark on how well they take care of themselves.

It is usually recommended to solve problems in this more collaborative fashion, but in the effort to protect the child who will not care for teeth, loved ones can also set aside "family money" to pay the dentist bill, which could impact on the family budget. In these more tenacious instances, it will be necessary to reduce money spent on toys and limit recreational activities. The child can also be informed that, in order to help protect his teeth, it is necessary to stop purchasing food that promotes tooth decay. The child can then decide whether it is preferable to assume greater personal responsibility for teeth brushing, in that he is directly or indirectly carrying some of the cost.

When the child shifts to adequate self-care, the family budget and protective patterning can then be readjusted accordingly. While generally it is advisable to solve these problems conjointly, an apparent benefit to this intervention is that children readily learn how their actions influence the future in ways not previously considered. Parents attempt to persuade the child by saying, "We might all enjoy spending family money on toys and outings rather than on regular trips to the dentist's office."

We presume that diagnosed persons can learn to function autonomously and acceptably when problems that reinforce their diagnostic patterns are resolved. For example, are diagnosed children comfortable with their tooth decay, or are they unhappy about being ordered around and treated as incompetent? Is it that they do not care about cavities because the occurrence of cavities is beyond their "event horizon," or is it the case that they have not yet been exposed to social patterns that would help them to develop regular teeth brushing? Does their neurological ADHD prevent them from adequately caring for themselves, or are they reinforced by concern, worry, and disturbance when they respond diagnostically?

In our learning model we also address the prevalent ADHD behavior of quitting after making a commitment. For example, if the diagnosed child repeatedly quits after signing up for various activities, parents can indicate that the family will pay only part of the entrance fees for future activities, and only reimburse the child when the activity is completed. When quitting occurs in relation to team sports, it is also helpful to talk with the child about the impact of her actions on other team members who rely on her participation.

However, caution is advised when imposing unilateral solutions to these problems, due to the possibility of significant side effects. For example, while having a child pay for the repeated failure to follow through with commitments (i.e., karate classes, music lessons, etc.) can sometimes help increase follow-through, using that strategy too frequently and harshly can also increase the risk that the child will be reluctant to try new activities. Quitting may often mean that the child is experiencing excessive failures or social conflict; and resolving those problems will yield better results than deciding how to coerce the child to commit.

Additionally, our learning model can help to increase chore completion for diagnosed persons using less pressure and recriminations. For example, rather than constantly remind and cue diagnosed children to put clothes in the laundry, and introduce additional rewards and punishments to increase the probability of those actions, parents can request that the child put clothes in the laundry before a designated time (a mutual decision) so that clothes will be washed regularly. The parent is willing to help the child, but in a way that puts less pressure on the parent. Clothes will be washed when the child takes the initiative to do the identified routines.

Family members are encouraged to take care of one another so that no one is unreasonably exploited or left to needlessly struggle with work. Parents also inform that a cooperative pattern will provide more free time for leisure activity, both together and apart, and also increase the likelihood that the child will have clean clothes. Diagnostic responding can diminish by showing appreciation when he contributes to the laundry routine, and also by resolving other conflicts that impede cooperation during laundry days. The child's social importance and concerns are retained as much as possible.

Some parents will fret that the child will continue to wear dirty clothes (because of neurological ADHD), but we anticipate that this unfortunate outcome will occur whenever wearing dirty clothes continues to be reinforced. Examples include: when parents constantly make derisive comments about his unacceptable appearance, when they fail to notice when he is neat and clean, when they intermittently wash his clothes at non-designated times in order to rescue him, or when they angrily coerce him to wear certain clothes.

Finally, we have also observed that diagnosed children do what is often called "spacing out" or "getting side tracked" in the morning when getting ready for school instead being on time. In order to remedy this problem by using our learning model, parents can help diagnosed children recognize that they already sometimes do the necessary behaviors when they prepare for an activity they enjoy (e.g., visiting an amusement park). A solution to the difficulty of getting ready on time may be as simple as encouraging the child to repeat the same behaviors during their morning school routines, and show appreciation when he is cooperative.

If problems in the morning continue, and she expresses a willingness to change, parents can ask why this is the case (to reinforce the responding). Parents can then help her figure out how to achieve the stated goal without increasing her reliance on parental initiative and effort (same as trips to an amusement park). It might also be decided that getting clothes and other essentials ready the night before immensely helps the morning routine. These children are not less able to be time organized, but rather, getting ready for school is similar to preparing for an execution.

A learning intervention helps child identify positive eventualities that will be incorporated as they become more resourceful and efficient while preparing for school. Parents can also comment that if the family leaves the house on time, they will get paid in full and extra money can be spent on activities that everyone enjoys. These benefits would not occur if the child were to miss the bus, and therefore require parental transportation or a taxicab.

However, there may be a low probability of success unless children and parents identify and resolve what is disturbing them about their daily itinerary. For example, parent might be frenetic and irritable in the morning, and child might be reacting negatively when parent seems more attentive to his or her own schedule than to the child. The child may at times personalize the parent's irritability rather than understand that those behaviors relate to other problems of the parent. In some instances a diagnosed child is anxious about separating from the parent, and/or concerned about being teased and mistreated by peers or teachers, etc. It is very important that parent(s) and child solve problems occurring at school so that avoidance behaviors will diminish.

We observe that the morning routine is usually very difficult for family members who operate under tight time schedules, as the parent's job as well as other children in the family need punctuality. If one family member does not cooperate, everyone is affected. Conditioning a child to awaken to an alarm clock set by him (rather than parent waking him) can, for example, allow participants to avoid a push/pull interaction, and permit the child greater autonomy.

A potential indirect benefit of our approach is that loved ones will feel less overworked. Promoting self-reliance rather than perpetual functioning as the diagnosed child's keeper will be less taxing over the long term. Since diagnosed individuals often respond to social requirements by doing the easiest and quickest solution, regardless of the inconvenience to others (e.g., using a shirt sleeve instead of reaching for a tissue, leaving tools out after finishing a project, leaving cabinet doors open unless hiding something, etc.), it may be necessary for others to compensate, remind, direct, fix problems, and carry out most of the work. Reliance on others to perform work, as traditionalists advise, will burden most parents; future spouses of diagnosed persons will not appreciate such social training either.

We suggest that in many scenarios ADHD behaviors can be extinguished by encouraging parents and teachers to adopt a "natural consequences" approach rather than "tighten controls" in order to protect diagnosed children from themselves—a common traditionalist recommendation. For example, diagnosed children will quickly realize that tardiness results in missing breakfast and going hungry, as well as penalties at school.

Resolving sibling conflicts

An intervention based on shaping self-reliant/collaborative interacting can be incorporated to help reduce the frequency of conflicts between diagnosed individuals and other siblings at home, which is a great concern for families with diagnosed children. Generally, when diagnosed families with more than one child seek intervention, sibling conflict is often extreme and frequent (Mash and Johnston, 1983). We observe, however, that ADHD responding lessens in relation to resolving sibling conflict.

For the most part, when there is sibling conflict in families, older siblings tend to shun, belittle, and disapprove of younger siblings—who will respond by learning subtle forms of provocation. However, it is not unusual for (clever) older siblings to believe themselves to be victimized by their younger siblings' unacceptable acts, nor is it uncommon for the recipient of misconduct to suffer a pejorative reaction from a parent when the parent believes that the older child had modeled the unacceptable action. An additional concern is that frequent blaming of a child in the family can compel the child to overreact to teachers (and others) when criticized or faulted.

In many instances, families with diagnosed children exhibit triangular patterns. These patterns occur not only between siblings and parents, but also between the child and both parents (i.e., particularly if there are step-parents), as the remaining adult is placed in the predicament of siding either with spouse or child in a no-win situation. Avoiding taking sides or triangular scenarios during conflict is extremely important, because resentment in the family will increase and foster collusions predicated on the exclusion or suffering of others. Moreover, if parents end these conflicts by inducing further suffering, children will likely retaliate and copy that solution. Likewise, the strategy of punishing the children "equally" will typically not help the children learn acceptable conflict resolution, and depending on circumstances, inadvertently favor one of the children as well.

Because provocation and intrusiveness (leading to conflicts) are included in the ADHD diagnostic set, ill will is frequently present in families requesting treatment. Moreover, if the diagnosed child behaves like the spouse, birth parent, or grandparent (annoyingly) it is often the case that the parent will align against the child and overreact when conflicts erupt. Diagnosed children are likely to enact ADHD behaviors when they become jealous or when they compete for social importance, so it is not surprising that rivalries occur with great intensity.

When using our intervention, parents allow siblings time to resolve discord on their own, stop interactions that could lead to physical harm, direct verbalizations towards both children, and speak calmly and non-critically in order to establish group rapport. Any deviation from such an approach is usually viewed as a "side take" or assignment of blame. A more neutral approach also reduces the possibility of alienating the "faulted" child, and reinforces the other child to pattern as victim (even though he or she may have instigated or hit first). Instead of focusing on identifying the culprit, parents shift to helping the children find mutually satisfying solutions to problems. The children suggest behavioral changes that might resolve the quarrel, and learn to invite siblings to interact in more congenial ways.

It is helpful to talk with the children about the reasons for the acrimony, but parents must not be critical towards one child and aligned with another. The slightest disparaging remark or alignment with one child can increase conflict and defensiveness and forestall a mutually positive resolution. Despite the apparent unfairness of taking a neutral position when one child is clearly in the wrong, it is usually the most effective way to intercede. It is often difficult to determine what sparked the conflict (which could have rumbled on for years); therefore this approach is quite reasonable.

We observe that parents risk conditioning increased sibling conflict when they try to determine who caused the fight. In this social pattern one child is reassured about his importance and the other child is shut out. In the same way, the alleged perpetrator is also reinforced when dominating the coddled child and aggravating the blaming parent in the process, or when putting the parent on the defensive by accusing the parent of favoritism. Parents will sometimes go to extremes to prove to the blamed (older) child that the accusation was false. If the adult continues to promote unilateral or biased solutions, complaints and comparisons will ensue (e.g., you gave *him* more). Many diagnosed children will learn to control the parent by declaring that "You always take his side." If the parent tries to equalize, he may risk reinforcing even more complaints in the future.

Many events are likely to reinforce the quarreling. For instance, the blamed child will continue to behave aggressively against a sibling (knowing full well that a reprimand is forthcoming for the sibling). Fighting, it is expected, punishes the victimized (usually younger) sibling for having been born, or for usurping family importance. The (older) child might also behave aggressively, in that the brother or sister is often annoying or gets him into trouble with parents.

While the problem could easily be solved by not responding to the provocations of the younger child, older children often regard less dominating solutions as equivalent to letting the younger child win. Moreover, if the parent maintains a disapproving and insensitive attitude towards the (older) child, the older child may remain angry with the parent for assigning blame; thus continual fighting is likely to be reinforced. Moreover, if the older child anticipates blame, regardless of circumstance, he will not recognize any advantage in refraining from antagonistic behavior.

Younger children (even if physically hurt) can also be reinforced when they provoke older siblings, especially if they behaved in a critical and dismissive manner. Physical pain is often insignificant, because the weaker child establishes a level of ascendancy when older child receives parental disapproval. In these scenarios, we also find that when a child notices that a sibling is being reprimanded, that child will goad the sibling even more in order to disrupt him.

Even though some sibling conflict seems less related to the provocation of parental involvement, and more about breaking monotony, or anger about other concerns and taking out frustrations on each other, sibling conflict seems related to parental approach and arbitration in many instances. This sequencing of events is evident even when the parent is not at home (e.g., when children are with babysitter, or when father is at work). Parental involvement can subsequently occur when the parent arrives home and is told about the ruckus that had occurred earlier.

Sibling rivalry and disruption not only increase involvement from the parent, but under some conditions punish the parent for having done a displeasing act at an earlier time. A child can punish a parent for being critical towards him by mistreating a sibling, *especially* if the action typically bothers the parent. A child might also be compelled to antagonize a sibling when the parent does something positive for the sibling, when sibling copies a disliked parental behavior, and/or when the parent has refused an earlier request.

Generally, sibling conflicts punish parents for perceived transgressions such as divorce, not spending enough time together, and/or preferential treatment to another individual in the household. If the child interprets others as denying, rejecting, and mistreating, and/or is frequently angry with one or both parents, inducing family conflict may be a powerful way to retaliate and keep everyone else unhappy as well.

As a rule of thumb, if the parent becomes distressed about fighting, it will reinforce the behavior. Parents often feel disgruntled about how they handled conflict, and in many instances, both parents and children are reinforced by making amends after a dispute. Sibling rivalry also makes it difficult for parents to maintain discretionary authority; the fighting essentially monopolizes the family agenda. At times it is only the parent who is dismayed when children do not get along; meanwhile, siblings continue to be reinforced by fighting and bickering.

We observe that quarreling is conditioned within families in a multitude of situations and circumstances: when there is a lull or requirement to wait, when parents are busy elsewhere, or when preparing to relax or do some other enjoyable activity. Siblings are generally aware of behaviors that reduce conflict (i.e., they sometimes treat each other kindly and share), intervention therefore orients to identify the parameters in daily family patterning that reinforce the (sometimes subtle) wrangling.

Kvols (1998) recommends plenty of parental involvement when helping children learn diplomacy. For instance, upon hearing complaints or tattling rather than specify a resolution, they redirect the children to talk together. They ask "Would you like to talk with her about what you think would make it better?" As a way to foster mutually acceptable accommodations, parents can also ask "Do you think both of you will be happy doing it that way?"

If children persist in identifying alternatives that are unreasonable (e.g., to give away the sibling), it is important to identify what interferes the ability compromise. On many occasions it will be necessary to wait for the situation to ease before any verbal exchanges can be productive, and siblings sometimes will not accept even the reasonable ideas of the other child, because they do not want the sibling to receive acknowledgment. Attentiveness and immediate memory are also likely to be impaired when interactions remain stressful (Horner and Hamner, 2002).

The more a parent pleads with children to stop, or lectures them about fighting, takes responsibility for resolving complaints, is resentful about children's lack of reciprocity after "all that is done for them," responds to conflict as a personal failure, becomes unduly reactive, continues to align with one child, insists that the children like each other, or frets about what "others" will think, the more conflicts will increase. Delving into the parent's psychosocial history in order to resolve the above mentioned concerns may first be necessary before they are able to recognize a noteworthy reduction in sibling conflict.

In sum, when implementing our approach, parents are encouraged to nonchalantly redirect interactions towards other topics when squabbles begin, or encourage the children to do separate activities without assigning blame, if cooling off seems helpful. We also recommend that parents stop acting as "judge and jury," and refrain from providing solutions for the children to enact. Parents (as ambassadors) ask the children what they think will help to resolve the dilemma, and proceed to facilitate discussion. They model receptivity to suggested solutions, and help the children refine ideas calmly. Finally, they are advised to stop their own patterns of behavior that seem to reinforce fighting among family members. For instance, if they continue to blame each other in front of the children, those patterns will undermine their credibility to lead and will instead model an argumentative demeanor. Conflict can be lessened simply by giving children positive attention whenever appropriate and enjoying the children's company. Parent can also invite the children to participate by helping to decide what to do while parent is busy in the kitchen. Collaborative planning often reduces the occurrence of sibling conflict (and diagnostic responding), in that the parent has reinforced children's importance by *not* giving them the impression that parent is indifferent.

Increasing cooperation

It is essential for parents not to alienate the child, as the goal is to maintain the child's interest in collaborative problem solving. If talking within the family has often resulted in frustration, disappointment, and disapproval, and/or if the parent has often "pulled rank" and controlled family resources when disturbed by the child's behavior, the child will not be conditioned to share concerns. Defensiveness, over reactivity, and escapism are likely to occur if the child learns to associate the parent with criticism, accusation, and badgering. To counteract the problem, parents can suggest the following: "I must sound like I'm hassling you." "What do you want to do?" "What can I do differently so I don't sound like I'm being critical?" "Please tell me about your concerns." "What is getting in your way?" "What can we do to make that happen for you?" "What changes can we make so that it is easier for us to talk?" "How do you feel about what I have been saying?" "Are you willing to do it that way?" Or: "Sometimes I mention things because I get worried, not because you are doing something wrong."

To build rapport parents ask the child to indicate changes to help the relationship become more like what the child prefers it to be. Facilitators can assure diagnosed persons that nothing dreadful will happen if their concerns are aired. If the child professes ignorance or withdraws, parent can ask, "What is giving you trouble?" and/or "What have you tried in the past in order to solve this problem?"

The parent encourages the child to give recommendations for change and shows receptivity to the child's suggestions. It can be helpful for the parent to adopt some of the vocabulary used by the diagnosed person so that discussions are relevant, familiar, and understandable. Parents can ask if child is willing to "take charge" of certain activities rather than coerce her to complete a chore, or ask her to help "protect" family property if misuse is a problem when friends visit. The goal is to increase her family status, not control her.

Parents can also apply reverse psychology and encourage her to discuss problems that would arise if she were to do *less* ADHD responding. Working harder, monopolizing less, or relying less on the efforts of others in response to requirements will not always be appealing. Rather than convince the child of the benefits of alternative patterns, reverse psychology may help the child reach the conclusion on her own. Many diagnosed persons eventually learn that increased self-sufficiency and cooperation is not a prescription for abandonment, denial, or further failure.

When changing conditioning, an approach similar to Kirsch and Lynn's (1999, 512) solution-focused intervention is recommended. The authors note that most solution-focused therapies "direct the client's attention to exceptions to the problem, thereby priming adaptive thoughts and behaviors." Such questions as "How would your life change if you had X?" would be applicable as well.

By intervening in this fashion, children learn that ADHD is something they *do*, not something that they *have*. Loved ones help them identify ways to respond differently in order to take care of themselves. For example, they might be asked, "Rather than drop out, what might work better for you when others sound critical?"

Parents can also offer guidance in more generalized forms (comprehensible to the child) when helping to extinguish diagnostic responding. For example, parents say "If you're the last one in the room, please close the door," instead of saying, "Please close the door." Or: "From now on would you be willing to put your dishes in the sink when you're finished eating?" rather than tell the child to put his dishes in the sink after each meal. Parents comment that it is "always" preferable to remove muddy shoes instead of telling the child to remove the shoes each time he enters the house. They note that helping makes life easier and more enjoyable for everyone, rather than associate helping with access to a specific privilege. A repetition of acceptable response patterns with less point of performance repeating is bound to follow.

In a situation such as sport, for example, after one can reasonably presume that the child knows the procedures, the parent is urged to wait for the child to assume the correct positioning before pitching a ball. To promote increased self-reliance, the parent is asked to remain tolerant while the child takes more time to do tasks less well (which can condition increased competency over the long term).

In a related matter, many child-rearing experts recommend giving children more discretionary authority, but some parents report that their child (diagnosed or not) does not always respond positively, even when given a choice. The child responds as if the parent *still* functions as controlling agent, and that the parent unilaterally decides on the possible choices.

To mitigate the problem of negative responding during "choice giving," the parent here again will suggest or encourage possible choices (whenever feasible) rather than compel the child to make a choice, or ask the child to help them figure out possible choices. A more accommodating style can elicit increased co-operation.

However, as we alluded above, it is not always feasible or reasonable to engage in open-ended mutually pleasing encounters. For example, the parent can tell the child that she can play with one of several toys, or ask "Do you want to leave these toys on the floor where they might get broken or thrown away, or would you like to pick them up?" On other occasions, parents will be more explicit about limitations and say "After these toys are picked up, we can play with the toys on the shelves." In other instances, parents will inform the child that "We haven't set money aside to replace that toy if it is lost or broken." Assertive interventions are sometimes necessary when an adult recognizes that the child is generating an extraordinary mess, or when the child shows neglect that will directly impact on others.

Parents can also present options in ways that facilitate the child towards more reasonable or socially acceptable behavior. For instance, a parent can state, "If you calm down, it might be easier to figure out a better solution." Similarly, a parent might tell the child, "You can keep complaining, but we still have time to play with the toys that are already off the shelves." Or: "We can finish now, or wait until tonight, but that might keep us from watching our movie."

As a way to facilitate mutual respect, loved ones can empathize with the diagnosed person's perspective, presume goodwill and competence, and alter language forms accordingly. For example, a parent might say, "Is it okay if I count on you to do that?" instead of "Don't forget!" or "I expect follow-through." Similarly, rather than point critically and say, "Clean this up again, it isn't right," the response can be: "Would you please take another look at this?" Or: "I wonder if you would do the family a favor and pick up all the pieces?"

When implementing our learning approach, parents routinely inquire whether it is best to ignore diagnostic responding or take some other action to immediately stop the behavior. The answer is "that it depends." That is, while sometimes ignoring problematic ADHD behaviors will help reduce the frequency rates of the actions over time, and not alert the child to new ways to in-furiate, unearth, or undermine parent, in some situations ignoring strategies will amplify diagnostic responding to a deleterious level. In that case it will be nec-essary for the parent to respond by limiting or redirecting (rather than overlook).

Parents can also defuse diagnostic responses simply by remaining calm and self-assured rather than frustrated and fuming. Whether to not respond, redirect, or forcefully coerce is a judgment call; parents are asked to evaluate risks and benefits. While diagnostic behaviors will likely diminish over time as long as those behaviors lose their mobilizing power, accommodations, and/or permit the avoidance of adversity, in the short-term, problems related to ADHD responding may require immediate resolution. Even when parents do not immediately inter-cede, they can nevertheless talk with older diagnosed children later on about recurrent problematic patterning. Without sounding berating, belittling, or criti-cal, the parent can solicit the child's help in order to resolve this type of diffi-culty.

But there are indeed benefits to waiting before engaging the child in conflict resolution. For example, the parent says during the ride home, "That was diffi-cult for both of us when we had to leave the toy store. What can we do so that it works out better the next time?" Discussing the problem when details are likely to be remembered may provide clear advantages, although it might be helpful to revisit this problem prior to the next excursion to the toy store as well.

By allowing for a gap between the performance of the problem behavior and attempts to solve the identified problems, there is less probability that prob-lem behaviors will inadvertently be reinforced. If time is set aside for mutually agreeable verbal interaction, alternative possibilities can thoroughly be dis-cussed. Daily life often unfolds too quickly for this to occur; problems associ-ated with shopping trips, for example, can be addressed proactively by asking diagnosed children to identify how to make waiting less problematic (e.g., bring a small toy) before leaving the house. Parents can also include the child in some of the shopping decisions in order to reinforce participatory behaviors (e.g., what to buy, when to visit a certain store, etc.). This will help make shopping trips less associated with loss of discretionary control.

Another way for parents to facilitate mutual accommodating during shop-ping is to emphasize that it is more pleasurable to complete errands if everyone cooperates. Parents highlight the advantages to making sound economic deci-sions. For example, money saved can be used for other purchases that the diag-nosed child and other family members appreciate.

Rather than focus on negatives, or threaten to put a red mark on the diag-nosed child's hand to indicate a penalty for shopping trip non-compliance (Barkley, 2001), the learning approach is a mutually reinforcing interaction where the child is urged to focus on positive events related to cooperation. Par-ents learn to ask questions rather than provide answers, and diagnosed persons learn to initiate rather than react to parental directives.

Only as a last resort are parents to consider coercion or explicitly telling the child what to do, in for example, shopping at the child's favorite store after other shopping is completed, or buying the child's favorite foods after other purchases have been made. Similarly, parents might sometimes decide to temporarily (or definitively) leave a store until problems are resolved, by telling the child, "Let's solve this outside so we don't disturb others."

When the learning approaches discussed above work effectively, the parent is no longer the only one preoccupied about meeting expectations. The diagnosed child will also show interest in cooperating, and behaving in ways that parallel initiated and enjoyed activity. Rather than posit that ADHD explains a child's lack of concern to coordinate with others over time, we uphold that context and circumstance reinforce intrusiveness, avoidance of requirements, and/or reliance on external initiatives. For intellectually competent diagnosed persons, social conditioning can very reasonably account for the child's apparent time blindness and other ADHD patterns. This new intervention helps children share ideas, appreciate socially valued achievements, and problem solve in positive ways.

Chapter 8

ADHD Responding in School

The likelihood of an ADHD diagnosis rises markedly when a child's difficult behaviors occur and are reported in school. Because it is scientifically tenuous to regard ADHD as a neural biological problem if difficult behaviors occur only under circumscribed conditions, a child's problematical experiences in school often tip the scales and cue an ADHD diagnosis. Teachers and parents are more likely to suspect that neurological ADHD is the underlying cause of the child's difficulties, even though diagnostic responding had not been a significant disruptor within the family.

When children do not readily conform, or if they monopolize social resources inordinately through rambunctious, hazardous, and non-participatory behavior, professional help is often sought; this tendency heightens when persons outside the family work with the child in school settings where conformity and achievement are crucial. A low probability of goodness of fit between ADHD behavior and school success suggests a mismatch between ADHD behaviors and the requirements and expectations imposed in most formal settings.

Children will also recognize significant adjustment difficulties in school that had not previously taken place. Pfiffner and Barkley (1998) note that poor functioning in school is the primary reason that parents bring their adolescents to treatment, because the child's immediate well-being is jeopardized by school failure. Perhaps the parent's employment is also threatened when the parent must leave work early to address school problems. Disapproval from sources outside the family can assault the parent's competency, thus calling for immediate solutions.

When younger diagnosed children repeat ADHD behaviors, they tend to be immaturely cute and entertaining, usurp attention, overstep boundaries and disregard instructions, especially in public places. However, we know that incessant giggling about nonsense will generate different consequences in school compared to the same behavior during family meals. Annoying others, lack of focus, giving up quickly, and shirking responsibility can lead to severe outcomes with teachers who must manage large groups of students. Manifest ADHD behavior certainly elicits concern from parents, but the child will duly get sent out of the classroom when behaving the same way with a teacher as he does at home. The classroom structure imposes that teachers expect greater self-reliance and accommodation than a typical family unit, and the diagnosed child can become disheartened and discredited when he fails to meet expectations.

When diagnostic behaviors repeat in school, problems will intensify. Teachers have little extra time to convince, prod, and induce accommodating responses from children who have been conditioned towards extremes of monopolizing and avoidance. These behaviors can manifest particularly strongly, because many diagnosed children have not yet learned to function cooperatively within the family, and school functioning requires adaptation to a group agenda. Teachers will complain that the student is fidgety, does not follow instructions, leaves his seat (to sharpen a pencil), does not assume responsibility, or will not abide by routines or an itinerary.

Barkley (2000) reports that the most important problem for ADHD children in school is lack of productivity. Diagnosed children are three times more likely to fail a grade at school than non-diagnosed persons (Barkley, 1998e). At elementary school they lack fine motor skills, are less ready to read, or have no knowledge of basic math'concepts (Barkley, Shelton, et al., 2002). Weiss and Hechtman (1993) have also observed that up to 30% of diagnosed children will drop out of high school, and on average, they score 10-30 points lower on school achievement tests (Barkley, DuPaul, and McMurray, 1990). However, the question begs whether their problems are caused by biological delay called ADHD, or are resultant from having *learned* a behavioral pattern that is a significant mismatch for school success.

In either case, as problems at school escalate, there is the likelihood that the child will become a beacon for negative attention at home; the child's school difficulty tends to monopolize and preoccupy the household. Problems at school increase problems at home, as loved ones admonish each other, assume blame for their child's failures, have difficulty with the teacher's disapproval of their child, and consequently grow more frustrated and impatient with the child.

If the child is able to function acceptably under less demanding circumstances, traditionalists will assert that school expectations often draw the child's inherent condition to the surface. Their approach is to immediately introduce a detailed contingency management program to tighten controls, engage the child in point of performance cueing, and keep the child medicated throughout the school day. Parents are encouraged to micromanage and coerce in order to increase school achievement. For example, traditionalists sometimes recommend that diagnosed teens not be permitted to drive the family car or play video games until grades improve and medication is taken. These recommendations are dogmatic despite the lack of consensus among medical peers on best practice techniques regarding diagnosed teens and school achievement (DuPaul and Stoner, 2003).

We therefore question whether traditional school interventions are effective in the long term; diagnosed individuals may simply be learning to study mechanically so that access to resources will not be lost. ADHD diagnosed individuals learn to study under conditions of parental insistence; they learn to do schoolwork under duress. As noted throughout this work, increased stringency can also increase the probability that they will learn to thwart their parents from usurping control.

In some instances, they will remain secretive about their school day, avoid contact with parents, and not inform them about what they enjoy, so that those activities will not be withheld when they are punished. Many diagnosed students become adept at sneaking and outmaneuvering if relationships become adversarial. Numerous parents report that, as discussion turns to school or schoolwork, the walls rise and the child becomes defensive, possibly yawns, avoids, or feigns weariness.

We acknowledge that the advice to induce productivity with amphetamines, constant monitoring, punishment, and bribes affects diagnosed students relatively quickly; however, compliance achieved under coercion or compensatory conditions will be unlikely to repeat when the pressure and enhancements cease. Those tactics might also result in even greater avoidance of schoolwork when the child eventually has enough discretionary authority to refuse, in that schoolwork has been paired with persistent negativity. Students might also decline to do schoolwork unless they receive extra compensations, including money.

We observe that a vicious cycle is evident where participants learn to counteract each others' attempts to coerce. Parents and teachers following traditional dictums are left with the problem of countering ongoing diagnostic responding by offering further compensations, coercions and enticements in order to reinforce acceptable school behaviors. Moreover, using the traditional approach to increase school productivity will require a monitor to conscientiously manage the child's resources; unless such an arrangement is maintained across a wide range of conditions, consistent school achievement will likely decrease.

Even though interventions such as the Irvine Paraprofessional Program produce positive short-term results in school performance (Kotkin, 1995; Arnold et al., 1997), adherents neither, as a matter of routine, delve into the shortcomings of the program, nor do they assess side effects very rigorously. For example, do the diagnosed students become conditioned to rely on the paraprofessional to sit with them, facilitate assignments, and organize their behavior? Do these interventions train children to be less persistent, in that giving up correlates with greater compensation or involvement from the aide? Are these children conditioned to wait for instructions rather than utilize their own resources?

Efforts to shape self-reliant functioning often appear to be secondary during traditional interventions. For instance, Pfiffner and Barkley (1998) recommend giving diagnosed students a second set of books to compensate for forgetfulness. They also encourage individuals to obtain a coach or mentor to help them coordinate and meet school requirements. However, specific techniques to help diagnosed students track their books and function autonomously are not outlined.

Traditional intervention is designed above all to contain symptoms and prevent harm; conversely, training for self-reliance allows parents to help diagnosed children learn to self-manage effectively in the classroom. While acknowledging that it may be initially necessary to move the child's desk closer to the teacher (Pfiffner, Barkley, and DuPaul, 2006), the learning intervention highlighted in this book works just as diligently to help the child function acceptably within the group. The assumption that continuous contingency management and "special conditions" are always necessary may also keep expectations low and increase reliance on external assistance.

Although traditionalists argue that the school environment lacks immediate reinforcers to stimulate diagnosed persons, we think that students may be immediately reinforced whenever they behave in ways that promote higher grades. The fact that a particular behavior can increase the probability of a more distant future outcome (such as an acceptable report card) does not negate the possibility that the behavior is also immediately reinforced as it is enacted. Reinforcement is not relegated only to times when someone explicitly gives, for example, a report card, a payment, complimentary acknowledgment, nor is it related to a designated (arbitrary) outcome such as receiving a diploma or making parents proud. All our behaviors may be immediately conditioned to occur more or less often, depending on what (immediately) sequences with our actions.

And despite that extra rewards and medication can, in the short-term, increase school achievement, it does not logically follow that lack of school achievement for diagnosed persons is caused by a chemical imbalance, or the failure to provide sufficient immediate rewards and punishments. The etiology of a problem is not determined by the fact that particular interventions work. For example, alcohol often helps a person function with less anxiety, and giving an alcoholic a reward for not drinking might diminish the drinking, but we learn nothing about potential ways to account for his or her anxiety when observing these effects.

Individuals can continue behaviors that increase their grades day by day even though an end state (however defined) will not occur for months or years. Every time an action contributes to the posited end state (e.g., a high grade, a completed collection of baseball cards, etc.), its probability of recurrence increases when equivalent situations are encountered. It will be necessary to observe diagnosed persons over time before it is possible to discern which event sequences are reinforcing their actions.

For example, discovering that a teacher is not grading homework assignments may significantly reduce the probability that students will complete the next assignment—despite whether the teacher assigns work the next day or several weeks hence. As many therapists can attest, events occurring many years ago may still influence responding in present situations in remarkable ways.

On the other hand, traditionalists doggedly maintain that diagnosed persons can only show unabated achievement when tasks provide *immediate* reinforcement. Activities that are uncorrelated with diagnostic responding allegedly have "built in" immediate reinforcements (e.g., computer games). It is claimed that schoolwork has relatively few of these provided compensations; that is why diagnosed persons have so much trouble motivating for these tasks.

However, one might also ask how it is decided that a person is operating under conditions of immediate or delayed reinforcement, or that students who perform well in school are better able to withstand delay. For example, what if we found that a more distant future event such as beating the game before a peer (who the diagnosed person will not see or talk with for a month) significantly influences his achievement rates with that activity? What if a non-diagnosed successful student stops achieving when his social life becomes more active? Is he now more influenced by smaller, immediate rewards due to a surge of inhibitory failures? What if school productivity improves for this formerly serious student only when his parents introduce tightly controlled contingency management? Is it that he now requires concrete external representation of parameters due to a recent contracting of an inhibitory problem?

In the above scenarios we can reasonably claim that both the high achiever in school and the diagnosed person who exhibits non-assigned achievements show conditioned patterns of behavior. In addition, one might argue that the social acceptability of the behavior tells us nothing about the extent to which delayed gratification is taking place.

For example, high achieving students may report that they enjoy learning about a particular subject, that they like it when they answer questions correctly during class, that they do non-vocal verbal responses pertaining to parent and teacher reaction to their work. These students may also indicate that they imagine getting into a prestigious college, and also fantasize about qualifying for a high paying job and being able to buy stuff. They state that they become excited about a promised monetary reward from a grandparent for each high grade. But these students are not delaying better; behavior consistent with school achievement has been conditioned, including the occurrence and content of specific mental responses that also influence their achievements.

In similar ways, otherwise competent *diagnosed* students who achieve less well in school are doing behaviors consistent with having the teacher approach their desk more often. They may also report doing non-vocal verbal behavior about content related to their plans when the school day ends. Avoidance of schoolwork and unacceptable school behaviors is reinforced by *not* putting themselves in the position of trying to please and then failing. Lower achievement may be the end result, even though they elicit great concern from teachers and parents. However, for both achieving and non-achieving students, each behavioral act is likely to be immediately conditioned by the sequencing of situations and circumstances related to the expressed behaviors.

As a way to empirically explore the parameters that influence each student's behavior, we might investigate how various conditions will affect school productivity. For example, variables such as substituting the teacher, changing conditions under which assistance is given, varying the managed consequences, introducing different subject matter, revising curriculum for increased success rates, altering the possibility of college admission, and introducing a boyfriend or girlfriend, can be assessed.

Understated or remarkable changes can also influence behavior significantly. For example, achievement rates at school can alter in an extreme way when a serious student discovers that her parents do not have enough money to pay for college. In contrast, a diagnosed poor achiever may begin to improve in school when his "perfect" sister starts to experience problems in that setting.

However, even though an individual is asked directly about what is influencing his school behavior (including questions about non-vocal verbal content and imaginings) he may not be able to account for what happens any better than an observer who has studied his actions. For example, many individuals do not recognize that their under-achievement or misbehavior in class protects them from trying and failing, nor do they understand that when they are content with others, confident, and eager to please, they often bring home assignments and complete them with relative ease.

Furthermore, even if it is the case that diagnosed students do not achieve in school because of failure to consider future consequences, we can still argue that differences in conditioning rather than inhibitory delay account for their failures to respond thusly. This argument is tenable because ADHD empiricism has not established that diagnosed persons are permanently less able to learn various mental responses. Traditional explication is even weaker, since no one has established that regard for future consequences at strategic times adequately accounts for less diagnostic functioning in school or at home. It has also not been established that diagnosed persons achieve relatively poorly in school because they do those precursor actions less often throughout the day.

In our learning model we alternatively explore interactional patterns that increase diagnostic responding. For example, when the child reacts to a parent who shows high anxiety responses (and discomfort) related to an expectation to succeed and achieve, these children perceive their parents as unhappy and stressed. Their diagnostic patterning is in stark contrast to the parent, and they might explicitly indicate that they refuse to be frazzled like the parent as they live their lives. They learn *not* to achieve so that their lives are not so scheduled and confining. In other circumstances a child may be excessively constrained within the home, and school is a context where it is safer for the child to be more careless and emotional. The child in this case transgresses in ways that occur less often in his intimidating household.

However, others find it safer to lash out towards milksop parents than towards school personnel. These children do quiet withholding when disgruntled with teachers; they become non-participatory at school. They may still qualify for diagnosis, but their psychology will be markedly different from diagnosed children who more frequently act out in school. Others may be reinforced to underachieve, in that poor school functioning distracts parents from other concerns, and some may shy from achievement, in that they doubt that they can adequately match the successes of other family members.

In this sense each child's history of reinforcement needs to be examined when determining the specifics of diagnostic patterning in particular situations. In this framework inattentiveness, under productivity, and other avoidant behaviors in school are recognized as the child's solutions to the adversity he has been facing in school. For example, in our view, the diagnosed student may be exhibiting alienation, preoccupation, or evasion when not fully immersed during class, rather than exhibiting a neurological inability to remain focused.

Facilitating autonomy and school success

For many diagnosed persons, excessive reliance on reminders from others to do necessary schoolwork becomes the daily routine. Typically these children are doing very little to increase the likelihood of completing work assignments, since it is the job of loved ones and teachers to safeguard, cue, and systematize. Anyone but the diagnosed child must sort things out and direct action.

However, even when traditionalists attempt to train diagnosed students to self-manage in school, contingency management and coercion are still embedded into their programs (Pfiffner, Barkley, and DuPaul, 2006). During these interventions, students are asked to observe and record their responses. The student's self-evaluations are then compared to the teacher's record to check for precision; the child is *reinforced with contingency management* for reliable and "honest" reporting of his classroom behavior (Barkley, Copeland, and Sivage, 1980; Edwards et al., 1995; Hoff and DuPaul, 1998; Barry and Messer, 2003). Successes have been noted, but generally these programs have not met expectations (Pfiffner, Barkley, and DuPaul, 2006).

We believe, however, that autonomous competency in the classroom can be improved by ensuring that trainees maintain discretionary authority as much as possible during the program. This is vital if we expect them to repeat certain behaviors when their arms are not being twisted. Until the program also helps the child learn necessary behaviors in situations they encounter without the program, training will be insufficient. By accentuating mutual respect and adaptation to *in vivo* conditions, we are likely to observe a development of self-management that does not occur with traditional intervention.

Interestingly enough, positive outcomes related to self management are being reported with some programs designed for diagnosed children. For example,

Hinshaw, Henker, and Whalen (1984b) report that self-evaluation was more effective in improving diagnosed children's cooperative behavior with peers on the playground than external reinforcement. These findings indicate that increasing discretionary influence for diagnosed children during problem solving has advantages over management systems that permit less discretionary input.

Similarly, Naglieri and Gottling (1997) also yield comparable results when students participate in their "Cognitive Assessment System" for mathematics, a program to facilitate planning, self-monitoring, and independent functioning. Special care is taken to avoid students' reliance on teachers' explicit directives or cues. The authors report positive outcomes with a wide range of students, including those diagnosed with ADHD.

Consequently, rather than focus on bribing the students with rewards that merely disrupt the chance for behaviors to repeat when rewards are withdrawn, program designers can focus on conditioning new behaviors without adding contingencies. Students can receive acknowledgment from the teacher and ultimately, higher grades, by learning effective self-managing behaviors.

In our approach, the program leader attempts to resolve concerns related to participation as an important first step *without* utilizing contingency management to induce participation. We expect that students will be reinforced to stay enrolled without bribes or threats. Students and teachers collaborate and identify which behaviors will be enacted in particular situations and circumstances, and the curriculum is designed in relation to their joint efforts.

Program facilitators or teachers would function as consultants who help students accomplish self-managing behaviors that they deem worthwhile or agreeable. Leaders would *not* role model as monitors who focus on insuring compliance to "honest reporting." Programs would instead be designed to help students resolve their own problems and concerns.

By not making additional contingencies dependent on program compliance, students are not reinforced to cheat the system. There is now no necessity for a warden. Students are reinforced when their coding is a reliable indicator of teacher grading, in that they are learning to be successful at school. They only cheat themselves by lying to the teacher. Because students and teachers share the same goal, it is advantageous for students to code honestly so that the teacher can help them make accurate self-appraisals.

If cheating is evident, or if the student has problems while functioning within the program, those concerns can be addressed; it is not that these problematic behaviors require punishment or withholding of contingencies, but they do require a resolution of what reinforces the negative responses. The student can be asked if he is apprehensive or self-conscious about failing; we do not presume that additional negative consequences will help him resolve what is problematic for him. Relationships will become less adversarial as teachers provide mentoring.

Student participation will permit them to better anticipate teacher evaluation. By allowing teachers to review their coding, students learn that they can effectively predict their grades. Since all students know that they will receive a grade, the program is a means for students to enhance their school performance and simultaneously maintain discretionary authority. Self-management is highlighted as a benefit rather than a chore.

Opponents will contend that students most in need of self-management will be the least likely to volunteer or continue to participate because of ADHD, but we counter argue that other problems might account for any lack of enthusiasm (diagnosed or not). Collaboration to resolve such problems before reaching the conclusion that ADHD disability hampers self-management is therefore a reasonable endeavor.

We believe that traditional classroom self-managing programs are unlikely to succeed because students are not learning to respond acceptably without stringent monitoring and extra rewards. Intervention from the outset can instead orient to condition behaviors in situations that will recur as the child progresses through the grades, so that they will progressively function without monitors. The usual consequences for poor school functioning need not be abandoned, but diagnosed individuals may indeed be shaped to function competently as most others in response to typically occurring conditions.

While Pfiffner, Barkley, and DuPaul (2006) claim that total transfer of management of the program from teacher to student is unrealistic, and that reinforcement with managed contingencies is a necessary and important variable for treatment effectiveness, this may not be the case. Perhaps it is only when the child learns certain behaviors in response to the extra rewards and/or withholding of privileges that traditional monitoring becomes a necessity that cannot be removed without significant recidivism. Perhaps only when managed contingencies are employed in the first place, does the continuance or removal of those contingencies become so influential. Rather than assert that the training alone is insufficient, perhaps reinforcing the training with contingency management interferes with the possibility of successfully removing it.

In our alternative intervention, students are encouraged to discuss problems; they are not commanded. For example, instead of forbidding a diagnosed student to interact with a child who frequently gets into trouble, the facilitator will ask the diagnosed child, "Are you sure you want to put yourself in that position by spending so much time together?" Or say, "What do you want to do if the other child starts talking or fooling around?" All participants work to identify adversities that occur at school and tend to reinforce high frequencies of ADHD responses.

In this regard, Clark et al. (1988) have found that peers more often withdraw from those who are ADHD diagnosed; moreover, diagnosed students typically have fewer friends (Blachman and Hinshaw, 2002), and are more often victimized by peers (Deater-Deckard, 2001). Not surprisingly, they often suspect that peers want to behave aggressively towards them (Milich and Dodge, 1984) and as a result, therefore tend to respond aggressively rather than calmly when conflict flares (Turber, Heller, and Hinshaw, 2002). Such events as these may conspire in making school an unappealing place for these children, and thus reinforce ADHD responding.

Therefore, it will be necessary to reduce the diagnosed child's concerns about failure, social exclusion, appearing stupid in front of others, and/or suspicion of peers. The child's preoccupation with other activities, or concerns about problems at home can also influence school functioning for diagnosed students. Often it will be necessary for the child to discriminate between situations at home with parents and siblings, and events occurring in school with teachers and classmates. Making these important distinctions helps the child stop repeating family behaviors that lead to more troublesome consequences when enacted in the school setting. For example, parents can observe, "I know you're not happy with the teacher, but will *not* doing the work get you what you want?"

Facilitators can also help younger diagnosed students develop routines regarding schoolwork by encouraging them to put homework assignments on the kitchen table where they can be easily seen, by suggesting that they start homework at predictable times such as when entering the house, or right after a snack, and by helping them learn to put their homework assignments in places that will increase the likelihood of bringing them back to school and handing them to the teacher. It is crucial that the plan be workable and designed in order for the diagnosed child to act autonomously.

Teachers can assist by allowing the child to be an active participant in designing assignments whereby she is encouraged to contribute more without the teacher simultaneously adding contingencies that are not already part of the basic school program. The objective is to decrease reliance on teacher surveillance. The major task is to figure out what increases or decreases the frequency rates of less acceptable ADHD behaviors, and this can differ from one diagnosed person to the next. For example, a child may sabotage the teacher's discretionary authority by responding with ADHD patterns; after teacher or peer provocation, a child may also be vehemently defended by her parents when complaining about peers or teachers who allegedly teased or mistreated her. A drama at school can then take over the household during the evening hours.

Diagnosed children get into significant trouble when they rile others in school, but they also elicit worry from teachers, principals, and parents. Those outcomes may continue to reinforce the behaviors, despite reprimands and possibilities of retention, which can eventually alienate and discourage them even more (Pagani et al., 2001). Similar to family patterning, the child can increase the consternation of those around her, protect adequacy and hope by *not* trying, and have her own workload reduced when ADHD responding in school.

Diagnostic responding with schoolwork may continue to be reinforced with great frequency despite that school achievement is lowered. Pfiffner and Barkley (1998) contend that a failure to bring home school assignments is related to memory problems due to delays caused by ADHD, but one can also posit (much like Freud) that forgetting is a solution behavior (or reinforced response), and more socially effective than saying no directly. For instance, when failing to bring home an assignment, the diagnosed person also has more time for other self-initiated activities, and can successfully avoid the assignment without suffering the consequences of explicit disobedience.

In light of these concerns, perhaps different categories can be imposed to account for the behaviors exhibited by diagnosed children in school. For instance, many of these children react to a lack of acceptance, or have a long history of difficulty mastering particular school content. Intervention can shape alternative ways to respond when those problems arise, instead of attempting to contain a posited "disinhibited" neurobiology. These students will benefit from an intervention that develops positive relational patterns with teachers (and peers) as well as exposure to success rates that incite persistence and further independence.

Other, albeit eccentric, changes can also be introduced in school to help diagnosed students achieve without utilizing traditional interventions. For example, if the younger child enjoys playing with tweezers, teachers can help the child develop fine motor skills through using that implement. The child then learns to use a pencil with content previously introduced while the child was working with the tweezers. Along these same lines teachers can help diagnosed persons learn math and reading by using their trading cards and video games rather than ban trading cards altogether from the classroom.

We can also help diagnosed children recognize similarities between tasks they competently complete, and tasks they have not yet mastered. For example, when drawing a diamond, a student may be able to construct the first and second angles, but have difficulty forming the third angle, in that she is required to identify a midpoint in order to accurately construct the final aspect of the drawing. Trying to discriminate this midpoint often results in children giving up or making inaccurate lines.

In contrast, the same child (after practice) shows more skill when operating a video game character that must carefully approach certain hazards, jump onto moving objects, and anticipate the movement of objects and other events that have not yet happened on the screen. Many diagnosed children eventually learn the proper movements without complete external representation during video game activity, and some of those competencies do not differ much from learning to draw the final angle of a diamond. By helping the child recognize similarities between school requirements and competencies already being demonstrated, assigned activity becomes less adverse and more practicable.

It may also be advantageous if the diagnosed child identifies instances of success at school. He can be encouraged to replicate the calmness, persistence, and self-reliance he has demonstrated with other subject matter. Students can anticipate what might happen if they were to show greater systematic effort, less self-doubt, and more persistence before giving up, as they tend to do with some school tasks.

Since diagnosed persons make the attributions and designations that they want certain outcomes to occur, they may also emit the same behaviors that are frequently observed when they pursue their interests. Such an intervention helps make problems less insurmountable, and helps the child recognize that she is competent enough to succeed. Therefore, prior to settling on a disability explanation, teachers are encouraged to study the child's behavior in many scenarios to look for instances of competency that supercede the child's posited delay.

Generally, teachers are encouraged to increase instances of independent successes, introduce remedial work to improve basic skills, and alter the content and pace of the curriculum so that learning curves are progressive. It will often be necessary to reduce class size to contour the curriculum in order to accomplish those goals. Teachers are advised to pay close attention to the relationship they are forging with the child, and to include the child's point of view when deciding the curriculum. Conversely, frequent disapproval for not producing enough work is not the most effective strategy, and tends to reinforce the child to react defensively and negatively. Teachers can, wherever possible, allow the child to take the lead and initiate during instructional sessions, and interact in a manner that presumes that the child is competent enough to succeed.

Rather than criticize or tell them what they *must* do when talking with diagnosed students about their school difficulties, teachers can help them to identify for themselves what they can do. The teacher would provide enough guidance to prevent floundering, and be impressed when the child derives solutions. Children can be asked if they are comfortable with what currently takes place in school. They can identify what interferes with school achievement, and think about what might happen if certain adjustments were made (e.g., stay after school, ask a question rather than give up, talk with the teacher, work consistently rather than procrastinate or rush, etc.). We presume that interventions are more helpful and effective when diagnosed children help make these determinations instead of hearing them from others.

These questions are also designed to help diagnosed children recognize that they must learn to live with the consequences of their actions. Achieving to conform becomes secondary as the emphasis shifts towards having diagnosed children increasingly take care of themselves by changing response patterns linked with schoolwork. In some instances children will indicate that they resent parental coercion and preoccupation with the level of their school achievement, in that their parents are too critical and seldom interested in spending time with them in enjoyable or helpful ways. The learning approach outlined here ameliorates the identified conflicts.

If the child complains that schoolwork is "boring" and that he "can't" imagine doing schoolwork in a positive fashion, this could mean that other problems loom large in the background and need to be resolved, such as the child's concerns about lack of competence, powerlessness, or fear of seeming ignorant. In these scenarios it is crucial to tolerate mistakes, to help parents pay attention to successes, and help them change their emphases so that the child will accommodate on a regular basis. It will often be necessary to help the child learn that it is not dangerous or threatening to submit to what others want. Parents work to increase the child's contributions in order to reduce passivity, complaints, and withdrawal.

Teachers too, can urge diagnosed students to specify the sequence of steps in order to complete a lengthy project instead of assigning or designating the steps; this strategy helps them learn to break complexity into smaller units. Not only will they have more opportunities to decide the assignment format (e.g., book reports), but they will also be eager to continue to be creative after assignments are completed. Work is less associated with rigidity and coercion.

Dunlap et al. (1994) agree that task productivity and attentiveness can be increased when students are given choices regarding schoolwork. If, for example, the child likes motorcycles, the teacher incorporates that content into curriculum when possible, and builds a positive rapport with the child by finding material about motorcycles. This pattern of interacting reinforces the diagnosed child's importance to the teacher, as well as role models how to accommodate to another person's point of view.

When diagnosed students are adept or well-informed about specific activities (e.g., video games, trading cards, information about animals, historical events, certain school subjects, etc.), they are asked to share that information, and act as mentor with other peers and adults "a la Montessori." This procedure not only helps to shape new learning, but also explains material to others in order to reverse a unilateral power situation. Diagnosed children have the opportunity to coach others (instead of always being helped), and classmates can characterize the diagnosed child in a new light as competent and knowledgeable. By encouraging peer mentoring, diagnosed children will also less often equate time spent in school with ineptitude, ostracism, loneliness, or estrangement. DuPaul and Eckert (1997) agree that peer tutoring has produced reasonable benefits for diagnosed persons, but having them tutor others is also advantageous because their competency is reinforced.

The child learns to repeat the same non-diagnostic responses with school-related content that had previously elicited negative, non-normatively paced, or avoidant reactions. Increasing the child's social importance and acceptability in school (e.g., greeting the diagnosed child enthusiastically, soliciting the child's help when the teacher would like assistance, etc.) can reduce diagnostic responding remarkably.

However, we must first jump the hurdle of the previous instructional patterns associated with diagnosed students that have thus far impeded learning. For example, diagnosed students rush through assignments or give up quickly when they first encounter disappointment or difficulty. Their response ameliorates aversive conditions and permits escape from completing a unilaterally imposed task that threatens their adequacy but does not help them learn the material.

Some diagnosed students will also focus on every mistake made by teacher or parent, thereby taking every opportunity to reverse the power arrangement. However, with so much correction taking place, student and teacher will often struggle and not work together effectively. For these children submitting to instruction becomes a sign of weakness, incompetence, or inferiority. Rather than learn the lesson, they expend more energy identifying what is *wrong* with the lesson.

For others, once a particular mistake is made, insecurity and self-doubt loom large, setting off a chain reaction of incorrect responses. The child gets "hung up" and is preoccupied with making the same blunders; and, similar to when individuals are told *not* to think about pink elephants, the error increases in frequency, thus adversely influencing learning rates. But getting "hung up" occurs in the general population as well. A person can, for example, initially mispronounce a word and have the same difficulty time and again, despite repeated corrections.

While many different scenarios are possible, often diagnosed children respond as if failure is inevitable. Some will anxiously tap their head with their pencil, cover their face, and/or scribble over their work presuming that it is not good enough. Participation will often decrease, and sometimes there will be long pauses where no ideas are forthcoming. The child becomes stressed and inordinately concerned about failing and not measuring up. Questions are not asked so that deficiencies will not be exposed (including failures to pay attention), and when returning to the lesson at a later time, it is as if nothing at all has been retained. Moreover, when others become frustrated with the slow learning curve, the situation only worsens.

We observe that many diagnosed students approach complex assignments as if others are imposing suffering and/or the certainty of failure. However, rather than accept the notion that diagnosed persons have "too much noise in their heads" to adequately complete tasks requiring multi-step planning and thoughtfulness, we adopt a positive view. Teachers can demonstrate acceptable procedures, keep verbalizations to a minimum, and ask questions to help the child identify strategies.

It will often be the case that the child has not yet learned basic problem solving tactics, such as altering only one parameter at a time. For example, when applying these techniques to improve oral reading, the diagnosed child can be encouraged to identify where the syllables in a word are, and mask sections of the word only initially. If teachers and loved ones continuously provide the external representation and mask for them, children will simply not learn how to be self-reliant when encountering complexities.

In a related matter, we observe that diagnosed children rely on their fingers while doing basic arithmetic. They do so in order to provide the solution just as when they demand parents to provide answers to various problems, or to spell a word rather than use the dictionary. Myriad forms of conditioning apparently allow for diagnosed children to feel relatively secure, but rarely do these solutions develop their competency to function with less help.

However, in our learning approach, diagnosed children are encouraged to close their eyes while finger counting in order to develop "mental" skills. This response substitutes for the more common "overwhelmed" reaction. After becoming comfortable with this procedure, the child then imagines counting on fingers without moving the fingers; strategies are eventually introduced to help the child visualize similarly using numbers.

The child is also given the opportunity to practice basic math computations *without* cards or paper and pencil (including multiplication tables). The parent or teacher presents sequences of numbers orally for the child to compute, and increases the complexity of the sequences as the child masters the simplest items. The child also practices spelling orally (including identifying words spelled out loud by others).

Likewise, in order to carry out a required sequence of actions independently, the parent first does homework with the child. The next time the parent sits beside the child, engaged in some other activity so that the child has company, but learns to complete the assignment with greater independence. The parent can say, "How about I do my house bills while you complete some of these school items?"

We observe an example of the benefits that correlate with maintaining an individual's discretionary authority when diagnosed individuals return to school as adults and show improved achievement relative to their childhood school experience. Without managed contingencies or simplified conditions, these adults often achieve within the school setting. Successes occur even though nothing has changed neurologically to account for the improvement; their behavior is now more time organized and acceptable. Poor educational achievement remains a problem for many diagnosed children, but some do return to school as adults and show improved functioning.

Consistent with the learning approach, Locke (1991) has coined the expression "motivation hub," which refers to personal goals, commitment to those goals, and self-efficacy. He claims that these variables are often the most influential determinants of action. Moreover, when studying the relationship between assigned and personal goals, Locke and Latham (2002, 709) claim that "assigned goal effects are mediated by personal or self-set goals that people choose in response to the assignment, as well as by self-efficacy." It is in this sense that the learning approach orients to shape self-reliance or "self-efficacy," and incorporate personal goals into assigned activity, because doing so helps people achieve, according to Locke and Latham's research.

Parents meanwhile can assist the child in recognizing that independence and mastery in the school setting will ensure that the child flourishes when the parent is not around. They can explicitly impart the message that life will improve for her if she learns stepwise autonomy. The parent is interested in helping the child, but it is in her best interest to gradually manage her own affairs with less reliance on them.

However, parents are always prepared to provide the necessary assistance to facilitate school achievement during the school years. For example, as a way to make cumbersome written tasks less daunting and enjoyable, parents can volunteer to transcribe as the child dictates. The parent responds positively to what the child says and helps him clarify ideas whenever necessary. Over time, he will associate less negativity with written work assignments, and parents can gradually remove themselves from the activity as competence develops. Parents can also intermittently celebrate and encourage the child's success without telling him in advance. Parents acknowledge accomplishments and impart the message that it is a pleasure to offer subsidy and other accommodations to a serious student; students receive special status rather than restrictions or controls.

Even when helping a younger diagnosed child with homework, a parent can act as a facilitator. For example, the parent requests the child's opinion about what to do first when starting an assignment. The parent checks to see whether the child agrees with any suggestions that the parent has made before proceeding, as this also reassures the child that her discretionary authority is respected. Similarly, rather than command the child to start an assignment, the parent can say, "This might be a good time for you to do some homework, since we are going out later."

However, we have seen that low grades could be clues to unhappiness: the child may be punishing parents for transgressions (e.g., abandonment, divorce, etc.). Some diagnosed children mimic the parental inactivity at home, and others have no achieving role model. However, very often the case is that diagnosed persons have learned to "save face" by not exerting effort. They do not want to risk giving up the notion that they would achieve high marks if they tried.

To help the diagnosed child respond positively to homework, parents can reframe activity as an "opportunity to practice" or "sharpen" skills. The parent indicates that practicing schoolwork is like practicing baseball before and after games. There is usually not enough time during school to sufficiently master the material or show the coach (or teacher) "what you can do," so practice is beneficial. Intervention is designed for the child to regard "homework" as a chance to hone skills. We expect that the child will participate more and more as the negativity associated with homework fades.

Without doubt this collaborative learning approach is quite different from Barkley's (1998f, 254) recommendation, for example, to inform the child that he or she has "30 minutes" to complete a class assignment, homework, or a chore, or advice to assign a school monitor at the point of performance—who will "remind" the child and check that compliance has occurred. Our approach also differs from the recommendation that teachers constantly tell him to "think aloud, think ahead;" and we do not advise teachers to continuously cue the child to recite rules for proper conduct, especially when transitions are introduced (Pfiffner, Barkley, and DuPaul, 2006, 555).

For example, if the child wants to play, speak with friends by telephone, or watch television in the evening, but has left work undone, rather than withhold the privilege of television until work is finished, or telling the child what *must* happen, parent can discuss with child the advantages of completing work sooner. By finishing assignments in the earlier evening hours, the child can relax without pressure. The child will feel less burdened by time constraints; parents will be available to consult with her during the early evening, and she can complete the work without becoming exhausted. Such a situation enhances both the work and the child's leisure time, and she will understand the benefits if they are positively noted.

Loved ones can also help to resolve complications that interfere with attempts to persuade. For instance, friends will only be available immediately after school. A break between the end of school and the start of homework will also yield beneficial results. Some assignments may, for example, be too difficult, and thus likely to end in failure. Perhaps the child enjoys monopolizing parent's time in the evening, or becomes angry and reinforced to *not* conform for various reasons. Resolving these problems is a crucial first step before imposing the order that work be done or else privileges will be denied. We suggest that it is entirely possible to sway diagnosed children to act in ways consistent with parental instruction using less supervision and involvement from the parent by incorporating what the child finds acceptable.

Even if parents realize only tolerable results at first, it's progress if the child enacts the plan with fewer parental cues. For example, the child may not scurry off to do homework immediately after school, but will, however, complete the work early in the evening. Routines are important so that diagnosed children can proceed independently when parents are not around. In this regard, Mac Iver, Stipek, and Daniels (1991) report that when students believe they have ability in a subject, they show increased persistence and achievement. Once success is associated with a particular activity, many do fewer ADHD behaviors.

Frequent problems to resolve

Since functioning at school is the most restrictive and demanding set of circumstances imposed on a child, it is not surprising that ADHD behaviors occur most often in the classroom, especially if other problems exist that impair their chances for success in school. Children who rely on their parents to remind and arrange for them, and/or have learned to avoid adversities and restrictions will often have problems adjusting to the classroom environment. A significant percentage of diagnosed children also show encoding and learning problems, so success at school can be fairly difficult. Moreover, McGee, Williams, and Feehan (1992) have pointed out that if ADHD behaviors continue beyond the preschool years, the child will probably have problems with reading when they start primary school.

Spencer, Biederman, and Wilens (1998) report that approximately 30% of diagnosed individuals have some learning disability, but it is expected that after learning ADHD patterning, learning rates of material presented in school are impeded. That interpretation is consistent with Fergusson and Horwood's (1992) findings: that early attentional problems increase the probability of later reading difficulties. Moreover, if various functional problems increase the likelihood that children will learn to respond with ADHD patterns, and those patterns hinder the mastery of school content, then we would expect a correlation between ADHD and so-called "learning disabilities." This alternative account seems just as reasonable as the traditional assertion that persons with limited educational attainment (and frequent learning problems) pair with each other, which then creates a "genetic linkage" between neurological ADHD delay and learning disability (Barkley, 2000).

Interestingly enough, many relatively bright diagnosed children do not show significant problems at school until it becomes more difficult to succeed. They may get by with very little inconvenience or threat to their adequacy upon first entering school, because they either learn very quickly or already know the material. Some of these children have also gained notoriety from others that they are smart enough to succeed without having to study. Although as success becomes harder to attain due to increasingly complicated curricula, which requires more time to complete (e.g., homework, preparation for exams), increased failure will induce diagnostic responding. However, other bright children may show diagnostic patterning earlier if the curriculum is too easy and repetitious; these children may have learned very early to extricate themselves from the vacuity and redundancy of the classroom.

Nevertheless, it is not always the case that ADHD behaviors occur more frequently at school. There are numerous ADHD protocols reporting that some children do more diagnostic responding at home than in academic settings. Given traditional understandings, how this is possible, or on what neurological grounds do we account for those data? While it is claimed that parent-only ADHD is more likely to indicate a predominately oppositional pattern, even though the child qualifies for diagnosis (Barkley, 2006b), one might alternatively claim that a child learns diagnostic responding in one or both settings relative to a multitude of histories and co-occurring problems. Some children repeat family behavior at school, while others respond markedly differently with teachers than with parents. Moreover, some individuals do ADHD at school and at home, and still manage to maintain respectable grades.

Despite the variations, students who most often do ADHD patterns at school are plagued by escalating social difficulties in that setting. For example, research shows that students labeled as rejected, hyperactive, or immature will behave intrusively, will frequently disrupt others, and act provocatively in order to repel or incite others even more (Coie et al., 1991; Dodge, Bates, and Petit, 1990; Lancelotta and Vaughn, 1989; Pope, Bierman, and Mumma, 1991). We observe a vicious cycle in which the diagnosed child learns a more extreme pattern in reaction to being shunned; the more a child behaves in extremes, the more others will recoil.

If the child has learned atypical responses at home, the behaviors will likely repeat in school when conditions that cue the responses recur. For example, when the teacher shows characteristics similar to a problematic parent, the child will be over reactive towards that teacher. If a diagnosed child characterizes a teacher as uncaring, excessively demanding, blaming, critical, or controlling, and casts a similar light on one or both parents, ADHD classroom behaviors will likely increase. The child will be less eager to please, and he may tune out, rush through requirements, and lash out at teacher—identical to the scenario at home.

For this reason a positive approach is necessary when helping diagnosed children adjust to the school environment; this view coincides with Seligman et al. (2005), who also advise positive interventions. The child focuses on the personal and social advantages that correlate with school achievement and the acquisition of knowledge.

Moreover, and paradoxically, to focus on negative events may also increase the probability that they will occur. That is, the more the parent tries to protect the child from fearful outcomes, the more those categories of action get identified and inadvertently fostered. A practical example of this effect occurs when people are told not to laugh. As Kirsch and Lynn (1999, 512) point out, "the attempt to suppress a particular thought or action increases the propensity to engage in the thought or action." Extrapolating from those findings, less school achievement may be inadvertently cued, to some extent, by parental preoccupations.

However, we acknowledge that the child's difficulties in school also spur the parent to be increasingly anxious and negative. In order to stop this unhelpful spiral, it is important for parents to focus on desirable behaviors, since focusing solely on forbidden acts will not help the child be more effective. In addition, a child who is regularly exposed to refusals and negative categories will also imitate that pattern and likely adopt negativity as a modus operandi.

It is noteworthy that Northup et al. (1997) found that using peers to correct the negative behavior of diagnosed students only served to worsen their behavior. If, however, parents and teachers attend to the child's achievement in relation to reasonable school functioning during the school day instead of repeatedly harping "Don't misbehave," or "Don't forget your homework," they become superb role models.

As a rule, when the option exists to either focus on what the child does positively to solve a school problem compared to focusing on behaviors they should avoid, identifying the positive acceptable behaviors will be most effective. For example, facilitators can ask the child what behaviors she would do in order to feel comfortable in school. If she decides on a problematic reaction (e.g., to yell at the teacher), the facilitator can explore whether the child would be satisfied with the consequences of a yelling reaction. However, outrageous replies usually indicate that a child is testing the parent or facilitator, or are related to avoiding an adult's attempt to induce problem solving because other problems are present. Although adults can encourage and persuade the child, focus is on helping the child identify actions that she is *ready to do*.

We anticipate that positive intervention and focus on success will increase the probability that diagnosed children will achieve at school much like their success with other content they associate with mastery and enjoyment. In this context Kirsch and Lynn (1999) discuss how to increase participation and achievement in a manner consistent with our learning intervention. They claim:

> Ensuring that positive feedback will be experienced during treatment can be facilitated by the expectancy that improvement will begin with small, gradual changes. This allows small increments, such as those produced by random fluctuations, to be interpreted as signs of therapeutic success. Relatedly, the assignment of easy initial tasks ensures early successes, which bolster the client's confidence in treatment (p. 511).

A positive approach can also be implemented when a diagnosed child shows a parent a performance report from school. When reports are made available, parents can ask the child what he thinks about it. The parent can ask the child to clarify likes and dislikes, tell the parent whether changes are warranted, and suggest whether alternative behaviors can help solve identified problems. Instead of encouraging parents to impose coercive conditions or offer their own solutions, social exchange centers on what the child identifies as problematic. The child may initially show negativity and avoidance due to past admonishments, but by making the exchange less adversarial and invasive, consultative problem solving will likely develop. The child learns to identify behavioral acts that promote desired outcomes instead of staying preoccupied and upset by parent's digging for information, impingements, and decisions on his behalf.

The procedure of daily teacher reports of diagnosed children is frequently used and recommended in the traditional intervention (Kelley, 1990; Pfiffner, Barkley, and DuPaul; 2006; Robin, 2006), but this strategy is problematic unless the parent is sensitive to the situation. Relationships between teachers and students can become negative and suspicious when teachers frequently draw parents into problems that could reasonably be solved discretely. We have observed that parents become distressed when school problems too often spill into the evening hours; thus no ostensible improvement is made. However, teachers are required to inform parents about the child's school difficulties as well as send home uncompleted work. Information about the child's school functioning might help the *parent* more effectively help the child, but it is important to keep a watchful eye on whether increased monitoring is hurting rather than helping.

Because many parents become more responsive when their children have difficulty at school, or will visit the school to support their child, his "war stories" at school may often mobilize parents in the same ways as when he runs into the street or puts fingers into light sockets. Children are conditioned to repeat behaviors that result in parental advocacy (even on an intermittent basis) during exchanges with teachers and administrators.

We do not condone that parents ignore school problems or be kept uninformed about the child's progress, but sometimes very subtle parental reactions to the child's school-related behaviors can be highly influential in determining the frequency with which ADHD behaviors are evident in school. Parental championing can significantly influence the child's persistence, productivity, avoidance, and patterns of inciting others when the child is at school. In this sense, although a diagnosis of ADHD requires that the unwanted behaviors occur in two different settings, home and school are rarely discrete venues.

However, because the classroom is even more conducive to imperious management than home life, in that monitoring is easier with a captive audience, it is not surprising that unilateral forms of discipline are used widely and endorsed for both diagnosed and non-diagnosed students alike. The classroom is generally a self-contained environment where surveillance occurs with relative ease. Except for very young children who have fewer opportunities to function independently, the classroom permits monitoring that apparently exceeds the typical home scenario. Because the classroom allows for extensive monitoring, and the possibility of quick and consistent contingency management, the school setting is highly conducive to approaches advocated by traditionalists.

It is often the case that teachers and parents are scolded for not doing more stringent contingency management. Many traditionalists assert that teachers must become adept at using "behavioral methods" as a "prerequisite" for teaching diagnosed students (Barkley, 2000). Recommendations are given as if it is factual that those methods are the only correct way to proceed. For example, Pfiffner and Barkley (1998, 452) assert that the ADHD-inflicted must have more structure, more frequent and salient positive consequences, more consistent negative consequences, and more compensation to offset inherent deficits. They recommend that professionals bring "handouts" to team meetings to "instruct school personnel" about ADHD from the perspective of the biological determinist model that necessitates these recommendations.

Teachers are recommended to move diagnosed students closer to the front in order to minimize distractibility and isolate them from such distractions as peers and extraneous sounds. They are advised that rules and instructions should be presented clearly, briefly, and made visible and external. Teachers might place cards in front of diagnosed students for them to be constantly cued about classroom requirements, and students can be given a device which vibrates when they go off task. Students are encouraged to use a computer, and/or write content on paper as much as possible, rather than struggle (and fail) to use their executive functioning. Often it is necessary to buy a second set of books to counter the student's pattern of forgetting materials at school. Students might also be required to take fewer courses if it is an available option (Barkley, 2000).

Everyone is directed to supervise the diagnosed child's school behavior closely, and use contingency management to control the disinhibited child. Not only are teachers encouraged to manage children with contingencies such as big deals, peg systems, lotteries, auctions, team contingencies, class movies, special privileges, etc., but they are also recommended to employ the same methods to monitor their own behavior as well. For example, teachers are encouraged to move bingo chips from one pocket to another when they give praise to a diagnosed child (Barkley, 2000).

We observe, however, that when traditionalists advise contingency management to handle school feedback (Pfiffner, Barkley, and DuPaul, 2006), problems are inevitable. The side effects associated with controlling another person's resources unilaterally will come into play when parents are instructed to react as traditionalists recommend. Disruptions are created when parents withhold rewards based on the teacher's version of an event, and problems can escalate further when explicitly negative consequences are introduced to deal with unacceptable teacher reports, as Robin (2006) recommends.

However, since these stringently managed systems keep parents abreast of what the child does each day and can provide quick and very detailed information, traditionalists continue to recommend those strategies (Anastopoulos, Rhoads, and Farley, 2006). Daily teacher reports are a mainstay of the traditional school intervention with diagnosed students. Since parents usually want to know what happens at school, and do not want to find out too late if their child's failure is imminent, we notice that many parents are receptive to coercive interventions. Most traditionalists claim that daily reports can be advantageous if handled constructively; they usually see no problem tying school achievement to resources made available to the child, which resembles getting paid for adequate job performance.

Although again, when parents decide that allocation of resources depends on the adequacy of the child's school reports, we see that the parent functions more as assessor rather than consultant. If the parent reacts negatively and withholds the child's resources in relation to school compliance, the reports will lead to numerous problems. The child may also react as if the parent is siding with the teacher when complaints result in reprisal, and are taken at face value. The child will become reinforced towards secrecy and other clandestine behaviors in an attempt to maintain access to basic privileges. Passive resistant behaviors such as forgetting and losing schoolwork will also escalate, in that those behaviors can often effectively impede unilateral coercion methods. While traditionalists claim that problems with reporting systems can be squelched by increasing accountability and punishment whenever the child seems to "manipulate," such as insisting that the teacher did not give a report, or that no homework was assigned (Pfiffner, Barkley, and DuPaul, 2006), we observe that patterning revolves around who outmaneuvers who most successfully, and requires that, when in doubt, parents make negative attributions.

These interventions also put the parent in the middle when problems occur between diagnosed children and teachers. Children will likely depict events at school in ways that keep them in a favorable light, while teachers will indicate that something very different occurred. Under those circumstances, if the parent blames the child (when parent did not see what happened) child/parent relationships can become strained and alienated.

Conversely, if the parent becomes critical of the teacher, the parent then runs the risk of undermining the teacher's credibility, which could also reinforce non-cooperative behaviors. These triangles introduce the same problems discussed earlier regarding conflicts among family members. Diagnosed students (often blamed at home), are reinforced when the parent takes their side against the teacher; this is a significant departure from the typical family pattern.

Given these concerns, the strategy of sending students home with daily reports is fraught with problems, particularly when parents abide by traditional recommendations. Often parents get the explicit or tacit message that they are abdicating their responsibility when they do not take punitive action. However, when they react dogmatically, they also put themselves in the position of warden, judge, and jury.

We would therefore refrain from telling parents to "inspect" the child's daily school report, as advised by Pfiffner and Barkley (1998, 475) and alternatively suggest that parents tactfully *discuss* reports with the diagnosed student. Parents can refer to the reviewing of the report as a problem-solving activity, or a way to celebrate successes that the teacher has identified. Ultimately, the child must deal with the contingencies imposed by the school (since the parent cannot change the outside world). But parents can say, "What can we do so that it won't happen to you again?" If or when the child is avoidant, then that reaction is important to address and resolve. It is unlikely that discussing these reports will be helpful if the diagnosed person responds defensively. Again, we do not advise intervention via inspection; such a strategy only puts the diagnosed child on the defensive. We want him to learn to function self-reliantly and confidently in school so that school is a desirable place to attend.

Alternatively, we would arrange so that behavioral change is compatible with both parent and diagnosed child's agenda. If it is deemed helpful to have the student obtain the teacher's signature indicating that homework had been written down accurately in the assignment book before leaving school, as well as obtain the parent's signature indicating that homework has been completed, instead of presenting this monitoring system as a way to curb sneaking and untrustworthiness, the procedure can be framed as a means of preventing the child from being labeled as capricious. He will also be reassured that his work has been adequately transcribed and completed by consulting with teacher *and* parent. The expectation is that he will find this procedure helpful rather than controlling (i.e., "we encourage this solution because we care about you").

Similarly, rather than intercede in a fashion that implies that the parent does not trust the child's competence by saying, "When you finish, I have to check your work," the parent can ask the child if he would "share" what he is learning. Parents can also comment that it is helpful for them to stay up to date with the curriculum in order to better assist him when he wants their assistance in the future. They can also say, "If you would like me to review your work today, let me know." Likewise, when responding to mistakes, they might remark, "I'm not sure I understand this answer; what do you think?" With this approach, parent conferencing orients to build the child's esteem and prowess rather than suggest inadequacy.

Curry (1970) exemplified the problem of rescuing ADHD children when describing an intervention with a bright young student who became conditioned to receive extra attention due to having a reading difficulty. The problem was solved not by increasing the help given, but by regulating the attention she received from her reading failures. Moreover, in some instances, diagnostic responding at school provokes attentiveness not only from family members in the household, but also from non-custodial parents as well, who will rarely be contacted at other times. Responses might reinforce ADHD responding dramatically (i.e., father finally gets involved).

Much anxiety can be elicited and the typical evening routine can potentially reinforce low productivity in the classroom instead of extinguishing the behaviors. Sometimes working parents find it overwhelming to spend excessive amounts of time helping their diagnosed child complete work not finished during school. Evening encounters can become strained, which will only increase ADHD responding when the child works with the parent to complete what "should have been finished earlier." Guilt and making up after frustrating exchanges can also reinforce the recurrence of the problematic behaviors.

However, we observe that parents with their own history of school difficulty, or apprehension about their child's well-being, do not have an easy time training their children to complete schoolwork independently. In some instances parents react to the child's school difficulties as threats to their own adequacy as caretakers. When such reactions occur, parents are likely to intervene intrusively, and overprotect or overreact to stop problematic behaviors quickly. In addition, some parents also go to extremes to not repeat mistakes committed in their childhoods by their own "negligent" parents. They think that their child's current difficulties will do irreparable harm to them; immediate solutions become imperative in this case. Such parents are likely to regard an approach that shapes independence as "too risky," especially if they cannot notice immediate improvement that could more easily be induced with amphetamine medication and coercion.

In contrast to the traditional intervention

Instead of working solely to have the school accommodate to the child, the learning intervention works just as intently to adjust the child to school. Rather than permanently change institutional limits, expectations, and school rules in order to remedy a posited fixed delay, there is an ongoing effort to change the child's pattern of responding so that he or she adapts to school without special accommodation.

Even if it is sometimes advantageous initially to simplify, compensate, externally represent, and provide instructional aids such as signs and notes, props, why not try to persuade diagnosed students to implement solutions independently? Why not encourage diagnosed children to help design and place the signals? Have them contribute as much as possible when identifying actions that help them achieve effectively in school, rather than immediately impose solutions without their input. Focus on reducing special accommodations rather than presume that they will always be necessary.

However, the general traditionalist recommendation is that consequences be given quickly, frequently, and with higher magnitude on a permanent basis. Often there must be richer incentives and rapid changes compared to non-diagnosed persons. Moreover, when assiduously implementing traditional policy, it may be necessary to segregate diagnosed children into self-contained classrooms, which permits intensive supervision and control over parameters thought to influence symptom severity (Pfiffner and Barkley, 1998).

While these groupings might facilitate the management of diagnosed persons (Barkley, 1993), it is questionable whether such groupings reinforce diagnosed children to copy each other and increase ADHD behavior. For example, in their longitudinal review of adolescent delinquency programs, Dishion, McCord and Poulin (1999) report that most of these programs increase delinquent acts. Adolescents reinforce each other to continue delinquent acts when they are placed with other teens who also behave unacceptably.

By extrapolating from those findings we discover that while homogeneous grouping permits specially-trained teachers to oversee and manage the classroom in a structured way, there is also concern that diagnosed students will reinforce each other to behave similarly through imitation. This problem is evident when teaching diagnosed children social skills with other children who show conduct problems (Antshel and Remer, 2003). In light of these concerns, Budman and Gurman (1988) assert that placing individuals in heterogeneous therapy groups is often a preferable way to induce change. Homogeneous grouping does not guarantee that individuals will recognize alternative ways to live in the world, and group members tend to assist each other when there is diversity.

We therefore choose to err on the side of caution when referring diagnosed children to homogeneous classrooms. The distinct advantage of being exposed to cooperative/self-reliant students is one important reason for keeping many children in mainstream classrooms. This approach can, however, adversely influence non-diagnosed children, so any decision about placement must weigh benefits to the individual against benefits to the classroom as a whole.

A conflict of interest also occurs when a decision has to be made about removing a child who misbehaves from the classroom. We suspect that ignoring, redirecting, or imposing a less punitive response will effectively reduce the behavior's frequency over time, but the entire class must endure the behavior until it disappears. Not only is this difficult for students, but the teacher responsible for the entire class is under strain as well. Teachers do not want to allow a bad example to be set, nor do they want other students to believe that one individual is "getting away" with misbehavior. As is often the case, there is a need to balance between what is best for the individual and what is best for the group.

However, Pfiffner and Barkley (1998) are convinced that most of the problematic behaviors associated with diagnosis are not attempts to gain teacher's attention. They go on to say that modulating the teacher's pattern of attending will not generate appreciable changes in the classroom. Time out procedures, response cost, and loss of privilege, they say, must be imposed by others for adequate results to be obtained. They emphasize that response cost procedures have been the only psychosocial interventions to produce the same benefits on academic performance as stimulant medication.

O'Leary and O'Leary (1972) are more reluctant to use punishment in the classroom, but they also observe that some students seem to benefit from watching another student receive punishment for unacceptable behavior (i.e., vicarious learning). They claim that, if used carefully, punitive action can promote acceptable outcomes.

Traditionalists claim that the diagnosed child's behavioral problems are generally unrelated to attention seeking, but is this empirical fact, or is it an interpretation that is consistent with traditional assumptions and tacit presumptions about biological determinism? Even if it were the case that diagnostic behavior is not purely a quest for attention, it does not follow that neurological delay causes the unacceptable acts; they could have been learned in relation to other event sequences apart from increasing attention rates from teachers. Moreover, when we assert that ADHD behaviors are conditioned, this is not the same as saying the child seeks attention. He or she may not be able to identify any contingencies as reinforcing a particular action.

Traditionalists assert that negative strategies are viable options for increasing school success, given the nature of ADHD, but it is essential to first define the criteria used to make that assessment. Immediacy of conformity is not necessarily the only way to evaluate the effectiveness of an intervention, because side effects can be extensive. For example, smacking the back of the child's hand may get him to comply sooner, but what are the long-term consequences of slapping him to gain obedience? Will a diagnosed child not incorporate that same behavior into his repertoire, or should we expect him to transcend such a response? Might we also be concerned that the child learns to dislike and avoid schoolwork even more, treat others as he had been treated, and show greater anxiety? Immediate compliance may have been obtained, and apparently, short-term success is a traditionalist credo.

Even if forced compliance discipline is the quickest way to induce school achievement, it might also be prudent to evaluate other school interventions over extended periods, in relation to numerous criteria and side effects, before settling on a forced compliance approach. Diagnosed students could indeed be learning various behaviors in response to the traditional strategies, even though rapid compliance is observed through use of coercion and amphetamines. If numerous problems and side effects relating to traditional intervention in the classroom are not fully evaluated by particular dependent variables, then further study is warranted.

For instance, Proctor and Morgan's (1991) system of confiscating tickets from disruptive junior high students, and rewarding students who still have tickets (by permitting free talking as a privilege) may inadvertently reinforce the behavioral act of talking with friends in the classroom, in that the reward seems to compel the unwanted behavior. Similarly, urging parents to give a child snacks or offer television time as reward for homework or acceptable school reports (Pfiffner and Barkley, 1998; Cunningham, 2006) might also inadvertently reinforce eating sweets and watching television, in that a "forbidden fruit" effect occurs when employing the Premack Principle.

Additionally, Pfiffner and Barkley's (1998) recommendation to force students to do tedious simple copying tasks as punishment may also reinforce negative responses to writing assignments, and subsequently reduce the frequency of those behaviors when the punishment and monitoring is removed. Students subjected to this discipline also learn to categorize teacher assignments as senseless, or as attempts to induce suffering rather than activities to facilitate learning. This might also undermine the chances for subsequent positive responses to teacher instruction and assigned work.

Along these same lines, O'Leary and O'Leary (1972, 151) discuss problems associated with punishment in the classroom. They claim that punishment is more likely to be helpful in increasing acceptable behaviors when children know precisely what they have done wrong and are explicitly informed about what substitute behaviors to enact. They note that punishment should be used "sparingly" so that the classroom will not become an aversive environment. Over-use of punishment can result in students becoming immune to it through "adaptation." Noteworthy too, is that the teacher can inadvertently risk truancy or avoidance behaviors such as "not paying attention, day dreaming and being restless" (i.e., behaviors already reinforced to occur too frequently in the diagnosed population). The authors also assert that punishments increase defiance if students are angered by the penalties, and thus learn to be irksome and aggressive if teachers role model those responses.

O'Leary and O'Leary (1972) recommend other positive ways to discipline within the classroom. Teachers are encouraged to take special precautions to reduce side effects and harm when disciplining. Any negative statements should be "soft reprimanding or reprimanding in a manner so that only the child concerned can hear the reprimand" (p. 155).

In much the same fashion, Skinner (1968, 98) notes that students could "counterattack" teachers when punished. He claims that students may become "impertinent, impudent, rude, or defiant." Students might also "annoy" the teacher, "shuffle their feet" or "snap their fingers," or resort to being "unresponsive" when operating under aversive conditions, which interestingly enough, represent the core ADHD symptoms.

Given the problems arising from negative discipline, we are concerned that more problems are created than solved in many instances. Disapproving or critical exchanges strain and disrupt the diagnosed student's relationship with the teacher such that displeasing the teacher is reinforced rather than achieving a passing grade. Spiteful rather than compliant behavior can be conditioned, and many diagnosed students may be reinforced to fail rather than allow the teacher to "win."

Pfiffner and Barkley (1998) are likely to recommend coercion, but they add that, preferably, teachers should use "response cost" rather than add negatives. They caution that legal and ethical concerns also come into play when negative interventions are imposed. However, as touched on earlier, inducing behavior with "response cost" may eventually become equivalent to *all* negative strategies (including punishment). Not gaining access to withheld positives results in the child responding as if being mistreated or denied, despite a surface attempt to be benign.

In closing, our recommendations to shape competent autonomous functioning are consistent with Ferber's (1985) advice to parents on how to solve childhood sleep problems. Ferber says that a child must learn to sleep under conditions without parental assistance. If children are conditioned to sleep with the parent in bed beside them, holding them, or singing to them, they will not learn to sleep without the parental cues.

Ferber encourages parents to extricate themselves from the child's sleeping pattern. When the parent is extracted, either immediately or incrementally, the child becomes less dependent on parental availability in order to sleep. During the intervention the child realizes that crying, complaining, fearfulness, etc., no longer sequence with parent returning to the former sleep patterns, and eventually no one needs to rock, sing, or coddle in order for sleep to occur (i.e., self-reliance is conditioned).

By following Ferber's recommendations, parents do not immediately enter the room to quickly stop the histrionics (i.e., unless extenuating circumstances necessitate parental involvement). Conditioning self-management takes longer and relates to an initial escalation of problematic behaviors, but the result is permanent: the child falls asleep without the aid of mother or father. Shaping diagnosed children to function increasingly self-reliantly/collaboratively utilizes Ferber's recommendation of independence, while the traditional intervention tends toward the perpetuation of external reliance.

Since many diagnosed children are conditioned to fulfill schoolwork only when instructed by others to start, or if someone sits beside them to provide company and assistance, parents and teachers may slowly move away from this arrangement by responding positively to instances of autonomous functioning and initiative with schoolwork, and by congratulating the child when problem solving and organizational skills are demonstrated. Children meanwhile are encouraged to inform parents about what hinders school achievement, and parents help the child feel free to discuss all topics.

If, for example, the child complains about the teacher's actions, the parent can say "Sometimes situations aren't handled very well. What do you want to do to make things better for yourself when the teacher behaves in that way?" The disgruntled diagnosed child is asked to identify protective actions to take when the teacher behaves in a way that is awkward for the child to confront (e.g., fails to write assignments on the board). Regardless of whether the child states initially that she does not know *what* to do (often the case), parents can rephrase questions in various ways to elicit responses.

Traditionalists continue to insist that diagnostic behaviors within school are resultant from neurological events called ADHD. From the learning paradigmatic perspective, however, the diagnosed student's behaviors at school are understood as *conditioned* reactions that often occur in response to the adversity regularly observed in school settings. The learning approach orients to identify ways to reinforce school achievement with less dependence on medicine or directive management. The child does not receive the messages that school achievement is only possible with either threats or payments; that school performance is primarily the parent's responsibility, or that parents must carry the major burden in order for the diagnosed child to succeed in school. Through the combined and sympathetic efforts of loved ones, the diagnosed child, and teachers, the ADHD diagnosed child can ultimately gain greater skill and confidence to succeed in the school setting.

Chapter 9

The Case of Jimmy

As a way to further clarify differences between the alternative learning intervention and the traditional approach, we will here elaborate upon the case example of six-year-old "Jimmy" (Hathaway, Dooling-Litfin, and Edwards, 1998). The authors describe a traditional intervention with a "pure ADHD" case in detail, upon which we are able to highlight the points of divergence.

When Jimmy's parents presented for intervention, they also reported having had difficulty raising his rambunctious older brother; not unexpectedly, traditionalists were immediately alerted to the possibility that the family had a genetic propensity to show ADHD problems. Reports about Jimmy's brother appear to support a genetic interpretation.

Conversely, from the learning paradigmatic perspective, the parental report relates to a behavioral rather than genetic set of assumptions and tacit presumptions; it prompts an analysis of the contingencies of reinforcement that increase rambunctious behaviors for both children in Jimmy's family. It may, however, also be true that their biological patterns raise the probability of learning diagnostic behaviors, but we do not posit *biological causality*. A learning paradigm (that includes biology) can also reasonably account for behavioral consistencies where similar reinforcement histories occur for both siblings.

In the learning paradigm there is an attempt to identify behavioral acts between parents and children that condition Jimmy and his brother to show high frequencies of ADHD behaviors. Investigators would note which events increase and decrease the frequency rates of various diagnostic responses. During the investigation we think it is sometimes helpful to include the perspective of Jimmy's brother in the evaluation, since siblings are privy to contingencies of reinforcement not always apparent to other family members and intervening professionals. This information may in some instances be useful; for example, help to identify which of Jimmy's behaviors tends to persuade parents to acquiesce.

Since there was no significant hostility between Jimmy and other family members, we suspect that he has learned to do ADHD rather than other more overt forms of defiance. However, as long as his hyperactivity and lack of responsible behaviors provokes parental anxiety, concern, comment, and accommodation, the greater will be the frequency rates of those behaviors. Family responding is the key parameter requiring analysis and revision.

Inquiry into whether Jimmy's parents also imitate their own parent's discipline patterns or whether they act in opposite extremes to prevent repeating problems that occurred in their own childhoods is a necessary exercise as well. Exploring these concerns will help Jimmy's parents change relational patterns within the family more easily, as they will explicitly recognize how their own histories of reinforcement and cultural origins have influenced their current behavior.

In our view, Jimmy's parents have neither caused nor taught him diagnostic behaviors; both Jimmy and his brother were atypical in that they were unusually motoric as toddlers. We expect that this characteristic will increase the probability of diagnostic patterning in many families; however, not all active toddlers qualify for diagnosis. Even if Jimmy were initially more active than other children, it is unreasonable to claim that his initial patterning demonstrated incipient ADHD, in that many false positives and negatives are possible when using activity levels to predict later diagnosis.

From the learning paradigmatic perspective, high activity increases the probability of learning ADHD responding. For example, there may have been a large number of interactions pertaining to constraint: attention would thus have been based on protection, and Jimmy might have learned to receive inordinate concern when behaving in amplified ways.

Jimmy's subsequent ADHD behaviors in the classroom, at recess, and while on family excursions are understood as repetitions of past conditioning. It is important to investigate events at home and school that continuously reinforce responses consistent with ADHD. We acknowledge that his high activity levels and provocative behaviors are problematic for those around him, but again, we assert that his behaviors are not definitively caused by neurological disinhibition. Jimmy and loved ones are participating in a biopsychosocial pattern that need not follow a fixed and inevitable course. It remains possible that alternative behavioral patterns can be shaped, despite Jimmy's troublesome starting point.

Jimmy's parents are encouraged to report the conditions under which Jimmy's diagnostic responding typically occurs: does the behavior manifest when parents are busy with other activities? when they arbitrarily shift Jimmy into a new setting (i.e., pressure an agenda)? when social exclusion is likely? Rather than accept without question that Jimmy is helpless to stop his own diagnostic functioning, or insist that his ADHD behaviors are unintentional, we focus on what reinforces behavior, such as sabotaging the discretionary influence of others or exuberant attention seeking. If we reframe his ADHD behavior as avoidant, desperate, insecure, and/or shirking, we can use the more reasonable learning approach, and begin to grapple with contexts and events that have shaped Jimmy's life thus far.

During daily functioning, frequent diagnostic responding has made it extremely difficult for Jimmy's family to either exclude him or curb his enthusiasm. His early behavior of running into the street and putting objects into electrical sockets suggests that he initially learned to provoke concern or notoriety by placing himself in jeopardy. Traditionalists will typically claim that his parent's reactions are consequences of his neurological ADHD, but we suggest that Jimmy's outlandish and dangerous behavior has been and continues to be reinforced by events.

Traditionalists have assessed that both the lagging behind and speeding ahead that occurs during family transitions is caused by the same neural biological delay, but the discrepant actions can be understood as reinforced responses: when running ahead, the child gets others to move quickly and take notice; by lagging behind, the child protests and sabotages. An important task for loved ones and practitioners is to identify the parameters that account for Jimmy's acceptable as well as diagnostic responding under various conditions.

While Jimmy sometimes pleases others, he also does not accommodate to his parents' requirements unless extra inducements are offered. Jimmy does not conform in acceptable ways, so parental involvement is crucial to discriminating which sequences of events are conditioning his under-accommodating pattern (which rarely finds him doing the routine behaviors they would like him to do). Jimmy's parents have the most contact with him, thus they are the agents of change; it is their actions and reactions that are likely to significantly impact on his ADHD frequency rates.

For example, if Jimmy's parents were to report that phone calls correlate with ADHD, they would be advised to discuss with him about changing circumstances when phone calls occur. They might mutually decide that he find a toy and sit beside them rather than interrupt a call (Kvols, 1998). As a way to further increase the probability of acceptable behavior, Jimmy and his parents can also address problems pertaining to his intolerance, insecurity, and jealousy when his parents talk on the phone.

If Jimmy continues to interrupt phone conversations, rather than stop the call or reprimand Jimmy while on the phone, Jimmy's parents can move to a quieter room in order to deflect annoying or hyperactive reaction. Avoiding anger and disapproval is essential when diagnostic patterns are emitted; those responses only foster a continuance of disjointed social behavior and unease.

By deriving a mutually reinforcing plan (despite repeated trials), we expect that Jimmy and his parents will enact the newly identified behavioral sequences and alter their negatively entrenched routines. Jimmy's parents can remark that all family members appreciate uninterrupted time to talk with friends and Jimmy is given the same courtesy.

When his parents report that, in comparison, Jimmy makes his brother seem calm and controlled, we would ask if Jimmy's older brother has, over time, calmed down in direct relation to Jimmy's escalating diagnostic behaviors. This scenario might be predicted developmentally, but the change may also relate to a pattern where siblings stake out their own territories within the family. Jimmy and his brother may be learning to live in diametric ways to prevent instances of direct competition.

While Jimmy might be receiving increased concern from others when rambunctious, his older brother meanwhile may be developing an increasingly sedate and cooperative family pattern. Jimmy's ADHD responding could also be a way to protect himself from trying (and failing to achieve) as competently as his brother. Observations over time may reveal that when Jimmy had not responded to a request for help, his brother had more often been willing to behave precisely the opposite of Jimmy.

However, in some families the birth of a sibling may exacerbate an older child's ADHD responding, in that diagnostic responding shifts attention away from the baby. The behaviors that get conditioned relate to myriad factors that can differ from one family to the next. An older sibling might begin more inattentive behaviors as the younger sibling becomes more hyperactive. Siblings can also team up and behave similarly. A learning paradigm does not purport that merely one psychosocial pattern can explicate the majority of cases.

Conceptual problems

Currently, Jimmy is characterized as a "well meaning" child who permits his "impulses" to get the better of him (p. 316). That assertion is put forward by traditionalists as fact. Jimmy's family is encouraged to accept the premise that, rather than intentional misbehavior, his ADHD relates to the reduced ability to withhold prepotent responses.

What seems to go unnoticed is that this is simply a characterization of behavior relating to traditional beliefs about what causes ADHD patterns. Participants are indoctrinated into the perspective that Jimmy has difficulty containing himself because of an inner dysfunction. He is seen as a victim of a bodily problem that accentuates inconsiderate and negligent behaviors, despite that treating professionals do not empirically demonstrate whether impulsive acts *actually have* different internal antecedents than behavioral acts that are not negatively characterized.

Given such a pronounced shortcoming, a more parsimonious understanding of Jimmy's behaviors is invoked here instead. Rather than understand Jimmy's ADHD behavior as a unique set of acts that differ from "intentional misbehavior, coercive defiance cycles, or deliberate aggression associated with ODD" (p.

316), the behaviors are alternatively understood as similar to any other learned set of responses. The criteria for making the distinction between intentional misbehavior and ADHD behavior have never been specified. That reason alone indicates that the dichotomy is meaningless for its lack of a valid empirical basis. It is not possible from this vantage point to decide if Jimmy has or has not *intended* to do a particular behavioral act, or whether his *impulses* get the better of him. In the traditional view, Jimmy's ADHD behavior is presumed to be caused by a neural biological disinhibition; no other possibilities are explored.

Traditionalists highlight that Jimmy seems "eager to please," but they do not clarify how he has earned that characterization. However, they do emphasize the characterization because it supports the notion that Jimmy's unacceptable ADHD behavior is beyond his control. That is, because he sometimes behaves in socially acceptable ways, the problematic behaviors must not be his "fault." In the traditional view, Jimmy's more agreeable behaviors can be *intentional*, but his disagreeable ADHD behaviors are *always* caused by neural biological delay. He is eager to do socially desirable behaviors, but he must be neurologically disinhibited if he puts keys into electric sockets.

However, rather than endorse the traditional views, the learning approach delves into the conditions under which Jimmy seems eager to please, and when he responds with diagnostic patterns. For example, is he eager to please when his brother is being reprimanded? When he is increasing the probability that his parents will say yes to him? Or when he makes a first impression? Jimmy's eagerness to please (just like his ADHD behavior) is understood as probable under certain conditions, in that he does not always behave exactly the same. For example, why isn't he eager to pick up his toys as soon as he is finished playing with them? Why is he not eager to make his bed (and please his parents) even though many mentally deficient individuals are trained to do those behaviors habitually (and without external cue or prior contemplation) by age six?

Once again, Jimmy is not "less able" to enact routines that his parents would prefer, but rather, other behaviors have been conditioned instead. The behaviors that disqualify him for diagnosis are conditioned, we suggest, as easily as putting on socks before shoes without the requirement to pause and consider as a series of actions. That is, Jimmy can learn to routinely stop at the curb rather than run into the street, if it were not for the contingencies of reinforcement that maintain his dangerous behavior. If his parents doubt the veracity of this statement, they might only refer to how quickly he stops in numerous other situations and circumstances.

When we scrutinize Jimmy's behavior in this alternative fashion, it is important to identify instances of responding that contradict his posited delays. For example, does Jimmy frequently put away personal belongings when he does not want his brother to have access to a particular object? If he sometimes behaves thusly, what makes that sequence of behavior neurologically easier than routinely putting away his toys? We think that the traditionalist neurological account is untenable unless they can specify why hiding objects from others requires less behavioral control than placing toys in particular places, or making one's bed each day.

Curiously, despite many trials and reminders, Jimmy still "forgets" to do various behaviors that his parents have instructed him to do. Traditionalists may stress that the natural environment does not give Jimmy enough help or immediate reinforcement, but we can focus on all the behaviors that Jimmy "remembers" to enact in that same natural environment. For example, the report that he is eager to please indicates that he can indeed be considerate of others. Apparently, he does not *always* annoy others, nor is he always non-responsive to instructions, or insecure when not the center of attention.

Traditionalists say that they are able to predict non-symptomatic behavior when activities reinforce, when events are salient, and when individuals maintain their interest, but that assertion says nothing more than at times he behaves problematically, and other times he does not. Usually those mitigating parameters are not independently defined other than to observe that Jimmy is not doing ADHD, and is responding acceptably in certain conditions.

Moreover, if traditionalists can discount all instances of non-diagnostic responding by claiming that something about the activity provides him with compensatory assistance or that he is interested, it is not clear how we might ever identify true competency. It may always be possible to claim that he was probably interested, or that something salient, externally represented, or immediately reinforcing exists whenever he behaves contrary to ADHD. Diagnosed persons, according to traditionalist assumptions, may excel at history, mathematics, and music; they can competently organize gatherings, outmaneuver others, play chess, and so on, and *still* be given a label implying a functional delay that mimics frontal lobe injury.

However, even if we accept the full range of traditional claims, then the remedy for ADHD may simply be that of finding a way to make activities more interesting, since ADHD problems diminish at these times. This raises the empirical question as to whether this can best be accomplished (according to criteria) with stimulant medication and contingency management, or by shaping Jimmy to function effectively on his own with less coercion and monitoring from others.

Our concern is that even though his behavior might become more compliant by raising the stakes and ingesting a medication, he might also remain infantilized and unenthusiastic about what others require during traditional treatment, especially if extra inducements are thinned out. Additionally, the stimulant he takes each morning can also produce side effects—and not yield long-term improvements—as he becomes accustomed to its effects, both biologically and psychologically.

Implementing an alternative model

By exploring his learning history we determine the patterns that raise parental, sibling and teacher concerns. In Jimmy's case reconditioning can make a significant difference in his future competency. No reports as yet indicate that he exhibits other troublesome functional complications; he does not have an intellectual limitation, severe language impairment, brain damage, or any medical problem to impede his achievement potential. Moreover, Jimmy sometimes shows acceptable attentiveness, organization of behavior over time, persistence, and pacing of responses in some situations and circumstances.

Traditionalists will claim that Jimmy has become the focal point of family interaction because he cannot inhibit, but this is not necessarily true: his behavior is more likely to be reinforced when he encounters a wide range of adversity. Even though he has not been overtly aggressive with his family and has only been aggressive at school, he has done many outlandish behaviors that are impossible to ignore. The behaviors mobilize and arouse others and maintain his parents' preoccupation with him and little else.

A number of questions can be asked when Jimmy's family presents for intervention. For instance, of all the possible behaviors to enact if one were disinhibited, why does he run into the street without looking; and why does he put keys into electrical outlets? Why wouldn't a disinhibited individual be just as likely to do positive disinhibited behaviors such as "blurting" out compliments? We observe that many *non-diagnosed* adolescents also do perilous behaviors that might be accounted for in various ways without invoking a neurological delay. Why then assume a delayed biology when accounting for Jimmy's risk taking pattern?

Although Jimmy's parents might have obtained immediate results from their "active" parenting, one could also claim that he has also been accidentally conditioned to be extraordinarily reliant on his parent's efforts, intent on risk taking, and reinforced to provoke and annoy them. As long as Jimmy behaves irresponsibly and dangerously, he remains the focal point of the family and his parent's active management is constantly tested and challenged. His parents do more to induce acceptable behaviors and Jimmy continues to do ADHD, which essentially counters the restraints and restrictions his parents impose, and simultaneously increases their concerns.

In a learning framework, it is less and less probable that Jimmy's diagnostic responding will diminish when repetitious lecturing, critical comment, eagle-eye scrutiny, and vehement and negative responses are the norm. The "active" management style being used by Jimmy's parents reinforces rather than reduces his ADHD pattern. The aforementioned parental responses may also draw greater attention to unwanted behaviors, and make it less likely that Jimmy will pattern differently.

Jimmy does not require the kind of "active" parenting he is receiving; but it is essential to change what reinforces his unacceptable actions. For example, his diagnostic responding may be reinforced when his parents relent, become hysterical, angry, protective, or caustic. Such responses may result in Jimmy monopolizing his parent's time and energy, increase his own discretionary authority, and disrupt relationships such that he is unlikely to accommodate to the pace or content of others. He is, inevitably, also learning that others will accommodate him and reduce their expectations when he presents as inept and blundering. The question of *who controls who* is appropriate when we confront ADHD behaviors in this manner.

In general, Jimmy's ADHD patterning may limit the extent to which others are able to deny, ignore, or constrain him. If others disapprove of his actions, he might censor them by doing ADHD. Jimmy and his parents are in a "cat-and-mouse" arrangement that traditionalists assert the parents will win (if they are stringent and insist on medication), although long-term data raises doubt about those assertions.

Rather than claim that Jimmy lacks control when he behaves outlandishly, the outcomes that sequence with bizarre actions may account for their increased frequency rates. For example, Jimmy could be reassured about his importance to others when his risk taking produces drama. If he is displeased that others are reluctant to interact with him, diagnostic responses may effectively force them to be involved, and punish others for having failed to be receptive. Since there is the possibility for a fiasco at any moment, it is difficult for family members to exclude him. Jimmy's "impulses" may get the best of him, but it also seems that those behaviors are frequently reinforced. Traditionalists would likely counterclaim and assert that Jimmy's parents are only reacting to his neurological disinhibition, but we argue here that the evolving interactions are shaping and reinforcing the frequency rates of the problematic behaviors.

Divergent accounts and solutions

His parents also noted that Jimmy's problems have begun to escalate as he ages. Traditionalists say that this relates to external requirements exceeding his biological limitations. Because they provide no independent determinant, we suggest that patterns of immature intrusiveness and reliance on others usually become increasingly unacceptable as the child grows older and there is greater expectation to conform.

Persons who learned ADHD responding will typically have increasing psychosocial difficulty the longer they behave like younger children, especially when it is necessary for them to function in school. Loved ones often become less tolerant when children are old enough to contribute and accommodate, but will not, and instead continue to monopolize available resources and incite others when conflicts of interest occur. Young children are not self-reliant, nor do they have deep consideration for the perspectives of others; it becomes particularly distasteful as older children, adolescents, and adults continue this behavior.

If we attempt to solve this problem by providing stimulant medication and stringently forcing him to comply, we may discover that he changes relatively quickly. However, the consequences of the interventions becomes problematic over time if the medication loses its potency or produces side effects, or if parents, spouses, teachers, and employers cannot deal with the extra requirement of having to manage and direct him at each point of performance. The more "active" interventions will get him to conform for the moment, but they are unlikely to produce generalized effects. We also find that he shows more ADHD when his parents struggle to impose stringent tactics, or when distracted by other matters.

Jimmy is not being trained to rely on his own directives and resources to acceptably meet societal expectations if others continue to monitor, medicate, and coerce him to reduce the frequency of diagnostic patterns. Since he will increasingly have to function autonomously during adolescence and into adulthood, he will have greater difficulty meeting expectations at that time. Because Jimmy's parents now utilize traditional methods, he is likely to continue problematic behaviors when *not* taking stimulants, when unique accommodations do not occur, and when his parents are less involved. Moreover, depending on what happens when his parents attempt to restore control, they may also be inadvertently shaping avoidant, under-assertive, or coercive behavior as well.

However, by accepting the traditional disability model, Jimmy's parents are told that age-consistent maturity cannot occur; the intervening professional recommends focusing on compensating for an insufficient neurology, giving up the goal of shaping age-consistent self-sufficiency and applying less coercion. Traditionalists surmise that Jimmy drums on desks, makes noises, and does not persist in school or at home due to his underlying neurological substrate. He is simply less able to resist disruptive action.

They conclude that Jimmy must rely on the initiatives of others (primarily parents). As long as he shows an inability to persist in response to parental requests and is frequently troublesome, provocative, intrusive and sometimes dangerous, his parents must follow him from one point of performance to another. His parents are convinced (by default) that they have to constantly medicate and monitor him, direct his every action, and make his environment explicit in order to compensate for his posited hampered ability to organize. Moreover, they will also have to anticipate problems when he emits particular responses.

Instead of shaping Jimmy to self-manage more effectively, he becomes accustomed to working under the influence of stimulant medication or when others tell him exactly what to do. He has fewer opportunities to engage in what traditionalists call "frontal lobe" functioning, because his parents have become his perpetual keepers. He will undoubtedly experience severe difficulties when those who have heretofore taken interest in his overall well-being are no longer available to remind, entice, and direct him through his day.

For the reasons mentioned above, the alternative learning approach is a better option for intervention for significant numbers of diagnosed persons and their families. Children like Jimmy can be spared a lifetime of psychotropic drugs and reliance on others, especially if these strategies are started early and rigorously maintained for a long time. Traditionalists will likely claim that their methods will at least get Jimmy to complete more schooling and reduce secondary problems, compared to allowing "natural consequences" to unfold without systematic management. However, our learning approach is indeed prescriptive, and it is not neglectful. It is a compromise between relentless management and disengaged permissiveness; both strategies, we strongly suspect, would over the long term disallow Jimmy from learning self-reliance, self-respect and courtesy towards others.

However, Jimmy's parents are being encouraged to participate in therapeutic consultation, group support, and are asked to read about ADHD from the perspective of biological determinism. This type of involvement will purportedly help them apply behavioral modification in its classical form. They will be advised to offer rewards and impose punishments for non-compliance. They will learn to tighten consequences so that training is consistent and enacted with immediacy and vigilance. Jimmy's parents will be asked to intercede at crucial points so that Jimmy will quickly be directed towards socially acceptable or correct behavior. He will be told what to do and what will happen to him regarding his actions. Furthermore, Jimmy's stimulant medication will likely increase his productivity at school and help him function with increased precision. He will generally be easier to manage, and will tend to be immersed rather than fidgety. He is likely to become engrossed in assigned as well as non-assigned activities.

His parents may be convinced that they are compensating for an inhibitory delay that prevents his frontal lobe activity (or executive functions) from being deployed. Associates of Jimmy's will believe that these interventions will always be required due to the nature of his ADHD; moreover, they should not expect recovery. In terms of the immediacy of results, there is little about which to complain.

On the contrary, since reinforcing self-reliant/collaborative interacting can be very complicated and subtle compared to medicating, commanding a specific behavior, and contingency management, it is usually very difficult to provide Jimmy's parents with a formula similar to that of the traditional intervention (e.g., designing a behavioral chart, medicinal prescriptions, and so on). The learning alternative model advocates coordinated behavior between Jimmy and his parents.

His parents will be asked to reinforce cooperation rather than compliance and urged to foster independent achievement. For example, they might comment, "Look what you did all by yourself!" when he shows self-sufficiency. Jimmy's parents will be asked to systematically diminish their constant orchestrating and unilateral management during daily patterning so that he learns to behave acceptability with fewer prompts, maneuvers, bribes, and threats.

It is improbable that an intervening professional can anticipate the potential problems and verbal exchanges in Jimmy's household that either facilitate or impede self-reliant/collaborative interacting. In that regard, the learning intervention is highly contingent upon the ability of Jimmy's family to repeat what is learned during therapy sessions. This often requires everyone to change their behavior in sometimes understated and thoughtful ways: For example, to talk with Jimmy in order to check for his agreement rather than presume that he is comfortable with the presented content or parental instruction.

We know that subtle changes can influence social patterning in sometimes extreme ways. Minor variations in word selection, voice tone, and inflection result in significantly different interactional patterns that will increase or decrease the probability of ADHD reactions. Slight deviations can determine whether participants will continue to compete for discretionary authority, or negotiate in ways that are respectful of multiple perspectives.

If Jimmy's parents are too insistent and keep trying to convince him to relinquish his diagnostic behaviors, they may end up reinforcing ADHD instead. Interactions can be juxtaposed with questions that respect and integrate his perspective into the social exchange. For example, his parents might ask, "Would you be willing to be more careful when closing that door?" "How about we think of another idea?" or: "Are you sure you want to do that to yourself?" Similarly, to help him better understand the psychology of his responses, they might ask, "Do you think your teacher is behaving in the same way as I do when I get upset?"

Although upon hearing these recommendations, Jimmy's parents will worry that Jimmy will act out even more with less inducement of immediate compliance and without the certitude that parents should be in control. They will often be correct. They may also assert that they turned out "ok" when their parents managed them coercively, so why shouldn't their children be treated the same? Jimmy's parents will worry that not sustaining him on stimulant medications will decrease his work productivity and increase his boisterousness. Moreover, they do not want to be regarded as negligent by teachers and professionals if they do not follow the traditional protocol; they already feel exploited by their diagnosed child. They are desperate for quick resolutions and receptive to the disability perspective for providing unequivocal advice.

The traditional intervention does have considerable advantages. A highly detailed system of compensatory management (and medication) often effectively protects the child for the time being, and is a much less difficult proposition to implement. In contrast, there is little incentive to adopt a different intervention that, from the outset, encourages individuals to allow more mistakes to be made over the long course of shaping self-reliance.

Shifting to a self-reliant/collaborative model simply seems more complicated, time consuming and awkward. Jimmy has not yet been conditioned to

248 The Case of Jimmy

take care of himself in age-consistent ways without parents' constant coaching for six years, so he will not immediately show age-consistent maturity because others are coercing him less. For example, asking him to consider what will help him brush his teeth without parental reminder may yield some initial positive effects, although we do not expect the problem to be solved in one trial, nor do we think that brushing teeth will become routine without resolving other problems.

Moreover, Jimmy will not necessarily be keen to relinquish his irresponsible behaviors. His contributing more means others will accommodate less. If parental reminding, contingency management, and organizational assistance reinforce Jimmy's importance to his parents, conditioning him to function autonomously will be an uphill battle. He will complain and counteract his parents' active management when they thwart his initiatives, but he may also associate self-reliance with reduced social significance.

He might also fear abandonment when others are less eager to immediately solve problems for him. Increased diagnostic responding may occur, in that those actions have sequenced with parental defense and rescue. If he were to become more autonomous and cooperative, his parents would have time to focus elsewhere (on siblings, for example). In an attempt to address this problem, his parents can ask him if he is afraid that they will forget about him if he took better care of himself.

Given our conceptual framework, Jimmy's reactions are likely to remain consistent with ADHD, especially if more mature ways of obtaining notoriety within the family have not been developed. In this way, ADHD behaviors are difficult to extinguish when contingency management is withdrawn. Jimmy may initially assume that he has permission to avoid school work, because he has heretofore learned to work instrumentally for particular contingencies that are no longer offered. He will likely resent being denied these extras.

Jimmy's grades in school may also initially drop during the alternative learning approach, although precautions can be taken to minimize the probability. For example, his parents can incrementally and very conservatively shape self-reliance rather than change all routines at once. If he already takes medication it is reasonable to wait until the school year is complete and withdraw the medication slowly, but only after his school routines have improved.

If problems heighten, Jimmy's parents may nevertheless complain that therapy gives Jimmy license to do whatever he wants, because he is less fearful that his parents will impose punitive measures. His parents might lament that he now does fewer expected behaviors even though overt conflicts are subsiding. Moreover, they may also receive disapproval from school personnel, friends and family about being too lenient (or negligent) if parents have ceased the medication.

However, if we presume that Jimmy can learn greater autonomy, and can be reinforced to behave in that way in future, very different (reasonable) results can be noted. We can condition him without the interminable requirement that others (particularly mother) must participate in a labor-intensive way that merely perpetuates his dependence on her.

Moreover, if he also resents the harping associated with doing what others expect, he will be unwilling and avoidant, thus making it less likely that he will carry out an assigned task independently. Given that possibility, we can alternatively encourage Jimmy to identify a reason to do a stipulated task that has nothing to do with parental coercion. For example, does he find it more comfortable to get into a "made" bed when going to sleep?

In an effort to foster independence, we might also ask him to help the family keep the house neat and clean, and let him know that his assistance is greatly appreciated. If he indicates willingness, he can at some point be encouraged to identify environmental cues that he can utilize to help him remember to make his bed without parental involvement. Given previous attempts to resolve problems that have thus far reinforced him to not make his bed (e.g., he is angry about the nagging, his mother continues to straighten the bed for him, etc.), the more collaborative interaction (which must be repeated) helps reinforce a new pattern of behavior without resorting to traditional remedies.

It is probable that Jimmy will become increasingly difficult to coerce, medicate, and supervise as he gets older; therefore the traditional intervention is short-sighted. Those approaches may be even more detrimental if, all along, more competent self-reliant/collaborative responding could have been shaped had there been a concerted effort to develop the behaviors. Commanding continuous compliance over time will not bode well for him when he leaves his primary family, because he will not have learned how to respond acceptably on his own.

Moreover, given that Jimmy is a bright individual, there is the reasonable probability that he will discover how to outsmart authority figures so that they have greater difficulty commanding him or imposing a regime of rigorous contingency management. There is an increased risk that Jimmy will respond to parental management strategies (including punishment) as vindictive rather than helpful. That sequencing of events will also likely increase the probably that he will, during adolescence, regard his parents as meddling or obstructive; he will thus learn complex strategies to further outmaneuver and avoid them. Traditionalists claim that their methods will effectively subdue his disinhibitions, but these kinds of side effects seem more probable with traditional interventions. Moreover, even if the methods tame him effectively, we are not assured that he is learning the quality of initiative valued by employers and spouses.

However, Jimmy is still only six years old; it is usually only later in childhood or adolescence that the more avoidant (ADD) responses will escalate. But as the transition from hyperactivity to inattentiveness occurs, his parent's intervention techniques may become increasingly bothersome, thus instigating a vicious cycle of avoidance and coercion in order to reestablish and maintain parental control.

Alternative interpretations of diagnostic responding

Jimmy's present pattern of attention provoking, desire for help when problems arise, self-doubt about acceptability, and monopolizing behavior, are a mismatch in the school setting, where others expect conformity without protest. In this regard, Jimmy's demands and insecurity become increasingly problematic because he is expected to accommodate to others and proceed to develop skills. Either Jimmy will gradually be shaped to do assigned work on his own and defer to others' instruction, or his patterning will become increasingly atypical, disruptive, and incompatible with the demands placed on him at home and in school. If he does not learn self-assurance, self-direction, and appeasement, he will always require a monitor to intervene and censor.

However, beyond early childhood, it is not easy for most of us to learn new behaviors for living. Having learned atypical patterns as a young child is a serious and difficult problem; it is therefore imperative that Jimmy learn to be more congenial before his negative behaviors grow in tenacity, before his behaviors have become too complex, and before his biological substrate is less malleable.

The early conditioning of an ADHD pattern hinders his current possibilities for success, especially in the school setting. His pattern of getting "sidetracked" by "more interesting things" (p. 313) is translated to mean that he regularly escapes from the constraint of imposed agendas and finds solace in self-determined, non-evaluated activities. This pattern may get reinforced, in that alternative activities are less rule-bound and less likely to expose his inadequacies. Additionally, when teachers and parents exert effort to keep him engaged, their actions may also inadvertently reinforce the "sidetracking" patterns.

Rather than presume that Jimmy is less able to resist being diverted, his "off task" responses (e.g., imaginings, doodling, playing with pencils, etc.) are reinforced in relation to escaping from the uncomfortable conditions in the classroom. If Jimmy is detached, he no longer must contend with the activity initiated by his teacher and is able to avoid potential failure. Moreover, he might receive help from his teacher when he approaches to urge him to resume working.

Traditionalists note that his "imagination play" during school illustrates inhibitory difficulties (p. 314), but the behavioral acts may just as likely be conditioned, in that "imagining" permits him to do unfettered responding. If he is confined or deprived by having to sit in the classroom, he does the next best option: he imagines playful behaviors. This interpretation contrasts with the traditional view which we think is contradictory, in that it highlights Jimmy's ability to do imaginative play, yet simultaneously claims that diagnosed children generally touch objects because they lack imaginative ability (Barkley, 2000).

Not surprisingly, it is also reported that group activity can increase diagnostic responding. We observe that Jimmy is more secure and settled when he is the center of attention and when the social agenda accommodates to him. If Jimmy is insecure or has difficulty with a loss of social importance when in a group, discomfort ensues—an intolerance of others is his reaction to being unable to maintain discretionary authority.

As a result, Jimmy may have difficulty, especially when his teachers give presentations to the whole class, since his social significance is likely to be reduced. The requirement to function as part of a team or group may also expose him to critique and disapproval, and those factors can contribute to making group participation an aversive activity. Generally, we can assert that whole group situations are more likely to cue the diagnostic extremes of inattentiveness or intrusiveness because individuals often feel powerless, overwhelmed, or underappreciated.

One way to address Jimmy's problematic responses in group circumstances is to have his family engage him in regular discussions, outings, and have meals together as a cohesive unit. By helping Jimmy learn to behave more acceptably during these communal family activities, his participation in other groups (e.g., classrooms, sports, etc.) will also improve.

Regular group participation in the family can, over time, diminish Jimmy's tendency to drift away to "do his own thing," since patterning in one setting is likely to repeat in other group contexts. Positive responses to his contributions, soliciting Jimmy's point of view, and inviting him to join in will also shape his confidence as an essential member of the group. Teachers meanwhile can allow Jimmy to take the lead in small and larger classroom groups to make those situations more comfortable and inviting.

Given the available source data, we are concerned that Jimmy is not very self-assured. He may therefore do ADHD responding when others seem to be detached. His insecurity can accentuate clowning and other rambunctious behavior, in that he does not anticipate being noticed, enjoyed, or included without going to extremes. We also expect his diagnostic responding to escalate when he encounters shunning or disapproval, in that intrusiveness functions as retaliation when he is rejected or cast aside. Instead of learning to peacefully resolve social frustrations and disappointments, he has learned to do ADHD.

Thus, it is important to recondition Jimmy to react less negatively to situations where others are not immediately available or approachable. Rather than for him to react as if he is being discounted or rejected when others are preoccupied, we can help him interpret situations in less personal ways, and assist him in recognizing that their unavailability has nothing to do with his importance to them. We can help him learn effective and positive ways to gain group inclusion.

Jimmy is, however, inclined to annoy, impose, rush, delay, avoid, give up, and disengage when encountering adversity in various settings and circumstances. He is not usually aggressive, hostile, or malicious, but he continues to diverge with his teacher and parents when they expect conformity in particular behavior, such as making his bed, completing assignments, and putting away belongings. Jimmy's behavior is escalating in school, which in turn further disrupts his home life. Jimmy talks when his teacher wants him to be quiet, and he seldom follows instructions. There are more complaints, disciplinary action, and very poor grades as he repeats diagnostic responding across contexts. On some occasions he is even asked to leave the classroom.

Clearly, very different sequences of events are happening as he does ADHD outside his household, although the responses continue to be reinforced durably enough to prevent them from being extinguished. Despite grievances from school personnel, his ADHD responding apparently protects him from trying and failing, reminding others that he exists, and deflecting restriction and censure. As in the general population, Jimmy seems to repeat behavior patterns learned early in childhood and infancy, and those patterns might not extinguish easily, despite their being problematic.

However, by making changes when possible such as pairing schoolwork with pleasure and enjoyment, and encouraging Jimmy to identify the conditions under which he will put homework into his backpack, and do it after school, the probability is that school productivity will increase. Traditional remedies will therefore become less necessary if schoolwork is more often paired with success. Jimmy may moreover learn new routines to enact autonomously.

Additionally, rather than consider his inattentiveness to detail as indicative of weak mental functioning, not attending to detail may indeed be a reinforced pattern. For instance, when tasks are completed carelessly, they can end more quickly, and adequacy can be protected when completing before others. Finishing may be reinforced compared with doing the activity more slowly and conscientiously, especially if the task is not straightforwardly easy. Not identifying details might also be an indirect way to resist accommodating to requirements, particularly when others urge that tasks be completed to a specified standard— much like what occurs when Jimmy is directed to clean up his mess in the house.

However, we might inquire into whether Jimmy shows the same difficulty discriminating details when he worries about being cheated by others, when apprehensive that his brother might have touched or hidden his toy. We would investigate whether he notices details that prevent him from losing his turn or increasing his chances of winning, or if he notices details when examining collectibles.

Parents can ask if Jimmy fails to notice new toys in the therapist's office, or when people commit mistakes. Does he discriminate the finer details while playing video games, and notice details of a situation in which his brother has more of something? Is he equally inept at articulating details when he lies in order to avoid punitive action? How does a biological determinist explanation account for Jimmy's close observation of minutiae, or discern between instances when he makes finer discriminations and times when he does not?

We would also study Jimmy's imitative behaviors when he does an activity that he initiates and enjoys as a way to identify a best-case scenario for that functioning. For example, does he regularly imitate his brother's negative behaviors to the chagrin of his parents? If he is able to imitate his brother without difficulty, we cannot argue that he is somehow inherently "less able."

In the situation where discrepancies in learning competencies are observed, we would entertain other explanations rather than ascribe Jimmy's difficulties to an ADHD delay. For example, when addressing his handwriting problems, we would ask if he forms his letters per his teacher's instructions. In that he seems to have a history of less often doing as he is told, he might not be practicing his handwriting consistently in the designated way. Rather than conform to teacher directives and imitate precisely (thus giving his teacher full discretionary authority and risking failure to meet expectations), he forms his letters idiosyncratically. We do not discount the possibility that Jimmy could have trouble mastering handwriting because of a bodily impairment, but ADHD, as understood by traditionalists, is not the cause of his handwriting problems. It has not been ruled out that he has difficulty learning handwriting because he has already learned ADHD responding.

Although if Jimmy frequently provokes others by doing unskillful, loud and abrasive actions, and/or defers to others to solve problems, it is not surprising if he is not developing a variety of fine motor skills that are usually shaped by experience. If he responds quickly rather than accurately, and procrastinates or avoids evaluative situations, we are not surprised that his writing is not age-consistent. Like many who do ADHD, he is unlikely to develop mastery of required tasks at the same pace as others, or to learn to write neatly enough to receive a critique of his work.

In the same manner, rather than interpret his errors on the Continuous Performance Test (CPT) as indicative of attentional and inhibitory problems (Murphy et al., 2001), his errors might also be interpreted consistently within a learning paradigm. That is, he has been conditioned to respond to these tasks through the quickest and easiest solutions rather than via vigilant and meticulous responding. The slightest distraction often triggers an escape reaction.

If it is true that Jimmy has a fixed lesser ability to do "interference control," it is necessary to rule out the possibility that he can successfully "tune out" his parents when they instruct him to do a chore while he does a task he has initiated, or whether he has substantial difficulty tuning out an antagonistic peer or sibling, despite the likelihood that his parent(s) told him on numerous occasions to *not* react. Finding functional inconsistencies in different situations therefore brings a biological disability formulation into serious question.

In our view, Jimmy requires exposure to new kinds of conditioning to shape behaviors other than ADHD. Intervention explores in myriad ways which historical events make it difficult for Jimmy's parents to foster cooperative/self-reliant patterns. As a way to alter Jimmy's provocative pattern, his family can introduce more rigorous consistency and routine into daily patterning, in for example, predictable meal times, routine time slots for homework, bedtime, playtime with parents, and parents' leisure time together. Routines help family members cooperate, avoid disappointment, and organize behavior effectively.

Jimmy's parents can also role model patience so that family members do not coerce each other by loud or forceful mannerisms in order for them follow requests or directives.

Jimmy's parents can emphasize that in "our family we don't behave that way" so that Jimmy learns that 'respect' is a two-way affair. They can solicit Jimmy's perspective when personal concerns are askew so that he will learn those behaviors too (e.g., mirroring and reflexive listening). Establishing affable patterns at home promotes concern for others rather than emphasizes personal indulgence.

Exploring family relationships

Although not specified in the case presentation, we would inquire into whether triangular relationships exist, in which one parent protects Jimmy after he has behaved ineptly against the other parent, his brother, or a teacher. We can assess whether others wait long enough for him to initiate an acceptable behavior, or if they hurriedly direct his actions without any systematic attempt to shape autonomy. Do they often give him several rapid-fire directives in succession (e.g., "leave the dog alone, pick up the toys, start your homework"), and do such rapidly paced injunctions exacerbate and/or perpetuate his inattentive response patterns?

Inquiry into whether Jimmy's older brother belittles, coerces, and omits him, and whether those interactions adversely influence his response to disapproval and the relationships he develops outside the home is worthy of investigation. Assessing whether Jimmy reminds his parents about their own negative characteristics, what they don't like about each other or an extended family member (and whether such similarities undermine the building of a comfortable relationship with him) would also be interesting questions. We would investigate whether one or both of Jimmy's parents report ambivalence regarding the necessity to care for him, whether they subtly undermine each other, or whether Jimmy is indulged in order to make up for a past misfortune, since that pattern will frequently make it difficult to refuse him when he complains or struggles.

Furthermore, we would assess the frequency with which Jimmy's parents role model diagnostic responding. Do Jimmy's parents blame each other for his diagnostic patterning? Do those reactions reinforce the behaviors, and give him license to externalize blame and complain about others? Does Jimmy's father intervene in a domineering and critical way? And does he allow Jimmy to suffer in order to "learn?" Does Jimmy's mother over accommodate, harp, give in, rescue, but then complain afterwards about feeling overwhelmed and slighted by Jimmy's irresponsibility and lack of appreciation? We would inquire into whether his mother receives extra help from family members (husband) whenever she is oppressed by Jimmy's behavior, and whether there is frequent spousal avoidance in the household.

We would orient ourselves in order to fully scrutinize his current lifestyle, including when he transitions with his family outside of the house. After identifying problematic situations, changes that foster autonomy and cooperation are introduced. For example, Jimmy can be helped to determine when it is safe to cross the street, and permitted to take the lead more often when making street-crossing decisions. He can be asked to identify the sequence of behaviors to enact to cross the street safely.

Guiding Jimmy towards understanding what reinforces his careless behaviors, and asking him whether he wants to continue to put himself at risk when he accompanies his parents in various situations is a plausible venture. Jimmy and his parents together can identify ways to deal with circumstances that correspond with his provocations and other diagnostic responses.

If Jimmy agrees that he would like to change his behavior, he can outline an "implementation intention," which would specify "what" and "when" he will do a particular sequence of actions. For example, Jimmy might agree to wait for his parents at the curb (instead of provoking them by darting into the street). He can also agree to look both ways and notify others when it is safe to cross.

Given Jimmy's age, it is initially helpful if these implementation intentions are made close in time to the actual behavior in order to increase their effectiveness. If Jimmy's parents deem it necessary to continue to hold his hand, such an intervention can be framed as a means of making "everyone safe," rather than a restriction or an insinuation that he is incompetent. Parents can put their arms around him affectionately while crossing to highlight physical contact as caring rather than coercive or restrictive. As acceptable street-crossing behavior becomes more and more conditioned, Jimmy will be able to cross particular streets with progressively less assistance or preempting.

Like many of us, Jimmy learns to behave in ways consistent with how others have characterized him. Parental descriptions and interpretations of his actions are extremely influential. For example, if Jimmy's parents observe him engaging in unacceptable activity, rather than yell "Stop sneaking!" his parents can simply redirect him to a different activity without dramatically expressing that he has committed a "sneaking" transgression. They can also ask him if something troubles him or prevents him from being forthright about his wants. Generally, it is important for all family members to avoid "bad mouthing" of any kind, as this is known to impede mutually acceptable patterning.

Even subtle reactions, such as smiling when an ADHD behavior is momentarily cute, can reinforce behaviors that are obnoxious and unwanted when repeated in other situations. When Jimmy bumps into objects, makes loud noises, mispronounces words, engages in bathroom humor, or shows gullibility, parents can extinguish those behaviors by reducing their social importance. Very understated parental responses may be reinforcing his intrusiveness, evasiveness, risk taking, clownishness, or complaints.

Within this framework an essential part of conditioning non-diagnostic responses is to urge Jimmy's parents to *not* discuss his ADHD behavior either in front of him or in the midst of other people. For example, parents should avoid saying "He is so hyper I can't keep up with him." "I'm so afraid he is going to get hurt; nothing seems to stop him." "I was just like that when I was his age." The act of discriminating and highlighting diagnostic behaviors may condition them to occur more often.

There are numerous empirical studies indicating that individuals who focus on *not doing* particular behaviors tend to amplify the frequency rates of those responses. Instead, it is important to highlight Jimmy's more mature, safer, less inciting, and agreeable behavioral acts. We want to raise his profile for having made self-sufficient and competent decisions.

Jimmy will learn that others love him even if they have changed how they take care of him, which is now different from when he was much younger. Remarks such as "Now that you know what to do, we can do all kinds of things we couldn't do before," expresses this shift in attitude. Jimmy's parents can be powerful agents of change once they recognize the numerous ways to help extinguish his diagnostic patterning, and thus reinforce self-reliance and collaborative interacting. Calm and non-critical mannerisms, redirecting strategies, more talk, less negativity, and consistent patience are strategies for parents to incorporate. They change social patterns so that Jimmy learns more socially acceptable ways to resolve *his own concerns.*

Jimmy will often imitate what he observes, so he will be unlikely to ascribe negative attributions to the behavior of others when his parents role model *positive* social exchanges. For example, when they set limits, he may report that his parents protect rather than deprive or doubt him. He will recognize that situational occurrences have interfered with plans made rather than presume that his parents have "lied" to him. Our learning approach orients to increase the probability that these positive responses will occur.

However, Jimmy's *history* of not coordinating action with others in mutually acceptable ways means that he has numerous problems when dealing with the outside environment. It may be that, for example, when crossing the street, Jimmy identifies his own destination (and wants to arrive as quickly as possible), but he does not discern that the car driver does not notice him. If Jimmy is patterned to attend only to his own point of view and not coordinate with others, conflict and sometimes dangerous encounters will ensue as those responses repeat, including when as a teen, he begins driving.

Frequent self-reliant/collaborative interacting will give him opportunities to practice identifying multiple points of view and sequelae associated with various actions. Such training will help him to learn to wait his turn in the classroom, let drivers pass him, and adjust the pace of his actions to better coincide with loved ones. Jimmy's parents will observe his responses keenly (both said and unsaid), and talk with him about his objections, reluctance, and detachment—so that social patterning will remain coordinated.

Summing up

In the learning model ADHD behavior is something that is *done*, not a thing one possesses. Rather than characterize ADHD from a biological perspective, and encourage dependency on the initiatives of others (and medication), those same behaviors are framed as conditioned responses that may be reinforced or extinguished. The decision to ingest medication is a pragmatic concern based on a risk analysis and the resources of the participants, rather than a necessity for rectifying a medical condition that causes the problematic behaviors.

We design intervention so that Jimmy learns to respond to disappointment, exclusions, difficulty understanding, irrelevance, constraint, imperatives to behave in particular ways, and a wide variety of adversity, by responding less disruptively. In that respect, our learning approach represents a *compromise* between Jimmy's interests and the interests of others. That is, coerce him less, but at the same time shape him to give more. For example, instead of saying, "You did a good job reading that book," parents can say, "It seemed like you enjoyed reading that book." Similarly, rather than, "You were a really good boy today," they can say, "I really enjoyed being with you today." A less evaluative manner helps Jimmy establish satisfying relationships with other adults and peers without inducing apprehension about performance or adequacy. We expect that these changes will help reduce diagnostic patterns in remarkable ways when repeated frequently enough to take hold.

However, it will often be the case that self-reliant/collaborative patterning will not initially repeat when the family returns home after therapy appointments, as the old circumstances will typically cue the old behaviors. To address these problems, therapists can role model the recommended strategies during therapy sessions, and help the family practice alternative problem solving whenever possible. For example, if there is difficulty getting Jimmy to come to dinner, Jimmy's parents can notify him that dinner will be served in five minutes. Instead of reminding him a second time five minutes later, they can attempt to shape Jimmy to cue himself so that he arrives on time without additional involvement from either parent.

Each instance of self-initiated time-organized behavior is one less instance of ADHD patterning. Jimmy is eventually shaped to organize his own actions by, for example, looking at his watch, and approaching his parents before being cued to discover when mealtime starts, so that he will be ready at the designated time.

However, if Jimmy resembles many other diagnosed children, he will probably initially react negatively when asked to participate in solving problems. He might say that a particular question is "too hard," complain that the problem is "boring," or say "I don't know." Much patience is required by parents; they will have to restate questions in different ways in order to receive contributions from the diagnosed child, especially at the beginning of the intervention.

Jimmy may often squirm and fidget during attempts to convince him to deal with a particular agenda. However, rather than understanding those actions as concomitants of neurological disinhibition, any moving and rocking on his part might relate to situational discomfort (e.g., interrogation, criticism, or the requirement to discuss problems). Restless movements may become so habitual, that immediately as he sits down, his legs wiggle, and twitching increases. Jimmy may react thusly as soon as topics related to "school" are mentioned, because the word cues a flight reaction or apprehension about the impending event.

Despite initial hardships, shaping active contribution can be facilitated by responding positively when Jimmy is more participatory, even minimally, during collaborative exchanges. If the interaction goes well, Jimmy will do significantly more talking than previously. Jimmy's parents are encouraged to be concise and/or make the interaction seem like a "volley," since Jimmy is likely to be conditioned to stop listening and/or emit distracting behaviors if he suspects that his parents are verbally dominating the interaction. For example, when his parents start to pressure or correct him, offer convoluted explanations, proselytize, or make assertions without seeking his agreement.

We conclude that ADHD patterning is inconsistent with biological determinism because most diagnosed persons *can* do the delayed behaviors some of the time, especially when initiating activity they enjoy. Instances of competency make ADHD diagnosis starkly dissimilar to other biologically-determined functional impediments. Moreover, because the frequency and severity of ADHD behavior also seems to change in relation to events, a learning paradigm is a plausible alternative for Jimmy and other diagnosed children.

Some parents and practitioners will, however, find it unconscionable to question traditional conceptualizations and treatment interventions, given the codification of such beliefs. Biological determinists have always been adamant that others build on their model rather than explore alternatives and potentially impede the progress already made. Although there is some historical basis for asserting their position, new paradigms cannot be established without somehow disrupting the status quo.

Even though the traditional view is for the time being recognized as best practice and evidence-based, there is much room for improvement. Despite all the medications and treatment offered to those diagnosed with ADHD, we observe that most individuals continue to show the same behavioral patterns throughout their lifetimes. While this could mean that the disorder simply cannot be alleviated by any means, it could also indicate that the ways in which the behaviors are understood and changed have been inadequate.

On the other hand, psychotherapeutic interventions will encounter many more obstructions than the traditional intervention using medicinal treatment; this is unavoidable because the learning intervention requires extensive client participation. Therefore, a limited number of clients (and therapists) will benefit from a psychologically-based approach to shape non-diagnostic functioning. Conditioning individuals towards mutually acceptable patterning is often multi-faceted and complicated, and much can go wrong. For example, asking too many questions in succession, the slightest blaming or critical tone, giving unsolicited advice, repetitiously initiating verbal exchange about disruptive content, pressuring for affirmation, and so on, may only increase diagnostic responding.

Forced compliance discipline is easier, because dominating others rather than coordinating perspectives (when they have the clout to do so) is straightforward and simplistic. A militaristic approach often effectively induces conformity, despite the many associated side effects. Most parents know how to coerce their children quite well, when for example, they tell a child: "I'll give you ten dollars if you finish your work." Or "I'll take away your toys if you don't pick them up right now." Fewer parents are familiar with a socialization process that elicits cooperation and self-reliance when, for example, persuading a child to take turns rather than demanding obedience.

We acknowledge that it is easier to manage a diagnosed individual who is rendered more attentive and less active by stimulant medications. By making tasks easier and making consequences of non-compliance more extreme, acceptable responding is evoked. However, one need not posit the existence of a neurological delay when accounting for the aforementioned findings.

It may be more accurate to suggest that diagnosed persons are changing in relation to the distinct environments constructed and maintained by the managing parties. Some individuals may continue living with parents well into adulthood for this reason, as they have not learned to function competently without help. Some diagnosed persons, moreover, enlist in the armed forces, hoping that a military routine will provide or organize for them. In this case they are resigned to the notion that they cannot provide for themselves or develop self-discipline. Although traditionalists claim that their outcomes are the most efficacious, we think that that assertion is premature.

Like the therapist's obligation to break patient confidentially only to protect the health and safety of clients, there may at times be extenuating circumstances whereby medication and dogmatic solutions are reasonable and justified. However, in our learning model, we limit interactions that are obedience-based, and operate to reduce the problems associated with traditional methods. We expect that our approach will better equip diagnosed persons for greater independence and cooperation over the long run, especially when started in early childhood.

Works Cited

Abikoff, H. "An Evaluation of Cognitive Behavior Therapy for Hyperactive Children." In Lahey, B., and A. Kazdin (eds). *Advances in Clinical Child Psychology* 10 (p. 171–216). New York: Plenum, 1987.

Abikoff, H. "Interaction of Ritalin and Multimodal Therapy in the Treatment of Attention Deficit Hyperactive Behavior Disorder." In Greenhill, L. L., and B. B. Osman (eds.) *Ritalin: Theory and Patient Management.* Larchmont, NY: Mary Ann Liebert, 1991.

Abikoff, H., and R. Gittelman. "Does Behavior Therapy Normalize the Class Room Behavior of Hyperactive Children?" *Archives of General Psychiatry* 41 (1984): 449–54.

Abikoff, H. and R. Gittelman. "Hyperactive children treated with stimulants: Is cognitive training a useful adjunct?" *Archives of General Psychiatry* 42 (1985): 953–61.

Abikoff, H., J. McGough, B. Vitiello, J. McCracken, M. Davies, J. Walkup, et al. "Sequential Pharmacotherapy for Children with Comorbid Attention-Deficit/Hyperactivity and Anxiety Disorders." *Journal of the American Academy of Child and Adolescent Psychiatry* 44, no. 5 (2005): 418–21.

Acosta, M. T., M. Arcos-Burgos, and M. Muenke. "Attention Deficit Hyperactivity Disorder (ADHD): Complex Phenotype, Simple Genotype?" *Genetics in Medicine* 6 (2004): 1–15.

Ahmann, P. A., S. J. Waltonen, K. A. Olson, et al. "Placebo-Controlled Evaluations of Ritalin Side Effects." *Pediatrics* 91 (1993): 1101–6.

Amen, D. *Healing ADD: The Breakthrough Program That Allows You to See and Heal the Six Types of Attention Deficit Disorder.* New York: Berkley Books, 2001.

Anand, G. "Canada Halts Adderall Sales, Citing Deaths." *The Wall Street Journal* (10 February 2005): B1–2.

Anastopoulos, A. D., L. H. Rhoads, and S. E. Farley. "Counseling and Training Parents." In Barkley, R. A. *Attention Deficit Hyperactivity Disorder: A Handbook for Diagnosis and Treatment,* 3rd ed. (p. 453–78). New York: Guilford Press, 2006.

Anastopoulos, A. D., T. L. Shelton, G. J. DuPaul, and D. C. Guevremont. "PT for Attention Deficit Hyperactivity Disorder: Its Impact on Child and Parent Functioning." *Journal of Abnormal Child Psychology* 21 (1993): 581–96.

Anastopoulos, A. D., J. M. Smith, and E. E. Wien. "Counseling and Training Parents." In Barkley, R. A. *Attention Deficit Hyperactivity Disorder: A Handbook for Diagnosis and Treatment* (p. 373–93, 2nd ed). New York: Guilford Press, 1998.

Angier, N. "How Biology Affects Behavior and Vice Versa." *New York Times* (30 May 1995): C1, C5.

Angold, A., A. Erkanli, H. L. Egger, and E. J. Costello. "Stimulant Treatment for Children: A Community Perspective." *Journal of the American Academy of Child and Adolescent Psychiatry* 39 (2000): 975–84.

Antshel, K. M., and R. Remer. "Social Skills Training in Children with Attention Deficit Hyperactivity Disorder: A Randomized-Controlled Clinical Trial." *Journal of Clinical Child and Adolescent Psychology* 32 (2003): 153–65.

Applegate, B., B. B. Lahey, E. L. Hart, L. Waldman, J. Biederman, G. W. Hynd, et al. "Validity of the Age of Onset Criterion for ADHD: A Report from the DSM-IV Field Trials." *Journal of the American Academy of Child and Adolescent Psychiatry* 36 (1997): 1211–21.

Arnold, L. E. "Treatment Alternatives for Attention Deficit Hyperactivity Disorder." in National Institutes of Health (NIH) *Consensus Statement: Diagnosis and Treatment of Attention Deficit Hyperactivity Disorder.* no. 16–18, 1998.

Arnold, L. E., H. B. Abikoff, D. P. Cantwell, C. K. Conners, G. Elliot, L. L. Greenhill, L. Hechtman, et al. "NIMH Collaborative Multimodal Treatment Study of Children with ADHD (the MTA): Design Challenges and Choices." *Archives of General Psychiatry* 54 (1997): 865–70.

Arnold, L. E., M. Elliot, L. Sachs, H. Bird, H. C. Kraemer, K. C. Wells, H. B. Abikoff, et al. "Effects of Ethnicity on Treatment Attendance, Stimulant Response/Dose, and 14-Month Outcome in ADHD." *Journal of Consulting and Clinical Psychology* 71, no. 4 (2003): 713–27.

Aviram, R. B., M. Rhum, and F. Levin. "Psychotherapy of Adults with Comorbid Attention-Deficit Hyperactivity Disorder and Psychoactive Substance Use Disorder." *Journal of Psychotherapy Practice and Research* 10 (2001): 179–86.

Ball, J. D., M. Tiernan, J. Janusz, and A. Furr. "Sleep Patterns among Children with Attention Deficit Hyperactivity Disorder: A Reexamination of Parent Perceptions." *Journal of Pediatric Psychology* 22 (1997): 389–98.

Ballinger, C. T., C. K. Varley, and P. A. Nolen. "Effects of Methylphenidate on Reading in Children with Attention Deficit Disorder." *American Journal of Psychology* 141 (1984): 1590–93.

Bandura, A. "Influence of Models' Reinforcement Contingencies on the Acquisition of Imitative Responses." *Journal of Personality and Social Psychology* 1 (1965): 589–95.

_____. "Self-Efficiency: Toward a Unifying Theory of Behavioral Change." *Psychological Review* 84 (1977): 191–215.

Bandura, A., D. Ross, and S. Ross. "Transmission of Aggression through Imitation of Aggressive Models." *Journal of Abnormal and Social Psychology* 63 (1961): 575–82.

Bargh, J. A., and T. L. Chartrand. "The Unbearable Automaticity of Being." *American Psychologist* 57, no. 7 (1999): 462–79.

Barkley R. A. "A Review of Stimulant Drug Research with Hyperactive Children." *Journal of Child Psychology and Psychiatry.* 18 (1977): 137–65.

_____. *Hyperactive Children: A Handbook for Diagnosis and Treatment.* New York: Guilford Press, 1981.

_____. "Hyperactive Girls and Boys: Stimulant Drug Effects on Mother-Child Inter-actions." *Journal of Child Psychology and Psychiatry* 30 (1989): 379–90.

_____. *"ADHD in Children and Adults with Russell Barkley,"* sponsored by New England Educational Institute, Brattleboro Retreat, and the University of Massachusetts Medical School Office of Continuing Education, 1995.

_____. "Behavioral Inhibition and Executive Functions: Constructing a Unified Theory of ADHD." *Psychological Bulletin* 121 (1997): 65–94.

_____. "History." in Barkley, R. A. *Attention Deficit Hyperactivity Disorder: A Handbook for Diagnosis and Treatment,* 2nd ed. (p. 3–55). New York: Guilford Press, 1998a.

_____. "Primary Symptoms, Diagnostic Criteria, Prevalence, and Gender Differences." in Barkley, R. A. *Attention Deficit Hyperactivity Disorder: A Handbook for Diagnosis and Treatment,* 2nd ed. (p. 56–96). New York: Guilford Press, 1998b.

_____. "Associated Problems." in Barkley, R. A. *Attention Deficit Hyperactivity Disorder: A Handbook for Diagnosis and Treatment,* 2nd ed. (p. 97–138). New York: Guilford Press, 1998c.

_____. "Comorbid Disorders, Social Relations, and Subtyping." in Barkley, R. A. *Attention Deficit Hyperactivity Disorder: A Handbook for Diagnosis and Treatment,* 2nd ed. (p. 139–63). New York: Guilford Press, 1998d.

_____. "Developmental Course, Adult Outcome, and Clinic-Referred ADHD Adults." in Barkley, R. A. *Attention Deficit Hyperactivity Disorder: A Handbook for Diagnosis and Treatment,* 2nd ed. (p. 186–224). New York: Guilford Press, 1998e.

_____. "A Theory of ADHD: Inhibition, Executive Functions, and Time." in Barkley, R. A. *Attention Deficit Hyperactivity Disorder: A Handbook for Diagnosis and Treatment,* 2nd ed. (p. 225–60). New York: Guilford Press, 1998f.

_____. *ADHD in Children, Adolescents and Adults: Diagnosis, Assessment, and Treatment.* New England Educational Institute Cape Cod Summer Symposia Audio Cassettes. New England Educational Institute, Pittsfield, MA, 2000.

_____. *ADHD: An Intensive Course on the Nature and Treatment of Children and Adolescents with Attention Deficit Hyperactivity Disorder.* Presented at the New England Educational Institute, Pittsfield, MA, 2001.

_____. "Mental Health Outcomes of Attention Deficit Hyperactivity Disorder." Presented at the University of Massachusetts Medical School: Grand Rounds Lecture Series. 01-17-2002.

_____. "History." in Barkley, R. A. *Attention Deficit Hyperactive Disorder: A Handbook for Diagnosis and Treatment,* 3rd ed. (p. 3–75). New York: Guilford Press, 2006a.

_____. "Primary Symptoms, Diagnostic Criteria, Prevalence, and Gender Differences." in Barkley, R. A. *Attention Deficit Hyperactive Disorder: A Handbook for Diagnosis and Treatment,* 3rd ed. (p. 76–121). New York: Guilford Press, 2006b.

_____. "Associated Cognitive, Developmental, and Health Problems." in Barkley, R. A. *Attention Deficit Hyperactive Disorder: A Handbook for Diagnosis and Treatment,* 3rd ed. (p. 122–83). New York: Guilford Press, 2006c.

_____. "Etiologies." in Barkley, R. A. *Attention Deficit Hyperactive Disorder: A Handbook for Diagnosis and Treatment,* 3rd ed. (p. 219–47). New York: Guilford Press, 2006d.

_____. "ADHD in Adults: Developmental Course and Outcome of Children with ADHD, and ADHD in Clinic-Referred Adults." in Barkley, R. A. *Attention Deficit Hyperactive Disorder: A Handbook for Diagnosis and Treatment,* 3rd ed. (p. 248–96). New York: Guilford Press, 2006e.

_____. "A Theory of ADHD." in Barkley, R. A. *Attention Deficit Hyperactive Disorder: A Handbook for Diagnosis and Treatment*, 3rd ed. (p. 297–334). New York: Guilford Press, 2006f.

Barkley, R. A., A. Copeland, and C. Sivage. "A Self-Control Classroom for Hyperactive Children." *Journal of Autism and Developmental Disorders* 10 (1980): 75–89.

Barkley, R. A., and C. E. Cunningham. "Do Stimulant Drugs Improve the Academic Performance of Hyperkinetic Children? A Review of Outcome Research." *Clinical Pediatrics* 17 (1978): 85–92.

_____. "The Effects of Methylphenidate on the Mother-Child Interactions of Hyperactive Children." *Archives of General Psychiatry* 36 (1979): 201–8.

Barkley, R. A., G. J. DuPaul, and M. B. McMurray. "A Comprehensive Evaluation of Attention Deficit Disorder with and without Hyperactivity." *Journal of Consulting and Clinical Psychology* 58 (1990): 775–89.

Barkley, R. A., and G. Edwards. "Diagnostic Interview, Behavior Rating Scales, and the Medical Examination." in Barkley, R. A. *Attention Deficit Hyperactivity Disorder: A Handbook for Diagnosis and Treatment*, 2nd ed (p. 263–93). New York: Guilford Press, 1998.

_____. "Diagnostic Interview, Behavior Rating Scales, and the Medical Examination." in Barkley, R. A. *Attention Deficit Hyperactivity Disorder: A Handbook for Diagnosis and Treatment*, 3rd ed. (p. 337–68). New York: Guilford Press, 2006.

Barkley, R. A., G. Edwards, M. Laneri, K. Fletcher, and L. Metevia. "The Efficacy of Problem-Solving Communication Training Alone, and their Combination for Parent-Adolescent Conflict in Teenagers with ADHD and ODD." *Journal of Consulting and Clinical Psychology* 69 (2001): 926–41.

Barkley, R. A., M. Fischer, C. S. Edelbrock, and L. Smallish. "The Adolescent Outcome of Hyperactive Children Diagnosed by Research Criteria: I. An Eight-Year Follow-Up Study." *Journal of the American Academy of Child and Adolescent Psychiatry* 29 (1990): 546–57.

Barkley, R. A., M. Fischer, R. Newby, and M. Breen. "Development of Multi-Method Clinical Protocol for Assessing Stimulant Drug Responses in ADHD Children." *Journal for Clinical Child Psychology* 17 (1988): 14–24.

Barkley, R. A., M. Fischer, L. Smallish, and K. Fletcher. "The Persistence of Attention Deficit Hyperactivity Disorder into Young Adulthood as a Function of Reporting Source and Definition of Disorder." *Journal of Abnormal Psychology* 111 (2002): 279–89.

Barkley, R. A., D. G. Guevremont, A. D. Anastopoulos, and K. E. Fletcher. "A Comparison of Three Family Therapy Programs for Treating Family Conflict in Adolescents with Attention Deficit Hyperactivity Disorder." *Journal of Consulting and Clinical Psychology* 60 (1992): 450–62.

Barkley, R. A., J. Karlsson, S. Pollard, and J. Murphy. "Developmental Changes in the Mother Child Interactions of Hyperactive Boys: Effects of Two Doses of Ritalin." *Journal of Child Psychology and Psychiatry* 26 (1985): 705–15.

Barkley, R. A., T. L. Shelton, C. Crosswait, M. Moorehouse, K. Fletcher, S. Barrett, et al. "Preschool Children with Disruptive Behavior: Three-Year Outcome as a Function of Adaptive Disability." *Development and Psychopathology* 14 (2002): 45–67.

Barry, L. M., and J. J. Messer. "A Practical Application of Self-Management for Students Diagnosed with Attention Deficit Hyperactivity Disorder." *Journal of Positive Behavioral Interventions* 5, no. 4 (2003): 238–48.

Beacon Health Strategies. "Strattera: FDA Warning." *The Lighthouse Times*, 8 May 2005.

Begley, S. "New Hope for Battling Depression." Retrieved 6 January 2004, from *The Wall Street Journal Online*. http://online.wsj.com/article_email.

Belkin, L. "Office Messes." *New York Times Magazine*. 18 July 2004.

Bergman, A., L. Winters, and B. Cornblatt. "Methylphenidate: Effects on Sustained Attention." In Greenhill, L. L., and B. B. Osmon (eds.) *Ritalin: Theory and Patient Management* (p. 223–32). New York: Mary Ann Liebert, 1991.

Berk, L. E. "Children's Private Speech: An Overview of Theory and the Status of Research." In Diaz, R., and L. E. Berk (eds) *Private Speech: From Social Interaction to Self-Regulation* (p. 17–54). Hillsdale, NJ: Erlbaum, 1992.

Bhatara, V. S., M. Feil, K. Hoagwood, B. Vitiello, and B. T. Zima. *Concomitant Pharmacotherapy in Youths Receiving Antidepressants or Stimulants.* Poster presented at the 47th annual meeting of the American Academy of Child and Adolescent Psychiatry, Washington, DC, 2000.

Biederman, J. "Attention Deficit Hyperactivity Disorder: A Life-Span Perspective." *Journal of Clinical Psychiatry* 59, Suppl. 7 (1998): 4–16.

Biederman, J., S. V. Farone, T. Spencer, T. E. Wilens, D. Norman, K. A. Lapey, E. Mick, B. Lehman, and A. Doyle. "Patterns of Psychiatric Comorbidity, Cognition, and Psychological Functioning in Adults with Attention Deficit Hyperactivity Disorder." *American Journal of Psychiatry* 150 (1993): 1792–98.

Blachman, D. R., and S. P. Hinshaw. "Patterns of Friendship among Girls with and without Attention Deficit Hyperactivity Disorder." *Journal of Abnormal Child Psychology* 30 (2002): 625–40.

Bloomquist, M. L., G. J. August, and R. Ostrander. "Effects of School-Based Cognitive-Behavioral Intervention for ADHD Children." *Journal of Abnormal Child Psychology* 19 (1991): 591–605.

Bor, W., R. M. Sanders, and C. Markie-Dadds. "The Effects of the Triple P-Positive Parenting Program on Preschool Children with Co-Occurring Disruptive Behavior and Attentional Hyperactive Difficulties." *Journal of Abnormal Child Psychology* 30 (2002): 571–87.

Braaten, E. B., and L. A. Rosen. "Self-Regulation of Affect in Attention Deficit-Hyperactivity Disorder (ADHD) and Non-ADHD Boys: Differences in Empathic Responding." *Journal of Consulting and Clinical Psychology* 68 (2000): 315–21.

Braswell, L., G. J. August, M. L. Bloomquist, G. M. Realmuto, S. S. Skare, and R. D. Crosby. "School-Based Secondary Prevention for Children with Disruptive Behavior." *Journal of Abnormal Child Psychology* 25 (1997): 197–208.

Braun, J., R. S. Kahn, T. Froehlich, P. Auinger, B. P. Lanphear. "Exposures to Environmental Toxicants and Attention Deficit Hyperactivity Disorder in US Children." *Environmental Health Perspectives*. Doi: 10.1289/ehp.9478: http://dx.doi.org/) Online 19 September 2006.

Breggin, P. "MTA Study Has Flaws." *Archives of General Psychiatry* 58 (2001): 1184.

_____. "A Critical Analysis of the NIMH Multimodal Treatment Study for Attention Deficit Hyperactivity Disorder (The MTA Study 2003)." http://breggin.com/2003/04/MTA.

Bridges, A. "Safety of ADHD Drugs Questioned." *Telegram & Gazette.* 5 January 2006: A6.

Brody, J. "TV's Toll on Young Bodies and Minds." *Telegram & Gazette.* 9 August 2004: C1 & C4.

Brown, R. T., and S. B. Sexson. "Effects on Methylphenidate on Cardiovascular Responses in Attention Deficit Hyperactivity Disordered Adolescents." *Journal of Adolescent Health Care* 10 (1989): 179–83.

Budman, S. H., and A. S. Gurman. *Theory and Practice of Brief Therapy.* New York: Guilford, 1988.

Buhrmeister, D., L. Camparo, A. Christensen, L. S. Gonzalez, and S. P. Hinshaw. "Mothers and Fathers Interacting in Dyada and Triads with Normal and Hyperactive Sons." *Developmental Psychology* 28 (1992): 500–9.

Buss, A. H., and R. Plomin. *Temperament: Early Developing Personality Traits.* Hillsdale, NJ: Erlbaum, 1984.

Caine, E. D., Ludlow, C. L., Polinsky, R. J., & Ebert, M. H. "Provocative drug testing in Tourette's syndrome: D- and L- amphetamine and haloperidol." *Journal of the American Academy of Child Psychiatry* 23 (1984): 147–52.

Campbell, S. B. "Hyperactivity: Course and Treatment." In A. Davids (ed.), *Child personality and psychopathology: Current topics* (Vol. 3). New York: Wiley, 1976.

Campbell, S. B. *Behavioral Problems in Preschool Children.* New York: Guilford Press, 1990.

Campbell, S. B., Endman, M., & Bernfield, G. "A three year follow-up of hyperactive preschoolers into elementary school." *Journal of Child Psychology and Psychiatry* 18 (1977): 239–49.

Campbell, S.B., Ewing, L.J. "Follow-up of hard to manage preschoolers: Adjustments at age 9 and predictors of continuing symptoms." *Journal of Abnormal Child Psychology and Psychiatry* 31 (1990): 871–99.

Carlson, C. L., Pelham, W. E., Milich, R., & Hoza, B. "ADHD boys' performance and attributions following success and failure: Drug effects and individual differences." *Cognitive Therapy and Research* 7 (1993): 269–87.

Charach, A., Ickowicz, A., & Schachar, R. "Stimulant treatment over five years: adherence, effectiveness, and adverse effects." *Journal of the American Academy of Child and Adolescent Psychiatry* 43, no. 5 (2004): 559–67.

Chase, E. "FDA: Antidepressants must carry 'black box' warning." *Massachusetts Psychologist* 1, November (2004): 9.

Christakis, D. A., Zimmerman, R. J., DiGiuseppe, D. L., & McCarty, C. A. "Early television exposure and subsequent attentional problems in children." *Pediatrics* 113 (2004): 708–13.

Chronis, A. M., Chacko, A. Fabino, G. A., Wymbs, B. T., & Pelham, W. E., Jr. "Enhancements to the behavioral parent training paradigm for families of children with ADHD: Review and future directions." *Clinical Child and Family Psychology Review* 7 (2004): 1–27.

Clark, M. L., J. A. Cheyne, C. E. Cunningham, and L. S. Siegel. "Dyadic Peer Interactions and Task Orientation in Attention Deficit Disordered Children." *Journal of Abnormal Child Psychology* 16 (1988): 1–15.

Coie, J., Dodge, K., Terry, R., & Wright, V. "The role of aggression in peer relations: An analysis if aggression episodes in boys' play groups." *Child Development* 62 (1991): 812–26.

Conners, C. K. "Forty years of methylphenidate treatment in attention-deficit/hyperactivity disorder." *Journal of Attention Disorders* 6, Suppl 1 (2002): S17-S30.

Conners, C., Levin, E. D., Sparrow, E., Hinton, S., Erhardt, D., Meck, W., Rose, J., & March, J. "Nicotine and attention in adult attention deficit hyperactivity disorder." *Psychopharmacology Bulletin* 32 (1996): 67–73.

Connor, D. F. "Other Medications in the Treatment of Child and Adolescent ADHD." In Barkley, R. A. *Attention Deficit Hyperactivity Disorder: A Handbook for Diagnosis and Treatment,* 2nd ed (p. 564–81). New York: Guilford Press, 1998.

Connor, D. F. "Preschool attention deficit hyperactivity disorder: A review of prevalence, diagnosis, neurobiology, and stimulant treatment." *Developmental and Behavioral Pediatrics,* 23, 1S (2002): S1-S9.

Connor, D. F. "Stimulants." In R. A. *Attention Deficit Hyperactivity Disorder: A Handbook for Diagnosis and Treatment,* 3rd ed. (p. 608–47). New York: Guilford Press, 2006.

Connor, D. F., Glatt, S. J., Lopez, I. D., Jackson, D., & Melloni, R. H., Jr. "Psychopharmacology and aggression. I: A meta-analysis of stimulant effects on over/covert aggression-related behaviors in ADHD." *Journal of the American Academy of Child and Adolescent Psychiatry* 41, no. 3 (2002): 253–61.

Connor, D. F., & Steingard, R. J. "New formulations of stimulants for attention-deficit hyperactivity disorder: Therapeutic potential." *CNS Drugs* 18, no. 14 (2004): 1011-30.

Consumer Reports. "Drugs vs. talk therapy." October 2004, 22–29.

Consumer Reports. "Mental Health: Does Therapy Help?" November 1995, 734–39.

Crawford, N. "ADHD: A Women's Issue." *Monitor on Psychology* 34, no. 2 (2003): 28–30.

Cunningham, C. E. "COPE: Large-Group, Community-Based, Family-Centered Parent Training." In Barkley, R. A. *Attention Deficit Hyperactivity Disorder: A Handbook for Diagnosis and Treatment,* 3rd ed. (p. 480–98). New York: Guilford Press, 2006.

Cunningham, C. E., & Barkley, R. A. "The interactions of hyperactive and normal children with their mothers during free play and structured tasks." *Child Development* 50 (1979): 217–24.

Cunningham, C. E., Benness, B., & Siegel, L. S. "Family functioning, time allocation, and parental depression in the families of normal and ADHD Children." *Journal of Clinical Child Psychology* 17 (1988): 169–78.

Cunningham, C. E., Boyle, M. "Preschoolers at risk for attention deficit hyperactivity disorder and oppositional defiant disorder: Family, parenting, and educational correlates." *Journal of Abnormal Child Psychology* 30 (2002): 555–69.

Cunningham, C. E., Bremner, R. B., & Boyle, M. "Large Group community-based parenting programs for families of preschoolers at risk for disruptive behavior disorders: Utilization, cost, effectiveness, and outcome." *Journal of Child Psychology and Psychiatry* 36 (1995): 1141–59.

Cunningham, C. E., & Cunningham, L. J. "Student-Mediated Conflict Resolution Programs." In Barkley, R. A. *Attention Deficit Hyperactivity Disorder: A Handbook for Diagnosis and Treatment,* 3rd ed. (p. 491–509). New York: Guilford Press, 1998.

Cunningham, C. E., & Cunningham, L. J. "Student-Mediated Conflict Resolution Programs." In Barkley, R. A. *Attention Deficit Hyperactivity Disorder: A Handbook for Diagnosis and Treatment,* 3rd ed.). (p. 590–607). New York: Guilford Press, 2006.

Curry, D. R. "Case studies in behavior modification." *Psychology in the Schools* 7 (1970): 330–35.

Dane, A. V., Schachar, R. J., & Tannock, R. "Does actigraphy differentiate ADHD subtypes in a clinical research setting?" *Journal of the American Academy of Child and Adolescent Psychiatry* 39 (2000): 752–60.

Danforth, J. S., Barkley, R. A., & Stokes, T. F. "Observations of interactions between parent and their hyperactive children: An analysis of reciprocal influence." *Clinical Psychology Review* 11 (1991): 703–27.

Deater-Deckard, K. "Annotation: Recent research examining the role of peer relationships in the development of psychopathology." *Journal of Child Psychology and Psychiatry* 42 (2001): 565–79.

Diagnostic and Statistical Manual of Mental Health Disorders. Fourth Edition. Test Revision. Washington, DC: American Psychiatric Association, 2000.

Diller, L. *Running On Ritalin. A Physician Reflects On Children in Society and Performance in a Pill.* New York: Bantam Doubleday Dell, 1998.

Diller, L., *Should I Medicate My Child? Sane Solutions for Troubled Kids With and Without Psychiatric Drugs.* New York: Basic Books, 2002.

Diller, L. "Bitter Pill." *Psychotherapy Networker.* Jan/Feb. (2005): 56–72.

Diller, L., "Kids on drugs: A behavioral pediatrician questions the wisdom of medicating our children." http://www.salon.com/health/feature/2000/03/kid_drugs/ index.html.

Dishion, T. J., McCord, J., & Poulin, F. "When Interventions Harm." *American Psychologist* 54 no. 9 (1999): 755–64.

Dodge, K., Bates, J., & Petit, G. "Mechanisms in the cycle of violence." *Science* 250 (1990): 1678–83.

Doherty, S., Frankenberger, W., Fuhrer, R., & Snider, V. "Children's self-reported effects of stimulant medication." *International Journal of Disability, Development and Education* 47 (2000): 39–54.

Douglas, V. I., "Higher mental processes in hyperactive children: Implications for training." In R. Knights & D. Bakker (eds.), *Treatment of Hyperactive and Learning Disordered Children* (p. 65–92). Baltimore: University Park Press, 1980a.

Douglas, V. I. "Treatment and training approaches to hyperactivity: Establishing internal or external control." In C. Whalen & B. Henker (eds.) *Hyperactive Children: The social ecology of identification and treatment* (p. 283–318). New York: Academic Press, 1980b.

Douglas, V. I., Barr. R. D., Desilets, J., & Sherman, E. "Do high doses of stimulants impair flexible thinking in attention-deficit hyperactivity disorder?" *Journal of the American Academy of Child and Adolescent Psychiatry* 34 (1995): 877–85.

Draeger, S., M. Prior, and A. Sanson. "Visual and Auditory Attention Performance in Hyperactive Children: Competence or Compliance?" *Journal of Abnormal Child Psychology* 14 (1986): 411–24.

Dubey, D. R., O'Leary, S., & Kaufman, K. F. "Training parents of hyperactive children in child management: A comparative outcome study." *Journal of Abnormal Child Psychology* 11 (1983): 229–46.

Dunlap, G., dePerczel, M., Clarke, S., Wilson, D., Wright, S., White, R., et al. "Choice making to promote adaptive behavior for students with emotional and behavioral challenges." *Journal of Applied Behavioral Analysis* 27 (1994): 505–18.

DuPaul, G. J., Anastopoulos, A. D., Kwasnik, D., Barkley, R. A., & McMurray, M. B. "Methylphenidate effects on children with attention deficit hyperactivity disorder: Self-report of symptoms, side-effects, and self-esteem." *Journal of Attention Disorders* 1 (1996): 3–15.

DuPaul, G. J., R. A. Barkley, and D. F. Connor. "Stimulants." In Barkley, R. A. *Attention Deficit Hyperactivity Disorder: A Handbook for Diagnosis and Treatment,* 2nd ed. (p. 510–51) New York: Guilford Press, 1998.

DuPaul, G. J., Barkley, R. A., & McMurray, M. B. "Response of children with ADHD to methylphenidate: Interaction with internalizing symptoms." *Journal of the American Academy of Child and Adolescent Psychiatry* 33 (1994): 894–903.

DuPaul, G. J., & Eckert, T. L. "The effects of school-based interventions for attention deficit hyperactivity disorders: A meta-analysis." *School Psychology Review* 26 (1997): 5–27.

DuPaul, G. J., McGoey, K. E., Eckert, T., & VanBrakle, J. "Preschool children with attention-deficit/hyperactivity disorder: Impairments in behavioral, social, and school functioning." *Journal of the American Academy of Child and Adolescent Psychiatry* 40 (2001): 508–15.

DuPaul, G. J., & Rapport, M. D. "Does methylphenidate normalize the classroom performance of children with attention deficit disorder?" *Journal of the American Academy of Child and Adolescent Psychiatry* 32 (1992): 190–98.

DuPaul, G. J., & Stoner, G. *ADHD in the schools: Assessment and interventions strategies* (2nd ed.) New York: Guilford Press, 2003.

Dweck, C. S. "Implicit theories as organizers of goals and behavior." In P. Gollwitzer and J. Bargh (eds.). *The psychology of action: Linking cognition and motivation to behavior.* New York: Guilford Press, 1996.

Dyme, I. Z., Sahankian, B. J., Golinko, B., & Rabe, F. "Preservation induced by methylphenidate in children: Preliminary findings." *Progress in Neuropsychopharmacology and Biological Psychiatry* 32 (1982): 190–98.

Edwards, G., Barkley, R. A., Laneri, M., Fletcher, K., & Metevia, L. "Parent-adolescent conflict in teenagers with ADHD and ODD." *Journal of Abnormal Child Psychology* 29 (2001): 557–72.

Edwards, L., Salant, V., Howard, V. F., Brougher, J., & McLaughlin, T. F. "Effectiveness of self-management on attentional behavior and reading comprehension for children with attention deficit disorder." *Child and Family Behavior Therapy* 17, no. 2 (1995): 1–17.

Elia, J., Borcherding, B. G., Rapoport, J. L., & Keysor, C. S. "Methylphenidate and dextroamphetamine treatments of hyperactivity: Are there true nonresponders?" *Psychiatry Research* 36 (1991): 141–55.

Faraone, S. V., Biederman, J., Jetton J. G., & Tsuang, M. T. "Attention deficit disorder and conduct disorder: Longitudinal evidence for a familial subtype." *Psychological Medicine* 27 (1997): 291–300.

Faraone, S. V., Monuteaux, M. C., Biederman, J., Cohan, S. L., & Mick, E. "Does parental ADHD bias maternal reports of ADHD symptoms in children?" *Journal of Consulting and Clinical Psychology* 71 (2003): 168–75.

Ferber, R. *Solve your child's sleep problems.* New York: Simon and Schuster, 1985.

Fergusson, D. M., & Horwood, L. J. "Attention deficit and reading achievement." *Journal of Child Psychology and Psychiatry* 33 (1992): 375–85.

Fiedler, N. & Ullman, D. G. "The effects of stimulant drugs on curiosity behaviors of hyperactive boys." *Journal of Abnormal Child Psychology* 11 (1993): 193–206.

Fine, S., & Johnston, C. "Drug and placebo side effects in methylphenidate-placebo trial for attention deficit hyperactivity disorder." *Child Psychiatry and Human Development* 24 (1993): 25–30.

Fisher, R., Ury, W. L. & Patton, B. *Getting to YES: Negotiating. Agreement Without Giving In.* (2nd ed.). New York: Penguin Books, 1991.

Flecher, M. Barkley, R. A. & Smallish, L., "A sequential analysis of the mother-adolescent interactions of ADHD, ADHD/ODD, and normal teenagers during neutral and conflict discussions." *Journal of Abnormal Child Psychology* 24, (1996): 271–97.

Frayne, C. A., & Latham, G. P. "Application of social learning theory to employee self-management of attendance." *Journal of Applied Psychology* 72 (1987): 387–92.

Freeman, W., Phillips, J., & Johnston, C. *Treatment effects on hyperactive and aggressive behaviors in ADHD children.* Paper presented at the meeting of the Canadian Psychological Association, Quebec City, June 1992.

Gadow, K. D. "Relative efficacy of pharmacological, behavioral, and combination treatments for enhancing academic performance." *Clinical Psychology Review* 5 (1985): 513–33.

Gentry, D. B., & Benenson, W. A. "School-to-home transfer of conflict management skills among school-age children." *Families in Society: The Journal of Contemporary Human Services* 74 (1993): 67–73.

Gerdes, A. C., Hoza, B., & Pelham, W. E. "Attention-deficit/hyperactivity disordered boys' relationships with their mothers and fathers: Child, mother, and father perceptions." *Development and Psychopathology* 15 (2003): 363–82.

Gerrard, L, & Anastopoulos, A. D. *The relationship between AD/HD and mother-child attachment in early childhood.* Paper presented at the annual meeting of the American Psychological Association, Washington, DC, August 2005.

Gittelman, R., Abikoff, H., Pollack, E., Klein, D. F., Katz, S. & Mattes, J. "A controlled trial of behavior modification and methylphenidate in hyperactive children." In C. Whalen & B. Henker (eds.). *Hyperactive Children: The Social Ecology of Identification and Treatment* (p. 221–43). New York: Academic Press, 1980.

Gittelman, R., Klein, D. F., and I. Feingold. "Children with Reading Disorders-II: Effects of Methylphenidate in Combination with Reading Remediation." *Journal of Child Psychology and Psychiatry* 24 (1983): 193–212.

Gittelman-Klein, R., Klein, D. F., Katz, S., Saraf, K., & Pollack, E. "Comparative effects of methylphenidate and thioridazine in hyperkinetic children: I. Clinical results." *Archives of General Psychiatry* 33 (1976): 1217–31.

Gittelman, R., Mannuzza, S., Shenker, R. et al. "Hyperactive boys almost grown up I. Psychiatric status." *Archives of General Psychiatry* 42 (1985): 937–47.

Gollwitzer, P. "Implementation Intentions: Strong Effects of Simple Plans." *American Psychologist* 57, no. 7 (1999): 504–15.

Goodman, R., and J. A. Stevenson. "Twin Study of Hyperactivity-II: The Aetiological Role of Genes, Family Relationships and Perinatal Adversity." *Journal of Child Psychology and Psychiatry* 30, no. 5 (1989): 691–709.

Greene, R. *The Explosive Child*, 2nd ed. New York: Harper Collins, 2001.

Greene, R., & Ablon, J. *Treating Explosive Kids.* New York: Guilford Publications, 2005.

Greenhill, L. L., Jensen, P., Abikoff, H., Blumer, J. L., DeVeaugh-Geiss, J., Fisher, C., et al. "Developing strategies for psychopharmacological studies in preschool children." *Journal of the American Academy of Child and Adolescent Psychiatry* 42, no. 4 (2003), 406–14.

Greist, D. L., Wells, K. C., & Forehand, R. "An examination of predictors of maternal perceptions of maladjustment in clinical-referred children." *Journal of Abnormal Psychology* 88 (1979): 277–81.

Gualtieri, C. T., Hicks, R. E., and Mayo, J. P. "Hyperactivity and homeostasis." *Journal of the American Academy of Child and Adolescent Psychiatry* 22 (1983): 382–84.

Gunnar, M., Mangelsdorf, S., Larson, M., & Hertsgaard, L. "Attachment, temperament and adrenocortical activity in infancy." *Developmental Psychology* 25 (1989): 355–63.

Haenlein, M., & Caul, W. F. "Attention deficit disorder with hyperactivity: A specific hypothesis of reward dysfunction." *Journal of the American Academy of Child and Adolescent Psychiatry* 26 (1987): 356–62.

Hall, R. J. "Cognitive behavior modification and information-processing skills of exceptional children." *Exceptional Education Quarterly* 1 (1980): 9–15.

Hallowell, E. M., and J. J. Ratey. *Driven to Distraction.* New York: Touchstone, 1995.

Harris, G. "Proof Is Scant on Psychiatric Drug Mix for Young." *The New York Times.* (November 23, 2006): p. A1, A28.

Hathaway, W., J. K. Dooling-Litfin, and G. Edwards. "Integrating the Results of an Evaluation: Eight Clinical Cases." In Barkley, R. A. *Attention Deficit Hyperactivity Disorder: A Handbook for Diagnosis and Treatment,* 2nd ed. (p. 312–44) New York: Guilford Press, 1998.

Higgins, E. T. "Beyond pleasure and pain." *American Psychologist* 52 (1997): 1280-1300.

Hinshaw, S. P. "Stimulant medication and the treatment of aggression in children with attentional deficits." *Journal for Clinical Child Psychology* 20 (1991): 301–12.

Hinshaw, S. P. *Attention deficits and hyperactivity in children.* Thousand Oaks, CA: Sage, 1994.

Hinshaw, S. P., Buhrmester, D., & Heller, T. "Anger control in response to verbal provocation: Effects of methylphenidate for boys with ADHD." *Journal of Abnormal Child Psychology* 17 (1989): 393–407.

Hinshaw, S. P., Henker, B., & Whalen, C. K. "Cognitive-behavioral and pharmacological interventions for hyperactive boys: Comparative and combined effects." *Journal of Consulting and Clinical Psychology* 52 (1984a): 739–49.

Hinshaw, S. P., Henker, B., & Whalen, C. K. "Self-control in hyperactive boys in anger-inducing situations: Effects of cognitive-behavioral training and of methylphenidate." *Journal of Abnormal Child Psychology* 12 (1984b): 55–77.

Hinshaw, S. P., Henker, B., Whalen, C. K., Erhardt, A., & Dunnington, R. E. "Aggressive, prosocial, and nonsocial behavior in hyperactive boys: Dose effects of methylphenidate in naturalistic settings." *Journal of Consulting and Clinical Psychology* 57 (1989): 636–43.

Hoff, K. E., & DuPaul, G. J. "Reducing disruptive behavior in general education classrooms: The use of self-management strategies." *School Psychology Review* 27 (1998): 290–303.

Hollenbeck, J. R., Williams, C. R., & Klein, H. J. "An empirical examination of the antecedents of commitment to difficult goals." *Journal of Applied Psychology* 74 (1989): 18–23.

Horner, M. D., & Hamner, M. B. "Neurocognitive functioning in posttraumatic stress disorder." *Neuropsychological Review* 12 (2002): 15–30.

Hoza, B., Owens, J. S., Pelham, W. E., Swanson, J. M., Conners, C. K., Hinshaw, S. P., et al. "Parent cognitions as predictors of child treatment response in attention-deficit/hyperactivity disorder." *Journal of Abnormal Child Psychology* 28 (2000): 569–84.

Humphries, T., Kinsbourn, M., & Swanson, J. "Stimulant effects on cooperation and interaction between hyperactive children and their mothers." *Journal of Child Psychology and Psychiatry* 19 (1978): 13–22.

Hyde, J. S. "The Gender Similarities Hypothesis." *American Psychologist* 60, no. 5 (2005): 581–92.

Ialongo, N., Horn, W., Lopez, M., and Greenberg, G. "The effects of psychostimulant medication on self-perceptions of competence, control, and mood in Attention Deficit Disorder Children." *Journal of Clinical Child Psychology* 23 (1994): 161–73.

Jensen, P. S. "ADHD comorbidity findings for the MTA study: New diagnostic subtypes and their optional treatments." In J. E. Helzer (ed.), *Defining psychopathology in the 21 century; DSM-V and beyond* (p. 169–192). Washington, DC: American Psychiatric Press, 2002.

Johnston, C., & Freeman, W. "Attributions of child behavior in parents of children with behavior disorders and children with attention deficit-hyperactivity disorder." *Journal of Consulting and Clinical Psychology* 65 (1997): 636–45.

Johnston, C. J., Pelham, W. E., Hoza, J., & Sturges, J. "Psychostimulant rebound in attention deficit disordered boys." *Journal of the American Academy of Child and Adolescent Psychiatry* 27 (1988): 806–10.

Kazdin, A. E., Holland, L., & Crowley M. "Family experience of barriers to treatment and premature termination from child therapy." *Journal of Consulting and Clinical Psychology* 65 (1997): 453–63.

Kelley, M. L. *School-home notes: Promoting children's classroom success.* New York: Guilford Press, 1990.

Kirsch, I., and S. J. Lynn. Automaticity in Clinical Psychology. *American Psychologist* 57, no. 7 (1999): 504–15.

Klein, R. G., & Mannuzza, S., "Hyperactive boys almost grown up: III. Methylphenidate effects on ultimate height." *Archives of General Psychiatry* 45 (1988): 1131–34.

Klingberg, T., Fernell, E., Olesen, P. J., Johnson, M., Gustafsson., P., Dahlstrom, K., et al. "Computerized training of working memory in children with ADHD- A randomized, controlled trial." *Journal of the American Academy of Child & Adolescent Psychiatry* 44, no. 2 (2005): 177–86.

Knights, R. M., & Viets, A. "Effects of pemoline on hyperactive boys." *Pharmacology, Biochemistry and Behavior* 3 (1975): 1107–14.

Kohlberg, L. Stage and sequence: the cognitive development approach to socialization. In Goslin, DA (ed.): *Handbook of socialization theory and research* (347–480). Chicago: Rand McNally, 1969.

Kotkin, R. A. "The Irvine Paraprofessional Program: Using paraprofessionals in serving students with ADHD." *Intervention in School and Clinic,* 30, no. 4 (1995): 235–40.

Kvols, K. J. *Redirecting Children's Behavior.* Seattle WA: Parenting Press, 1998.

Ladnier, R. D, Massanari, A. E. "Treating ADHD as attachment deficit hyperactivity disorder." In: Levy T. M. (ed.). *Handbook of attachment interventions* (p. 27–65). San Diego: Academic Press, 2000.

Lancelotta, G. X., & Vaughn, S. "Relation between types of aggression and sociometric status: Peer and teacher perceptions." *Journal of Educational Psychology* 81, no. 1 (1989): 86–90.

Latham, G., Erez, M & Locke, E., "Resolving scientific disputes by the joint design of crucial experiments by antagonists: application to the Erez-Latham dispute regarding participation in goal setting." *Journal of Applied Psychology* 73 (1988): 753–72.

Latham, G., Mitchell, T. R., & Dossett, D. L. "The Importance of Participative Goal Setting and Anticipated Rewards on Goal Difficulty and Job Performance." *Journal of Applied Psychology* 63, no. 2 (1978): 163–71.

Latham, G. P., Winters, D., & Locke, E. A. "Cognitive and motivational effects of participation in goal setting." *Journal of Organizational Behavior* 15 (1994): 49–63.

Latham, G. P., & Yukl, G. "Effects of assigned and participative goal setting on performance and job satisfaction." *Journal of Applied Psychology* 61 (1976): 166–71.

Lawlis, F. *The ADD Answer: How to Help Your Child Now- with questionnaires and family centered action plans to meet your child's specific needs.* New York: Viking, 2004.

Leary, M. R., & Miller, R. S. *Social psychology and dysfunctional behavior.* New York: Springer Verlag, 1986.

Lengfelder, A., & Gollwitzer, P. M. "Reflective and reflexive action control in frontal lobe patients." *Neuropsychology* 15, no. 1 (2001): 80-100.

Lepper, M. R., D. Greene, and R. E. Nisbett. "Undermining Children's Intrinsic Interest with Extrinsic Rewards: A Test of the Over-Justification Hypothesis." *Journal of Personality and Social Psychology* 28 (1973): 139–87.

Locke, E. A. "The motivation sequence, the motivation hub and the motivation core." *Organizational Behavior and Human Decision Processes* 50 (1991): 288–99.

Locke, E. A., Alavi, M. & Wagner, J. "Participation in decision-making: An information exchange perspective." In G. Ferris (ed.) *Research in personnel and human resources management* 15, p. 293–331. Greenwich, CT: JAI Press, 1997.

Locke, E. A., and G. P. Latham. "Building a Practically Useful Theory of Goal Setting and Task Motivation." *American Psychologist* September 57 (2002): 705–17.

Loney, J., Langhorne, J., & Peternite, C. "An empirical basis for subgrouping the hyperkinetic/minimal brain dysfunction syndrome." *Journal of Abnormal Psychology* 87 (1978): 431–44.

Loney, J., & Milich, R. "Hyperactivity, inattention, and aggression in clinical practice." In D. Routh & M. Wolraich (eds.), *Advances in developmental and behavioral pediatrics* Vol. 3, p. 113–47. Greenwich, CT: JAI Press, 1982.

Louv, R. "Nature Deficit: Is ADHD research overlooking the green factor?" Health and the Environment. *Orion,* July/August (2005): 70–71.

Mac Iver, D. J., Stipek, D. J., & Daniels, D. H. "Explaining within-semester changes in student effort in junior high school and senior high school courses." *Journal of Educational Psychology* 83 (1991): 201–11.

Mannuzza, S., Klein, R. G., Bessler, A., Malloy, P., & LaPadula, M. "Adult outcome of hyperactive boys: Educational achievement, occupational rank, and psychiatric status." *Archives of General Psychiatry* 50 (1993): 565–76.

Martens, B. K., & Hiralall, A. S. "Scripted sequence of teacher interaction." *Behavior Modification* 21, no. 3 (1997): 308–23.

Mash, E. J., & Johnston, C. "A comparison of the mother-child interactions of younger and older hyperactive and normal children." *Child Development* 53 (1982): 1371–81.

Mash, E., & Johnson, C. "Parental perceptions of child behavior problems, parenting self-esteem, and mothers' reported stress in younger and older hyperactive and normal children." *Journal of Consulting and Clinical Psychology* 51 (1983): 68–99.

Masserman, J. H. *Behavior and neurosis.* Chicago: University of Chicago Press, 1943.

Mathews, A. & Abboud, L., FDA Raises Concerns about ADHD Drugs. *The Wall Street Journal.* June 29, 2005. D1, D5.

Mattes, J. A., Boswell, L., & Oliver, H. "Methylphenidate effects on symptoms of attention deficit disorder in adults." *Archives of General Psychiatry* 41 (1984): 1059–63.

Mattes, J. A., & Gittelman, R. "Growth of hyperactive children on maintenance regimen of methylphenidate." *Archives of General Psychiatry* 40, no. 3 (1983): 317–21.

McBurnett, K., Lahey, B. B., & Swanson, J. M. "Ritalin treatment in attention deficit disorder without hyperactivity." In L. L. Greenhill & B. B. Osmon (eds.). *Ritalin: Theory and patient management* (p. 257–65). New York: Mary Ann Liebert, 1991.

McGee, R., S. Williams, and M. Feehan. "Attention Deficit Disorder and Age of Onset of Problem Behaviors." *Journal of Abnormal Child Psychology* 20 (1992): 487–502.

McGee, R., Williams, S., & Silva, P. A. "Behavioral and developmental characteristics of aggressive, hyperactive, and aggressive-hyperactive boys." *Journal of the American Academy of Child and Adolescent Psychiatry* 23 (1984): 270–79.

McMahon, R. J. "Diagnosis, assessment, and treatment of externalizing problems in children: The role of longitudinal data." *Journal of Consulting and Clinical Psychology* 51 (1994): 68–99.

McNeil, C. B., Eyberg, S. M., Eisenstadt, T. H., Newcomb, K., & Funderburk, B. "Parent-child interaction therapy with behavior problem children: Generalization of treatment effects to the school setting." *Journal of Consulting and Clinical Psychology* 55 (1991): 169–82.

Mechan-Mayne, A, Yuan, J., Hatzidimitriou, G., Xie, T., Mayne, A., McCann, U., Ricaurte, G. "Amphetamine treatment similar to that used in the treatment of adult ADHD damages dopaminergic nerve endings in the striatum of adult non-human primates." *Journal of Pharmacology and Experimental Therapeutics* 315, no. 1 (2005): 91–8.

"Methamphetamine will deliver 'a forest fire of brain damage.'" *Worcester Telegram,* 8/2/2004, 3C.

Meichenbaum, D., & Turk, D. C. *Facilitating treatment adherence: A practitioner's guidebook.* New York: Plenum, 1987.

Milich, R., Carlson, C. L., Pelham, W. E., & Licht, B. G. "Effects of methylphenidate on the persistence of ADHD boys following failure experiences." *Journal of Abnormal Child Psychology* 19 (1991): 519–36.

Milich, R., & Dodge, K. A. "Social information processing in child psychiatric populations." *Journal of Abnormal Child Psychology* 12 (1984): 471–90.

Milich, R. A., and J. Kramer. "Reflections on Impulsivity: An Empirical Investigation on Impulsivity as a Construct." In Gadow, K., and I. Bialer (eds.) *Advances in Learning and Behavioral Disabilities* (Vol. 3, p. 57–94). Greenwich, CT: JAI Press, 1985.

Moline, S., & Frankenberger, W. (2001). "Use of stimulant medication for treatment of attention deficit/hyperactivity disorder: A survey of middle and high school students' attitudes." *Psychology in the Schools* 38, no. 5 (2001): 569-84.

MTA Cooperative Group. "Moderators and mediators of treatment response for children with attention-deficit/hyperactivity disorder: The Multimodal Treatment Study of children with attention-deficit/hyperactivity disorder." *Archives of General Psychiatry* 56, no. 12 (1999): 1088–96.

MTA Cooperative Group. National Institute of Mental Health Multimodal Treatment Study of ADHD Follow-up: Changes in Effectiveness and Growth After the End of Treatment. *Pediatrics* 113 no. 4, April (2004): 762–69.

Murphy, D. A., Pelham, W. E., & Lang, A. R. "Aggression in boys with attention deficit-hyperactivity disorder: Methylphenidate effects on naturalistically observed aggression, response to provocation, and social information processing." *Journal of Abnormal Child Psychology* 20 (1992): 451–65.

Murphy, K. R., "Psychological Counseling of Adults with ADHD." In Barkley, R. A. *Attention Deficit Hyperactivity Disorder: A Handbook for Diagnosis and Treatment* 2nd ed. (p. 582–91). New York: Guilford Press, 1998.

Murphy, K. R. "Psychological Counseling of Adults with ADHD." in Barkley, R. A. *Attention Deficit Hyperactivity Disorder: A Handbook for Diagnosis and Treatment,* 3rd ed. (p. 692–703). New York: Guilford Press, 2006.

Murphy, K. R., Barkley, R. A., & Bush, T. "Executive function in young adults with attention deficit hyperactivity disorder." *Neuropsychology* 15 (2001): 211–20.

Murphy, K. R., and M. Gordon. "Assessment of Adults with ADHD." in Barkley, R. A. *Attention Deficit Hyperactivity Disorder: A Handbook for Diagnosis and Treatment,* 2nd ed. (p. 345–69). New York: Guilford Press, 1998.

———. "Assessment of Adults with ADHD." in Barkley, R. A. *Attention Deficit Hyperactivity Disorder: A Handbook for Diagnosis and Treatment,* 3rd ed. (p. 425–50). New York: Guilford Press, 2006.

Naglieri, J. A. & Gottling, S. H. "Mathematics instruction and PASS cognitive processes: An intervention study." *Journal of Learning Disabilities* 30 (1997): 513–20.

Neergaard, L. "New warnings set on antidepressants." *Worcester Telegram & Gazette, 8/21/04*, A1, A7.

Nelsen, Jane. *Positive Discipline.* New York: Ballantine Books, 1987.

"Methamphetamine will deliver 'a forest fire of brain damage.'" *Worcester Telegram, 8/2/2004*, 3C.

Nigg, J.T. "Is ADHD a Disinhibitory Disorder?" *Psychological Bulletin* 127, no.7 (2001): 571–98.

Nigg, J. T., & Hinshaw, S. P. "Parent personality traits and psychopathology associated with antisocial behaviors in childhood attention-deficit hyperactivity disorder." *Journal of Child Psychology and Adolescent Psychiatry* 39 (1998): 145–59.

Northup, J., Jones, K., Broussard, C., DiGiovanni, G., Herring, M., Fusillier, I., & Hanchey, A. "A preliminary analysis of interactive effects between common classroom contingencies and methylphenidate." *Journal of Applied Behavioral Analysis* 30, no. 1 (1997): 121–25.

O'Connor, T. G., Heron, J., Golding, J., Beveridge, M., & Glover, V. "Maternal Antenatal Anxiety and Children's Behavioral, Emotional Problems at 4 years. Report from the Avon Longitudinal Study of Parents and Children." *British Journal of Psychiatry* 180 (2002): 502–8.

O'Leary, K. D., & O'Leary, S. G. *Classroom Management: The Successful Use of Behavior Modification.* New York: Pergamon Press, 1972.

Olivero, H. "Many young men seek thrill in pill." *Worcester Telegram and Gazette,* January 19, 2004, C1.

Pagani, L., Tremblay, R., Vitaro, F., Boulerice, B., & McDuff, P. "Effects of grade retention on academic performance and behavioral development." *Development and Psychopathology* 13 (2001): 297–315.

Parker-Pope, T. "The Dangers of Second-Hand TV: What You Watch Can Affect Your Kids." *The Wall Street Journal,* April 13, 2004.

Parrott, A. C. "Does Cigarette Smoking Cause Stress?" *American Psychologist* 54, no. 10 (1999): 817–20.

Pelham, W. E. "The effects of stimulant drugs on learning and achievement in hyperactive and learning disabled children." In J. K. Torgesen & B. Wong (eds.), *Psychological and educational perspectives on learning disabilities* (p. 259–95). New York: Academic Press, 1985.

Pelham, W. E., & Bender, M. E. "Peer relationships in hyperactive children: Description and treatment." In K. Gadow & I. Bailer (eds.). *Advances in learning and behavioral disabilities* Vol. 1, p. 365–436. Greenwich, CT: JAI Press, 1982.

Pelham, W. E., & Bender, M. E. "Attention deficit and conduct disorders." In Hersen, M. (ed.). *Pharmacological and Behavioral Treatments: An Integrative Approach* (p. 108–48). New York: Wiley, 1986.

Pelham, W. E. Jr, Greenslade, K. E.,Vodde-Hamilton, M., Murphy, D. A., Greenstein, J. J., Gnagy, E. M., Guthrie, K. J., Hoover, M. D., & Dahl, R. E. "Relative efficacy of long-acting stimulants on children with attention deficit-hyperactivity disorder: a comparison of standard methylphenidate, sustained-release methylphenidate, sustained-release dextroamphetamine, and pemoline." *Pediatrics* 86, no. 2 (1990): 226–37.

Pelham, W. E., McBurnett, K., Harper, G. W., Milich, R., Murphy, D. A., Clinton, J., & Thiel, C. "Methylphenidate and baseball playing in ADHD children: Who's on first?" *Journal of Consulting and Clinical Psychology* 58 (1990): 130–33.

Pelham, W. E., & Milich, R. "Individual differences in response to Ritalin in classwork and social behavior." In L. L Greenhill & B. B. Osmon (eds.), *Ritalin: Theory and patient management* (p. 203–21). New York: Mary Ann Liebert, 1991.

Pelham, W. E., Murphy, D. A., Vannatta, K., Milich, R., Licht, B. G., Gnagy, E. M., Greenslade, K. E., Greiner, A. R., & Vodde-Hamilton, M. "Methylphenidate and attributions in boys with attention-deficit hyperactivity disorder." *Journal of Consulting and Clinical Psychology* 60 (1992): 282–92.

Pepper, S. C., *World Hypotheses.* Berkeley, CA: University of California Press, 1966.

Pfiffner, L. J., and R. A. Barkley. "Treatment of ADHD in School Settings." in Barkley, R. A. *Attention Deficit Hyperactivity Disorder: A Handbook for Diagnosis and Treatment,* 2nd ed. (p. 458–90). New York: Guilford Press, 1998.

Pfiffner, L. J., R. A. Barkley, and G. DuPaul. "Treatment of ADHD in School Settings." In Barkley, R. A. *Attention Deficit Hyperactivity Disorder: A Handbook for Diagnosis and Treatment,* 3rd ed. (p. 547–89). New York: Guilford Press, 2006.

Pisecco, S., Huzinec, C., & Curtis, D. "The effect of child characteristics on teacher's acceptability of classroom-based behavioral strategies and psycho-stimulant medication for the treatment of ADHD." *Journal of Clinical Child Psychology,* 30 (2001): 413–21.

Polivy, J., & Herman, C. P. "If at first you don't succeed: False hopes of self-change." *American Psychologist* 57 (2002): 677–89.

Pope, A., Bierman, K. L., & Mumma, G. H. "Aggression, hyperactivity, and inattention-immaturity: Behavior dimensions associated with peer rejection in elementary school boys." *Developmental Psychology* 27 (1991): 663–71.

Popper, C., "Combining methylphenidate and clonidine: Pharmacologic questions and new reports about sudden death." *Journal of Child and Adolescent Psychopharmacology* 5 (1995): 157–66.

Prince, J. B., Wilens, T. E., Spencer, T. J., Biederman, J. "Pharmacotherapy of ADHD in Adults." In Barkley, R. A., *Attention-Deficit Hyperactivity Disorder: A Handbook for Diagnosis and Treatment,* 3rd ed. (p. 704–30). New York: Guilford Press, 2006.

Proctor, M. A., & Morgan, D. "Effectiveness of a response cost raffle procedure on the disruptive classroom behavior of adolescents with behavior problems." *School Psychology Review* 20 (1991): 97–109.

Quay, H. C. "Attention Deficit Disorder and the Behavioral Inhibition System: The Relevance of the Neuropsychological Theory of Jeffrey A. Gray." In Bloomingdale, L. M., and J. Sergeant (eds.) *Attention Deficit Disorder: Criteria, Cognition, Intervention* (p. 117–26). New York: Pergamon Press, 1988.

Rapport, M. D., Denney, C., DuPaul, G. J., & Gardner, M. J. "Attention deficit disorder and methylphenidate: Normalization rates, clinical effectiveness, and response prediction in 76 children." *Journal of the American Academy of Child and Adolescent Psychiatry* 33 (1994): 882–93.

Rapport, M. D., DuPaul, G. J., Stoner, G., & Jones, J. T. "Comparing classroom and clinic measures of attention deficit disorder: Differential, idiosyncratic, and dose-response effects of methylphenidate." *Journal of Consulting and Clinical Psychology* 54 (1986): 334–41.

Rapport, M. D., Jones, J. T., DuPaul, G. J., Kelly, K. L., Gardner, M. J., Tucker, S. B., & Shea, M. S. "Attention deficit hyperactivity disorder and methylphenidate: Group and single-subject analyses of dose effects on attention in clinic and classroom settings." *Journal of Consulting and Clinical Psychology* 16 (1987): 329–38.

Rapport, M. D., & Kelly, K. L. "Psychostimulant effects on learning and cognitive function: Findings and implications for children with attention deficit-hyperactivity disorder." *Clinical Psychology Review* 11 (1991): 61–92.

Rapport, M. D., & Moffitt, C. "Attention deficit/hyperactivity disorder and methylphenidate. A review of height, weight, cardiovascular, and somatic complaint side effects." *Clinical Psychology Review* 22, no. 8 (2002): 1107–31.

Ratey, J. J., Greenberg, M. S., Bemporad, J. R., & Lindem, K. J. "Unrecognized attention-deficit hyperactivity disorder in adults presenting for outpatient psychotherapy." *Journal of Child and Adolescent Psychopharmacology* 2, no. 4 (1992): 267–75.

Redman, C. A., & Zametkin, A. J., "Ritalin and brain metabolism." In L. L. Greenhill & B. B. Osmon (eds.), *Ritalin: Theory and Patient Management* (p. 301–9). New York: Mary Ann Liebert, 1991.

Reeve, E. & Garfinkel, B. "Neuroendocrine and Growth Regulation: The Role of Sympathomimetic Medication." In Greenhill, L. L., & Osman, B. B. (eds.) *Ritalin: Theory and Patient Management* (p. 289-300). Larchmont, NY: Mary Ann Liebert, 1991.

Rie, H., Rie, E., Stewart, S. & Ambuel, J. "Effects of methylphenidate on underachieving children." *Journal of Consulting and Clinical Psychology* 44 (1976a): 250–60.

Rie, H., Rie, E., Stewart, S. & Ambuel, J. "Effects of Ritalin on underachieving children: A replication." *American Journal of Orthopsychiatry* 46 (1976b): 311–22.

Robin, A. L. "Training Families with ADHD Adolescents." In Barkley, R. A. *Attention Deficit Hyperactivity Disorder: A Handbook for Diagnosis and Treatment* (p. 462–97). New York: Guilford Press, 1990.

Robin, A. L. "Training Families with ADHD Adolescents." In Barkley, R. A. *Attention Deficit Hyperactivity Disorder: A Handbook for Diagnosis and Treatment,* 2nd ed. (p. 413–57). New York: Guilford Press, 1998.

Robin, A. L. "Training Families with Adolescents with ADHD." in Barkley, R. A. *Attention Deficit Hyperactivity Disorder: A Handbook for Diagnosis and Treatment,* 3rd ed. (p. 499–546) New York: Guilford Press, 2006.

Rosenthal, R., & Jacobson, L. *Pygmalion in the classroom.* New York: Holt, Rinehart & Winston, 1968.

Rutter, M. "Brain damage syndromes in childhood: Concepts and findings." *Journal of Child Psychology and Psychiatry* 18 (1977): 1–21.

Rutter, M. "Attention deficit disorder/hyperkinetic syndrome: Conceptual and research issues regarding diagnosis and classification." In Sagvolden, T. & T. Archer (eds.). *Attention deficit disorder: Clinical and Basic Research* (p. 1–24). Hillsdale, NJ: Erlbaum, 1989.

Safer, D. J., "Relative cardiovascular safety of psychostimulants used to treat attention-deficit hyperactivity disorder." *Journal of Child and Adolescent Psychopharmacology* 2 (1992): 279–290.

Safer, D. J., & Allen, D. J. "Factors influencing the suppressant effects of two stimulant drugs on the growth of hyperactive children." *Pediatrics* 51 (1973): 660–67.

Safer, D. J., Allen, R. P., & Barr, E. "Depression of growth in hyperactive children on stimulant drugs." *New England Journal of Medicine* 287 (1972): 217–20.

Safer, D. J., Zito, J. M., & Fine, E. M. "Increased methylphenidate usage for attention deficit disorder in the 1990s." *Pediatrics* 98 (1996): 1084–88.

Safren, S. A., Otto, M., Sprich, S., Winett, C., Wilens, T., & Biederman, J. "Cognitive-behavioral therapy for ADHD in medication-treated adults with continued symptoms." *Behaviour Research and Therapy* 43 (2005): 831–42.

Sallee, F. R., Stiller, R. L., Perel, J. M., et al. "Pemoline-induced abnormal involuntary movements." *Journal of Clinical Psychopharmacology* 9 (1989): 125–29.

Scantling, S. R. *Extraordinary Sex Now.* Doubleday: New York, 1998.

Schachar, R., & Tannock, R., & Logan, G. "Inhibitory control, impulsiveness, and attention deficit hyperactivity disorder." *Clinical Psychology Review* 13 (1993): 721–39.

Schein, E. H. *Process Consultation.* Reading, MA: Addison-Wesley, 1969.

Schlozman, S. "The New Pharmacopoeia." *Newsweek.* April 25, 2005, 56.

Sebrechts, M. M., Shaywitz, S. E., Shaywitz, B. A., Jatlow, P. Anderson, G. M. & Cohen, D. J. "Components of attention, methylphenidate dosage, and blood levels in children with attention deficit disorder." *Pediatrics* 77 (1986): 222–28.

Seligman, M., Steen, T., Park, N., & Peterson, C. "Positive Psychology Progress: Empirical Validation of Interventions." *American Psychologist* 60, no. 5 (2005): 410–23.

Shelton, T. L., Barkley, R. A., Crosswait, C., Moorehouse, M., Fletcher, K., Barrett, S., et al. "Multimodal psychoeducational intervention for preschool children with disruptive behavior: Two year post-treatment follow-up." *Journal of Abnormal Child Psychology* 28 (2000): 253–66.

Sherman, D. K., McGue, M. K., & Iacono, W. G. "Twin concordance for attention deficit hyperactivity disorder: A comparison of teacher's and mother's reports." *American Journal of Psychiatry* 154 (1997): 532–35.

Shure, M. B. *Raising a Thinking Child.* New York: Pocket Books, 1994.

Silver, L. B. "Attention-deficit/hyperactivity disorder in adult life." *Child and Adolescent Psychiatric Clinics of North America* 9, no. 3 (2000): 511–23.

Sinha, G. "Out of Control?" *Popular Science,* June, 2001, 48-52.

Sinha, G. "Training the Brain: Cognitive Therapy as an alternative to ADHD drugs." *Scientific American* 293 (2005): 22–23.

Skinner, B. F. *Science and Human Behavior.* New York: The Macmillan Company, 1953.

Skinner, B. F. *The Technology of Teaching.* New York: Appleton-Century-Crofts, 1968.

Sleator, E. K., and W. E. Pelham. *Attention Deficit Disorder.* Norwalk, CT: Appleton-Century-Crofts, 1986.

Smith, B. H., Barkley, R. A., & Shapiro, C. J. "Combined Child Therapies." In Barkley, R. A. *Attention Deficit Hyperactivity Disorder: A Handbook for Diagnosis and Treatment*, 3rd ed. (p. 678–91). New York: Guilford Press, 2006.

Snyder, M., Tanke, E. D., & Berscheid, E. "Social perception and interpersonal behavior: On the self-fulfilling nature of social stereotypes." *Journal of Personality and Social Psychology* 35 (1977): 656–66.

Solanto, M. V. "Dosage effects of Ritalin on cognition." In Greenhill, L. L. & Osmon, B. B. (eds.), *Ritalin: Theory and Patient Management* (p. 45–68). New York: Mary Anne Liebert, 1991.

Spague, R., & Sleator, E. "Methylphenidate in hyperkinetic children: Differences in dose effects on learning and social behavior." *Science* 198 (1977): 1274–76.

Spencer, T. J., Biederman, J. Harding, M., O'Donnell, D., Farone, S. V., & Wilens, T. W. "Growth deficits in ADHD children revisited: Evidence of disorder associated growth delays?" *Journal of the American Academy of Child and Adolescent Psychiatry* 35 (1996): 1460–69.

Spencer, T. J., Biederman, J., & Wilens, T. "Pharmacotherapy of ADHD with Antidepressants." In Barkley, R. A. *Attention Deficit Hyperactivity Disorder: A Handbook for Diagnosis and Treatment,* 3rd ed. (p. 552–63). New York: Guilford Press, 1998.

Spencer, T. J., Biederman, J., Wilens, T. W., Harding, M., O'Donnell, D., & Griffin, S. "Pharmacotherapy of attention-deficit hyperactivity disorder across the life cycle."

Journal of the American Academy of Child and Adolescent Psychiatry 35 (1996): 409–32.

Spencer, T., Wilens, T. E., Biederman, J., Faraone, S. V., Ablon, S., & Lapey, K. "A double blind crossover comparison of methylphenidate and placebo in adults with childhood onset attention deficit hyperactivity disorder." *Archives for General Psychiatry* 52 (1995): 434–43.

Stambor, Z. "Psychologist calls for more research on adolescents' brains." *Monitor on Psychology.* 37, no. 9 (2006): 16.

Stellar, B. Vorsatze und die Wahrnehmung Gunstiger Gelegnheiten "Implementation intentions and the detection of good opportunities to act." Munich, Germany: tuduv Verlagsgesellschaft, 1992.

Stephens, R. S., Pelham, W. E., & Skinner, R. "State-dependent and main effects of methylphenidate and pemoline on paired-associate learning and spelling in hyperactive children." *Journal of Consulting and Clinical Psychology* 52 (1984): 104–13.

Sternberg, R., Grigorenko, E., & Kidd, K. "Intelligence, Race, and Genetics." *American Psychologist* 60 (2005): 46–59.

Strauss, A. A., & Lehtinen, L. E. *Psychopathology and education of the brain-injured-child.* New York: Grune & Stratton, 1947.

Swanson, J. M. "Paired-associate learning in the assessment of ADD-H children." In Bloomingdale, L. M. & Swanson, J. M. (eds.), *Attention deficit disorder: Current concepts and emerging trends in attentional and behavioral disorders of childhood.* (p. 87–123). New York: Pergamon Press, 1989.

Szatmari, P., M. H. Boyle, and D. R. Offord. "ADHD and Conduct Disorder: Degree of Diagnostic Overlap and Differences among Correlates." *Journal of the American Academy of Child and Adolescent Psychiatry* 28 (1989): 865–72.

Szatmari, P., Offord, D. R., & Boyle, M. H. "Correlates, associated impairments and patterns of service utilization of children with attention deficit disorder: Findings from the Ontario Child Health Study." *Journal of Child Psychology and Psychiatry* 30 (1989): 205–17.

Tarkan, L. "Attention Disorder Advice, by One Who Knows." *New York Times.* August 26, 2003, Section F, p. 6, C. 3.

Tarkan, L. "Autism Therapy Is Called Effective, but Rare." *New York Times.* October, 22, 2002. Section D, p. 1.

Taylor, E. A. *The overactive child.* Philadelphia: Lippincott, 1986.

Taylor, E., Chadwick, O., Heptinstall, E., & Danckaerts, M. "Hyperactivity and conduct problems as risk factors for adolescent development." *Journal of the American Academy of Child and Adolescent Psychiatr,* 35 (1996): 1213–26.

Taylor, E., Schachar, R., Thorley, G., Wieselberg, H. M., Everitt, B., & Rutter, M. "Which boys respond to stimulant medication? A controlled trial of methylphenidate in boys with disruptive behavior." *Psychological Medicine* 17 (1987): 121–43.

Thomas, A., & Chess, S. *The dynamics of psychological development.* New York: Brunner/Mazel, 1980.

Thurber, J. R., Heller, T. L., & Hinshaw, S. P. "The social behaviors and peer expectation of girls with attention deficit hyperactivity disorder and comparison girls." *Journal of Clinical Child and Adolescent Psychology* 31 (2002): 433–52.

Tourette's Syndrome Study Group. "Treatment of ADHD in children with tics: A randomized controlled trial." *Neurology* 58 no. 4 (2002): 527–36.

Tyre, P. "Finding What Works." *Newsweek* April 25, 2005, 54–56.

Wahler, R. G. "The insular mother: Her problems in parent-child treatment." *Journal of Applied Behavior Analysis* 13 (1980): 207–19.

Webster-Stratton, C. W., & Hammond, M. "Maternal depression and its relationship to life stress, perceptions of child behavior problems, parenting behaviors, and child conduct problems." *Journal of Abnormal Child Psychology* 16 (1988): 299–315.

Weiss, B., Dodge, K. A., Bates, J. E., & Petit, G. S. "Some consequences of early harsh discipline: Child aggression and a maladapted social information processing style." *Child Development* 63 no. 6 (1992): 1321–35.

Weiss, G., & Hechtman, L. T. *Hyperactive children grown up.* New York: Guilford Press, 1986.

Weiss, G., & Hechtman, L. *Hyperactive children grown up: ADHD in children, adolescents, and adults,* (2nd ed.). New York: Guilford Press, 1993.

Werner. E. E. "Risk, Resilience, and Recovery: Perspectives from the Kauai Longitudinal Study." *Development and Psychopathology* 5 (1993): 503–15.

Whalen, C. K., Henker, B. *Hyperactive Children: The Social Ecology of Identification and Treatment.* New York: Academic Press, 1980.

Whalen, C. K., & Henker, B. "The social worlds of hyperactive (ADDH) children." *Clinical Psychology Review* 5 (1985): 447–78.

Whalen, C. K., & Henker, B. "Therapies for hyperactive children: Comparisons, combinations, and compromises." *Journal of Consulting and Clinical Psychology* 59 (1991): 126–37.

Whalen, C. K., Henker, B., Castro, J., & Granger, D. A.) "Peer Perceptions of Hyperactivity and Medication Effects." *Child Development* 58 (1987): 816–28.

Whalen, C. K., Henker B., & Dotemoto S. "Methylphenidate and hyperactivity: Effects on teacher behaviors." *Science* 208 (1980): 1280–82.

Whalen, C. K., Henker, B., Hinshaw, S. P., Heller, T., & Huber-Dressler, A. "The messages of medication: Effects of actual versus informed medication status on hyperactive boys' expectancies and self-evaluations." *Journal of Consulting and Clinical Psychology* 59 (1991): 602–6.

Whalen, C. K., Jamner, L. D., Henker, JB., Delfino, R. J., & Lozano, J. M. "The ADHD spectrum and everyday life: Experience sampling of adolescent moods, activities, smoking, and drinking." *Child Development* 73 (2002): 209–27.

Wheeler, M. A., Stuss, D. T., & Tulving, E. "Toward a theory of episodic memory: The frontal lobes and autonoetic consciousness." *Psychological Bulletin* 121 (1997): 331 54.

Whitaker. J. "A Proposal Before the Florida Legislature: Stop Drugging Our Kids." *Health & Healing* June, 2005, p. 1–2.

Wiener, C. *Attention Deficit Hyperactivity Disorder as a Learned Behavioral Pattern: A Return to Psychology.* Lanham, MD: University Press of America, 2007.

Wilens,T., Biederman, J. "The stimulants." In Shafer, D. (ed.), *The Psychiatric Clinics of North America* (p. 191–222). Philadelphia: W. B. Saunders, 1992.

Wilens, T., Biederman, J., Mick, E., & Spencer, T. "A systematic assessment of tricyclic antidepressants in the treatment of adult attention-deficit hyperactivity disorder." *Journal of Nervous and Mental Disease* 183, no. 1 (1995): 48-50.

Wilens, T. E., and T. J. Spencer. "The Stimulants Revisited." *Child and Adolescent Psychiatric Clinics of North America* 9, no. 3 (2000) 573–603.

Wilens, T. E., Spencer, T. J., & Biederman, J. "Pharmacotherapy of Adult ADHD." In Barkley, R. A. *Attention Deficit Hyperactivity Disorder: A Handbook for Diagnosis and Treatment,* 2nd ed. (p. 592–606). New York: Guilford Press, 1998.

Wood, R. E. & Bandura, A. "Social cognitive theory in organizational management." *Academy of Management Review* 14 (1989): 361–84.

Zeiner, P. "Body growth and cardiovascular function after extended (1.75 years) with methylphenidate in boys with attention-deficit hyperactivity disorder." *Journal of Child and Adolescent Psychopharmacology* 5 (1995): 129–38.

Zentall, S. S. "A Context for Hyperactivity." In Gadow, K. D., and I. Bailer (eds.) *Advances in Learning and Behavioral Disabilities* Vol. 4, p. 273–343. Greenwich, CT: JAI Press, 1985.

Author Index

Subject Index